CORNWALL SINCE THE WAR

CORNWALL SINCE THE WAR

The Contemporary History of a European Region

Edited by

Philip Payton

Director, Institute of Cornish Studies, University of Exeter

INSTITUTE OF CORNISH STUDIES

Sardinia Pilchardus
(The Pilchard)

DYLLANSOW TRURAN

First published 1993 by
Institute of Cornish Studies,
Trevithick Centre, Trevenson Road,
Pool, Redruth, Cornwall, and
Dyllansow Truran,
Trewolsta, Trewirgie, Redruth, Cornwall.

ISBN 1 85022 073 5

Typeset at the Institute of Cornish Studies

Printed and bound in Great Britain
by Short Run Press Ltd, Exeter

For the peoples of
Croatia and Bosnia-Hercegovina,
in the hope that
all the small nations and regions of Europe
will one day find their proper place.

By the same author:
Pictorial History of Australia's Little Cornwall
The Story of HMS Fisgard
The Cornish Miner in Australia
The Cornish Farmer in Australia
Tregantle and Scraesdon: Their Forts and Railway
The Making of Modern Cornwall

(*contributed to:*)
The Australian People
Cornish Studies For Schools
European Security: Towards 2000
Political Ideologies Since 1945
The New Maritime History of Devon

(*edited:*)
Cornish Carols From Australia
Cornish Mine Disasters
Cornish Studies: One
St Ives Mining District: Volume II

CONTRIBUTORS

Colin Bristow is Visiting Professor at the Camborne School of Mines, University of Exeter.

Lyn Bryant is Principal Lecturer in the Department of Applied Social Science, University of Plymouth.

Bernard Deacon is Tutor/Assistant Staff Tutor in the Open University.

John Hurst is Senior Tutor in the Department of Continuing and Adult Education, University of Exeter.

Adrian Lee is Associate Dean in the Faculty of Human Sciences, University of Plymouth.

Peter Mitchell is Senior Research Officer in the Planning Department, Cornwall County Council.

Philip Payton is Director of the Institute of Cornish Studies, University of Exeter.

Ronald Perry was formerly the Head of the Faculty of Management, Cornwall College.

Gareth Shaw is Senior Lecturer in the Department of Geography, University of Exeter.

Allan M. Williams is Senior Lecturer in the Department of Geography, University of Exeter,

Malcolm Williams is Lecturer in the Department of Applied Social Science, University of Plymouth.

Contents

ACKNOWLEDGEMENTS

I am indebted first of all to Bernard Deacon, Adrian Lee and Ronald Perry, that small team which assisted in sketching-out the preliminary plans for *Cornwall Since the War*, helping to decide upon content, balance and themes. The other contributors, of course, are also deserving of my thanks and appreciation, not only for their individual Chapters but also for their advice, patience and forebearance over many months. Similarly, I should like to thank the many others who have read, re-read and commented extensively upon the various Chapters, offering numerous suggestions which have measurably improved the quality of this book.

At the Institute of Cornish Studies, I should like to thank my Secretaries, Elizabeth Jackson and Heather Oliver, for their assistance and support, as well as acknowledging the ready assistance of our Computing Development Officer, Colin French. In particular, an especial debt of gratitude is due to Adamu Sabo who with irrepressible enthusiasm and painstaking skill computer type-set *Cornwall Since the War*.

Acknowledgement is also due to those publishers who have given permission to quote from their titles; individual acknowledgements are referenced in full in the notes to each Chapter but if any omissions or mistakes have occurred in this respect apologies are offered in advance and errors will be corrected in any future editions.

And finally, I should like to thank Phil Monckton of Cornwall & Isles of Scilly Press for permission to reproduce as our front cover illustration his superb photographic evocation of 'Trelawny's Army' in full-cry at Twickenham - surely the quintessential expression of the Cornish identity in the 1980s and 1990s?

Philip Payton
4th November 1993
Feast of St Cleer

INTRODUCTION

Philip Payton

It is only within the last half-decade or so that contemporary Cornwall has attracted the serious attention of historians, social scientists and others interested in examining the nature and consequences of rapid change since 1945. This book is the result of a research project initiated at the Institute of Cornish Studies (part of the University of Exeter but funded jointly by Cornwall County Council and situated in Cornwall) as a strand of a wider strategy to focus upon contemporary issues, and brings together a team of writers already well-known for their disparate contributions to Cornish Studies and Cornish public life. The aim is to present a critical contemporary history of Cornwall since 1945, examining the impact of change upon the Cornish economy, society and culture.

The three arms of the University of Exeter in Cornwall - the Institute of Cornish Studies, the Camborne School of Mines, and the Department of Continuing and Adult Education - have each been involved with this project, as has the University's main campus at Exeter. Additionally, there are three contributions from scholars at the University of Plymouth, while others are from a research analyst at Cornwall County Council, a tutor at the Open University, and a former Head of the Faculty of Management at Cornwall College. In the absence of a unified University of Cornwall, these individuals and their parent institutions form an important part of what we may call the Cornish academic community. Publication has been undertaken in a similarly co-operative manner, bringing together the Institute of Cornish Studies (with its own modest publishing programme) and the major Cornish publisher Dyllansow Truran.

Although *Cornwall Since the War* makes no claim to be definitive (more work needs to be done, for example, in areas such as fishing, transport, education, fine art, the environment, and health-care) it does marshall and re-assess much recent research, as well as presenting a wide range of new material. Inevitably, it raises at least as many questions as it answers, an important objective being to stimulate further debate and suggest new avenues for further research. The book also reflects the common determination of its contributors that Cornwall should be afforded due consideration and given proper place in the developing discussion of European regional diversity. There is, however, no 'staff answer' (as the Military would say) to which contributors to this work have been required to adhere. Although the perpetuation of 'difference' despite (or even because of) rapid change since 1945 is a strong editorial theme that permeates the book, each contributor has been encouraged in the spirit of academic freedom to develop her/his own perspective. There are, indeed, contrasting perspectives within these pages - not least with regard to the double-edged sword of tourism with which (if one may mix one's metaphors) the Cornish have long had a love-hate relationship - and its hoped that these contrasts will inform the wider debate that *Cornwall Since the War* may generate. Individual contributors, of course, are responsible only for their own views, while the editor does not necessarily agree with each and every of the opinions advanced herein.

A shortcoming of many books compiled from the contributions of various writers is that they tend to be just that - compilations, ad hoc constructions in which 'chapters' are in reality discrete articles and where common themes and developing arguments are difficult to discern. Mindful of this difficulty, we have attempted to structure *Cornwall Since the War* in such a way that underlying themes are developed and reinforced as the book proceeds. To this end, the book - in addition to the free-standing Introduction and Conclusion - is organised in three distinct sections:

Part One, **The Cornish Context,** identifies contemporary Cornwall as 'a suitable case for treatment', explaining how and why its is that scholars have been drawn in recent years to examine the 'Cornish question', and setting Cornish Studies as an area of inter-disciplinary study in the wider context of academic development and debate since the War. Here Cornish Studies is seen as having escaped the narrow confines of antiquarianism and 'Celtic Studies', in particular developing a social science and becoming part of the scholarly movement concerned with contemporary European diversity. Part One also presents a broad sketch of Cornwall as it was circa 1950 - at the beginning of the era under discussion - identifying the fabric of Cornish life, its economy, society and culture, but also pin-pointing inherent tensions in a 'tight little island' on the eve of dramatic change.

In Part Two, **The Impact of Socio-Economic Change,** a broad analysis is presented of changes to the Cornish economy in the years since 1945, changes that occurred against the background of structural changes in the wider British economy and the introduction by central governments of interventionist Regional Development and other policies. Although the socio-economic characteristics of Cornwall altered almost beyond recognition, this did not mean (as the policies had intended, and the planners had hoped) that Cornish economic ills were at last remedied or that Cornwall had been brought (as some observers had imagined) to the same socio-economic condition as the South East of England. Not only had the inherent problems of a peripheral economy been perpetuated but in fact the nature of peripherality itself had become more complex. This exposed the shortcomings of the conventional wisdoms regarding the approach to Cornish economic problem-solving and also precipitated a range of 'opposition' policies which were voiced with increasing clarity from the mid-1970s but which did not visibly affect local policy-making until the late 1980s and never seemed to penetrate the consciousness of central government.

Two contrasting but, surprisingly, increasingly complementary strands of the Cornish economy - tourism, and the extractive industry - are singled-out for closer examination. Both are seen to have changed enormously since the War, and both have prompted heated debate on their desirability or otherwise as 'flagships' of the Cornish economy, areas of contention ranging from environmental concerns to problems of long-term sustainability. Intriguingly, the arrival of 'heritage' or 'cultural' tourism finds an area of common interest between these two hitherto distinct (and sometimes mutually-hostile) economic activities, while also attempting to provide some answers to the long-term issues. A principal indicator (and, indeed, precipitator) of post-War change has been in-migration into Cornwall from outside, and Part Two explores this phenomenon in some detail as well as assessing its critical impact upon the Cornish housing market and thus the house-purchasing or even shelter-seeking aspirations of the indigenous Cornish. As a result of this post-War change and the pressures that it has exerted, but also reflecting a much deeper and distinctive historical inheritance, the contemporary Cornish family is seen as exhibiting small but discernable behavioural differences from those elsewhere, while also acting as an important vehicle for the sense of Cornish ethnic identity.

In fact, Part Three, **A Re-defining Identity**, examines the response of the Cornish identity to the changes considered in Part Two. Here massive in-migration, the growth of mass tourism, the arrival of the 'branch factory' economy, pressures on the housing market and thus the family, had led not (as some had feared) to the submergence of the Cornish but to the construction of both socio-economic survival strategies for individual Cornish families (notably in the area of housing) and a coherent set of 'opposition' economic policies. This, as Part Three indicates, has led in turn to a sharpening of Cornish ethnic identity and an enhanced popular consciousness, exhibited in a range of behaviour from the growth of anti-metropolitanism in politics to the extraordinary 'Trelawny's Army' phenomenon in the Rugby Union County Championship.

Part Three shows that although the ethnonational movement remains small, its influence should not be under-estimated, while the propensity for wider ethnic mobilisation in certain conditions is demonstrated in the widespread concern for the territorial integrity and identity of Cornwall itself - exhibited, for example, in the anti-'Tamarside' and Euro-constituency campaigns, or more modestly in the attempts to assert the constitutional significance of the Duchy of Cornwall and Stannary Law. Cornish 'difference' and - specifically - the manner in which it has been recast since the War is observable generally in Cornish political life in the behaviour of parties and voters (where Cornwall is identified as having a distinct regional identity), and most acutely in the fascinating ideological debate within the Cornish language movement where competing groups fiercely contest each other's philosophical assumptions. Cornish literature, too, has responded to changing circumstances, Sir Arthur Quiller-Couch's legacy being perpetuated by a range of writers but with the appearance in recent years of indigenous authors such as Myrna Combellack and Alan Kent emphasising Cornwall's distinctive place within the wider Western literary and cultural tradition.

Ultimately, it is concern for that place in Western tradition which characterises the mood of this book. As well as possessing its own historically significant links with both the Commonwealth and the United States of America, Cornwall has an enduring (indeed, re-defining and strengthening) regional identity which not only emphasises its status as a distinct component of the United Kingdom but also (aided, perhaps, by the connections with Celtic but non-British Ireland and Brittany) establishes its credentials as a European region.

PART ONE:

THE CORNISH CONTEXT

CHAPTER 1

POST-WAR CORNWALL: A SUITABLE CASE FOR TREATMENT?

Philip Payton

THE RISE OF CORNISH STUDIES

Why study contemporary Cornwall? The question is one posed often to the team responsible for this book, not least by Cornish enthusiasts who point to the fascination of 'old' Cornwall with its hidden mysteries, intriguing evidences, and tantalising glimpses of peoples gone before. Besides, they argue, surely the real Cornwall, or at least Cornwall as the land of 'difference', lies rooted firmly in the dim and distant past, with modern Cornwall a sad and pale imitation as the homogenising agencies of mass communications, mass tourism and mass in-migration make it more or less like anywhere else?

The answer, as we shall see, is that - despite those 'homogenising' agencies - Cornwall has stubbornly maintained its sense of separate identity. Indeed, the post-War years have in several respects seen a heightening of Cornish consciousness, perhaps as a reaction to those forces identified above and comparable to the emergence of ethnic and territorial awareness observable elsewhere in Europe and North America. And yet, even if there has been an enhancement of identity, the socio-economic condition of post-War Cornwall has become increasingly parlous - particularly for those indigenous Cornish who find themselves caught in a peculiarly Cornish low wage/high house price nexus. Similarly, a growing concern for the territorial expression of the Cornish identity (manifested, for example, in the various campaigns to preserve the Tamar border or achieve a Cornish Euro-constituency) has occurred against the background of both the diminishing powers of local government and an increasing tendency to organise public and private agencies on a Devon-and-Cornwall ('Devonwall', to its detractors) or South West basis.

There are paradoxes here that invite investigation, and fortunately one important element in the development of Cornish Studies in recent decades has been an increasing willingness to address contemporary issues. But it was not always thus. As an academic discipline, Cornish Studies grew out of the pre-

1914 and (especially) inter-War 'Cornish Revival', which was itself a component of a wider 'Celtic Revival' that had emerged in Brittany, Ireland, Wales, Scotland, and the Isle of Man. Inevitably, therefore, not only was Cornish Studies then defined narrowly as as an element of 'Celtic Studies', but also its early practitioners and adherents shared the ideological assumptions and perspectives of the Cornish Revivalists. Put simply, the Revivalists ignored (even rejected) nineteenth-century notions of a Cornish identity based on industrial prowess and technological advance, and - in the face of the traumatic effects of rapid de-industrialisation that lay all around them - looked back to a Medieval, pre-industrial Celtic-Catholic Cornwall for their model for the future.[1] Thus Cornish Studies was concerned principally with the mechanisms of language 'Revival' and, like the Old Cornwall movement, busied itself in an antiquarian quest to gather all the fragments of identity before they were lost in the rush to post-industrial modernity. From re-discovering old Celtic crosses to recording snippets of dialect speech, Cornish Studies turned away from the crises of modern Cornwall to embrace the more reassuring and seemingly timeless world of 'Arthur's Realm'.

After the War, Cornish Revivalists proved readier to address the problems of modern Cornwall (leading, amongst other things, to the foundation of the political movement, Mebyon Kernow), while Cornish historians moved their sights from more ancient themes to begin the investigation of Cornwall's industrial period. Industrial archaeology emerged as a maintream element of Cornish Studies (Geoffrey Ordish[2] had already commenced the painstaking photographic recording of Cornish engine-houses, while A.K. Hamilton Jenkin had begun the social history of Cornish mining [3]), and authors such as John Rowe, A.C.Todd and D.B.Barton emphasised the specifically Cornish aspects of the industrial experience, including the extraordinary 'Great Migration'.[4] However, the full accommodation of contemporary Cornwall within the compass of Cornish Studies was not achieved until the establishment in 1970 of the Institute of Cornish Studies (part of the University of Exeter, but funded jointly by Cornwall County Council), with Charles Thomas as its first Director.

Rejecting any limiting definition of his subject, Thomas insisted that Cornish Studies was '. . . the study of all aspects of man and his handiwork in the regional setting (Cornwall and Scilly), past, present and future'.[5] The incorporation of the emerging Cornish Biological Records Unit within the Institute broadened this definition still further to include consideration of the physical and natural environment. As Thomas argued, 'The development of society, industry and the landscape in our fast-changing world is as much of concern . . . as the history of those vast topics in the recent and remote past'.[6] In his inaugural address as Professor of Cornish Studies, Thomas re-emphasised this approach, but went further still to suggest that part of the role of Cornish Studies was to furnish a critique of those policies and forces that were moulding the socio-economic characteristics of contemporary Cornwall. In effect, Thomas was arguing for the development of a critical Cornish social science, and indeed by the 1980s Cornwall was beginning to attract the attention of political scientists, economists, geographers, sociologists and anthropologists, as well as modern historians, each with their own disciplinary perspective to offer. By the early 1990s such an approach had become a central plank of the Institute of Cornish Studies' activities, and this study is of course one example of that new focus.

At the same time that Cornish Studies was shedding its antiquarian image, so scholars in other disciplines were becoming more aware of the significance of regional and ethnic studies. Hitherto dismissed as parochial and folkloric dilettantism, at best an obsession with the minutiae of local history, such studies were now seen as affording important insights into the patterns of territorial diversity (cultural, political, and socio-economic) that had become increasingly evident in Western states since the late 1960s and 70s. This in itself was a measure of a major shift in academic thinking since the War, with an earlier insistence upon a fundamental homogeneity of Western states and societies now replaced by a new conventional wisdom which emphasised the persistence, indeed resurgence of diversity.

HOMOGENEITY OR DIVERSITY?

In the 1950s and 60s social scientists in the West saw the defeat of fascism in the Second World War as the final demise of ethnicity as a major determinant in Europe of political and social behaviour. Ethnic consciousness was considered to be increasingly irrelevant (even distasteful) in the consolidating 'civic cultures' of Western Europe (and North America and the 'White Commonwealth'). Within these 'civic cultures', the legitimacy of institutions and the emergence of consensus politics, together with improved political participation, enhanced socio-economic and geographical mobility, and evermore sophisticated communications, made for increasingly homogeneous states in which any residual territorial diversity was anachronistic and destined to disappear. However, the emergence in the late 1960s and 70s of separatist sentiment (and often community conflict) in areas as diverse as Flanders, Northern Ireland, Quebec, and the Basque Country, forced social scientists to revise their estimations of the nature of modern Western states. From this reassessment emerged the new orthodoxy which not only recognised the existence of regionalist and nationalist movements but also admitted that such phenomena were but one index of a broader pattern of territorial diversity in contemporary societies.

Elsewhere in the Western World, allied issues of ethnicity were also emerging, as in the United States where Indians (Native Americans) asserted their rights and identity with renewed confidence, or in Australia and New Zealand where the Aborigines and Maoris were similarly active. Extensive post-War immigration in Australia, first from continental Europe and latterly from South East Asia, had also challenged the 'Anglo-Celtic' homogeneity of Australian society (itself something of a myth, given the disparate impact of the

Irish, Cornish, German and other groups during the colonial era), with a resultant new perspective which emphasised Australian 'multi-culturalism'. Indeed, Antipodean multi-cultural policies were to some extent a model for British society as it moved to deal more adequately with its own post-War immigration (principally Afro-Carribean and Asian), UK policy shifting from benign assimilationism towards a more proactive multi-cultural accommodation.

An extensive literature emerged to document this diversity, with scholars anxious to both describe and explain the origin of territorial diversity and the reasons for its recent reassertion. Although some were content to focus upon the phenomenon of ethnonationalism, others were concerned to explore the broader pattern of diversity that was by now apparent, with commentators of note from Anthony Smith and Michael Hechter to Jim Bulpitt, Stein Rokkan and Derek Urwin pointing to the significance of historical state-building processes, particularly in Western Europe.[7] For some observers, within these state-buliding processes (many dating back to the Medieval and Renaissance periods) could be identified the root causes of contemporary ethnonationalism, while for others these processes had created in modern Western European states a fundamental dichotomy between 'centre' and 'periphery'. Although this dichotomy was obviously territorial, its determinents lay within the political, socio-economic and cultural power structures created by state-building processes, and its manifestations were many and varied - ranging from regional economic inequality to expressions of ethnic distinctiveness. Moreover, this 'centre-periphery' relationship was itself dynamic in quality, with Tarrow[8] and others postulating a series or phases of peripherality as states moved from one historical period to another. In this way, the relationship was never redundant but merely adapted to reflect the conditions of a newly-emerged period.

Interestingly, commentators observed that the degree of peripheral protest or regional restiveness varied between and sometimes even within states (Western Europe exhibited by no means a uniform pattern). This was seen as a measure of the success (or failure) of accommodating devices (devolved local authorities, decentralised regional governments, federal structures, and so on) constructed by the 'centre' to deal with the problems of its 'peripheries'. Generally, those states that had successfully accommodated their peripheral territories were those least likely to be faced by peripheral protest, although paradoxically - as Moynihan[9] has argued recently - those states that react belatedly to protest by attempting to devise new mechanisms of accommodation may serve only to exacerbate their own problems. In Western Europe, however, despite outbreaks of violence in areas such as Northern Ireland or the Basque Country, states had more or less been successful in establishing constitutional accommodations, whether it was the relatively venerable British practice of allowing Scotland its own institutions or the more recent and more radical restructuring of post-Franco Spain. And, although scholars had by now exposed the shortcomings of the homogeneous state paradigm, perhaps there was after all in the West an element of 'civic culture' pervasive enough to allow the democratic debate and resolution of territorial and ethnic issues.

But if this was true for the West, it was not at all applicable to the old Eastern Europe and Soviet Union (or, for that matter, to much of the Third World), where the attempts to embrace democracy in the late 1980s and 1990s had almost without exception failed to deal adequately with issues of territorial diversity. Interestingly, those social scientists who in the 1950s and 60s had observed (they thought) the end of ethnicity in Western Europe, were at the same time trumpeting the demise of diversity in the East. Although by the late 1970s this conventional wisdom did have its detractors (many pointing to the impact of the rapid expansion of the Soviet Union's Muslim population in Central Asia), the view that the post-War experience of the East had been one of a relentless imposition of Communist homogeneity survived even into the Gorbachev era. The impact of Marxist-Leninist ideology, the effect of one-party totalitarian rule, and the force of Moscow domination and economic/ military integration had led, it was assumed, to a considerable degree of homogeneity within both the internal and external Soviet empires. Not surprisingly, Western observers were encouraged in this belief (and in their distatse for expressions of ethnicity) by Soviet ideologists who stressed that ethnic consciousness was 'false consciousness'.

Inevitably, however, the emergence of 'glasnost' and 'perestroika' prompted an abandonment of this perspective, with the practical evidence of the 1990s pointing not only to the survival of diversity but also to the central importance of territorial and ethnic issues in moulding political behaviour in the East. Again, this had by now impressed Western scholars, and part of the rehabilitation of the academic study of ethnic and territorial diversity has been an acknowledgement of the significance of these phenomena in explaining the contemporary history of both parts of the European continent, West and East.[10] Equally, there is now a general recognition that these issues raise daunting questions for the future, not least with regard to European security (and the roles therein for bodies such as NATO and the European Union) as the disintegration of Yugoslavia illustrates graphically. But for many it has come as a surprise as well as a shock that the immediate memorials to post-Communist, post-Cold War Europe should be Vukovar and Sarajavo.

And yet, for those investigating the territorial dimensions of European states, the United Kingdom has proved a particularly difficult nut to crack. Despite the pioneering work of Rose[11] (who confidently redefined the United Kingdom as a 'multi-national state'), many of the subtleties and obscurities of the British case remain only partially explored - the division between 'North' and 'South' in England awaits to be fully researched, while the Channel Islands are only now coming under close academic scrutiny. Not surprisingly, within this general British difficulty, Cornwall has been an extraordinarily hard nut to crack, and it has been only in recent years - coincident with and dependent upon the inter-disciplinary broadening of Cornish Studies noted above - that the Cornish case has attracted serious attention. Even now, it is possible for otherwise careful observers to seriously misinterpret the basic fabric of contemporary Cornwall.[12]

Back in the early 1970s, before the elucidation of the British diversity had commenced in any determined manner, consideration of Cornwall by social scientists was always brief and often unsatisfactory. In 1971 Punnett's consideration of Cornish political behaviour was limited to a fleeting reference to the Liberal Party's 'Celtic fringe'[13] and a comment that 'Other minor parties exist, and a handful of Democratic Party, National Front, Mebyon Kernow (Cornish Nationalist movement), World Government and Socialist Party of Great Britain candidates contested the 1970 election, but with even less success than the Communists'.[14] Similarly, for Dowse and Hughes in 1972, Cornwall was of interest only for the evidence it afforded of the political psychology of the 'lunatic fringe'. They observed that 'A politician may be seriously disturbed psychologically and yet be constrained to act in ways very similar to other politicians. . .',[15] taking as their examples groups which appeared '. . . to many outsiders to attract "cranks"- the Communist Party, the various right-wing extremist groups, the Cornish and Welsh nationalists, etc . . .'.[16] In similar vein, Crick, arguing that what individuals entered in hotel registers (English, British, Welsh etc) was an intriguing insight into how citizens of the United Kingdom regarded their national identity, commented 'Once I read "Cornish" but I suspected, correctly, that it was a wag and not a nut'.[17]

Although other observers such as Pelling and Madgwick were prepared in the 1970s to admit to a Cornish political behaviour that was neither eccentric nor marginal, their treatment was equally brief and confused, their analyses flawed by an assumption that Cornwall was merely an integral part of a wider, homgeneous South West.[18] Although by the late 1970s Lee and Rallings were affording a more penetrating insight into the distinctive qualities of modern Cornwall, their work hardly affected wider discussions of territorial and ethnic diversity.[19] Even in the 1980s major contributions offered by commentators of the stature of A.D.Smith and Anthony Birch failed to take more than passing note of the Cornish situation.[20] Kearney's refreshing reassessment of British history[21], published in 1989, noted that Cornwall was deserving of more and better attention but was unable to provide it himself.

FROM GENETICISTS TO JOURNALISTS: DEFINING AN ETHNIC IDENTITY

Perhaps significantly, one of the first serious attempts to acknowledge the territorial importance of Cornwall and the ethnic identity of the Cornish came not from the United Kingdom, but from Australia. In 1988 the Australian National University produced its *The Australian People*, an encyclopedia of the nation, its people, and their origins. Described as '. . . one of the largest social science projects ever undertaken in Australia',[22] the encyclopedea tackled head-on issues of race and ethnicity. 'Race' as a concept was seen as both spurious and destructive, for it was based on '. . . the false belief that individual behaviour and social attributes are determined by the inheritance of certain physical characteristics'.[23] In other words, '. . . racial theory is racial prejudice . . .'.[24] In marked contrast, however, 'ethnicity' was considered a vital academic notion, although 'The concept of ethnicity is more difficult to grasp than that of race because it requires an understanding of social behaviour, which may vary over time . . .'.[25] The central characteristic of ethnic consciousness, it was argued, was a sense of identity: the shared but separate common origin, value-set, culture, religion, nationality, territory, region, or historical experience with which a community or individual chose to associate and affirm.

From this perspective, '. . . the Irish, Scots, Welsh, Cornish and others, often lumped together as persons of English-speaking background, are just as much "ethnics" as Greeks or Chinese'.[26] Territorial origin was of particular significance - '. . . living together for so long in a particular place that people possess a quite distinct history and background, as with the Cornish and Samoans'.[27] This recognition of the Cornish as a distinct ethnic group was reflected in the treatment that they received in the encyclopedia. Not only were the Cornish allocated their own Chapter, detailing their immigration and subsequent impact in colonial Australia,[28] but the English Chapter expressly 'Excludes Cornwall and Monmouthshire',[29] noting that Cornwall '. . . was something more than simply an extension of the South-West'.[30] It was also noted that the *Directory of Ethnic Community Organisations*, compiled by the Commonwealth Department of Immigration and Ethnic Affairs, included details of the several Cornish Associations active in contemporary Australia.

Although the pioneering work of Rallings and Lee (with its identification of distinctive Cornish political behavioural patterns) had highlighted Cornwall as a potentially rich field of endeavour for social scientists, academic research in Britain into Cornish 'difference' was led in the 1980s by geneticists who wished to test the biological affinities of the Cornish to other Celtic and non-Celtic peoples in north-western Europe. Not surprisingly perhaps, their findings showed that in some respects the Cornish were indeed biologically close to the other Celtic peoples, while in others they were less closely related, or in fact nearer to neighbouring Anglo-Saxon peoples. Thus '. . . such characteristics as head size, hair and eye colour point to greater affinities with the Celtic-speaking peoples of Wales, Ireland and Scotland, than with the neighbours of the Cornish to the east'.[31] But equally, 'On the other hand, the blood group evidence shows that the sample occupies a somewhat intermediate position between Celtic and Anglo-Saxon populations, but with a definite tendency to be aligned with the latter'.[32] However, the researchers urged caution in the discussion of their findings and considered that '. . . the biological evidence is not easy to interpret'.[33] Moreover, they acknowledged that genetic make-up was only incidental to ethnic identity and concluded that '. . . we would not presume to measure on the yardstick of heredity that which might more satisfactorily be assessed through genealogy, geography, dialect and culture'.[34]

In a conference in Plymouth in 1991 Malcolm Smith returned to these concerns, this time concentrating upon the blood group evidence. Locating the genetic data upon a two-dimensional plot, he showed that '. . . Cornwall holds a central position between the broad spread of the other Celtic populations to the left, and the Anglo-Saxon and other continental populations (including the Scandinavians) to the right and top'.[35] But this was even truer (surprisingly) for the southern Irish, located as they were amongst the Anglo-Saxon/Scandinanvian cluster, and once again Smith was led to cautious and qualified conclusions. He considered that 'In the Cornish case, admixture with immigrants from England during historical time does not seem well supported by evidence',[36] noting that in the 1851 Census 90% of the adult Cornish population had been born in Cornwall. In searching for possible explanations, he postulated that 'The area of intriguing murk which might hide the key to understanding the genetics is the colonisation and settlement of Cornwall from Wales and Ireland in the 5th and 6th centuries AD'.[37]

However, despite their cautious and inconclusive nature, Smith's remarks were siezed upon by an enthusiastic press which announced to the effect that there were no Celts left in Cornwall. BBC Spotlight declared that 'The Cornish are no more Celtic than your average Brummie', and newspaper articles handled the issue with a manner that one critic dismissed as 'racist glee'.[38] An embarrassed Malcolm Smith journeyed to Cornwall to put the record straight, but less than a year later new genetic evidence (again suggesting blood group affinity between the Cornish and their neighbours to the east) was interpreted by one journalist to mean that 'Bloodline ties Cornish to Devonians'.[39] This time there was an additional message: 'The Cornish might not like it, but . . . they are no different from the Devonians on the other side of the Tamar'.[40] Perhaps calculated to be provocative (or to assist in attempts to construct a 'Westcountry' identity), this assertion prompted a flurry of correspondence from irate Cornish readers, each pointing out that ethnic identity had little to do with biology and everything to do with culture, self-perception, and historical experience - including contemporary socio-economic conditions.

Whilst research in the area of genetics had led discussions of Cornish ethnicity into the arid and potentially dangerous area of spurious racial theories, the attendant debate had at least alerted sociologists and social anthropologists to the existence of a 'Cornish question'. Thus the late 1980s and early 1990s witnessed the first field-work in these areas in Cornwall. Mary McArthur found that 'There is evidence of a sharpening of conscious ethnic identity among Cornish people . . .'[41] and argued that the Cornish were a useful case study in which to test '. . . a number of theories of ethnic phenomena'.[42] She concluded that 'The Cornish are a named group or community, with a self-awareness (albeit of differing degrees) of a separate identity, being long established in a well-defined territory, and according to this definition do qualify for the label "ethnic group" or "ethnic community"'.[43] She added, 'It could be argued that the Cornish culture is today indistinguishable from the wider English culture but even if this were objectively agreed (which it is not), the degree of such differences are in any case immaterial'.[44] For McArthur, 'It is perception of difference, the importance attached to what may objectively be very small variations, which is relevant . . . it is not the attribute that makes the group, but the group that makes the attribute, important'.[45]

Caroline Vink, writing in 1993, attempted an anthropological analysis of what she termed the 'Cornish ethnoregional movement'. She considered that 'What makes Cornwall interesting is not so much the question of whether the ethnic roots claimed by the activists are genuine, but that there has been an emergence of an ethnoregional movement at all'.[46] The growth of the 'Cornish Revival' in the twentieth century had given form and content to the movement but 'Regional problems and economic deprivation are the fuel that can get the motor of ethnoregionalism running'.[47] Interestingly, she observed that for the ethnoregional activists, 'Their Cornish identity is an acquired identity. The awareness of a separate Cornish identity has arisen through their contacts with other activists, by living away from Cornwall or through other causes'.[48] Here Vink had anticipated the approach of Allan Ivey, who suggested the need for research into the social psychology of the Cornish ethnic identity, drawing upon 'identity theory' developed in the United States where individuals from Black communities were seen to have experienced systematic heightenings of ethnic consciousness as a direct result of encountering inequality and discrimination.[49] This, in turn, echoed the concerns of the Commission for Racial Equality which in 1992 had detected evidence of discrimination within Cornwall (prompting *The Times* to ask, 'Are the Cornish an ethnic minority?'[50]). The Commission had identified a '. . . substantial number of indigenous Cornish people who feel disadvantaged compared with "incomers" in relation to class, income, housing, employment . . .',[51] with one respondent - an advisory teacher - explaining that '. . . she fully accepted the view that the Cornish are an oppressed minority, and found that recognition of this fact in her work had proved to be a useful introduction to multi-cultural and and anti-racist education'.[52]

Similarly, the postulations of Vink and Ivey with regard to the Cornish were mirrored in Native American communities where a rediscovery of ethnic identity in response to decades of discrimination and inequality had led to 'The newer Indian culture . . . termed "Pan-Indianism" by anthroplogists'.[53] As Johnson remarked, this 're-invented' culture '. . . is expressed outwardly in social and political contexts, but perhaps most visibly by the ubiquitous "Powwow", which merges traditions of song and dance from various Indian cultures, heavily modified . . .'.[54] This process of 're-invention' (particularly the co-option and synthesis of cultural symbols from various sources) was not unlike that undertaken in Cornwall since 1945, the Powwow perhaps finding parallels in the Gorseth ceremony or the behaviour of 'Trelawny's Army' at Twickenham.

By 1992 the cues provided in the work of Rallings and Lee were at last being responded to by political scientists, and one major interpretation of modern Cornish history from a centre-periphery perspective concluded that '. . . given that it is the condition of periperality that has ensured the perpetuation of Cornwall's separate identity, one must reflect that the price of distnctiveness has been so often economic hardship and deprivation . . .'.[55] Here again was the link between ethnic identity and inequality, a connection also suggested by

Mary Buck *et al.* in their 1993 study of *Housing and Households in Cornwall*.[56] But such assessments inferred not only an inequality between Cornwall and England but also inequality within Cornwall itself - between the indigenous Cornish and the in-migrants. And yet to attempt to draw such a sharp distinction within the population of Cornwall was fraught with difficulty, and begged the question: 'just who are the Cornish?'

As long ago as 1890 the Cornish Association of South Australia volunteered an answer, identifying those who were Cornish by birth or descent and those who had acquired their Cornish credentials by virtue of 'long residence' in Cornwall.[57] Today, the London Cornish Association adopts similar criteria but distinguishes between those of Cornish parentage (ie born outside Cornwall but with at least one Cornish-born parent) and those of Cornish descent (a more distant connection), as well as a identifying those who have become Cornish 'by marriage'[58]. As Peter Mitchell notes in Chapter 6, the possibility of precise definition is made all the more remote now that the overwhelming proportion of the 'indigenous Cornish' in South East Cornwall has in fact been born across the Tamar in Plymouth. Nevertheless, Buck *et al.* sought objective definitions in setting the methodology for their project. Interviewees were considered Cornish if: a) they were born in Cornwall and had lived most of their life in Cornwall, or b) at least one parent was born in Cornwall and they had lived most of their life in Cornwall, or c) if b) obtained but they had migrated from Cornwall to return later.[59]

Perry *et al.* in their study noted that the 'returning Cornish' (those who had left Cornwall for career or other reasons but had now 'come home') were in socio-economic terms a distinct category when compared to both 'locals' (indigenous Cornish who had never removed from Cornwall) and non-Cornish in-migrants,[60] while anecdotal evidence suggests a fourth category consisting of those born outside Cornwall of Cornish parentage who decide to 'return' to Cornwall as a result of kinship ties or ethnic self-identification. As one interviewee explained to Vink, 'My mum is Cornish, but we have always lived on the wrong side of the Tamar. When I was a boy she would point in the direction of Cornwall and tell me "don't forget, that is home"'.[61] Similarly, the re-emerging international Cornish identity of the 1980s and 90s drew attention to an increasingly large body of Cornish-Australians, Cornish-Americans and others who saw themselves at one level as being 'Cornish'. In addition, evidence suggests that many post-War in-migrants have acquired 'Cornish' characteristics, whether consciously or unconsciously, while their off-spring not only take pride in their Cornish-born status but are also subjected to precisely the same distinctive socio-economic forces that socialise the children of more long-established families. Certainly, Buck *et al.* found indicators amongst in-migrants which '. . . might be taken as the achievement of a fairly high level of assimilation into a Cornish community . . .'.[62] As McArthur observed, '. . . unless the category of Cornish is submerged (which currently seems unlikely) it is possible that . . . the incomers of today will become (or produce) the Cornish of tomorrow'.[63] As early as the 1960s Mebyon Kernow was defining 'Cornish nationality' for membership purposes as the attribute of 'anyone who feels him or herself to be Cornish'.[64]

However, despite this fluidity of ethnic identity, ethnicity is a question of other-perception as well as self-perception. Thus not only may some in-migrants strongly resist the suggestion that they or their off-spring might become Cornish (particularly if this were to mean becoming 'less English') but equally many indigenous Cornish would find it diffcult to apply the 'Cornish' label to in-migrants with 'up-country ideas', 'Cockney accents' or other 'foreign' attributes (such as the ease with which they penetrate the Cornish housing market). At its most extreme, such an attitude is merely parochialism ('You're not really Cornish unless you're from west of Hayle River'[65]) but at its most sophisticated it represents a genuine concern that the pace and volume of post-War in-migration has been so vast that assimilation may not be possible or, indeed, that the in-migrants may impose their own standards on Cornish life.[66] And, as Malcolm Williams makes clear in Chapter 7, the underlying link between ethnicity and inequality has become crsytalized in the housing market, where the indigenous Cornish have become clearly disadvantaged as a result of in-migration. Perhaps not surprisingly, Perry *et al.* found that 25% of in-migrants had experienced some conflict with locals.[67] Intriguingly, the planning policy controvery in North Cornwall which in 1991 made UK national headlines was at one level a contest between indigenous Cornish and in-migrants, the former reserving their right to build new homes for themselves whenever and whereever they wished, and the latter determined to preserve their rural idyll at all costs.

In assessing the impact of the widespread post-War in-migration from England to rural Wales (an experience similar to that of Cornwall, but with the added dimension of language), Colin Williams has argued that 'Newcomers may be considered as an insidious threat to fragile local communities, but they are more profitably seen as a welcome development to strengthen local services, employment opportunities, and a diverse quality of life'.[68] However, this was only possible 'If the appropriate indigenous cultural infra-structure is established, with institutional safeguards and means of promoting the assimilation of newcomers into the community . . .'.[69] In Cornwall (unlike Wales) the cultural infrastructure is flimsy and does not (with the notable exception of BBC Radio Cornwall) enjoy state patronage or command the attention of big-business. Thus the mechanisms of assimilation noted by McArthur and Buck *et al.* must rest upon an inherent strength of ethnic identity in the Cornish community and, particularly, the readiness of the Cornish community to accommodate change. And yet such accommodation does not imply resignation or acquiesence, for - as Ronald Perry notes in Chapter 3 - one significant feature of Cornish activity in the 1970s and 1980s was the emergence of 'opposition economics' articulated by groups such as Cornish Alternatives to the Structure Plan and the Cornish Social and Economic Research Group. Here, indeed, ethnic identity became a valuable vehicle for the elucidation of Cornish socio-economic gievances, with the necessity of confronting and accommodating change leading not to the demise of that identity (as many had feared) but to its enhancement. As Hobsbawm explained rather quaintly in 1990,

> The Cornish are fortunate to be able to paint their regional discontents in the attractive colours of their Celtic tradition, which makes them so much more visible . . . . They are luckier, say, than Merseyside, which can mobilize in defence of the hard-hit local interests only the memory of the Beatles, of generations of Scouse comedians, and the proud tradition of its rival football teams . . ., Merseyside cannot blow a national trumpet. Cornwall can.[70]

Paradoxically, however, despite its apparent 'visibility', Cornwall failed generally to catch the eye of central government in the 1980s and 1990s, while Merseyside and other 'inner-city' conurbations were singled-out for particular attention by Westminster and Whitehall. A Minister was appointed to address the problems of 'inner-city' regeneration, special 'enterprise zones' were created to focus regional development on such areas, and European Community funding was sought - a process which culminated in 1993 in the designation of Merseyside as an EC Objective 1 region, acknowledging it as being amongst the poorest areas of the European Community (or Union, as it has become) and thus deserving of extensive grant aid. Ironically, Cornwall - with a Gross Domestic Product lower than that of Merseyside - failed to achieve Objective 1 status, a result of the government's insistence that for EC bidding purposes Cornwall and Devon be considered together as a 'sub-region'. In effect, Devon's relative affluence had obscurred the scale of Cornwall's problems. The government had prevented Cornwall from blowing its 'national trumpet' on the European stage, despite strenuous attempts by Cornwall County Council to present a separate Cornish case (reminding European observers that 'Many still see Cornwall as having a distinct "national" identity').[71]

For many Cornish activists this failure to attract the attention of central government created a sense of frustration and powerlessness, a mood that was caught by Linda Christmas in her perceptive portrayal of Britain in the 1980s:

> Cornwall does not wish to be ignored and does not wish to be hyphenated to Devon, as though 'Cornwall and Devon' were like Gilbert and Sullivan, nothing without each other, devoid of a separate identity. Cornwall is fed up with border blurring, with having more and more decisions that affect daily life decided on the other side of the Tamar[72].

Christmas also noted the link between identity and socio-economic protest, explaining, for example, that the Cornish '. . . were no longer happy to see potatoes dug out of the ground and taken to England to be put in plastic bags and sold back to them via Tesco. Why couldn't the value be added in

Cornwall?'[73] Similarly, as well as encountering the traditional Cornish criticism of the tourist industry (seasonal, low-paid employment), she detected a newer strand of concern:

> They told the story of how Cornwall's stall at British Travel Week had been surrounded by Hull, Bradford and Greater Manchester. They would like to find a way of attracting the kind of tourist who is interested in Celtic Cornwall, the kind of tourist who comes to appreciate Cornish culture . . . The lovers of sea and the surf are no longer enough.[74]

An academic journalist, Christmas had been drawn to Cornwall - like other acedemics - by its 'visibility' (or rather, 'difference'), that same quality described by Hobsbawm but all but ignored by central government. While the government was in the late 1980s and 1990s increasingly reluctant to respond to territorial issues that would emphasise diversity within the United Kingdom (vide its position on Scottish devolution), countenancing support for the 'inner-cities' on the presumption that this would foster socio-economic homogeneity rather than diversity, academic observers had no such reservations and in increasing numbers found Cornwall 'a suitable case for treatment'. From geneticists to journalists, academics were drawn to investigate the characteristics of contemporary Cornwall.

By the 1990s, then, Cornwall had at last captured the attention of scholars anxious to explore the new-found ethnic and territorial diversity of Britain and Europe, while Cornish Studies as an area of academic endeavour had both acquired an inter-disciplinary flavour and developed a social science equipped to handle contemporary issues. Research, although often tentative and preliminary, had consistently identified a Cornish 'difference' in areas as distinct as voting behaviour and kinship patterns, or even genetics! Moreover, as McArthur had intimated, Cornwall was itself a fertile ground within which scholars might operate, the Cornish case exhibiting a range of characteristics that in some respects typified the experience of Western European peripheries in the post-War era but in others areas was unique. In addition, within Cornwall observers were increasingly aware of new and complex conditions created by rapid socio-economic change since 1945, arguing that these conditions merited closer investigation. Central government might not have woken-up to the existence of a 'Cornish question', but the academic community had.

REFERENCES

1. see Philip Payton, *The Making of Modern Cornwall: Historical Experience and the Persistence of 'Difference'*, Dyllansow Truran, Redruth, 1992.
2. Geoffrey Ordish, *Cornish Engine Houses*, Vols. 1 & 2, Bradford Barton, Truro, 1967 & 1968. Although published in the 1960s these memorable volumes include many photographs taken before the War.

3. A.K.Hamilton Jenkin, *The Cornish Miner*, 1927, republished David & Charles, Newton Abbot, 1972.
4. John Rowe, *Cornwall in the Age of the Industrial Revolution*, Liverpool University Press, Liverpool, 1953, republished Hillside Publications, St Austell, 1993; A.C.Todd, *The Cornish Miner in America*, Bradford Barton, Truro, 1967; D.B.Barton, *A History of Copper Mining in Cornwall and Devon*, Bradford Barton, 1961, revised ed. 1968; D.B.Barton, *A History of Tin Mining and Smelting in Cornwall*, Bradford Barton, Truro, 1967, republished Cornwall Books, Exeter, 1989.
5. *Institute of Cornish Studies Bulletin No.1, June 1972.*
6. *ICS, June 1972.*
7. Anthony D.Smith, *Theories of Nationalism*, Duckworth, London, 1971; Michael Hechter, *Internal Colonialism: The Celtic Fringe and British National Development*, Routledge, London, 1975; Jim Bulpitt, *Territory and Power in the United Kingdom*, Manchester University Press, Manchester, 1983; Stein Rokkan and Derek W.Urwin, *The Politics of Territorial Identity: Studies in European Regionalism*, Sage, London, 1982.
8. Sidney Tarrow, *Between Centre and Periphery: Grassroots Politicians in Italy and France*, Yale University Press, New Haven, 1977,
9. Daniel P. Moynihan, *Pandemonium: Ethnicity in International Politics*, Oxford University Press, Oxford, 1993.
10. Victoria Syme and Philip Payton, 'Eastern Europe: Economic Transition and Ethnic Tension', in Michael Pugh (ed.), *European Security: Towards 2000*, Manchester University Press, Manchester, 1992; Philip Payton, 'Ethnic Consciousness', in Michael Foley (ed.), *Political Ideologies Since 1945*, Manchester University Press, Manchester, forthcoming 1994.
11. Richard Rose, *The United Kingdom as a Multi-national State*, University of Strathclyde Research Occasional Paper No.6, Glasgow, 1970.
12. For example, M.A.Havinden, J.Queniart and J.Stanyer, *Centre and Periphery: Brittany and Cornwall & Devon Compared*, University of Exeter Press, Exeter, 1991; for a critical review see *Journal of Interdisciplinary Economics*, Vol.4, No.2, 1992.
13. R.M.Punnett, *British Government and Politics*, Heinemann, London, 1968, 2nd ed. 1971, p78.
14. Punnett, 1971, p104.
15. Robert E.Dowse and John A.Hughes, *Political Sociology*, Wiley, London, 1972, p205.
16. Dowse & Hughes, 1972, p205.
17. Bernard Crick, 'An Englishman Considers his Passport', in Neil Evans (ed.), *National Identity in the British Isles*, Coleg Harlech Occasional Papers in Welsh Studies, No3, Harlech, 1989, p23.
18. Henry Pelling, *Social Geography of British Elections, 1885-1910*, Macmillan, London, 1962, p159; P.J.Madgwick, *The Politics of Rural Wales*, Hutchinson, London, 1973, p15.
19. Colin Rallings and Adrian Lee, 'Cornwall: The "Celtic Fringe" in English Politics', unpublished paper, ECPR workshop, Brussels, 1979; Colin Rallings and Adrian Lee, 'Politics of the Periphery - The Case of Cornwall', unpublished paper, PSA UK Politics workgroup, Aberystwyth, 1977.
20. Anthony D.Smith, *Ethnic Revival in the Modern World*, Cambridge University Press, Cambridge, 1981, p11; Anthony H.Birch, *Nationalism and National Integration*, Unwin Hyman, London, 1989, p70.
21. Hugh Kearney, *The British Isles: A History of Four Nations*, Cambridge University Press, Cambridge, 1989, p1 and p105.
22. James Jupp (ed.), *The Australian People: An Encyclopedia of the Nation, its People, and their Origins*, Angus Robertson, Sydney, 1988, dustcover notes.
23. Jupp, 1988, p2.
24. Jupp, 1988, p2.
25. Jupp, 1988, p2.
26. Jupp, 1988, p119.
27. Jupp, 1988, p119.
28. Philip Payton, 'The Cornish', in Jupp, 1988.
29. Jupp, 1988, pp372-373.
30. Jupp, 1988, p389.

31. R.G.Harvey, M.T.Smith, S.Sherren, L.Bailey and S.J.Hyndman, 'How Celtic are the Cornish?: A Study of Biological Affinities', *Journal of the Anthropological Institute*, Vol.21, No.2, June 1986.
32. Harvey *et al*, 1986.
33. Harvey *et al*, 1986.
34. Harvey *et al*, 1986.
35. Malcolm T. Smith, 'Cornish Genes and Celtic Culture', unpublished paper presented at Polytechnic South West, 1991.
36. Smith, 1991.
37. Smith, 1991.
38. *Western Morning News*, 18 November 1991.
39. *Western Morning News*, 29 August 1992.
40. *Western Morning News*, 29 August 1992.
41. Mary McArthur, 'The Cornish: A Case Study of Ethnicity', unpublished MSc thesis, University of Bristol, 1988, Summary, see also p100.
42. McArthur, 1988, Summary.
43. McArthur, 1988, p81.
44. McArthur, 1988, p81.
45. McArthur, 1988, p81.
46. Caroline Vink, 'Be Forever Cornish! The Emergence of a Cornish Ethnoregional Movement in the Twentieth Century', unpublished doctoral thesis, University of Amsterdam, 1993, Summary; see also Caroline Vink, 'Be Forever Cornish! Some Observations on the Cornish Ethnoregional Movement in the Late Twentieth Century', *Cornish Studies*, second series, No.1, 1993.
47. Vink, Amsterdam, 1993, Summary.
48. Vink, Amsterdam. 1993, Summary.
49. Allan Ivey and Philip Payton, 'Cornish Identity Theory: Denigration or Affirmation?', *Cornish Studies*, second series, No.2, forthcoming 1994.
50. *The Times*, cited in *Cornish Banner*, November 1992, No.70.
51. *Cornish Banner*, November 1992, N0.70.
52. Eric Jay, *Keep Them in Birmingham: Challenging Racism in the South West of England*, Commission for Racial Equality, London, 1992, p16.
53. Michael G.Johnson, *The Native Tribes of North America: A Concise Encyclopedia*, Windhow and Green, London, 1992, p197.
54. Johnson, 1992, p197; for a Cornish comparison see Bernard Deacon and Philip Payton, 'Re-inventing Cornwall: Culture Change on the European Periphery', *Cornish Studies*, second series, No.1, 1993.
55. Payton, 1992, p241.
56. Mary Buck, Lyn Bryant and Malcolm Williams, *Housing and Households in Cornwall: A Pilot Study of Cornish Families*, University of Plymouth, Plymouth, 1993; see also Mary Buck, Lyn Bryant and Malcolm Williams, 'Housing the Cornish: Containing the Crisis', *Cornish Studies*, second series, No.1, 1993.
57. *Commercial, Shipping and General Advertiser for West Cornwall*, 5 April 1890.
58. *London Cornish Association, Membership List*, 1993.
59. Buck *et al*, Plymouth, 1993, p23.
60. Ronald Perry, with Ken Dean and Bryan Brown, and with the assistance of David Shaw, *Counterurbanisation: International Case Studies of Socio-Economic Change in Rural Areas*, Geo Books, Norwich, 1986, pp89-101.
61. Vink, 1993, p62.
62. Buck *et al*, 1993, p51.
63. McArthur, 1988, p97.
64. Charles Thomas, *The Importance of Being Cornish in Cornwall*, Institute of Cornish Studies, Redruth, 1973, p14.
65. Gerald and Sylvia Priestland, *West of Hayle River*, Wildwood, London, 1980, p9.
66. Thomas, 1973; Perry *et al*, 1986.
67. Perry *et al*, 1986, p101.

68. Colin H. Williams, 'Assimilating Newcomers: an insidious threat or a welcome development?', in Llinos Dafis, *The Lesser Used Languages - Assimilating Newcomers*, Joint Working Party on Bilingualism in Dyfed, Carmarthen, 1992, p26.
69. Williams, 1992, p26.
70. Eric Hobsbawm, *Nations and Nationalism since 1870*, Cambridge University Press, Cambridge, 1991, p170.
71. Cornwall County Council, Devon County Council, Plymouth City Council, *Towards an Economic Strategy for Cornwall and Devon*, Exeter, 1992, p14.
72. Linda Christmas, *Chopping Down the Cherry Trees: A Portrait of Britain in the Eighties*, Penguin, London,1991, p262.
73. Christmas, 1991, p263.
74. Christmas, 1991, p263.

CHAPTER 2

CORNWALL CIRCA 1950

Ronald Perry

It was not until the early fifties, wrote David St John Thomas in his Publisher's Note to Hamilton Jenkin's *Cornwall and Its People*, '... that motorised tourists, television and other forces finally broke down old patterns ...'.

Many would agree, for the period seems enshrined in the collective memory as a golden age before, as the writer Robert Homan put it, '... the outsider came in such numbers and ruined everything'. Here is Homan's recollection of that era: 'The sound of a silver band drifting through the mist ... a choir in full cry with Wesley ... the roar of a rugby crowd as boots and fists fly'. To St John Thomas it was a time when he could catch a bus to St Just in Penwith and see no more strangers than in a north country mining community. But did the early fifties really witness the last of old Cornwall, or is this another case of nostalgia masquerading as history? St John Thomas and Homan were by no means the first, nor were they to be the last, to set the death of the Cornish spirit in the days of their own youth. For Philip Payton, in *The Making of Modern Cornwall*, on the other hand, the fifties have quite a different significance, marking the end of a great 'paralysis' that traced its origins back to the collapse of copper mining nearly a century earlier. Only recently, suggests Payton, has Cornwall perhaps broken free from a fossilised Victorian mould, with a new generation of post-War Revivalists seeking their 'Kernow Resurgent'. But again, they are not the first to seek a golden age in the future rather than in the past. The Cornish, as Harris the nineteenth-century mining poet once wrote, are eternal children of hope.[1]

This Chapter sets out to explore some of the realities behind such visions of the 1950s. But it should be made clear from the outset that it is only a preliminary scan of a largely unchronicled epoch.[2] For most historians of Cornwall pay scant attention to the twentieth century - one recent self-styled 'modern county' history, for instance, while full of illuminating insights about the distant past, spared just half a dozen pages for the last hundred years, four of them recording the decline of mining and fishing. Like most accounts of modern times this Chapter provides, in some ways, more of an agenda for further research than a body of agreed conclusions.

The Chapter starts by looking at Cornwall's distinctive settlement pattern of small, free-standing towns of equal and jealously guarded status and individuality. It examines the dimensions of that diversity - localised political loyalties, industrial specialisation, self-contained administrative, transport and retail catchments, a fragmented intellectual infrastructure. Then it considers Cornwall's unique mixture of economic activities: dairy farming, fishing, mining, china clay working, ship repairing, engineering, tourism, retirement immigration, and defence. In this context it analyses some contemporary assessments of its strengths and weaknesses - structural, locational, socio-economic. Differences are noted between the inner dynamics of a modernising elite of locally-owned medium-sized engineering and extractive firms (ignored in outside surveys) and a traditionalism, bordering upon self-destruction, in some other local trades. After a review of life in inland rural Cornwall, the tensions between conflicting views on coastal development - pre-industrial, industrial, post-industrial - are identified.

The Chapter ends by suggesting how poets and painters, novelists, historians and guide-writers conditioned the way that the Cornish looked upon themselves and that outsiders - planners and politicians, industrialists and investors - saw them. Now since the economist is not encouraged to stray into realms that cannot be strictly measured or analysed, perhaps a word is needed to explain such forays into the ill-illumined no man's land between art and economics. The aim here is not to present an over-arching cultural theory of Cornish history, nor a synthesis of humanistic and deterministic viewpoints, nor to treat a flourishing (or inactive) artistic life as an index of socio-economic wellbeing. An artist, whether Cornish or not, may dwell in Cornwall without acquiring the stigmata of 'Cornishness' and may, consciously or otherwise, belong to a wider cultural community. All that this Chapter does seek to suggest is that art may sometimes colour economics, just as economics may drive art.

A SEMI-URBAN SETTLEMENT PATTERN

We cannot hope to recapture the essential quality and diversity of Cornwall circa 1950 without taking account of its unusual configuration of urban and rural settlements. With under 1% of the UK population and a density of only 245 to the square mile compared with 750 for England and Wales, it might well have seemed a classic case of a rural peripheral region. But such comparisons ignored factors of great significance: an industrially-influenced east-west imbalance, a post-industrial concentration along the coast, an unusually uniform spread of small towns and a relative absence of the nucleated 'Anglo-saxon' village.

Cornwall owed this pattern to a variety of causes, geographic, climatic, geological and ideological. A narrow peninsula jutting into the Atlantic, isolated outcrops of copper, tin and china clay, a warm but humid climate, a coastline of spectacular cliffs and sandy bays: all these attributes spread farmers, miners, fishermen, defence personnel, tourists and retirees fairly thinly over the territory. Cornwall was not a polarised region like Devon, where two thirds of the population lived in the shadow of Plymouth, Torbay or Exeter and the rest in a sparsely-peopled agrarian hinterland. Nor was it a homogeneous region, like parts of rural Wales, Scotland or Ireland, with small agricultural market centres which provided a uniform range of services for the surrounding villages. Eastern Cornwall, it is true, was (apart from the corner abutting Plymouth) indeed a thinly peopled agrarian district, where 18% of Cornwall's population covered 57% of its surface at an average density of 80 to the square mile. But in the area from Penzance to St Austell 55% of Cornwall's inhabitants lived in a semi-urban concentration of 650 to the square mile. Of the bigger towns, only Saltash was located in the east and that place in part owed its population of nearly 8000 to a role as dormitory suburb of Plymouth. Of the 64 firms employing one hundred or more workers, only three were in the east, again at Saltash, where they served the distribution and building needs of a Plymouth-dominated area.

Cornwall's other leading towns had grown by producing specialised sets of goods and services, some of them sold to people all over the UK and across the world. Camborne-Redruth was the focus for mine-engineering, St Austell for china clay and its associated technology, Penzance-Newlyn for farming, fishing, tourism and art, Falmouth for ship repairing and holidaymaking, Truro for administration and commerce, Newquay for tourism *par excellence*. In the conventional models of industrial location used by geographers and central planners at the time, export activities concentrated in large central places. In Cornwall they did not. But a stereotyping centralist perspective insisted, in the 1948 White Paper on 'The Distribution of Industry', in pigeon-holing Cornwall along with remoter Wales and Scotland as under-developed and 'rural' and therefore inappropriate for status or assistance as an industrial Development Area .

The second factor determining Cornwall's settlement structure was people-led seaboard growth. Whereas, during the first half of the twentieth century, the population of Cornwall as a whole rose by 5%, that of the coastal parishes (enlarged in area during the process) increased by 55%. Newquay was the fastest growing Cornish town during that period, trebling in size to nearly 10,000 to become the premier seaside resort, with a third of Cornwall's employment in hotel and catering. Bude was second, in relative terms, rising from under 2000 to over 5000, and other expanding places included Looe (with a population of 3600), St Ives (8,600) and Penzance (20,000). Carbis Bay and St Ives were also the most popular retirement spots with 25% of their male population of pensionable age (double the UK norm) and other resorts with high levels of retirees included Newquay, Bude and Looe with 22% and Padstow, Fowey and Penzance with 18% to 20%. Families of defence personnel added to growth around Torpoint, Newquay, Padstow and Helston, and 1100 commuters travelled daily to Plymouth from Saltash and 750 from Torpoint.

Finally, there was the residue of Wartime expansion. Between 1939 and 1941 the civilian population of Cornwall shot up by 20% from 308,000 to

370,000 through an invasion of voluntary exiles (including some famous artists like Barbara Hepworth, Ben Nicholson and Naum Gabo), evacuees from the big cities, private schools transferred en bloc, refugees from Belgium and France and Land Army girls. In addition there were of course British and allied soldiers, sailors and airmen and, later on, German and Italian prisoners of War and Polish refugees. Not all of them went back after the War and most of those who stayed continued to live on the coast. While total population contracted to 330,000, at Newquay it remained 29% higher, at Looe 21%, Bude 18%.

MARKET TOWNS & INDUSTRIAL CENTRES

While coastal towns were increasing in population, most inland centres stayed at much the same level. Several of them - Lostwithiel, Launceston, Bodmin, Truro - had once been, or might consider themselves to be, Cornwall's nerve centre but there was no real sign of the development of any one place as a dominant capital. Launceston was a hub for local fanners and for public services, more influential than its population size of 4500 (slightly larger than Liskeard's) might suggest and with a retail catchment extending well into west Devon. Bodmin was the County Town, with the Assizes, the Regimental barracks, the County Mental Asylum and the old County gaol, but its population of 5800 had not increased much since the Victorian era and although the first meeting of Cornwall County Council took place in Bodmin in 1889, the second and all subsequent gatherings were held at Truro. When, in Edwardian times, County Hall was built there and the Nave of its Angllcan Cathedral was blessed in the presence of the Duke and Duchess of Cornwall, it seemed set to become Cornwall's capital. But, half a century on, its population of 13,000 only gave it fifth place in the hierarchy of towns, and a poor fifth at that, the other centres being in the 20,000 plus range, and ranking higher in terms of industrial employment and retail sales.

The bulk of Cornwall's industry was distributed between three places. Camborne-Redruth with Hayle was the traditional heart of mining and engineering with the largest remaining mining company as well as two explosives factories and a world-famous construction and mine equipment firm. But even the Camborne Redruth area, Cornwall's largest conurbation, was in many ways still a constellation of small interconnected villages with their own local traditions. The second industrial town, Falmouth, had taken over as Cornwall's biggest employer of skilled engineering manpower and many Camborne and Redruth men now commuted there to work in its shipyards. The other main centre was the china clay district of St Austell where English China Clays, by far Cornwall's greatest industrial employer, was a real political as well as economic force in the land, a powerful counterweight to the pull of the towns further west.

Each of Cornwall's main centres had a distinctive pattern of retailing. Of course the multiple chains, or 'Company Stores' as they were called then, had shown their faces on the high street in Edwardian times, and during the interwar years the incongruous facades of Montagu Burtons and Woolworths replaced traditional premises. But family owned haberdashers and drapers maintained Victorian standards of courtesty and service. Going shopping was a popular Saturday pastime, especially as car ownership accelerated in the 1950s. According to one survey, Penzance fulfilled a psychological need for a 'big town' where the people of Penzance could dress up to parade along its shopping streets, and Falmouth also more than held its own, with Cornwall's only Marks and Spencer's and a reputation for high class leather goods. Redruth housed the West End Department Stores, Cornwall's largest, which attracted people from a wide area, St Austell was the social and retail centre for the china clay area, and Launceston was widely known as the place to go for riding hats and boots. The smaller towns, too, were individual and vibrant, often boasting a market, with clearly defined market and early closing days, meeting places served by local bus networks, cafes, restaurants and small family shops offering locally produced goods. Bus and railway stations had an air of energy and purpose, local hospitals had beds and casualty units. People identified with their local town, which provided them with work in shops and factories and all the services they needed in an age when pastimes and leisure pursuits were more limited. Holidays were generally taken at home and were usually short, a time to cultivate the vegetable garden or spend a few days on the coast nearby.

PAROCHIALISM, REGIONALISM & CORNISH NATIONALISM

Politically, the industrial culture had long been allied to a tradition of anti-centralism at all levels of disaggregation: a distaste for Truro-rule as well as Whitehall-rule. Loyalties were localised. Cornwall's representatives at Westminster were known as good constituency members with no overriding ambitions and no ideological axe to grind. At County and district council level Independents, cast in the same mould, were 'elected' (often unopposed) and could be trusted to look after parochial interests. Apart from Truro, an Anglican isle in a Methodist sea (although it contained one of the largest Nonconformist chapels in Britain) Cornwall was also noted for its dislike of rigid ecclesiastical control from above and, as a corollary of its democratic nature, a tendency to rifts and dissensions. Despite dwindling membership, half a dozen denominations still co-existed and each town possessed a number of rival chapels, all struggling to maintain vast edifices as big as those of the northern manufacturing cities, erected in more affluent times before industrial decline, mass education, cinemas, wireless and the traumas of two World Wars eroded the old black and white divisions between good and evil. But in the immediate post-War years, both Methodists and Anglicans showed comparatively high levels of religious allegiance in Cornwall, compared with Britain as a whole, and the long-term decline of Cornish Methodism seemed to have abated while the Church of

England, although a minority church, was a growing minority - coloured still by the inter-War growth in 'Anglo-Catholic' and 'Celtic Revivalist' sentiment.

What might have given Cornwall a locally recognised rallying point, a platform from which to articulate territorial loyalties or political aspirations, would have been a thriving nationalist movement based upon the Celtic heritage, and for half a century or more a devoted band of enthusiasts had striven to construct one. Henry Jenner, through the publication of his study of the Conish language, and the admission of Cornwall into the ranks of the Celtic Congress, had begun the process, although his pre-industrial, monarchist and Catholic leanings did not make him the ideal leader of a Nonconformist, dissenting people who were exceptionally proud of their industrial achievements. Indeed, some early Revivalists, scholarly and refined, felt that Cornwall's industrial period was best forgotten, a rather sordid and money-grubbing interlude, an ugly blotch on the rich tapestry of Celtic-Cornish history.

The intellectual ferment of the great days of mining, when Cornwall was a focus of the advanced technology of its day, fairly bristling with talented engineers and inventors and a place of burgeoning distinction in the arts as well as the sciences, had left a heritage of learned institutes. But the intellectual infrastructure too was fragmented. If Truro could boast its Royal Institution and Museum, Penzance could rightly take equal pride in its (slightly more venerable) Geological Society, Falmouth could counter with its Polytechnic Society and Camborne its internationally famous School of Mines. Such societies, together with other professional mining, engineering, literary and antiquarian associations, kept alive a faith of Cornish people in their scientific and technical prowess for which, Philip Payton has argued, they had a deep psychological need.[3]

Some of the latent antipathy between believers in pre-industrial as opposed to industrial Cornwall dissolved during the inter-War period. Morton Nance and zealous members of his Old Cornwall Societies, with amiable electicism, welded stone age artefacts, quaint dialect sayings and pasty recipes into a Celto-Victorian synthesis, an example of which was an early meeting of the Cornish Gorseth when Jenner, Nance and the other Bards descended in their flowing 'pre-industrial' robes from the heights of Carn Brea to industrial Camborne to partake of a clotted cream tea served by ladies dressed as balmaidens. Even so, while Bards swore allegiance to Arthur the King and the Motherland of Cornwall, they did not stir the hearts and minds of the majority of the Cornish people. At a time when farming families lived on the poverty line and a third or more of industrial workers were on the dole, the niceties of the Cornish movement seemed mere dilettantism. And Cornwall-wide loyalties only surfaced occasionally, as when in the mid-1940s Plymouth made one of its periodic attempts to annex South East Cornwall, or when the Cornish rugby team was enjoying a run of good luck. This is not to say that Cornish patriotism did not exist and indeed flourish. The Cornish people were proud to be 'Cornish' but this did not necessarily stop many of them from 'being English' as well, and very few would have objected to the description 'British'. That many saw no great problem in accepting this dual or even triple nationality was displayed clearly during the War years. When John Legonna, a Cornish nationalist, bicycled around seeking someone to hide him so that he would not have to fight for England he found only one 'true Cornishman' to shelter him, the coppersmith Carkeeg of Hayle. To be Cornish, to be a Celt, Legonna concluded, was merely a sentiment, just a matter of '... taking the antique waters at some twilight spa'.[4]

In 1951, however, a group called Mebyon Kernow (Sons of Cornwall) was formed which, while recognising the value of Celtic roots and language as the necessary basis for building a national consciousness, nonetheless put more weight upon economic and political aims. To begin with they kept a low profile, preferring to work as a pressure group within existing parties, especially the Liberals who traditionally had shown more sympathy for devolution of power to the regions. But the 1951 election returned to power a Tory party which had little interest in regionalism. Such territorial divisions as they recognised, within government services or nationalised industries or for statistical purposes, related to a nebulous area known as the 'South West' with its ex-centric capital of Bristol, whose socio-economic links with Cornwall were minimal and whose cultural ties with the Cornish were non-existent.

INDEPENDENT CITY STATES

To sum up this account of the geography and politics of Cornwall, Cornwall was in no way, and never had been, a 'city region', where a dominant capital spread its tentacles of commerce and power down a hierarchy of smaller and subservient towns and villages. Nor was it a homogeneous rural region made up of small towns serving an agricultural hinterland. What gave the territory its distinctive character was its configuration of independent-minded, self-contained 'city states', of roughly equal size, each with its own jealously guarded personality, traditions and sphere of influence. This compartmentalised and heterogeneous structure displayed itself in many ways, some of which have been discussed already, some to be considered later: localised political loyalties, self-sufficient administrative units, separate public transport and retail catchments, a dispersed and specialised pattern of industry, free-standing port ownership and a fragmented intellectual infrastructure. Not all these decentralising characteristics were exclusive to Cornwall of course, but put together they amounted to a high degree of disaggregation which was not accidental, but reflected the individualistic and independent character of the Cornish people and their antipathy to large monolithic structures and strict hierarchies of control.

Local leaders recognised this diversity in their 1952 *Development Plan*,[5] the first to cover Cornwall as a whole. Recent local government reforms had given them more powers over key areas like education, but this did not lead them to flex their muscles and try to centralise. Instead they sought to perpetuate the traditional decentralised pattern of industry, commerce and higher learning. Any industrial expansion that occurred (which was not expected to be great) was apportioned between the existing centres of Camborne-Redruth, Falmouth and St Austell. An ambitious programme to enhance the intellectual infrastructure was shared between a College of Technology at Camborne, one for Art, Architecture and Commerce at Truro, an Agricultural Institute in the east and two residential centres for Adult Education and for Teacher Training in unspecified locations. These projects, inspired by the idealistic visions of early post-War years, all came to nothing. There were several reasons why they failed, not least of which were lack of money and of local commitment. But one problem was that of presenting such a disaggregated pattern to Whitehall administrators looking for large centres of industrial and academic excellence, to whom Cornwall was not an intriguing example of complementarity but a land of warring tribes, and such an attitude held up progress for decades to come.

THE STATE OF THE ECONOMY

Turning to the economic situation circa 1950, the first thing to be said is that it was a time of unaccustomed prosperity and demographic stability for Cornwall, an era of international retrenchment, when countries were recovering from the ravages of War, giving a chance to Cornwall's industries to meet the pent-up demand for their products in the absence of some powerful overseas competitors. Unemployment dropped to an historic low and workers were not forced to migrate en masse as in the past, although the young continued to leave in search of better prospects in a UK of full employment. But this loss was almost offset - in numerical terms at least - by an inflow of retirees and the small net deficit through migration was nearly balanced by an excess of local births over deaths.

As far as Cornwall's basic industries were concerned, agriculture prospered under a regime of price control, and mining revived after War broke out in Korea in 1951, when tin prices quadrupled. Ironically, Cornwall now suffered from a shortage of skilled men, and miners had to be brought in from Italy and elsewhere. Quarrying, by now a bigger employer than mining, was returning to pre-War levels of production and shipping out large quantities of granite and slate. Clay output, despite a lack of fuel, transport and labour, climbed 25% above the pre-War peak and over 60% of it was exported. Employment in engineering had risen to heights not known since the days of the Edwardian tin boom but this time the stimulus came not from local mines but from exports of mining and construction equipment and from repairing the world fleet of tankers. Tourism was on the upsurge again, propelled by a new kind of holiday-maker, the mobile self-caterer. Finally the building trade, after struggling with scarcities of materials and skilled labour, had attained the high pre-War levels of house construction, but with a different aim in sight. Before the War, private developers created growth along the coast, now public authorities financed slum clearance and municipal estates around the towns.

STRUCTURAL & LOCATIONAL QUESTIONS

The burning question in the minds of Cornwall's leaders was how long it all would last. Remembering the problems of the past, they were worried when unemployment rose above 2% in the towns or 3% in Redruth when, only two decades earlier, rates ten times higher were the norm. They were also naturally concerned whether the economy was sustainable over the longer term or whether they would once more suffer the collapse of basic activities. When foreigners, shattered by the War, returned to the market, would Cornwall's resources of food and raw materials, ship repairing and mine engineering, still be competitive, or would the territory once more be left high and dry? And how important was Cornwall's distance from the main UK markets?

Structurally, the Cornish socio-economic system was an early model of a post-industrial society in the sense that, because of the decline of mining and fishing and the growth of tourism and retirement activities, more than half the workforce had long been engaged in service trades, ever since the beginning of the twentieth century in fact. By 1950 mining and fishing, which had once occupied nearly half the working population, now had only one and a half per cent of that total whereas over 70% were in the service sector, including 15% in jobs connected with looking after tourists, retirees and other incomers. Nearly 20% were engaged in farming, about 5% in clay, stone and tin extraction, and a further 5% in engineering and ship repairing.

The economy was thus based upon an unusual, indeed unique, set of products and services. But, with the exception of food processing, it lacked the new range of mass consumer-oriented industries that had brought affluence to southern England and the Midlands, such as cars (the output of which increased more than fivefold from the mid-20s to the mid-30s), man-made fibres like rayon, Bakelite radios, vacuum cleaners, refrigerators and washing machines. Nor did Cornwall possess internal sources of funding for investment: local offices of banks, building societies and finance houses were all branches of up-country concerns. To explain why this was so, it is helpful to look at two surveys of the local economy which arrived at different answers and proposed different remedies: Cornwall's 1952 *Development Plan* and a 1947 study of Devon and Cornwall by the University College of the South West at Exeter.[6]

The *Development Plan* was the work of shrewd and pragmatic Councillors who had no experience in, and no appetite for, grand theoretical constructs or abstract model building, but it can be seen as containing the germs of two diametrically opposed spatial models-of Cornwall's role in the UK economy, one maritime, the other land-based. The first harked back to the days when Cornwall was an international centre of metalliferous mining and hard rock technology, with the sea as the main highway, and with one of the finest natural anchorages in Europe only a dozen miles from one of the world's busiest shipping lanes. Within the context of this view, the 'Report of Survey' of the Plan contained what is probably the most comprehensive and sympathetic account of Cornwall's ports and harbours and marine activities to be found in any plan issued before or since. But it also included a panoply of programmes for dual carriageways and bypasses which were part of a different view of the territory as a distant terminal of a land-based system, far from the main concentrations of population, industry and power, where everything of importance began and ended in central England. In one vision the sea was a unifying factor, a gateway to the wider world, in the second it was a barrier.

Then, as now, the maritime vision was a minority view. Geographical peripherality was seen as the main problem, roads as a key factor in a solution: 'Owing to Cornwall's geographic situation, good road communication with the remainder of the country is essential'.[7] The internal road system was little changed from horse and cart days. There was one strip of dual carriageway (around Redruth) and one set of traffic lights - at Newquay. The state of the roads leading to Cornwall were, the Planners politely reminded the government, such as to cause '. . . reluctance to continue the journey westwards'[8] and a critical component in its highway improvement programmes was a road bridge across the river Tamar that would cut nearly 30 miles off the land trip from Saltash to Plymouth.

No empirical studies were thought necessary, either in Cornwall or in the UK as a whole, to test the conventional wisdom that geographical peripherality was the main problem, nor that better roads were the best remedy. No doubt these propositions were considered self-evident, a simple matter of common-sense. Yet the Exeter study, which did research the issue, found no supporting evidence for these hypotheses from industrialists and concluded that the '. . . frequently expressed opinion' that higher road costs were a damaging locational problem should be '. . . treated with reserve if not suspicion'.[9] Far from suffering from locational deficiencies, the survey concluded, Devon and Cornwall offered a number of benefits to light manufacturers who were no longer tied closely to sources of iron and coal and who could take advantage of plentiful untapped supplies of female labour, cheaper land, a pollution-free atmosphere and a pleasant, largely union-free working environment.

The 'fundamental, pervasive' problem, according to the Exeter researchers, was not distance from the main markets or suppliers but a lack of competitive ability, of industrial enterprise. This they attributed partly to a long term drain of entrepreneurial talent and funds up-country, but principally to the channelling of local energies and capital into the tourist and retirement sector at the expense of manufacturing industry. Their remedy was, in line with the prevailing ideology of the middle 1940s, an interventionist one: strong local Distribution of Industry Panels who would avoid the parochial squabbles between rival towns which had spread new firms thinly around the territory in the inter-War years, and instead concentrate growth upon industrial estates in a few key centres where they could enjoy the benefits of external economies such as a range of local suppliers, subcontractors and utilisers of by-products.

Which set of explanations and solutions to choose: geographical peripherality and the 'roads to prosperity' philosophy or socio-economic peripherality and the growth-point paradigm? The two were not mutually exclusive and in later years roads and growth-points became part and parcel of the same model for economic development of the outer regions. A roads policy may have reflected an unspoken fear among Cornwall's leaders that its basic industries would fail again, for while the majority of visitors still came by train, more and more were arriving by road.

The hypothesis that tourism absorbed local energies seemed plausible, for it would have been logical if, during the depressed inter-War years, local business people preferred to cater for customers who arrived on their doorsteps rather than venturing into the outside world of cut throat competition. Capital was short in any case, for the vast profits made in mining's heyday had long ago been lost in new speculations or invested in other parts of the UK. In an economy which had been starved of capital for decades it hardly seemed wise to sink what there was into a local industry that had reached rock bottom. The only mines of any size still operating, South Crofty and Geevor, had been exploited to meet the UK's needs during two World Wars and neglected in between. Some of their workings dated back two centuries or more and were urgently in need of a massive injection of funds which could only come from outside Cornwall.

That said, the strength of the enterprise culture among local tourist operators should not be exaggerated. During the first half of the twentieth century much of the impetus came from the Great Western Railway which introduced the 'Cornish Riveria' and other express trains, extended local platforms to take the holiday rush, formed the 'Come to Cornwall Association' with local chambers of commerce and offered subsidies for every pound spent upon publicity by Cornish resorts. The Newquay Hoteliers' Association, possibly the most dynamic of the coastal groups, acknowledged that the G.W.R. had taught them the art of advertising, and collaborated with them in an Easter Holiday Campaign to extend the shoulders of the summer holiday season. However, Sir Felix Pole, General Manager of the G.W.R. in the inter-War years, thought the effort had come 20 years too late. It was a pity, he said, that some hotels were not blown up to make way for more modern facilities and he offered to help install the 'latest sanitary arrangements' in Penzance, a place where conflict between traditional maritime activities and tourism hindered the large scale schemes he had in mind.[10]

A MEDIUM SIZED INDUSTRIAL BACKGROUND

Small firms, it is often said, form the backbone of the Cornish economy. But the birth rate of new local manufacturers from the 1920s up to and including the 1950s was very low, and their contribution to employment growth minimal. Any discussion of the state of the enterprise culture in Cornwall Circa 1950 must take account the fact that the inner dynamic of the extractive and engineering sectors came, not from small enterprises but from a group of medium-sized companies employing from a few hundred to several thousand workers apiece. Each had its roots deeply embedded in Cornwall's industrial past; each was still owned and often run by direct descendants of the families who had founded it a century or more ago and each had survived, in some cases prospered and expanded, during the harsh times of the great depression, through policies of modernisation, diversification, takeovers or mergers. Between them they kept alive some of the old industrial spirit and engineering traditions of Cornwall.

For example Holman Bros, a small Camborne foundry through the 19th century, more than doubled its local employment between 1930 and 1950 to over 2000 by exporting mining and construction equipment around the world and opening depots or factories in the 1930s in South Africa, the Gold Coast and Canada. Silley and Cox, who started as shipbuilders in Falmouth after the packet trade was lost to Southampton in the 1840s, also more than doubled their workforce to over 2500 from pre-War days by turning from ship building to ship repairing and investing in modern dry docks. Harvey's of Hayle, founded by a local blacksmith in the later 18th century to supply cast iron pipes to the mines, was now a leading importer of coal and timber and embarking upon a series of acquisitions and mergers which were to make it Cornwall's largest builders' merchants with over 1000 staff. J & F Pool, another Hayle firm, who began in the early 19th century by supplying ironware to the mines, had switched trades to become one of Europe's leading specialist metal perforators, employing several hundred workers. Quarrying firms also showed considerable initiative and marketing skills in selling bulky products over long distances, and the 1947 *Handbook of Granite Masters* listed 37 Cornish enterprises, some of them known throughout the UK and abroad, compared with only six in Devon.

The giant of this group of locally owned firms was English China Clays, an amalgam of old clay families like the Martins, Varcoes and Loverings. Despite losing 40% of the market after the collapse of the American economy in 1930, they used the depression years to transform a primitive pick and shovel trade into a sophisticated modern processing industry. They acquired Charlestown foundry nearby to design and make their own equipment, built their own power station, set up laboratories to improve methods of refining clay and developing new uses for it, bought the port of Par, took over local transport firms and also two leading builders who had designed a modular housing system, the 'Cornish Unit', which the group marketed successfully throughout South West Britain and beyond. Although they had reduced the direct clay workforce by a quarter while expanding output by a quarter, they maintained group employment in the area at the pre-War peak of 5000.[11]

Menbers of the old families, the Holmans, Harveys and Pools, Loverings and Varcoes were still to the fore, moreover, chairing or directing their companies and leading social life in their localities. Many craftsmen and tradesmen in the area had been trained in their workshops and Cornwall's three Further Education Colleges that developed at Camborne, Falmouth and St Austell owed their origins to day-release classes for commercial and technical trainees from their apprentice schools. Son followed father and grandfather into the firm and an employment interview for a young applicant was something of a social occasion, taken up with enquiries about relatives who had once worked there. A good voice, a talent for a wind instrument or sporting ability gave a candidate a more than even chance, for the firms sponsored silver bands, choirs, horse shows, rock drill contests and all the other traditional festivities that reinforced the old triumphalist industrial culture.

Female participation in the industrial workforce was low. Seventy years earlier, 'independent balmaidens' had crushed the ore at the surface of the mines, but these had long ago disappeared. During the First and Second World Wars, women had taken over from skilled men in explosives and manufacturing works but once the War was over they retreated or sought work in the tourist industry. In the St Austell area they only made up a fifth of the workforce, in the Newquay district they accounted for a half.

LAST SMALLHOLDERS OF THE SEA

In assessing the dynamism of the Cornish economy around 1950, it is instructive to contrast the thrustful and outward looking approach of the group of firms considered above with the attitudes of another set of Cornishmen in a sector that faced real problems in the fifties. Fishing had enjoyed a flush of activity after the War in sea beds that had been rested, but when price controls on fish were lifted in 1950 the bottom fell out of the market overnight and what Commander Luard, Chairman of Cornwall's Sea Fisheries Commission, called a 'creeping paralysis' was crippling an industry burdened by obsolete vessels, out of date equipment and an ageing workforce. Over half the men were over 50 years old and youngsters fought shy of an occupation that offered meagre rewards for a tough and dangerous life when there was plenty of work ashore. 'In a matter of a few years from now', Luard warned, 'Cornish fishing will cease to exist' and those 'last smallholders of the sea', as he called them, with the traditions of grit and courage, independence and initiative, would be no more.[12]

What had caused the decline? At one time some fishermen had blamed the G.W.R said to favour 'clean tourists to smelly fish.' Now the G.W.R. had gone but other whipping boys had been discovered, including foreign governments who unfairly subsidised their mariners, outsiders from the east coast who overfished and scraped local beds bare, greedy dealers from up-country who kept all the profits, even the disloyalty of the fish themselves who deserted Cornwall's shores. All these factors were relevant, of course, yet time and again, as Hamilton Jenkin observed in the 1930s, fishermen had formed cooperatives to finance new boats and equipment, only to fail because of the disloyalty of their own members, '. . . so jealous of each other that they will not work together'. Compared with the attitudes of the engineering and extractive firms who had set out in the face of adversity to show, in the words of a Holman Bros. Director, '. . . what the tradition of mechanical inventiveness . . . in a small corner' of Britain could do, the reactions of the fishermen seemed ill-suited to survival in a profit-driven world of large-scale, capital-intensive industrial fishing. Mariners in other regions had successfully banded together to solve similar problems but, as a later study concluded, the Cornish seafarer's very characteristics of pride and independence, which isolated group from group, '. . . rendered large-scale cooperatives un-natural'.[13]

It would be quite wrong, however, to give the impression that traditional activities along the coast were all following a self-determined path to oblivion. Fowey, Par and Charlestown were shipping increasing tonnages of clay around Europe, as far as the Baltic and the eastern Mediterranean. Penryn and Newlyn (and to a lesser extent Porthoustock, Dean Point and Gweek) exported stone. Coasters still made their way to Penryn and up the Fal to dock in the heart of Truro with cargoes of grain, timber and cement, coal and fertilizer. Newlyn landed half of Cornwall's wet fish catch, Mevagissey a fifth and Looe around 15%. Falmouth had no coastal trade but its ship repair yards were busy.

Along the north coast, in contrast, traditional maritime life had been slowly ebbing away since the railways arrived, bringing holiday-makers but undermining coastal trade. Bude lost its commerce at the end of the nineteenth century, a storm washed away St Agnes harbour during the First World War and the G.W.R. closed Newquay's port in 1929. Although small colliers still put in to Padstow, its once thriving fishing business had almost disappeared. Portreath continued to import coal, Hayle was Cornwall's largest coal handler to feed its power station and Harvey's of Hayle was also the principal importer of timber and, increasingly, oil. Small boats, mainly crabbers, fished out of St Ives, Port Isaac and a few smaller places, but by and large the inhabitants of the north coast had gone over to the holiday trade.[14]

Except for some flourishing 'one commodity' harbours, however, Cornwall's ports were caught between the pincers of falling revenues and the rising costs of dredging and modernising. General cargoes were only two thirds of the already reduced levels of pre-War, coastal trade was being written off nationally as a serious form of inter-regional transport and the University College Exeter study concluded that only Plymouth might, possibly, have a future ag a trading port. The 1952 Plan, on the other hand, still believed that some Cornish harbours - Penzance, Hayle, Penryn, Truro - had a commercial future, provided they could be brought up to date, and called for a national plan to modernise coastal commerce. Unfortunately, it could not have chosen a worse time to make such a plea. A Conservative government had just been elected, planning was out of fashion, road transport swiftly denationalised and the British Transport Commission, which was supposed to hold a balance between land and sea transport, became a mere umbrella organisation.

In addition to this lack of interest at the UK level, the possibility of local cooperation to rationalise Cornwall's port structure was hampered by divided ownership. Some ports were in private hands like Par (owned by English Clays), Hayle (belonging to Harvey's) and Portreath (the property of a Cardiff company). Some were run by separate groups of Harbour Commissioners, as at Newlyn, Falmouth, Fowey, Looe and Padstow. Still others - Penzance, Truro and Penryn for instance - were operated by local authorities. Separate ownership of this kind was not a purely Cornish problem, but with even close neighbours like Penzance and Newlyn, or Falmouth and Penryn, belonging to different bodies, ideas of a coordinated strategy for Cornwall's ports seemed just a pipe dream.

INLAND RURAL CORNWALL

From the centre of any of Cornwall's towns it was only a short stroll to the open countryside or the sea, agricultural activities covered nine tenths of the territory's surface, and there was no sharp distinction between urban and rural life. But to talk of 'rural Cornwall' as a homogeneous entity is to gloss over important variations in socio-economic and cultural structures within Cornwall itself, as well as ignoring the differences between the area and agrarian regions such as East Anglia or the outer zones of Scotland and Wales.

As far as internal distinctions were concerned, Cornwall's villages grouped into three types. Along the seaboard, properties for retirees, second homers (not so plentiful then as in other places nearer to London) and holiday-lets sprouted across the headlands, while in the more picturesque fishing ports many locals had moved out to make way for Lobster Pot guest houses and Mermaid cafes. In the china clay area and the environs of the industrial parts of Camborne and Redruth, on the other hand, the population was largely Cornish born and bred and an old lifestyle prevailed in which farmworkers lived cheek by jowl with miners and shifted from one occupation to another from season to season or even day by day. In the remoter inland corners of Cornwall, mainly in the north, another way of life, nearer to the rural stereotype, existed, which will be described later.

By the early 1950s, Cornish farmers had reverted to their normal pattern of work after the changes imposed upon them during the War years when they had been told to plough up grass land and moor land for cereals to feed the country. Dairy farming ruled once more west of a line roughly from the Fal river northward to St Agnes. Stock rearing was more common to the east. Pockets of horticulture continued (albeit without government price support) in the Scillies, the 'golden crescent' from Penzance to Hayle and in parcels of land along the southern coast to the Tamar Valley. The remarkably small-scale nature of farming was also unchanged, indeed the landscape had not altered much from what Wesley might have observed from his horseback a couple of centuries earlier. Virtually all holdings were under 120 hectares and six out of ten under 20. The average size of a Cornish farm was threequarters that of Devon, half that of Britain.

There were about 11,000 holdings at that time and roughly the same number of full time male farm hands. In terms of regular employment, agriculture had become a male preserve. During the inter-War years, while the male full-time work force had fallen by about a quarter, the female had dropped by over a half to under a thousand and although the influx of Land Army girls brought it up again, it swiftly contracted to the 1939 level after the War. Farming was very much a family affair in which all members of the household, male or female, had to pull their weight. Wives and daughters controlled the interior of the farmhouse, looked after small livestock (and bed and breakfast guests), did the hand milking, helped with outside work on demand and increasingly did the mounting paperwork generated by officialdom. The farmer (95% of farm proprietors were men) and his sons did the heavy work, operated and maintained the machinery and did the buying and selling as well as working for other farmers or in the towns to make ends meet.

Despite the difficult nature of the terrain and their distance from the main consumer markets, Cornish farming communities, by working long hours and careful husbandry, held their own against the big mechanized estates to the east. But only with significant help from outside. A point worth emphasizing is that, sturdy independent yeomenry though they were, local farmers nevertheless operated within the supporting structure of one of the most state-regulated parts of the economy outside the public sector. The Milk Marketing Board promoted their dairy produce, built depots to absorb and process seasonal surpluses and transferred milk from farm to depot and thence to road and rail networks.

Yet the Cornish system of small family businesses in isolated 'Celtic' clusters of homesteads dictated a different socio-culture from that of the compact 'Anglo-saxon' villages of central and eastern England. There, under the watchful if benevolent eye of parson and squire, enclaves of a rural proletariat were increasingly being segregated from an inflow of bourgeois settlers, gentlemen-and-weekend farmers. Cornish rural society was more homogeneous, culturally and economically, especially in the remoter inland villages untouched by tourists, retirees or other urban refugees. A high proportion were Cornish born and bred and there were fewer distinctions between masters and men, especially since both had lived on the breadline for decades.

Because society was more egalitarian, however, this did not mean that social control was less strict. Apart from the Duke of Cornwall, there were no great dukes to set the tone, but there were titled landowners as well as landed gentry on local councils. The part they played is one of the many unresearched areas of the period, but their influence should not be forgotten. There were also the Methodist farmers. In the towns, it was said, the Minister ruled his Congregation, in the countryside the Congregation - or the Elders of the chapel - controlled the Minister. Preachers in the more isolated parishes still denounced cinemas, dance halls and public houses in the town, even whist drives in the village hall, as sinks of iniquity, hotbeds of vice, the Devil's snares for idle hands. The political, the practical and the pious went hand in glove. Local matters, it was agreed, were best left for locals to decide and leading farmers doubled as local preachers, Stewards of the Chapel, Parish or District or County Councillors. Community life was cemented through a myriad of activities and institutions, Sunday schools, Women's Meetings, Wesley Guilds, silver bands, rugby matches, chapel treats and feast days, ceremonies and festivities which provided occasions to parade the trophies and totems of Cornishness, from saffron buns and pasties to horse shows and ploughing contests, to renew kinship and friendship ties and reaffirm traditional values.

Life, of course, was not one long stream of unalloyed pastoral harmony. Rifts and dissensions broke out between Nonconformist denominations and quite small settlements had two or more rival chapels. Attendences were falling, everyone agreed there were too many chapels, no one could agree which one to close, and the temptation was to let Darwinian laws apply and wait for the weakest to go to the wall. What is more, the Welfare State was chipping away at chapel functions and younger people (and some older persons who had seen War service elsewhere) were losing their faith in the Manichean polarities of old style Methodism, and succumbing to the pluralist, relativist, post-Freudian ideas that were filtering through via town life and the media. The 1950s saw the end of many 'all age' schools as older pupils were bussed to new 'Secondary Modern' schools in the towns. Teaching staffs were changing. The village schoolmistress who lived among her school children and was probably of local stock was being replaced by someone from a more cosmopolitan background. Small wonder if some, especially the young, sought escape. Only a strong-willed and inflexible breed could have resisted the grueliing hardships of the pre-War years and these survivors held firm to the beliefs that had seen them through, to the moral superiority of a spartan life of teetotalism, strict sabbatarianism and work that involved muck and sweat. On Sundays the wireless was switched off, the playing fields were silent.

Character-building this life may have been, but to the young it seemed one of unremitting boredom and drudgery. Apart from the lure of city lights, perhaps magnified by denunciations from the pulpit, and the shake-out of farm labour through mechanisation, another reason why workers left the land was the appalling state of some rural housing, especially when they compared it with the new municipal estates, with their main drains, piped water and electric lights, that were springing up around nearby towns. Of course, it was much cheaper to build them there than in some remote corner of the countryside but another, and perhaps more compelling reason why property owners were loath to modernise or rebuild was the fear that, if they did, those homes would sooner or later end up in the hands of urbanites who would undermine a traditional and much-valued way of life.

To conclude this sketch of agrarian Cornwall, it might be said that the lifestyle it describes was a stereotype of farming communities throughout the world: a slow changing pace of life, traditional family work strategies, suspicion of the hererodox values of urban culture, a belief in the need for long hours of toil as part of the everyday pattern of existence, rigid sabbatarianism, a puritanical attitude towards leisure activities outside the framework of the local chapel. But Cornwall's land owners and small tenant farmers shared a belief in themselves as the last bastions of a distinctively 'Cornish' ideology, once shared with the local towns but now fast disappearing under the onslaught of the forces that St John Thomas outlined at the beginning of this Chapter. Which helps to explain why the 1952 *Development Plan*, much influenced by the old trilogy of farming, Methodism and Liberalism, made it crystal clear that new non-farming activities - whether residential, commercial or industrial - were not welcome in the agricultural interior.[15]

SEABOARD GROWTH

The rural populations were influenced by what they saw happening along the coast. In the 1952 Plan, E.M.Trembath, Newquay's Publicity Officer, had suggested that the annual total of visitors, which had grown rapidly since the War, could not be far short of half a million. Some time later, Cornwall's planners, in their appraisal of the holiday industry, estimated that the total by 1954 must have been nearer to one and a half million. One reason why even the experts underestimated tourist growth at the time was the changed character of the holiday trade. Before the War most visitors arrived by train and stayed in hotels or bed and breakfast places. Now more and more were coming by road (peak tourist traffic grew 80% in the 1950s) and choosing a more informal self-catering lifestyle in chalets or static caravans or in tents in fields and laybys. The hotel and 'B & B' sector was still growing but very modestly by under 1% a year, the grand total of annual visitors was increasing by 4%, but the self catering segment was mushrooming by 14% per annum.[16]

Defenders of the old maritime traditions were dismayed. A former Penryn port officer, making a return visit to Cornwall, was appalled to find St Ives '. . . all milk bars and pin tables'. What really distressed him, though, was to see once '. . . bold hearted, freedom loving mariners' reduced to touting for trade from passing tourists: 'Boat, sir? Boat, sir?' Of course many Cornish people were pleased to earn a bit of jam on their bread as they put it, but Commander Luard was horrified to think that his ports might degenerate into full time tourist centres. There had been a time, in the dying years of the nineteenth century, when Sir Arthur Quiller Couch had given tourism his qualified backing as the only available cure for Cornwall's dilemma: '. . . since we must cater for the stranger, let us do it well and honestly.' But with the inter-War years, and the onslaught of what he called the 'motorist hordes' of visitors, he became disillusioned: '. . . any people which lays itself out to exploit the stranger . . . runs a grave risk of deteriorating in manliness.' Service was equated with servility: 'I would rather see my countrymen poor than servile'.[17]

VISIBLE COSTS, INVISIBLE BENEFITS

In the harsh conditions of the inter-War depression beggars could not be choosers, and few could afford the luxury of Q.'s scruples. But by the fifties, when the going was good, people felt able to question the need for greater numbers of visitors, especially the new kind of mobile self-catering tourist. Cornwall was following a trail blazed in other regions by a motorised public with longer paid holidays, but Cornish memories of the days of its industrial prowess were more recent and so the opponents of tourism numbered not simply retirees, artists and writers, but also working-class supporters of an industrial culture. For them tourism symbolised an invasion of 'foreigners' which threatened the Cornish identity and a traditional social as well as economic life. They condemned it for marginalising the ordinary Cornish people in their own homeland, for relegating them to second class housing on the outskirts of picturesque ports and villages and for condemning them to second rate jobs as ice-cream vendors, car park keepers and deck chair attendants.

The point was, however, that the costs imposed by tourism were highly visible whereas the benefits it conferred were hidden. Traffic jams cluttered roads little changed since the days of horse and cart, rashes of chalets, shacks and caravans sprawled across headlands, but much of the revenue that visitors generated lay uncounted and unseen, outside the traditional hotel and bed and breakfast sector in shops, garages and hairdressers, in the hands of entertainers, small builders, transport workers and farmers. Already in the 1930s Hamilton Jenkin had asserted that the Cornish, far from being the misty Celts of the guide book, were a shrewd and calculating people, very polite to the visitor, but determined to extract the last penny of the 'new harvest of wealth which the gods have provided'. By the 1950s this harvest was becoming big business indeed, but equally a source of social irritation for many.[18]

The debate about the use of Cornwall's seaboard was not just a straight contest between those who wanted to preserve it for traditional maritime activities and those who favoured more tourism. A powerful and articulate body of opinion, opposed to any type of development, industrial or post-industrial, had long been active. Back in 1895, the National Trust's second purchase was Barras Head, to stop anyone putting up a duplicate of the massive King Arthur's Castle Hotel built nearby. The local section of the Council for the Protection of Rural England was the first to publish a survey of the destruction of the landscape, in 1930. A few years later the Cornish branch of the Federation of Women's Institutes seconded a motion at a National Conference to halt the 'rapidly increasing ruination' of the land. The Common and Footpath Society complained in 1935 that Cornwall's (and Devon's) Councillors were slow to protect bridleways and paths. The CPRE feared that nothing would be done because '. . . that virtue of sturdy independence so characteristic of the Cornish race may sometimes conflict with the need for cooperation in planning on a regional basis'. But Councillors also had to heed those who, in a time of desperate poverty, when many farmers earned less than a living wage, could not turn down any chance of making ends meet.[19]

After the War, however, the Planners, equipped with greater powers, were quick to regulate the proliferation of coastal sites. 'The magnificence of Cornwall's coasts', the 1952 Plan said, 'must never be marred by the hand of man'. Such restrictions still did not meet with unqualified approval however, and the conflict between traditionalists and anti-developers is well illustrated in two accounts of the same strip of west Cornish coastline circa 1950 by two artists (and friends), the newcomer and poet David Lewis and the locally-born painter Peter Lanyon. To Lewis the cliffs were a place where 'gulls white as wave spume' wheeled above 'colonies of pinks that harboured spiders shortlegged as beetles' while, as a background to these scenes, a distant church bell tolled for evensong. To Lanyon it was a meeting place of 'the commerce of man with granite', of 'tin and ocean', where 'men fished for food after labour beneath the sea bed'. New arrivals, he claimed, who had already made their money elsewhere, 'wail out that we destroy the beauty of their view' and the outsider's concept of beauty barred Cornish people from making a living off their own land.[20]

THE ARTIST'S VISION OF CORNISH CULTURE

Lanyon's was not a typical artistic response, however, and no description of Cornwall circa 1950 could be complete without recognising the impact of generations of painters, poets, romantic novelists, historians and guide writers who imprinted a vivid but lop-sided image of Cornwall on the minds of outsiders. From an economic and social point of view, their direct effect was benign. They sent modest ripples of affluence through the coastal villages, where they lived with the local population in a state of mutual tolerance. As Lewis remarked, the subculture of fishing boats and Primitive Methodist chapels was a world that turned on a different axis. While artists painted their pictures of boats and houses, locals painted the real objects in preparation for the coming season.

The Cornish, it must be noted, were never credited with much in the way of artistic talent or creative imagination by observers, Cornish and non-Cornish alike, who focussed upon what they did not do rather than upon what they did. In St Ives in 1949, Denys Val Baker, a prolific Welsh-born writer on the arts in Cornwall, started his *Cornish Magazine*, a conscious effort to pick up where Quiller Couch had left off fifty years earlier. It was not long, however, before one Cornish contributor was complaining that most of the articles were written by a 'passel of arty foreigners', to which two other Cornish-born readers replied that this was inevitable, since the Cornish suffered from a 'paucity and impotence' of imagination and had evolved 'no art, no architecture, no craftwork'. A relatively small population can hardly be expected to excel in all branches of culture and such judgements failed to take account of the output of regional novelists, some of them best-sellers in their days, throughout the decades of dire poverty. Bestsellers are a good indication of popular aspirations, and the Cornish novelists reflected the industrial work ethic and Nonconformist ideology of their times. For while repeated waves of evangelising Methodism and militant teetotalism may have swept pre-industrial music, dance and customs out of sight, it was surprising, as Merv Davey, the Cornish musicologist reported, how much was smuggled through within the pages of Methodist texts and hymbooks.[21]

St Ives at that time was, thanks to the influence of Barbara Hepworth, Ben Nicholson, Bernard Leach, and others attracted by their presence, a world focus for avant garde sculpture, painting and ceramics, while across the peninsula at Newlyn the Passmore Edwards Gallery was a reminder of the international reputation enjoyed half a century earlier by members of its school of artists. The largest art school in Cornwall circa 1950, at Falmouth, owed its inspiration to artists of Edwardian times. It was this heritage that, in decades to come, was to lay the foundations for an important structure of higher education in pure and applied art and design.

ART & INDUSTRY

If the artistic presence brought some material benefits, both short and long term, its effect upon external perceptions of Cornwall as place for modern industry was less constructive. Long ago Stanhope Forbes, doyen of the Newlyn School, had claimed that they painted with unflinching realism the life of their time and people in their natural environment. But the titles, so popular among the fashionable crowds who flocked to the Royal Academy, told their own story: 'Feeding the Fowls', 'By Hammer and Hand all Art doth Stand', 'Tucking a School of Pilchards', and many others portrayed a simple, God-fearing fisherfolk, rustic peasantry and honest craftsmen going about their time honoured pre-industrial rituals. Neither these artists, nor their patrons, nor the long line of literary trail-blazers who followed the footsteps of Tennyson, had any time for what Harris, the local miner-poet, called 'the heat, the cold, the sulphur and the slime' of underground work.

Philip Payton has argued that it was the publication of John Rowe's *Cornwall in the Age of the Industrial Revolution* in 1953 that sparked off interest in the mining heritage. But it was some time before industrial archeology took root in the popular mind. The notion that visitors would pay good money to see a 'horrific museum' - as one guide called it - of artefacts from the age of steam seemed laughable, the thought that, in a few decades, ruined engine houses and crumbling mine chimneys of the wastelands around Camborne and Redruth would be a potential 'World Heritage Site' would have seemed beyond belief. In guide books of the period, Cornwall's industrial areas were seldom mentioned except as its 'Black Country', to be avoided like the plague. St Just in Penwith, according to another guide, was just a dingy mining town, Redruth a depressing place, and the best thing about Camborne was the road leading out of it. Grim, grey, proletarian, industrial Cornwall had nothing to offer tourists seeking to escape a smokestack- ridden world, with the possible exception of the conical, white china-clay tips ('lunar landscapes' or 'the Cornish Alps' in guide-book language). Even so most holiday makers might have agreed with Jack Clemo, poet to the clay lands: 'Here on the sharp clay tip . . .. peaks of vision seethe with hostile potency'.[22]

OUT OF ENGLAND & INTO CORNWALL

What thrilled the visitor was another Cornwall, an intangible sense of crossing a spiritual boundary, of encountering an older and alien civilisation, a land of legend and mystery. 'Out of England and into Cornwall', is how Newquay's Publicity Officer described it, '. . . the slightly foreign atmosphere, the dialect, the Celtic air of remoteness are irresistibly attractive to the prosaic urban dweller.' As the *Blue Guide* to Cornwall of the period said, it offered '. . . all the climatic advantages ot Continental Residence without the drawbacks of fatiguing travel, foreign language, unusual habits or Strange Attendance'. If 'Celticity' did not touch Clemo and many inhabitants of an industrial culture, it fascinated other poets, novelists and guide writers, and their language and imagery had lost nothing of the ridiculous extravagance of earlier generations described by Bernard Deacon. The artist and writer Sven Berlin and the novelist Ruth Manning-Sanders saw the same stretch of coast described by Lewis and Lanyon in a lurid light. Berlin sensed processions of gods and devils, dragons and spectres, Manning-Sanders glimpsed giants heaving boulders up at witches perched on the crags.[23]

Some Cornish had long been happy to cash in on the visitors' undiscriminating appetite for the occult and the bizarre. As motorists drove off the Torpoint ferry, ancient seafarers, anxious to inform them of the difference between spriggans and piskeys, buccas and knockers, called out 'You're in a foreign country now'. The only piskeys in St Ives, however, as a fisherman told Val Baker, were those in the window of the tourist shops that lined the quayside and the attitude of many locals was summed up in the anecdotal reply to a visitor who asked what they did in the long winter evenings. 'We dream up new legends for you for next season.'

All this might seem mere harmless nonsense, but it had a more sinister side. Ruth Manning-Sanders and others put the visitors on their guard against the seemingly innocuous locals. They were a polyglot and unreliable race, some with swarthy faces and black hair and Spanish-sounding names like Jose and Jago, others tall, fair and blue-eyed, still others with flat mongolian pre-Celtic features. And although charmingly child-like when rewarded, they could quickly flare into anger, even violence, when thwarted. Apart from this conditioning of unwary outsiders, such a constant recycling of a bogus culture did little to ease relations between grass-roots Cornish and members of the Cornish movement. If the latter were occasionally caricatured in the local press as middle-aged eccentrics prancing about on damp hillsides in fancy dress, part at least of the blame must be laid on generations of whimsical novelists and romantic guide writers.

CONCLUSION

Cornwall circa 1950 was still - historically, culturally, politically and economically - something of a tight little island, a land apart. An accelerating rate of contact with the outside world brought about by the expansion of railways, trade and tourism and the upheavals of two World Wars (and the intermarriage that resulted) had still left a local culture intact. Most Cornish felt comfortably part of a large extended family and made no attempt to analyse what made them feel 'different' from their neighbours.

Cornwall also possessed considerable economic advantages, a unique combination of economic activities: metalliferous mining, granite, clay working, fishing, dairy farming, ship repairing, construction and hard rock engineering, tourism, the retirement industry and defence. It was also a place of contrasts. In some ways it remained a museum of nineteenth-century values, of Nonconformist convictions and dissenting Liberal radicalism. The miner and the fisherman who flanked the shield on the County coat of arms may have been, in strict employment terms, reminders of past glories rather than current achievement, but local society was still inspired and driven by an intense pride in engineering prowess, a belief in the moral superiority of work that was hard, often dirty, sometimes dangerous or even deadly, in the virtues of thrift and temperance, in the obligation of individuals to take responsibility for their own salvation and destiny.

All this reflects the atrophy that Philip Payton has described. Yet at the same time Cornwall was, as always, a remarkably open society in economic terms, at the mercy of sudden upturns and downswings on the international scene. Because of this it was enjoying an unexpected taste of prosperity, exporting tin, granite, china clay and mining equipment all over the globe, repairing the world's shipping fleets. But this affluence depended upon swift responses to external change and the local socio-economic structure displayed some features which made its future problematic. At one end of the entrepreneurial spectrum was a modernising elite, dynamic and outward looking but confined to a fairly narrow range of markets. At the other end were groups with strongly entrenched, even self defeating, attitudes. In the middle were small businesses who were responding adequately to change without showing, or indeed needing to show, great inventiveness or originality.

In this respect the Cornish economy was not unlike that of the UK at that time. Tourist operators were able to cater for the new breed of mobile self-catering visitors at low cost or even no cost by putting up chalets, buying static caravans or opening fields to campers. Farmers, after decades of struggle, were content to follow directives that brought them a steady income. The birth rate of new manufacturers was low and the undergrowth of suppliers, contractors and processors which surrounded the leading firms was not producing many new products, partly because the local leaders tended to internalise their own engineering, marketing and research and development operations - English China Clays, with its vertically integrated structure from energy supply and product and equipment development through to docks and shipping was a text book example of this. If Cornwall's economy was still largely owned and operated by local people, this did not make it innovatory or incubatory, capable of spawning new enterprises, modern technologies or entering growth markets, as it was once in the great days of the mining boom. In a world where, for generations, people had lived close to the poverty line, horizons had become very close and aspirations limited. Tourism is a case in point. Being so close to home, many Cornish undervalued the quality of their own environment, its location, climate, beauty and the neighbourliness of local life. To them it often recalled hard days of failing industry, low wages, poor accommodation and wet, windswept winters. Outsiders' perceptions were altogether different: because they had a point for comparison they were better able to exploit Cornwall's attractions.

Moreover, Cornwall lacked its own sources of industrial funding. It had no locally based banks, insurance companies, finance houses or building societies. And it was further hampered by two factors, one internal, one external. Internally, the corollary of a democratic, egalitarian and cellular society with its structure of dispersed and self-contained settlements and its distaste for rigid hierarchies, whether religious, political or economic, was a reluctance to work together for the common good, a tendency towards schisms and parochial rivalries that sometimes, as the Cornish were the first to accept, made a mockery of the motto 'One and All' emblazoned under the County Shield.

The external limiting factor was a perception of Cornwall by potential up-country investors as a pre-industrial or a post-industrial land, lost in the mists of time and peopled by a sly but inefficient race, fit only for jobs as caretakers and attendants in a remote playground. If this reflected the urbanite's dismissive attitude towards a rural peasantry, it was strongly reinforced, in Cornwall's case, by generations of fanciful guide-writers and nostalgic poets and painters who generated a bank of images which were not merely aesthetic but which sent off powerful and negative signals to outside business investors. And while it is easy to see how this message could enter popular metaphor, it is more surprising how completely the picture of Cornwall as a sleepy, down-trodden place suffused academic writings such as the Exeter survey. True, these criticised 'foreigners' who came to taste the unhurried local life, only to condemn the inhabitants as stupid and backward. But this did not stop the researchers from informing readers that only after many years of residence would they come to understand '. . . that strange mentality of people in remote and rural parts'.[24]

REFERENCES

1. David St John Thomas in A. J. Hamilton Jenkin, *Cornwall and its People*, David and Charles, Newton Abbot, 1983, v; Robert Homan 'Treading on Corns', *Harpers and Queens*, 1981, pl74; Philip Payton *The Making of Modern Cornwall: Historical Experience and the Persistence of 'Difference'*, Dyllansow Truran, Redruth,1992.
2. The author is indebted to John Brock OBE, Richard Edward- Collins MBE, Effie Harvey, F. L. Harris, John Hurst, Peter Mitchell, F. R. Rayner, Frank Thomas, Joe Thomas and Tony Williams for reading an earlier draft and making valuable contributions.
3. Payton, 1992.
4. John Legonna in *New Cornwall*, Vol.14 p70.
5. Cornwall County Council *Development Plan: Report of Survey*, Truro, 1952.
6. Cornwall County Council, 1952; University College of the South West, *Devon and Cornwall: A Preliminary Survey*, Wheatons, Exeter, 1947.
7. Cornwall County Council, 1952, p234.
8. Cornwall County Council, 1952, p48.
9. University College of the South West, 1947, pp221-2 and p303.
10. Alan Bennett, *The Great Western Railway in West Cornwall*, Southampton, 1988, and *The Great Western Railway in East Cornwall*, Southampton, 1988.
11. Kenneth Hudson, *History of English China Clays*, David and Charles, Newton Abbot, 1968; R M Barton, *A History of the Cornish China Clay Industry*, D.B.Barton, Truro, 1961.
12. W B Luard, 'The Cornish Fishers', in Cornwall County Council, 1952, p72.
13. Hamilton Jenkin, 1983, pll7; Bernard Holloway, *English Engineers*, Holman, Camborne, 1951; University College of the South West, 1947, pl92.
14. Roland Roddis, *Cornish Harbours*, Christopher John, 1951; Richard Pearce, *The Ports and Harbours of Cornwall*, Warne, Truro,1963; Donald Rawe and Jack Ingrey, *Padstow and District*, Lodenek Press, Padstow, 1984; Cornwall County Council, 1952, pp49-62.
15. Thomas Shaw, *A History of Cornish Methodism*, D.B.Barton, Truro, 1967; John Probert, *The Sociology of Cornish Methodism*, Cornish Methodist Historical Society, Truro, 1971; Richard G.Jones in Sarah Foot (ed.), *Methodist Celebration*, Dyllansow Truran, Redruth, 1988, pp8-12; Michael Winter, 'The Twentieth Century' in Nicholas Orme (ed.), *Unity and Variety: A History of the Church in Devon and Cornwall*, University of Exeter Press, Exeter, 1991, ppl57-174.
16. E.H.Trembath, 'The Future of the Tourist Trade' in Cornwall County Council, 1952, p76; Cornwall County Council, *Survey of the Holiday Trade*, Truro, 1966.
17. Roddis, 1951; Luard, 1952; Sir Arthur Quiller Couch in Preface to *Cornwall: A Survey*, Council for the Protection of Rural England, Truro, 1930.
18. Hamilton Jenkin, 1983, p314.
19. Council for the Protection of Rural England, 1930.
20. Cornwall County Council, 1952, p75; David Lewis, 'St Ives: A Personal Memoir', in *St Ives 1939-44*, the Tate Gallery, London, 1985; Peter Lanyon, 'The Face of Penwith', *Cornish Review*, Vol.2.7, p7.
21. Frank Ruhrmund and Emma Harvey Jones in *Cornish Review*, Vol.5, p75; R Glynn Grylls in *Cornish Review*, Vol.1, p28; Merv Davey, *Hengan*, Dyllansow Truran, Redruth, 1983.
22. E.W.Martin, *A Wanderer in the West Country*, Phoenix, 1951; William F Burbidge, *On Rolling Wheels in the West*, Crowther, 1948; Jack Clemo, 'Clay Land Moods', *Penguin Modern Poets*, Vol.6, Penguin, London, 1964, p22.
23. Trembath, 1952; Ronald Clark, *We Go to the West Country*, Harrap, London, 1962; Hugh E Page, *Rambles in East Cornwall*, British Railways, London, 1949; Ruth Manning- Sanders, *The West Country*, Batsford, London, 1949; Bernard Deacon and Philip Payton, 'Re-inventing Cornwall: Culture Change on the European Periphery', *Cornish Studies*, second series,1, 1993; *Blue Guide to Cornwall*, Liddicoat, Truro, 1958.
24. University College of the South West, 1947, pl3.

PART TWO:

THE IMPACT OF SOCIO-ECONOMIC CHANGE

CHAPTER 3

ECONOMIC CHANGE AND 'OPPOSITION' ECONOMICS

Ronald Perry

For most of the second half of the twentieth century, Cornwall's economic policy-makers have accepted as their over-riding priority the generation of employment and the reduction of unemployment. Even in the immediate post-War years, when the number of people out of work was at historically low levels, fear of unemployment was never far from their thoughts, which is understandable in a region where heavy job losses had been the order of the day for the best part of a century. And already, by the early 1960s, mounting unemployment meant that most parts of Cornwall qualified for regional assistance as Development Districts. Later in the decade, when the government massively reinforced its regional aid programmes, all of Cornwall became a Development Area except for the South East corner abutting Plymouth, which was soon designated an Intermediate Area, receiving rather lower levels of help. Then, as unemployment totals climbed still higher at the end of the 70s, West Cornwall was granted the status of Special Development Area meriting top priority and in the mid-80s when Rural Development Areas were created, a veritable patchwork of regional aid evolved, some parts of Cornwall being recognised as Industrial Development Areas, some as Rural Development Areas, some as both.

What was the outcome of three decades of continuous, if fluctuating, support? As the following Table 3.1 shows, employment rose by 42%, a performance which would be the envy of most Assisted Areas. On the other hand, a four-fold increase in unemployment might dampen the spirits of even the most ebullient policy-maker. For every 100 jobs that were generated through so much effort by so many agencies (typically over 40 operated at any one time), 130 workers appeared on the labour market to claim them. This is only one of several seeming paradoxes thrown-up in the course of Cornwall's economic evolution over past decades. Why, for instance, is Cornwall's Gross Domestic Product per head only two thirds of the European Union norm, which apparently puts it on a par with southern Spain or Italy, and yet disposable household incomes are only a few percentage below the UK average?

TABLE 3.1
CORNWALL 1961-1991: GROWTH IN POPULATION AND LABOUR DEMAND AND SUPPLY

	1961	1991	Increase	% Increase
Population	339,000	473,000	127,000	39
Employment	131,000	186,000	55,000	42
Unemployment	5,000	20,000	15,000	300

Source: Census of Population, 1961 and 1991

And why, if earnings are three-quarters of those in prosperous Wiltshire at the other end of the South West Planning Region, are house prices only 10% below the Wiltshire figure? Have such conumdrums anything to do with the fast rate of Cornwall's population growth (entirely due to in-migration, as Peter Mitchell indicates in Chapter 6) and with the fact - still largely ignored by outside analysts and by many Cornish citizens - that two thirds of the incomers are working-age people and their children?

An underlying hypothesis of neo-classical market economics, on which government policies are (however tenuously) based, is that of economic rationality. Working age immigrants and their families do not, it is assumed, uproot themselves and settle in another area in large numbers if job prospects seem much worse than in their place of origin. But in Cornwall, apparently, they do. Of course economic as well as non-pecuniary factors are at work. The house price differential is such that some can sell their home, buy an equivalent or better one in Cornwall - and still have enough over to set up in business or look around for a job. Many trade what they see as a better quality of life for lower pecuniary prospects, helped perhaps by redundancy or early retirement payments. Some prefer life on the dole in a pleasanter environment.

Faced with behaviour which flies in the face of conventional thinking, the debate on Cornwall's development is often disappointingly sterile, a dialogue of the deaf. On one side centralist politicians, planners and industrialists share the same overriding priority - faster economic growth - the same mental map of a world divided into dynamic urban cores and moribund rural peripheries and the same diagnosis of the 'regional problem' - a lack of modern industry. From these common beliefs emerge a consensus on the way to solve the regional problem: an injection of new industry and an infrastructural face-lift - in particular better roads. In this way capital, enterprise and knowhow are supposed to cascade down the urban hierarchy to the remoter corners of the rural hinterland.

Not least of the skills employed by orthodox policy-makers is their ability to present these proposals as positive and progressive, while dismissing alternative views as negative, pessimistic, even reactionary. The established doctrine appears monolithic and coherent, if simplistic. The opposition viewpoint, on the other hand, is presented by shifting coalitions of people who may be united in an anti-metropolitan stance but are divided on what the problem is and how to solve it. Their mental maps are drawn on widely different scales, ranging from global pollution to the territorial integrity of Cornwall to not-in-my-backyard realignments of by-passes. Their imperatives vary as well: for some the overriding priority is ecological, for others ethnic, cultural or political. Given such diversity, these groups may identify areas of debate, raise issues, provide arguments, but they do not shape long-term trends.

The aim of this Chapter is not to present a mere taxonomy of 'opposition' thought, but to give due recognition to it as a valid alternative. And rather than working laboriously through the period year by year in an attempt to explore the interface between economic change and opposition planning, the Chapter divides into two sections. The first outlines upturns and downswings in the local economy, relates them to the hopes and fears they aroused and introduces some of the groups who articulated those feelings. The second examines strategies for economic growth: alternative transport policies; the role of people-led growth; the contribution to inward investment by national and international concerns; the impact of incoming small businesses; efforts to encourage informational activities; and opportunities in the intellectual infrastructure.

SECTION ONE: CORNWALL'S ECONOMY 1952-1992

THE EARLY FIFTIES

In the early fifties Cornwall enjoyed an unaccustomed taste of prosperity brought about by a healthy post-War demand for nearly all its basic activities - tin, granite and clay, ship-repairing and mining equipment, dairy and horticultural produce, tourism, the retirement industry, defence and construction. Only fishing was in the doldrums. Such affluence was of course relative, for Cornwall was still a poor territory compared with southern and central England, but in an era of full employment it was understandable if its leaders felt able to express, in their 1952 *Development Plan*, an air of cautious optimism. The long and painful process of demographic and industrial decline seemed at last to be over and the Plan envisaged something of a three speed economy. It forecast that tourism and retirement growth would resume along the coast, that employment would remain stable in the industrial towns, but that a gentle loss of population and jobs would continue in the inland rural areas. Overall,

Cornwall's employment and population were expected to rise slightly over the next twenty years.

As the 1950s wore on it became clear that only part of this scenario would be realised. Retirement immigration was on course, nearly offsetting a continued loss of younger Cornish people. Tourism was moving ahead by leaps and bounds, and the total of visitors, possibly of the order of one million in 1950, reached the two million mark around 1960. Tin mining received a boost when metal prices shot up after the outbreak of the Korean War in 1951. Clay working continued to expand. But other traditional activities, which had been working flat-out during the post-War boom, began to lose trade to up-to-date and aggressive competitors from elsewhere. Ship repairing was a microcosm of the failings of traditional industries at the time. In the mid-fifties the local historian James Whetter could point to Falmouth as a port known throughout the world for its repair facilities, including a brand new dry docks big enough to take the new supertankers. By the end of the fifties Falmouth - insufficiently modernised by world standards, complacently managed and plagued by labour troubles - was in serious trouble, with winter unemployment reaching 10%. The shake-out of farm labour was also greater than anticipated: over a quarter of the full-time male farm hands left the land.

To begin with, Cornwall got little help from the UK government in dealing with its problems. In the past the government, although not recognising Cornwall as sufficiently important to be a Development Area, had helped firms to move there to mop-up unemployment, but the apparatus of regional aid had been dismantled during the post-War boom and Cornwall's planners had to go it alone in promoting the area at conferences and trade fairs at home and abroad. Despite their efforts, however, unemployment kept rising and when, after 1960, a new kind of Assisted Area was devised by the government - Development Districts defined in terms of high unemployment rates - nearly the whole of Cornwall qualified for inclusion.

A SECOND INDUSTRIAL REVOLUTION

Then, just as Cornwall seemed to be sliding into yet another trough, its fortunes revived in a spectacular way and the years from the early 1960s until the aftermath of the Opec oil rise of the early 1970s were a time of increasing employment, mounting prosperity and rising population.

The twin motors of recovery were manufacturing and employment. Both, curiously enough, expanded (in full-time-equivalent terms) by the same amount and from the same initial base - from around 13,000 to over 20,000 jobs.

Manufacturing expansion in Cornwall was one of the more remarkable instances of a general upsurge in factory employment in the outer regions at a time when, in the UK as a whole, it was beginning its long term decline. In Cornwall, as elsewhere, the revival was almost entirely due to the decentralisation of units from the South East and the Midlands, for the birth rate of indigenous enterprises remained low. Branch plants (or 'branch factories' as they were also known) provided 60% of the new factories, two thirds of the extra employment, three quarters of the female jobs. The inflow reached its peak around 1971 and then, when it became clear that Plymouth would become an Assisted Area as well, declined at the expense of growth in that city. But the number of manufacturing jobs in Cornwall kept increasing for several years as firms which had already arrived built up their work-force.

Mining, too, was enjoying one of its periodic remissions as the price of tin escalated from £900 a tonne in 1961 to over £1500 later in the decade. South Crofty, the largest remaining mine, announced a programme of expansion that would nearly double its output by 1971. Geevor, the other survivor, financed by Union Corporation, the giant international mining company, raised output by 30% and - its share prices (49p in 1954) rose to £4.62 by 1970. The first major shaft to be sunk in Cornwall for 40 years was opened at Wheal Pendarves, drilling began at Mount Wellington, and Consolidated Goldfields announced a new venture at Wheal Jane - 'a really major mine, the biggest thing Cornwall had seen', according to Jack Trounson, the Chairman of Cornish Mining Development Association. Tin streaming resumed along the Carnon River and the Red River, Union Corporation converted a vessel for tin-dredging in St Ives Bay and English China Clays began drilling on Par Beach.[1] These coastal tinning activities were shortlived but there were plenty of other maritime developments to take their place. Fishing, which had reached its lowest ebb in the early sixties, revived as fish prices rose and as the limits reserved for local boats were extended. Trade in shell-fish benefitted from 1973 when Brittany Ferries linked Plymouth with Roscoff, allowing roll-on, roll-off lorries to drive direct to the expanding markets of Brittany and western France. The shipping world was in the throes of the container revolution and in 1971 an Act of Parliament empowered Falmouth Container Company to begin work on a port where cargoes could be transferred from giant containers to smaller coastal vessels or to rail and road terminals. Meetings were held to discuss the impact of offshore oil exploration in the Celtic Sea and Falmouth, Newlyn and Fowey were among the harbours expecting a share in the bonanza.

TOURISM & PEOPLE-LED GROWTH

In the midst of all this speculation, docks at Truro, Penzance, Portreath and elsewhere were filled in to provide car parks and sites for holiday homes for those other great users of the Cornish seaboard - the leisure and retirement industries. Tourist numbers pursued their upward path, climbing above three million in the early seventies for this was the age of the touring caravan when Cornwall became known not just for copper, tin and fish but for twenty-mile tail-backs along the roads leading to it. The opening of the road bridge across the Tamar, which cut nearly 30 miles off the road trip from Plymouth to Saltash, played a vital part and where tourists went, others followed - second homers, commuters, retirees, small business owners - often the same types of people at different stages of their careers. Secondary residences, modest by the standards of other coastal regions until the 1950s, mushroomed during the sixties. Commuting to work in Plymouth increased substantially, retirement immigration remained strong and a major new factor which took everyone by surprise was the mounting influx of working-age people and their families. Builders worked flat out to meet the demand for homes, schools, shops, offices, factories and roads. House prices doubled in the early 1970s.

There was a downside to the boom. Farm workers continued to leave the land through farm amalgamation as well as mechanisation, branch railway lines were closed (isolating the Lizard and huge tracts of North Cornwall from railheads), rural bus services cancelled and the number of manual local government workers fell. But, at the same time, a shift in government agricultural policy from quantity to quality increased the importance of dairying in the west and farm incomes and land prices rose, with knock-on effects upon suppliers, food processors and distributors. The decrease in employment in public transport was more than offset by an increase in the numbers involved in the motor trade. The fall in the number of blue-collar workers in local government was more than compensated by a rise in the number of office workers. In general, gains in manufacturing, tourism and people-led activities much more than counter-balanced losses in other sectors and labour demand was buoyant. There was even a brief moment in the summer of 1973 when the number of male jobs on offer compared with the number of registered unemployed, was more favourable in Cornwall than in the UK as a whole.

EUPHORIA - & SOME DISSIDENT VOICES

Such was the feeling of economic well-being that the regional economist Derek Spooner, investigating manufacturing growth in Devon and Cornwall, concluded that this 'rural periphery' was transforming itself into a part of the prosperous South East. Another analyst, John Blunden, noted suggestions that Cornwall was at the beginning of a considerable renaissance of mining. James Whetter, the Cornish historian, asserted that the local fishing industry was in as good a position as it has been for decades. And, as if to confirm this confidence, the South West Economic Planning Council (SWEPC) followed its 1967 draft strategy for the South West, optimistically entitled *A Region With A Future*, with a *Strategic Settlement Pattern* in which a broad swathe of development swept down from somewhere north of Gloucester past Bristol, Exeter and Plymouth all the way to Truro and beyond.[2]

Not all Cornish people were thrilled at this prospect. The Cornwall Conservation Forum, an amalgam of environmental groups, painted, in its 1973 *Cornwall's Choice*, a horrific vision of a territory swollen to bursting point with inmigrants, its natural resources and beauty squandered to meet their needs.

Professor Charles Thomas, Director of the newly-formed Institute of Cornish Studies, spoke of a 'beleaguered Cornwall' under '. . . erosive attack by social and economic factors too powerful to vanquish'. There were few true Cornishmen left, he believed, and precious little left of the old Cornwall. Len Truran, leader of Mebyon Kernow (MK), which had by now ceased to be a behind-the-scenes pressure group and had become a political party, sensed defeatism all around him: 'Never before has there been such disillusion, never before such despair as today'. The source of this despondency was what one Grand Bard of the Cornish Gorseth called the involuntary exodus of the Cornish and the voluntary influx of the English, said to take the better jobs, buy-up the choicer properties and destroy the Cornish identity.[3]

MK called for taxes on tourism, a moratorium on second homes and retirement immigration, action against local estate agents who marketed Cornish houses in national magazines to 'robots from the battery cage society'. It was also the first to identify and attack what it called the 'Devonwall' syndrome, the merger of Cornish services like the police and the water boards into Devon-and-Cornwall authorities with their headquarters (and higher-paid posts) in Devon. Of course this was part of a long term process. Local banks, insurance and finance companies had long been controlled from afar. Post-War nationalisations saw the end of Cornish gas and electricity companies. Defence cuts meant the amalgamation of the local regiment (the Duke of Cornwall's Light Infantry) with that of Somerset. But the arrival of main-frame computers had given a fresh impetus to centralisation; for instance, the transfer of the South Western Electricity Board's (SWEB) accounting and invoicing activities to Plymouth, which also became Cornwall's centre for certain specialist health services as well as the site of the District Hospital for East Cornwall. Already by the mid-70s only five of SWEB's 1400 Cornish employees were of managerial or higher executive grade, and while 69 Plymouth civil servants received professional day-release training, there were just six able to do so in the whole of Cornwall.

CORNWALL BETWEEN THE OPEC OIL SHOCKS

The oil price crisis of late 1973 brought to an abrupt end Cornwall's period of economic growth. The inflow of new factories dried up, tourist numbers dipped, in-migration slowed down, new housing starts halved within a year, unemployment rose from 3.5% to 12%. One of the main propellents of the boom, branch plant growth, was now a thing of the past for, with UK manufacturing employment already on the downward path and with a sluggish demand for existing products, manufacturers no longer needed to look at Cornwall for cheap sites or available labour. And although Regional Aid programmes continued, the government was becoming more concerned about the problems of inner-cities than about far-off rural areas. Of course Regional Aid, although it had been massively increased in the mid-60s, was not the only reason for the dispersion of manufacturing from urban to rural areas. Factory decentralisation had also occurred in places like East Anglia, where no Assisted Areas existed, and in countries like Japan and the United States which did not operate policies of the British kind. But Assisted Area status had at least put Cornwall on a level playing field compared with other assisted areas. Its problems, however, were more akin to those of the inner-cities themselves than rural Wales or Scotland. But population size disqualified towns like Camborne, Redruth or Penzance from Urban Programmes - although some Welsh valleys with similar towns managed to claim assistance.

All the same, and despite the economic shock waves from outside that hit Cornish industry, local employment proved to be more resilient than the rest of the South West Region or in the UK as a whole. The reason for this was that the other main driving forces of the earlier years picked up momentum again. Tourist numbers went on to achieve new records, achieving an all-time peak in 1978 at 3.4 million, worker-immigration resumed, employment in education, hospitals, banking and business services moved strongly upwards.

It was during this time, when economic signals seemed to be pointing in different directions, that Cornwall's leaders prepared, with a mass of consultative documents and a commendable degree of public involvement, their new *Structure Plan* for the development of Cornwall. They were not short of advice. Organisations already introduced in this Chapter, with many others, were ready with alternative plans for the future. The planners began their work in the aftermath of a period of expansion and optimism, but between 1976 and 1981 unemployment rose by 55% and the situation in West Cornwall was so bad that most of it was designated a Special Development Area. Yet if we compare Cornwall's employment total in 1981 with that in 1976, it was only fractionally lower. Employment fell by just 300 while unemployment rose by 6600.

Paradoxically, people-led growth was the key to both the buoyancy of employment and the rise in unemployment. Expansion in service sector occupations, including tourist-influenced activities, almost offset a 14% loss of manufacturing jobs combined with a further 5% decline in the farm work-force (mining employment remained stable). The SWEPC 1973 *Strategic Settlement Plan* pinned its hopes on an immigration-led approach: the task of local authorities, such a policy implied, was to accommodate the inflow of people and find jobs for them. Cornwall's Councillors were more guarded. They maintained an employment-led approach and presented to the public three scenarios, involving varying levels of employment growth. Two points may be made about these policy options. Firstly, although they all involved immigration growth as well, this was within a rather narrow range, from 7.5% to 12.5% over 15 years. Secondly, the top of this range was below the SWEPC projection, which in turn was below the actual rate of population growth experienced in the 70s. Cornwall was thus moderating immigration-led growth. And, as perhaps was to be expected, the public chose the middle path, which was well below the rate that was currently being experienced.[4]

It was during this period that another pressure group made its influence felt, the Cornwall Industrial Development Association (CIDA). CIDA included some important local industrial business leaders but although many were Cornish-born they had little interest in the political aims of Mebyon Kernow, nor much sympathy for the Greens. Indeed, one of the chief reasons for the formation of CIDA was to stem what they saw as a rising tide of anti-industrial feeling, with every fresh proposal, whether for mining, quarrying or clay working, food- or fish-processing, offshore oil exploration or tourism, meeting a blanket refusal. An anti-development feeling, CIDA believed, was permeating the attitudes of local planners and councillors and paralysing economic development.[5]

CIDA agreed with the Conservation Forum and Mebyon Kernow, however, in exposing the basic futility, even absurdity, of Whitehall policy. CIDA was the first to demonstrate statistically how the supply of incoming labour was exceeding the rising demand for workers, thus pushing up unemployment and helping to damp down wages.[6]

DEPENDENT INDUSTRIALISATION

The second Opec oil crisis wrought greater damage upon the Cornish economy than did the first. Tourist numbers dropped more sharply than in previous recessions, the net inward movement of migrants below the age of 55 fell by 60% and that of older newcomers by nearly 30%. But the major long-term casualty was manufacturing. In the middle of a UK depression that trebled national unemployment to over three million and wiped out a third of manufacturing jobs, most of Cornwall's manufacturing gain of the post-War years was lost. On the industrial estate between Camborne and Redruth, for example, branch plants of Heathcoats, a Devon-based textile company and Rank Bush Murphy, supplying television components to a Plymouth main factory, employed between them some 2500 workers. The textile factories closed after Heathcoats became part of Coats Paton, whose headquarters were in Scotland and the television plant, after becoming Rank Toshiba, followed suit. To make matters worse, the backbone of medium-sized, locally owned and controlled firms was crumbling away. The last vestiges of the integrated mining economy disappeared - brickyards, arsenic works, fuse making, powder mills. Long-established companies were submerged in the anonymity of national concerns or financial corporations like the Royal Bank of Scotland or Prudential Insurance. After nearly two centuries of trading and technological innovation the name of Harvey's of Hayle disappeared from the scene. Holman's, flagship of hard-rock technology, was a shadow of its former self. It had built its trade, as had so many traditional British firms, by following the flag to Empire and Commonwealth markets - where Cornish Cousin Jacks were to be found. Its massive new offices were the largest building in the Camborne-Redruth area. But now, like so many other companies, it found itself outpaced by foreign competitors and, after merging with two other medium-sized compressor manufacturers, was absorbed into a larger group with head-offices up-country. Silley Cox, the ship repairers, came under the control of the P&O shipping group, were then nationalised, nearly closed down, made a limited recovery and made further revivals under a property group and as part of a ship-building and house-building consortium.

The combined result of branch plant development, the collapse of some local firms and takeovers by outsiders was that, by the late 1970s, three quarters of the industrial workforce in Cornwall were under the control of head offices outside the territory. Cornwall was a classic case of dependent industrialisation, and authority over its own economic destiny was rapidly diminishing in the non-manufacturing sphere as well. 'Regional' bodies like South West Water and the Devon and Cornwall Constabulary were hiving-off vital functions with a consequent loss of local control (and of higher level jobs). Retailing was another sector where local ascendancy disappeared. In the 1950s the 'Fore Street' of most towns boasted a collection of Cornish-owned department stores, ladies and gentlemen's outfitters, ironmongers and other shops of some size and importance. By the 1980s most of these had closed down, been taken over by national chains or forced away from the prime shopping areas.[7]

DECLINE IN THE STAPLE TRADES

Adding to Cornwall's problems, other traditional mainstays like farming and defence were having to bear their share of national and international cuts. Although the farm work force had been declining in the mid-1980s, farmers' incomes had risen and land prices reached record levels in the mid-1980s. But they fell sharply after milk quotas were reduced and the impact on farmers' incomes was felt far beyond the farm gate by food processors and distributors, suppliers of fertilisers, feedstuffs and machinery. As for defence work, commuters from South East Cornwall provided a fifth of the labour force in Plymouth's naval dockyards where thousands of jobs were lost. Further west, even greater numbers worked for air bases near Helston and Newquay and, throughout Cornwall, a similar sized workforce was involved in sub-contracting for defence-related work.

Two final blows, psychological as well as material, were the sudden end of yet other of tin mining's false dawns and the loss of the clay industry's brain centre. In 1985 the bottom fell out of the international tin market and prices plunged from £9000 to £3000 a tonne almost overnight, rendering Cornwall's mines uneconomic. In spite of rescue operations, the industry was once more back to the worst of the inter-War days, with a few hundred workers on reduced wages in a couple of mines. Cornwall still produced a quarter of the UK's tin needs but Geevor was acquired by Cornwall County Council as a tourist attraction and Camborne-Redruth's relics of the tin-mining revolution were to be transformed into an open-air museum of industrial archaeology. The clay industry had to meet competition from overseas producers and from manufacturers of substitutes for clay. It survived by periodic slimming of its local workforce, by cutting out earlier diversifications into leisure activities and building operations and by concentrating upon the core product. During this period those well known features of the St Austell landscape, the conical white clay tips, were transformed into green mounds, but another landmark took its place - John Keay House, the giant (by Cornish standards) headquarters of English Clays International. At the end of the 80s, however, this last bastion, Cornwall's only private sector establishment with a range of sophisticated 'head office' functions, was lost when the company moved their brain centre to Reading. English China Clays, like Holmans before it, had fallen victim to Parkinson's Law of Purpose-Built Decay. Construction of prestigious new offices marked the beginning of a run-down of office staff.

In the past, when the going was hard in mining, fishing and farming, tourism had come to the rescue. But now - and for the first time in its long history - it failed to recover and bounce back again to new heights. That old standby, the traditional British family fortnight by the sea, which had been on the wane nationally for some decades, seemed at last to be reaching the end of its product life in Cornwall as well. Tourist totals bumped along at a lower level but never regained the levels of the late 1970s, and the holiday trade reacted in various ways. Some operators left the industry, altogether, converting their property into residential apartments or moving into a new boom activity - nursing homes and residential homes for the elderly. The number of Cornish people in such establishments nearly doubled during the 1980s as government policies favoured private sector accommodation at the expense of public provision, and already by the mid-1980s this sector employed more workers than mining and fishing put together. Most tourist proprietors, however, stayed in the trade and tried to attract more customers from the growth sectors of foreign visitors, business conferences and short breaks. But they found that Cornwall faced mounting competition from places nearer to the big cities which, a few years earlier, would never have been thought of as tourist honeypots at all - deserted cotton mills and derelict dockyards were now heritage complexes, workaday suburbs boasted leisure centres of tropical sunshine and simulated waves. In desperation promoters dreamed-up schemes to cover Cornish beaches with retractable plastic domes and convert old warehouses into Hawaiian sun palaces. These schemes did not come off, but Cornwall plunged whole-heartedly into the industrial archeology business with Methodist trails and plans to make the old mining hinterland of Camborne-Redruth a 'World Heritage Site'. And operators began to cash in more heavily on Celtic culture and made greater use of the Cornish language in promotional literature and road signs. Tourist attractions mushroomed and, according to one leading tourist operator, Cornwall could be regarded as 'one vast theme park'.

DEVELOPMENT-LED BOOM

When it comes to picking the moment to launch a new strategy Cornwall's planners do not seem to have much luck. In 1980 they had the misfortune to launch their *Structure Plan* - the culmination of years of detailed preparation and consultation - in the midst of a deep recession which upset many of their forecasts. In 1987/8 they produced their up-date of the plan (entitled the *First Alteration*) at the height of a frenzied property boom.[8] Population expansion, the fastest in the South West Region, produced the steepest rise in housing stock in the region, from 182,000 in 1982 to over 200,000 by 1988, with home prices doubling in real terms. This had happened before in the early 1970s, but what was new was the scope of the developments. As express roads finally crossed the borders of Cornwall, people from London and the Home Counties found they could easily slip down for a day or two, snap up their dream cottage, return for short holidays or weekends or commute to work - or communicate rather than commute - from their electronic telecottages.

Hitherto, most private building in Cornwall had proceeded on a relatively modest scale, a field of bungalows here, a couple of shops and a garage there. But changes in UK planning procedures made it simpler for developers to submit to local councils and, if their schemes were rejected, appeal to Whitehall and win the day. Large firms of UK or international standing had the resources to do this and the knowhow to plan on a massive scale and so planning officials had to work late into the night, processing applications described in terms which had become familiar to residents of central England but which were puzzling to Cornish ears. At the heart of most projects was a proposal for a large housing estate (local house prices were still below the levels of the prosperous parts of southern England from which most in-migrants came) but this was buried in a context of yachting marinas, golf courses, country house hotels, conference centres, arts and crafts complexes, heritage centres, even airports. Truro was a particular target, with blueprints for riverside business villages, man-made lakes, retail parks, superstores and shopping malls.

The key issue was now the size of the *Structure Plan*'s revised targets for housebuilding, for Cornwall was an extreme example of the UK's position: the health of the economy was measured by the prosperity of the building industry and the buoyancy of the housing market. The 1980 Plan had been conceived in more optimistic days when manufacturing growth and tourist expansion were setting the pace and was therefore employment-led. It estimated the number of extra jobs likely to be generated locally and set the targets for population and housing accordingly. But although employment projections had been down-graded during the late 1970s as economic prospects worsened, they still proved too optimistic for the 1980s. The 1987 *First Alteration* therefore set very moderate targets for employment growth, or - as in the case of tourism - refrained from giving any forecasts at all. To use the employment-led model, then, would have pointed to nil or very low targets for housing or population expansion, unless that expansion was limited to people who would not require jobs but would generate work, such as retirees, second homers and commuters. The prevailing philosophy of the government, however, was that all had a democratic right to choose to live (or at least to buy a house if they could afford it) wherever they wanted, whatever the employment situation, and the result of that policy was already clear. While the 1980 Plan's inward migration forecasts were on target, its employment projections were not and - as a consequence unemployment was higher than predicted.

Cornwall's employment-led strategy had failed because outside forces did not allow it to succeed. And since Cornwall's planning officials believed that Whitehall would not accept a policy that drastically reduced inward movement, the 1987 *First Alteration* was immigration-led. It fixed a target for population growth that was based upon rather lower levels of inward migration than were currently the case, and was forced to assume that enough extra work would result not merely to provide jobs for the enlarged workforce but also to bring down unemployment. Whereas in the 1980 Plan the labour market was used to regulate growth, in the 1987 *First Alteration* the housing market (determined by demand by in-migrants) was the moderator.

Such an indeterminate situation left the field wide open for competing claims. On one side expansionist groups, including the Housebuilders' Federation, argued - quite plausibly, given the state of planning regulations - that the Plan's projections for new homes were too low. Guidance from Whitehall was that local authorities should take account of 'demand for housing' and since there were millions of owner-occupiers in southern England who could make a sizeable untaxed capital gain by moving to Cornwall the sky was really the limit as far as housing demand was concerned. Opposing this viewpoint were ecological and anti-metropolitan groups and two new bodies, Cornish Alternatives to the Structure Plan (CASP) and the Cornish Social and Economic and Research Group (CoSERG). CASP called for a moratorium on new house construction except for local needs. To build for incomers would, they contended, only lead to more demands for schools, shops, roads and jobs which would in turn generate fresh pressures for yet more factories, infrastructure and more houses. CoSERG, in its book *Cornwall at the Crossroads*, argued that support for in-migration-led growth, combined Devon-and-Cornwall initiatives, and better roads to central England all stemmed from certain basic assumptions about Cornwall's weaknesses: that it was too small, too backward and too remote. These alleged weaknesses, CoSERG insisted, should be turned on their heads and perceived as strengths. Cornwall's human scale settlements, structures and institutions were a source of envy by outsiders and should not be swamped by population growth. The brain drain of its talent should be stemmed by encouraging small-scale but innovative enterprises that were market-leaders in design and technology. A 're-centralisation' perspective would see the territory as the centre or gateway to a maritime network, not the distant terminus of a landbased system.[9]

By this time Cornwall was clearly lagging behind the rest of the South West Region as far as economic growth was concerned, a poor performance that contrasted with western Brittany's, where local leaders had transformed a peasant society, backward and archaic, into a modern and vibrant economy. Symptomatic of the difference between the two areas was the fact that it was Breton farmers - not those of Devon or Cornwall - who showed the initiative to start up the freight and passenger service from Plymouth to Roscoff and then, even more surprisingly, Plymouth to Santander. The obscure port of Roscoff developed into something of a maritime crossroads, with sailings to Cork as well, while Plymouth and Falmouth lagged behind. Work by the Universities of Exeter and Rennes confirmed the contrast. Daniel Gadbin and Malcolm MacMillan identified a general lack of initiative to seek and grasp opportunities in Cornwall and Devon and an absence of coordination of such initiatives as there were. Brittany had developed a sense of regional identity and acquired regional clout which was altogether missing in Cornwall and Devon, according to Michael Havinden, one of the editors of the study, a view reinforced by Prince Charles' Conference on 'Cornwall: the Way Ahead', at which speaker after speaker denounced the apathy in local affairs and called for Cornwall to be galvanised into action on the lines of Finistere. Alexis Gouvennec, charismatic leader of Breton farmers and President of Brittany Ferries, was there to point out the way forward and from this conference issued a number of bodies, financed by public and private funds and aimed at energising the local economy on Breton lines, including the Devon and Cornwall Development Company and the Devon and Cornwall Fisheries Development Group. Another important institution created a little later was the Devon and Cornwall Training and Enterprise Council (TEC).[10]

At the end of the 1980s another damaging UK and world recession stopped the developer-led boom in its tracks and Cornwall shared in a new kind of slump that hit white collar activities in southern England harder than blue collar industries in the North. The inflow of tourists, retirees, commuters and small business owners, who mostly came from southern England, slowed down. Big developers pulled out of the area, small builders and builders' merchants fell on hard times and even went bankrupt, shop fronts were boarded-up and sub-offices closed down. The end of the boom punctured the new businesses so laboriously built up by enterprise agencies by the thousand. A decade earlier a collapse of Cornish manufacturing had left work study officers, factory managers, cost accountants and engineering technicians stranded without a job, but within a few years the service trades created enough vacancies to absorb a new inflow of workers as well as some of those displaced. This time, however, it was the turn of property conveyancers and valuers, interior decorators, double-glazing consultants and fitted-kitchen advisers to be left high and dry.

SECTION TWO:
AN ALTERNATIVE ECONOMIC CASE

LABOUR DEMAND DEFFICIENCY & 'IMPORTED UNEMPLOYMENT'

Through all the upheavals of the Cornish economy two factors at least remained constant: comparatively low pay and relatively high unemployment. The conventional explanation of such disparities is two-fold: an unfavourable industrial structure and labour demand deficiency. In depressed problem regions, the argument goes, a cumulative causation process is at work. As local industries contract and shed labour, workers migrate, thus further reducing the demand for local goods and services. Since Cornwall exhibits most of the features of such a region - low female activity rates, chronic unemployment, low earnings - it is treated as a typical case of labour demand deficiency due to structural decline. An alternative explanation, however, put forward by 'opposition' groups, directed attention to labour supply rather than labour demand. It was CIDA who first demonstrated statistically that employment was rising, not falling, and if unemployment was going up as well it was because the increase in labour supply outstripped the capacity of the local economy to provide more jobs. This notion was at first resisted by Department of Employment Officers but later confirmed in a study they commissioned by Robert McNabb. Employment in West Cornwall between 1961 and 1976 had increased by a surprising 26% at a time when in Britain as a whole it had gone down. Yet over the same period the unemployment rate in Cornwall rose five-fold, from 1.8% to 9.2% while in Britain it advanced from 1.1% to 5.5%[11]

Where then did the truth lie; on the labour demand or on the labour supply side, or perhaps on both? As Table 3.1 at the beginning of this Chapter suggests, the long term trend in labour demand was upward (although there were some depressed periods when it fell). But at the same time structural changes produced a mismatch between local labour supply and the kind of new skills required. A massive shake out of labour occurred in the traditional male-oriented activities of Cornwall involving the movement of goods out of the area: farming, fishing, mining, quarrying, clayworking, ship-repairing and hard-rock engineering. But these job losses were much more than offset, in purely numerical terms, by gains in female-related activities concerned with the movement of people into Cornwall: tourism, second homes, retirement immigration, commuting.

TABLE 3.2
CORNWALL: CHANGES IN EMPLOYMENT 1961-1991

		1961	1991	Increase
MALE	Full Time	65,600	68,500	2,900
	Part Time	2,200	4,300	2,100
	Self Employed	31,200	33,200	2,000
	Total Male	99,000	106,000	7,000
FEMALE	Full Time	20,900	36,900	16,000
	Part Time	5,900	32,400	26,500
	Self Employed	5,300	10,800	5,500
	Total Female	32,100	80,100	48,000

Source: Census of Population, 1961 and 1991

As Table 3.2 indicates, seven out of eight of the extra jobs were taken by females and nearly half by part-time female workers. Apart from this there was also an important mismatch within the male labour market between the skills required by incoming firms and the capacity of local men to provide them. Already, by the early 1960s, Associated Industrial Consultants were reporting a paradox of labour scarcity against a large theoretical labour surplus - a shortage of unskilled as well as skilled men and by the mid-70s CIDA was claiming that 'skilled men - there aren't any!' Of course, it would have been strange indeed if Cornwall had housed a reservoir of all the knowledge and skills required by employers coming to the area, and new factories brought in around 10% of their labour requirements, mainly managers and specialist operatives, from outside, supplemented by newcomers who came to Cornwall under their own steam. Employers soon became familiar with the sight of waiting rooms full, in holiday times, with visitors enquiring about permanent jobs and one CIDA survey showed that up to 50% of all the skilled men in new West Cornwall factories had arrived recently in Cornwall of their own accord.

To sum up thus far, employment opportunities rose by leaps and bounds compared with the situation in the UK as a whole and this, along with other factors such as lower house prices and environmental attraction, helped to attract a high rate of working-age in-migration, which in turn generated the demand for more jobs in the service sector. But the pattern of industry in Cornwall was biased towards lower pay and seasonal activities and its small scale structure meant that there were few higher-paid 'head office' jobs in banking, insurance and finance, higher education, research and development, marketing and advertising, the civil service, nationalised industries or public utilities. Employment expansion was lop-sided, part of what CIDA called the 'centralisation of brain and the decentralisation of brawn', accounting for a two-way traffic of worker migration. Parallel with the inflow there was a persistent exodus of the younger and better education elements of the population who were looking for better job prospects elsewhere.

TRANSPORT STRATEGIES

Cornwall's 1952 *Development Plan* contained the essence of two diametrically opposed perspectives: on the one hand the orthodox core-periphery vision of a remote terminal of a land-based network where everything of importance began and ended in central England and where the only hope lay in improving access - particularly by road - to the centre; on the other hand a view of a peninsula jutting into the Atlantic, only a dozen miles from one of the world's busiest shipping lanes and with one of Europe's finest natural anchorages, which could be, if not a maritime crossroads, at least an important gateway to the wider world. To support a land-based strategy Cornwall's leaders proposed an ambitious internal programme of dual-carriageways and bypasses and construction of a road bridge across the Tamar, while politely reminding the government that roads leading to Cornwall were such as to deter all but the most determined traveller from making the journey. As far as a maritime strategy was concerned, they called upon Whitehall to produce a ports policy that would recognise Cornwall's potential for coastal trade.[12]

The government was deaf to Cornwall's demands for a ports policy. The British Transport Commission, which might have constructed an integrated transport strategy, had become a mere umbrella group and by the end of the 1950s road vehicles had overtaken trains as the prime mover of both passengers and freight in the UK. In Cornwall peak holiday traffic on the roads rose by 80% during the 1950s but the real break-through came when the Tamar Bridge opened in 1961. Whitehall transport officials argued that Cornwall's forecasts of future traffic were over-optimistic but in the first full year 5000 vehicles a day crossed the Tamar and a quarter of a century later the figure was 28,500.

The railway network was everywhere under threat. Cornwall's leaders resisted the Beeching rail cuts of the mid-60s with some success, retaining the main route from Plymouth to Penzance along with links to the resorts of Newquay, St Ives, Falmouth and Looe, but the entire North Cornwall system was dismantled and thereafter rail transport was more or less neglected. The

1947 University College of Exeter survey had recommended that rail improvements (for business executives as well as freight) should take precedence over road and a study forty years later by Dr R. A.Gibb of University of Plymouth came to the same conclusion. But during the years between exactly the opposite took place and the low priority given to rail traffic with Cornwall can perhaps be judged by current average speeds of trains from Paddington: 103 mph to Bristol, 90 mph to Exeter, 77 mph to Plymouth, 67 mph to Truro.[13]

Road programmes, in contrast, took up an ever larger part of strategic plans and the lion's share of transport budgets. Yet surprisingly, in view of the vast sums spent upon them, no surveys were ever carried out to test the case for the roads and their construction was justified by a mixture of home-spun philosophy and ever more enthusiastic repetitions of the 'roads to riches' theses. Cornwall's 1952 Plan began the process with the maxim that Cornwall would have to pay the cost of new roads whether it built them or not. The 1970 *West Cornwall Study* accepted that no hard evidence existed of the effect of better roads on local agriculture or industry but asserted that they were vital for tourism. SWEPC's 1973 *Strategic Settlement Plan* - the apotheosis of the 'roads to prosperity' dogma - unveiled a belt of development either side of planned expressways from Gloucester to Hayle. Cornwall's Highways Department, in its 1983 *Roads to Prosperity*, argued the case for dualling the A30 from Exeter to Penzance so persuasively that Whitehall changed its mind and, encouraged by this success, pressed for dualling the A38 from Plymouth and talked of an 'Atlantic Highway' following the A39 along the north coast. Such programmes received enthusaistic support from local MPs, the Euro MP and agricultural, industrial, tourist and building interests and formed a keystone of Devon and Cornwall Development Company's *Strategy for Prosperity* and the South West Branch of the CBI's *Prosperity for the 90s*.[14]

This powerful orthodoxy was challenged by local branches of Friends of the Earth, Transport 2000, the Ecologists and the Council for the Protection of Rural England (CPRE) as well as by local bodies such as CIDA and CoSERG. While the 'Green' pressure groups concentrated more upon global threats to the environment, CIDA and CoSERG were more concerned with the centralising dynamic of road improvement and with the issue of opportunity costs, in other words whether the large sums spent on roads might have been more usefully invested elsewhere. They posed a number of questions, the most obvious being why, if roads were supposed to bring prosperity, Cornwall did not seem to reap any benefits in terms of higher earnings or lower unemployment. And why had manufacturers moved into Cornwall en masse during the 1963-73 period when, because of motorway construction elsewhere, Cornwall's competitive position in road transport was *worsening*, and then moved out of Cornwall when its road links improved? Why, again, had tourist numbers risen spectacularly when it was difficult to get to Cornwall and fallen when it became easier? One answer was that, no matter how good the roads became, freight charges and travel times were always going to be higher than for most other parts of the UK. For instance, a 1990 West Country Tourist Board (WCTB) survey found that visitors were still complaining about the long and tiring journey to Cornwall compared with other places. The WCTB's solution was, predictably, to widen the M4 and M5 and dual the road all the way to Penzance.[15] Another reason for the - to say the least - nebulous link between roads and prosperity was the centralising dynamic of road improvement. While faster road traffic helped Cornish firms to compete elsewhere they also, by the same token, helped a far greater number of outsiders to trade in Cornwall and, as critics pointed out, there was no *a priori* reason why gainers in Cornwall should exceed losers.

Arguments based on a simplistic roads-prosperity nexus were shaky but, undeterred, the roads lobby pressed on with their demands. 'Is it any wonder,' asked the Regional Manager of English Estates in 1989 'that inward investors and commercial developers are still reluctant to cross the Tamar with the low priority given to roads?' In fact, as CoSERG showed in its *Roads to Superjam*, they had received top priority. It was far easier for local authorities to get funding for roads than for rail, air or sea improvements, let alone than for cyclists or pedestrians. What is more, road network programmes were negotiated between local Highways officers and the Department of Transport, with Councillors generally rubber-stamping them. And once the bypasses and dual carriageways were built, other developments accompanied them - service stations, restaurants, industrial and housing estates, so that, instead of responding to the strategic needs of Cornwall, road programmes dictated them. And instead of giving priority to improving accessibility of local people to local services, they put a premium on mobility, and encouraged centralisation of services, thus reinforcing the need for yet more road transport. The tragedy, CoSERG concluded, was that Cornwall had always been a region of small communities which reduced the need for day-to-day travel over long distances. Yet this settlement pattern, of great long-term benefit for the future, was being destroyed in a self-fulfilling, but self-defeating, programme of road construction.

This raises the question of the opportunity costs of road building, an issue which was first explored by CIDA in its 1976 *The Economy of Cornwall*. Unlike some conservationists, CIDA did not reject road programmes outright, but suggested alternative and, in the long run, more effective ways of raising Cornwall's competitiveness. To illustrate this approach Dr Terry Thorneycroft of CIDA invented a new unit of 'Cornish currency' - the 'mile of Camborne bypass'. Cornwall was at that time having its first experience of new by-passes built to reduce congestion generated on the old by-passes and CIDA's unit of currency was introduced with a very serious intent: to demonstrate that many of the facilities under threat in Cornwall, or needing to be introduced, cost very little compared to the amounts spent on new roads. CIDA research had identified high class medical care as extremely important in attracting and retaining senior executives, and one mile of by-pass swallowed up an amount equivalent to the total annual capital expenditure budget for all hospital improvements for the whole of Cornwall. CIDA surveys also produced particularly strong support for developing an airport (including customs clearance facilities), maintaining the main-line railway to Penzance and enhancing Cornwall's ports. On the CIDA map, Cornwall was the centre of gravity of a maritime network, for the container revolution was in full swing and giant ships could have offloaded their cargoes at Falmouth onto smaller coastal vessels and CIDA called for roll on, roll off links with Ireland, Brittany, Western France and the Iberian peninsula, and for road access to Falmouth to be improved. CIDA saw the sea not as a barrier but as a highway to trade.[16]

But it was Breton farmers who made the obscure little port of Roscoff into a maritime crossroads and even ran a ferry direct from Plymouth to Santander as well as establishing links with Cork. For although interest in marine opportunies flared up from time to time in Cornwall, it seldom lasted long. In the early 70s oil exploration in the Celtic Sea aroused a great deal of excitement and a decade later Falmouth was handling about 5% of total British servicing for oil rigs, but only a comparatively small labour force was involved. In 1971 an Act of Parliament authorised a company to construct a container port at Falmouth, planned to employ 250 directly and another 1250 in spin-off jobs: a decade later the project was abandoned. In the mid-1980s a Norwegian shipping company investigated the potential of Falmouth as a passenger and freight ferry to Iberia but decided the return on investment was too low and criticised the 'appallingly poor road network' to the port.[17] The idea was revived in 1992, by which time the 'Atlantic Arc' had given the maritime dimension a new lease of life. The impetus, inevitably, came from Brittany, but membership of the Arc soon extended from Norway past Scotland, Wales and Ireland and down to the Algarve. In 1988 Cornwall made a bid for research support to investigate its sea-faring potential to the European Regional Development Fund, although the amount involved was dwarfed by its proposals for new roads. A year later Cornwall Agricultural Group called for construction of a deep sea port to import feedstuffs and fertilizers and export grain to be 'advanced with minimal delay'. All this gave fresh hope to Cornwall's port trade which, in relative terms, still seemed of some importance - Par was the South West Region's third port in tonnage handled (after Bristol and Poole), Fowey was sixth and Falmouth seventh. But these were in the main 'one cargo' ports. Par and Fowey exported clay, Falmouth imported petroleum products. Newlyn was the main fishing harbour along the entire south coast of Britain (80% of its product was re-exported via Plymouth) and Penzance was the sea link for passengers and freight with the Scillies.[18]

Plymouth Business School put this into perspective: Cornwall's share of British port trade was barely 1%, it pointed out, and Devon and Cornwall would be 'running with the wrong hounds' if they concentrated on backward, low-income and low-productivity regions of the Atlantic Arc. Only a supreme optimist, the School declared, would put much faith in such a venture. Peter Wills of CoSERG displayed this brand of optimism. A maritime strategy, he contended, would be a better way of allocating scarce resources than a road-based approach. Cornwall, Wills argued, would be increasingly disadvantaged in trading with a 'centre' that seemed to be receding rapidly eastwards towards *mittel-Europa*, whereas it would always be geographically advantaged in a marine network of commerce with the western seaboard of Europe. Updating CIDA's 'Camborne by-pass' currency, he calculated that just one mile of the new expressways under construction would pay for the refurbishment of one Cornish port, but the long-term benefit of such a maritime investment would be immeasurably greater.[19]

ROAD IMPROVEMENTS & PEOPLE-LED GROWTH: PANACEA OR PROBLEM?

Whatever doubts might exist about the impact of faster roads on industrial development in Cornwall, there was one sort of expansion where, all agreed, roads played a big hand: people-led growth. Where individuals disagreed was whether such growth constituted, on balance, an opportunity or a threat. Many issues are involved - environmental, cultural, ethnic - but this Chapter focuses on the quality and quantity of employment created, problems of planning for people-led expansion and the role of incoming firms and new business starts.

People-led growth is not of course new to Cornwall. It has long been a Mecca for artists and writers, holiday-makers, retirees and invalids, to which can be added such newer species as second homers, long-distance commuters who work far across the Tamar and networkers who communicate rather than commute to work in the outside world from their electronic cottages. Until the 1960s the inflow was offset by outward migration of Cornish workers. In the last thirty years Cornwall has witnessed, as Peter Mitchell demonstrates in Chapter 6, a large net inward movement of people, seven out of ten of whom are under retirement age.

The consensus view was that net inward migration is a good thing. CIDA, for instance, while criticising government policies which enticed manufacturing firms to Cornwall, favoured people-led growth. Subsidising factories which laboriously brought all their inputs to Cornwall, only to send their finished products back out again, defied economic logic. People-led growth, in contrast, involved the voluntary movement of individuals who were attracted by the natural and lasting advantages of Cornwall and not by artificial and temporary subsidies. Apart from CIDA, many sections of the local economy were also, understandably, enthusiastic about an inflow of new customers. Planners, enterprise agencies and academics stressed the fact that Cornwall had one of UK's fastest rates of population increase, and associated factors such as new house construction, as indicators of rising prosperity. For example, Plymouth Business School ran an annual index of well-being for the seven counties of the South West Region. In 1989, according to the School, this showed that Cornwall not only ranked seventh but that it was 'a very bad seventh'. In 1991 the School changed its mind; 'this is no longer true, for Devon now occupied bottom place'.[20] What caused this turnaround? Naturally there were shifts in a number of rankings and the biggest relative change - without which Cornwall would have remained firmly at the bottom - was in 'A' level results. More important, however, in real terms was the fact that Cornwall moved up relatively to Devon in population growth and new housing starts. Yet Cornwall was still last in male and female weekly earnings, yearly incomes, female activity rates, unemployment, GDP per head, and homes with no inside toilets. All of which raises questions about the influence of population-led growth on raising local standards. It undoubtedly generated jobs, though many of these involved lower-paid and lower-skilled part-time, seasonal and casual work and did little to raise Cornwall from the nether regions of the earnings league. It also led to higher unemployment since the inflow of worker migrants outstripped the rise in the number of jobs available.

PLANNING FOR PEOPLE-LED GROWTH

Is there any way of reducing the unfavourable influences of people-led growth upon unemployment and earnings? In answering this question it is useful to divide newcomers into two categories: job-givers and job-takers. Under the first heading come holiday-makers and retirees, commuters and networkers. Planners can estimate, within broad limits, the amount of work these in-migrants will generate. The contribution of incoming small business owners and self-employed professional workers and tradespeople is more problematic since some will give employment to dozens of local people while others work on their own or use no workforce outside the family who came down with them. They may even take work away from the existing local labour force.

The inflow of 'job takers' on a significant scale is a new phenomenon. Cornwall's traditional mining economy was inspired by home-grown entrepreneurs and innovators and worked by indigenous labour. The period since the 1960s, in complete contrast, has been characterised by a large-scale influx of industrial managers, engineers, skilled manual workers, clerks and typists, local government officers, teachers, health and social service workers, accountants and solicitors, artists and craftworkers and - more recently - architects, estate agents and surveyors. Why had most of these newcomers left areas where employment prospects were brighter and earnings higher to come to Cornwall? Not all had taken a drop in salary, of course, since although average earnings were lower in Cornwall there were still some better paid jobs on offer. But many had traded-off pecuniary losses against perceived quality-of-life gains, and house price differentials meant that owner-occupiers could make an untaxed capital gain as well. The role played by another group of in-migrants in the labour market is equivocal: the category identified in a survey by the present author as the 'partially employed' who come to Cornwall to follow a life style in which spells of employment or self-employment intermingle with periods of registered unemployment or non-employment. These may have amounted in the 1980s to as much as one sixth of the in-migrant flow.

This brief analysis of 'job givers' and 'job takers' highlights the problem that planners face in forecasting employment and unemployment levels in a situation where they have no control over key variables. There is no mechanism in a market-force economy for determining with any degree of precision what the effects of inward migration upon local earnings and employment and unemployment levels will be. It is particularly difficult in Cornwall because the proportion of self-employed, who may be job givers or job takers, is so high. In the 1980s it rose from 27% to 31% of the male workforce (for women it increased marginally to 13%). But, despite this uncertainty, planners feel forced to upgrade their forecasts of the contribution that people-led growth makes as employment fades in the traditional sectors of farming, mining, clay-working, ship-repairing, tourism and defence. With no real influence over the size or the composition of the inflow of people, however, the planners are increasingly working in the dark. How could they avoid a mismatch between the skill requirements of incoming industry and the capacity of the local pools of labour? Firms overcame this by bringing in key workers and recruiting from the inflow of skilled people who were moving to Cornwall of their own accord. A better solution would have been to train or retrain the local workforce and this problem was tackled by colleges and training agencies, but two factors made it difficult. The first was the collapse of traditional Cornish-owner companies that had provided the bulk of local apprentice and technical training. The second was the wide range of skills involved in the new industries - one survey identified over two hundred different technologies and processes. Following from this was the impossibility of forecasting what the skill requirements would be and therefore of gearing-up training programmes to meet future needs.

MANUFACTURING DECENTRALISATION AS A PROPELLANT OF LONG-TERM GROWTH

In the mid-1960s Cornwall found itself the beneficiary of a massively augmented package of regional aid, investment grants, employment subsidies, and training allowances as part of a government policy which involved the dispersion of factories from prosperous but congested areas of southern and central England to the outer regions of the UK. The results, in Cornwall's case, were particularly spectacular. Up until then Cornwall's planners had only received a dozen or so enquiries a year about new industrial sites: in 1967 there were nearly 100, in 1968 over 150. Manufacturing employment, which had fallen by 14% in the fifties, rose by nearly 60% up to the mid-70s.

Judging from these figures, the new regional policies were an outstanding success, especially when we consider that Cornwall was further in travel-time from any major centre of industry than almost all the other areas that were receiving the same levels of aid. Of course, regional programmes were not the only factor but they did put Cornwall on equal terms and help it to exploit its comparative advantages such as larger concentrations of female labour. The proportion of females in paid employment in Cornwall was as low as in any rural region, but Cornwall's semi-urban settlement pattern, a relic of its industrial past, meant that Camborne-Redruth and St Austell could accommodate factories up to 1000 strong. Falmouth, where skilled engineers were being laid-off from ship-repair yards, also offered advantages to male-employing firms. The Cornish climate and quality of life was another attraction that was fully exploited by planners in their promotion of the area. Surveys showed that entrepreneurs and skilled workers (and their families) in the South East viewed Scotland, the industrial north and rural Wales as 'foreign parts', cursed with a harsh climate. Cornwall on the other hand enjoyed a highly favourable reputation, usually the result of earlier holiday experiences.[21]

The factories that moved to Cornwall injected fresh capital, technology and employment into the local economy. According to some observers at the time they were ushering in a new industrial age. Other local bodies, however, including CIDA, did not share this optimism. CIDA's surveys showed that the industrial growth was cellular and compartmentalised and did not create an incubatory economy in which market leaders and technological innovators spawned large numbers of small local sub-contractors and suppliers. Instead each unit existed in technical as well as trading isolation from the rest, using its own already established network of up-country suppliers, distributors and customers, buying most of its components elsewhere, using marketing and research and development expertise from outside. Moreover, many of the jobs created in these firms were lesser-skilled and lesser-paid. It was no coincidence that two-thirds of the growth in manufacturing employment occurred in five sectors - mechanical and electrical engineering, clothing, footwear and textiles - which came within the bottom six in the UK for manufacturing operative earnings and within the top six for the proportion of females employed. (The sixth, in both cases, food and drink processing, was already well established in Cornwall.) What is more, many of the technologies and products were approaching the end of their useful life, as a study by Richard Payne showed. If some regions had managed to attract leading-edge industries which offered a future of self-generating growth, many of Cornwall's new plants already seemed relegated to the technological past.[22]

After the first Opec oil crisis local planners came under tremendous and prolonged pressure to persuade new plants to come to Cornwall at a time when the supply of suitable factories was drying up and when competition from other regions in the UK and Europe for such units was becoming ever more intense. In these circumstances their achievements were creditable but, with existing plants closing down and old-established Cornish manufacturers shedding labour, they had to run very hard just to stay in the same place. It is easy to see why they were willing to accept almost any factory which promised to create more jobs even if those jobs were not of high quality. It is also understandable if they cashed in on Cornwall's environmental attractions to promote the area at home and abroad, stressing its equable climate and easy-going pace of life.

Whether these policies were wise in the long run is open to question. Peter Gripaios has defended them on the grounds that we have to make the most of inward investment since nothing else is likely to solve the problems of peripheral areas. Cornwall's planners produced another argument. Surveys of people who stayed in Cornwall or came to Cornwall indicated that they were willing to trade-off lower-pay and less-skilled work against social and environmental attractions. A policy that provided low pay jobs, if nothing better was available, therefore seemed justified. But such a strategy does nothing to fulfil another objective of government policy - to bring local earnings levels up to UK norm. And, linked with this, factory expansion was associated with an influx of workers so large that unemployment levels actually went up rather than down. Cornish employers soon got used to seeing their waiting rooms fill up during the holiday season with skilled and unskilled visitors looking for jobs. If labour supply due to worker in-migration increased faster than a rise in labour demand due to the inflow of new factories then the process, CIDA argued, was self-defeating. It tended to keep earnings levels down and even widen the gap between centre and periphery, unless the skill input to the local economy helped to create self-generating growth. But this only happened in a few cases: one useful legacy of the branch plant expansion was a nucleus of small textile firms, employing some 150 workers, formed by executives and skilled workers left stranded when Heathcoats closed down.[23]

As for the emphasis on Cornwall's environmental attractions as a selling point for potential inward investors, an early criticism of this approach came in a 1972 survey by Peter Newby of factory owners in Devon and Cornwall: the appeal, he said, was not to business instincts but to a desire for leisure activities. As CoSERG later showed, promotional leaflets for would-be investors portrayed the local workforce as reliable, loyal and steady (if stubborn) with the lowest level of industrial unrest in the UK, very low absenteeism, minimal labour turnover. Augmenting this solid base was a big inflow of 'skilled graduates attracted by excellent living conditions'. This comforting picture was questioned at the Duke of Cornwall's 1987 Conference. The territory, complained one distinguished contributor, had become a cosy backwater for people wishing to do their own thing, a place of basket weavers and salad bowl turners, following which a procession of speakers rose to denounce the lethargy into which Cornwall had sunk and demand that it should be energised into action.[24]

Was there, CIDA and others asked, a better way of spending the large amounts of money spent on creating jobs in plants which seemed to have no real reason to be in Cornwall and which simply shifted materials down to the area and then laboriously sent them back again in a slightly modified form? Could the money be better spent on sectors where Cornwall enjoyed a comparative advantage - for example adding value to food and fish products, clay and tin, tourism and the retirement industry - activities which utilised raw materials already *in situ* or the movement of people who came at their own expense?

INCOMING SMALL BUSINESSES - A MODERNISING ELITE?

One unusual feature of Cornwall's manufacturing growth was the contribution made by incoming transfers of owner-managed firms and - especially - by newcomers setting-up business in Cornwall for the first time. Even at the height of branch-plant expansion, these independent firms provided 40% of the new units with more than 10 employees and a third of the extra jobs and as the inflow of branch factories dried up, and employment in some already established began to fall, the small firm sector took over the lion's share of job creation. According to a CIDA survey of the late 1970s, two fifths of employment in new small factories in West Cornwall was in owner-managed transfers, another two fifths in incoming new starts and one fifth in indigenous enterprises.[25]

When it became clear in the later 1970s that branch-plant decentralisation, at least by UK companies, was largely a thing of the past policy-makers looked with increasing enthusiasm on the contribution of small business people. Again, as with branch plant expansion, Cornwall's planners and enterprise agencies scored some notable successes. Indeed, without self-employment growth, the local economy would in 1980s have been in a poor state. The number of full-time male employees actually fell by 3800 but this was much more than offset by an increase of 7900 in the number of self-employed men, 1400 of whom employed others as well. But policy-makers searching desperately for a cure for mounting unemployment tended to over-rate the real successes that they achieved. New business starts in Cornwall were viewed as something of a modernising elite, a band of 'new frontiersmen' who would help to revitalise a moribund economy. As the region declined, the argument went, the more original and radical elements had departed, leaving behind a population who were loyal and reliable-enough but either basically content with their lot or else sunk into a resigned apathy. Either way they lacked innovative ability. 'Dynamic in-migrants' (to use a phrase from Cornwall's planners) were what was needed to galvanise the economy.

Did newcomers to Cornwall match up to such expectations? Outstanding successes can indeed be cited; cases of Cornish and incoming entrepreneurs who now employ some hundreds of local workers. Research by CIDA, the present author and others suggested, however, that incomers to Cornwall differed from the usual pattern in significant ways. To begin with, entrepreneurs in other parts of the UK tended to start up in their own home territory for sound economic and social reasons: they had useful contacts there and avoided adding the trauma and expense of moving home and family at a time when they were pre-occupied in adjusting to a new working life. The majority of new starts in Cornwall, in contrast, were involved in a complete displacement of home and workplace and surveys showed twin motives for setting up: 'to be one's own boss' and 'to escape the city rat race'. These newcomers were also relatively well-educated, well-qualified and experienced professionally in comparison with the local population, although their experience was often confined to specialised departments of large corporations rather than the jack-of-all-trade requirements of a small concern. But a survey by Derek Spooner in the early seventies concluded that their economic behaviour was satisficing rather than optimising, concerned with making a reasonable living rather than seeking to maximise efficiency, and studies in the later 70s by CIDA found that a large proportion of new factory owners began to look around for a suitable site, or even a suitable line of business, after they had already settled in Cornwall or while they were on holiday (many had second homes). While not choosing a life of total leisure, they were looking for a more leisured life-style away from the stresses and strains of town life. They brought something of a semi-retirement atmosphere to an area already known for its more relaxed pace. A survey by Gripaios in the 1970s of 200 nursery units built to encourage advanced technology and reduce long-term unemployment showed they increased employment substantially, by 60%, but very few involved new technology and none reduced long-term unemployment. The business life of West Cornwall firm was also much shorter than those in rural Devon.[26]

During the mid-80s Gareth Shaw and Allan Williams came to similar conclusions about the tourist industry. Most holiday businesses and shops in Looe, for instance, were owned by newcomers who had sunk their life-savings into ventures of which they had little prior knowledge, except through rose-coloured spectacles as former holiday makers during the boom days of Cornish tourism. In another review of the economy of Cornwall and Devon, Williams detected a 'low economic dynamism' in the small business sector, a serious lack of research and development and innovative capacity, and a small-scale agricultural sector lacking value-added agri-businesses. Phillips and Williams produced evidence that, after taking account of high failure rates, net new business formation in Cornwall and Devon was far lower than in Somerset.[27]

It is important to guard against expecting miracles from the small firm sector. UK research has shown that small entrepreneurs typically have little experience in their chosen trade, possess only moderate levels of education and are motivated more by a desire to be their own boss than by a drive for originality, high profitability or expansion. Only a third of them employ others, even fewer aim to increase their labour force and almost half fail within the first four years. If the Cornish experience is that new business starts achieved rather less than this, is this surprising? The newcomers were a self-selected group, anxious to escape the city treadmill, lured by promotional literature which stressed leisure rather than work, eager to be their own boss even if they had little knowledge of the trade they were entering. And despite all the road improvements, Cornwall was inevitably still disadvantaged in terms of road transport times and costs. That they were able to compete at all is a matter for congratulation. As a provider of jobs, the small business is essential. But, within the current context of regional policy, it is too much to expect it to be a spear-head of innovation and advanced technology.

THE INFORMATIONAL & INTELLECTUAL INFRASTRUCTURE: A STUDY IN FRUSTRATION

One essential set of activities for any region which seeks to shake off the shackles of peripheral dependence involves the creation, processing and transmission of high grade information - science-based industries, information technology, advanced education, research and development. Such activities tend to concentrate in a few centres and the history of attempts to reduce Cornwall's deficiencies is worth examining in some detail since it exemplifies the obstacles that Cornwall has to overcome: Whitehall's centralising philosophy, the superiority of its Devon neighbour and its own internal rivalries.

During the 1960s and 1970s the main thrust of regional policy, as far as Cornwall was concerned, involved decentralisaiton of factories. Manufacturing employment in the UK was falling, however, and office employment was rising rapidly, but few incentives were given to office firms to move to the Assisted Areas. Over 1000 such firms were persuaded to move out of London, creating over 150,000 jobs in the provinces, but none came as far as Cornwall. Yet the area seemed to offer advantages for office location: office rent and rates were only 15% of the level in central London, less than half those in Bristol, two-thirds of Devon's. Clerical staff costs were 25% below the London level, 22% below Bristol, 4% below Devon's. A CIDA survey identified reserves of female labour already trained in clerical tasks who were looking for jobs, particularly part-time work. And the Hardman Commission on civil servant decentralisation had found that the South West Region was one place where office workers wanted to go if they had to move. But Cornwall did not even feature on the Commission's map of possible office relocations.[28]

An important local initiative of the early 1980s which attempted to introde office-based activities to Cornwall was the South West Area Network Service (SWANS) Scheme. The notion came from Terry Thorneycroft of CIDA, working with Cornwall's planners, but soon extended to include Devon and Plymouth. Put very simply, SWANS involved a telephone tariff structure whereby, after paying an annual subscription, Cornish users would be charged at local rates for calls to cities such as London and Bristol and possibly Birmingham, Liverpool and Manchester. More advanced facilities including teleconferencing and viewdata could be added. Callers from those areas would also be charged local rates when telephoning Cornish subscribers to the scheme.[29] SWANS had all the hallmarks of an idea whose time was ripe. The convergence of advances in information technology and telecommunications had annihilated distance. Corporate networkers communicated to work from home as employees or consultants of national or international companies. Andrew Page of the Dartington Institute in Devon was developing the concept of a 'cottage office', a computer-based bureau with a range of sophisticated facilities which could also serve as a community meeting place for teleworkers. The SWANS idea fitted a model for Business Innovation Centres being disseminated by the European Commission, as well as being the prototype for

'Office Parks'.[30]

Cornwall, moreover, seemed ideally suited for such a scheme. It had long possessed a magnetic appeal for 'outworkers' such as artists and writers, it was attracting the new breed of teleworkers: designers, consultant engineers, technical writers and software developers. Its low office costs and reserves of clerical skills also fitted it to carry out 'back office' jobs - tasks involving ordinary office activities such as electronic mail, telephone answering, airline and other reservation and booking services, credit card operations, tele-shopping and mail-order. Message-intensive firms in the big cities could decentralise this kind of work to Cornwall. One such scheme was already operating from St Austell, financed 80% by Western Union, 20% by China Clays. Was it to be the spearhead of other ventures which would transform the area into what Thorneycroft called a 'Telecoms Riviera' - a mecca for long-distance telecommunications workers in a favourable environment?

Paradoxically, the liberalisation of telecoms networks that was taking place at the time in the UK meant that market forces were working precisely in the opposite direction. Advanced systems were planned for already information-rich areas, thus further disadvantaging outlying regions. What is more, the SWANS Scheme was seen as undermining British Telecoms' tariff structure, in which profits on trunk lines offset losses on local calls. And while the SWANS effect on its own might not have been catastrophic for BT, the progress of SWANS was closely watched by planners in other regions who would inevitably press to follow suit if it got off the ground. Nor did the Department of Trade and Industry (DTI) any longer favour projects which simply displaced jobs from the centre, rather than creating new work. Indeed, it was now preoccupied with city-centre problems and urban regeneration schemes: expenditure on such initiatives rose from £117 million in 1979 to £867 million in 1991.

SWANS depended upon 80% public sector finance, half from the UK, half from the EC but, without UK support, matching funds from EC would not be forthcoming. As for private sector support, a questionnaire survey of 1400 corporations with large London-based office staffs produced only five initial replies and, after over 350 further telephone contacts, only one positive response. Cornwall (and Devon) were perceived as 'too remote' even although the difference in telecoms terms was infinitesimal. A CIDA survey of 450 Cornish firms identified 36 who showed some interest, but in 23 cases telecoms costs were under 2% of total costs. Such small potential cost reductions did not overcome a reluctance to pay an advance subscription of some thousands of pounds. Another selling point - that customers in big cities would find it cheaper to call Cornish subscribers - did not of course produce direct cost saving for Cornish firms. Finally, local businesses were also concerned that, although Cornwall might be first in the field, other regions would soon follow and wipe out Cornwall's advantage.[31]

The SWANS idea thus came to nothing. The expense - of the order of £8 million - was apparently too high. Yet, to put this into perspective, it amounted to the cost of a few miles of dual carriageway. Alternatively, it could be compared with the £25 million spent on aid to the Assisted Areas of Cornwall, Plymouth and North Devon from 1972 to 1982, which created 1200 relatively low-level factory jobs.

Higher-level education and research is another sector where Cornwall has been more fundamentally disadvantaged than in advanced telecoms. It seems self-evident that the area can not hope to attract 'high-tech' or science-based industry without an appropriate intellectual underpinning, and yet the history of Cornwall since the War in this sphere is one of neglect and of missed opportunities. It all started promisingly enough, with ambitious proposals for a higher level infrastructure including an institution of art, architecture and commerce at Truro, a college of technology in the Camborne-Redruth area, together with full-time teacher training and adult education facilities and an agricultural institute somewhere in the territory. But internal rivalries and fragmentation of effort, the bugbear of Cornish policy-making, soon made themselves felt. The idea of a farm institute, for example, was not new, indeed it had been mooted as early as the 1850s, but as Lawrence Piper, long-time Principal of Cornwall College commented, '. . . the sticking point was that farmers in the east of the County could never agree to a development in the west and vice versa'.[32]

Nor was the concept of a Cornish University a novelty. Members of the local intelligentsia, including Q. (Sir Arthur Quiller-Couch), had discussed it seriously in the Edwardian era, only to conclude that 'the time was not yet ripe'. In the early fifties, however, Cornwall's leaders, in an imaginative gesture, acquired a large site at Trevenson in the mining heartland between Camborne and Redruth as a campus for a future College of Technology, and during the period of university expansion in the 1960s new hopes were kindled. Cornwall's claims were presented by local MPs to Quintin Hogg, then Secretary of State for Education. Councillors and Chambers of Commerce started to look for further suitable sites and Alderman K.G.Foster, Chairman of the County Council, felt able to claim that University status was only a few years away. Cornwall was disappointed in its hopes, but a fresh opportunity seemed to beckon when Polytechnics were set up in the 1970s and Dr Kenneth Farnell, Principal of Cornwall Technical College at the time, was optimistic about the chances. Yet, when Camborne School of Mines had to seek new premises, Cornwall's leaders had to fight tooth and nail to stop it from being lost to Plymouth or London. It was finally installed, at great cost to Cornwall's slender education budget, on the Trevenson Campus next to Cornwall Technical College. At about the same time a new Institute of Cornish Studies, funded by the County Council and University of Exeter, with Professor Charles Thomas as its Director, was started on the same campus.

All seemed set now for the creation of an Institute of Higher Education which grouped the various strands of advanced learning in Cornwall, and by now Cornwall Technical College itself was building up a sizeable corpus of full-time degree level students in scientific and technical graphics and radio journalism, together with substantial numbers of part-time students on advanced management and professional studies, teacher training, engineering and science courses, all of which led to recognition of the College as one of Higher as well as Further Education, equipped to design its own degree programmes under national supervision. All this was thrown away, however, in the mid-1980s when Falmouth School of Art came under threat of closure. After the War some of the big guns of the art world who lived locally, like Barbara Hepworth, Bernard Leach, Patrick Heron and Brian Wynter, had fought for degree-level diploma status for the School. Now, what Piper called 'a very small influential lobby'[33] stripped Cornwall College of its art and design work and transferred it to Falmouth, leading to the loss of the College's status as a centre for advanced work.

Later, the early 1990s saw the recognition of Plymouth Polytechnic as a University and the merger of the Camborne School of Mines with the Engineering Faculty of the University of Exeter. The Camborne-Exeter merger meant that the University of Exeter in Cornwall was, with its three component bodies (the Institute of Cornish Studies, the Camborne School of Mines, and the Department of Continuing and Adult Education), approaching something like a critical mass from which a significant expansion of Cornish Higher Education activity might be developed, offering exciting potential for the future. However, the crushing superiority of Devon's intellectual infrastructure over that of Cornwall was still self-evident, a tragic irony given the early emergence in the period of Cornish industrial pre-eminence of the Royal Cornwall Polytechnic Society, the Royal Geological Society of Cornwall, and the Royal Institution of Cornwall.

CONCLUSION: VISIONS OF THE FUTURE

It has become the fashion in policy documents to set out visions of the years ahead. Take for example that of the Chairman of Cornwall's Planning and Economic Development Committee: '. . . my vision of Cornwall's future is of a special place, where people want to live, where they can enjoy an improved standard of living and where their quality of life is enhanced by a beautiful environment'. South West Enterprise Limited (SWEL) has a vision to '. . . drive the region to the forefront of sustained economic, social and cultural growth'. SWEL's predecessor, the Devon and Cornwall Development Company, was more specific: 'Cornwall is ten to 15 per cent below the rest of the country. We want to see it ten to 15 per cent above.' Positive and optimistic plans accompany these visions. 'Strategies for Growth' and 'Action Programmes for Prosperity' abound. The only things missing are growth and prosperity themselves.[34]

Why is this so? The blame lies squarely, not with the genuinely enthusiastic promoters of these visions, but with the reductionist simplification of conventional dogma, which encourages them to believe in - and the public to demand - quick and easy solutions to extremely complex problems. The process of economic regeneration in Cornwall is a long-term affair, complicated and made more difficult by people-led growth. It requires a more subtle and long-term approach than the blunt and spasmodic application of the kind of regional policy instruments that have been outlined in this Chapter. Mainstream doctrine, with its aura of crisp and confident decision-making, seeks to eliminate doubt and uncertainty. What it achieves, in fact, is to increase risk and uncertainty among actors upon the Cornish economic stage. What this Chapter has tried to do is to re-introduce doubt about an orthodox theory which blinds its local proponents to the magnitude of the tasks that they set themselves, the greatly diminished powers that they have and the ephemeral nature of the benefits that they provide.

First, the sheer magnitude of the task. How, for instance, can Cornwall's GDP per head be raised from 15% below the UK norm to 15% above? It would involve a transformation of the Cornish economy from a lower-pay structure based on farming, tourism and personal services to a higher-pay pattern of leading-edge industries and information-rich activities - a 'High Tech' as well as a 'Telecoms' Riviera. The failure of the SWANS scheme illustrates the enormous obstacles to be overcome to achieve this aim in a market-force economy. And imagine for a moment that, by some wave of a magic wand, the Cornish people actually became 15% better off. Surely they would be swamped as the flood gates opened under pressure from people eager to get the best of both worlds, higher material standards of living and a superior quality of life as well? Unless, of course, as for example in Jersey, inward migration was contained. But this would imply a measure of local devolutionary self-government.

Turning to local control over economic decision-making, it could be argued that one objective - increased employment - has been achieved by the sacrifice of another - economic sovereignty. Already, at the beginning of the post-War period, decisions on farming and defence were made at Westminster, while local banking, insurance and finance were controlled from the City. But Cornwall still had the nucleus of an independent industrial structure in mining, clay-working, ship-repairing and hard-rock engineering. Since then, regional policies involving branch-plant insertion, coupled with the centralisation of some important Cornish activities in 'Regional' bodies, together with the collapse of some leading Cornish-owned firms, have greatly reduced the degree of local control over Cornwall's economic destiny. The satellite character of the local economy is displayed both in incomes and employment. Household incomes, at 94% of the UK level, do not at first sight look too bad. But the high proportion of residents who receive unemployment and other state benefits or pensions or live on investment income means that only 54% of household incomes are derived from employment, compared with 74% for England. And some of these earnings come from commuting to Plymouth or elsewhere. What is more, a significant share of employment is in activities where control resides in Whitehall or Brussels.

Agriculture, fishing and defence involve 26,000 workers directly, or

14% of the total workforce, and many thousands more are in up-stream or down-stream jobs that rely on those industries. To these we must add the 19,000 employees in local government who are subject to indirect interference from Whitehall, together with an ever greater number of employees in branch factories and shops or the offices of national networks of banks, insurance companies, estate agents, building societies and so on. Clearly the scope for local initiatives is closely circumscribed. From being, to some extent at least, an independent centre of the periphery in 1950, Cornwall has become a highly dependent periphery of the centre. In the language of Payton's analysis, a new condition of 'Third Peripheralism' had been created.[35]

As for the ephemeral nature of the benefits regional programmes have bestowed, it must be acknowledged, to begin with, that they are extremely small compared with the aid lavished upon Scotland, Wales, Northern Ireland or, more recently, the inner-cities. To match expenditure per head, Cornwall should receive something of the order of ten times as much. Be that as it may, what is more important in the long run is that the aid received, as the criticisms voiced in this Chapter have suggested, is largely misdirected. Policy-makers seem so busy serving and defending their system that they fail to notice that it simply is not working in the case of Cornwall. They judge their effectiveness by goals that they have defined themselves: the value of new European Community schemes approved, the mileage of bypasses and expressways constructed, the acreage of Science Parks and Business Campuses built, the number of branch plants installed, the volume of new business start-ups encouraged. But while better roads have undoubtedly boosted the volume of road traffic their overall effect on GDP per head is problematic, for in enhancing the competivity of local firms vis a vis central England they have made it easier to centralise control and distribution for organisations in both the public and private sector. Again, a short-term injection of capital involving the manufacture of products approaching their technological sell-by-date is of no help in the long run since it does not integrate with the rest of the economy nor produce spin-offs in the business sector. Neither are escapees from the urban treadmill, attracted by persuasive images of sunny coves and an easy pace of life, likely to recharge Cornwall's economic batteries.

A SMALL-SCALE APPROACH TO THE FUTURE

Is the lesson to be learned from the past forty years that the key to Cornwall's future does not lie in heroic visions and bold strategies which, for all their confident, up-beat tones, merely lead to higher unemployment and rock-bottom earnings? If Cornwall has to remain permanently locked into a scramble for external funds, could they not be used for long-lasting rather than short-lived gains: rail electrification, harbours, airports, first class hospitals and colleges? And should not attention be focussed upon enhancing the intellectual infrastructure, upon investing in human capital, so as to reduce Cornwall's socio-economic peripherality, without which the massive expenditure to lessen its geographical peripherality will achieve little lasting benefit?

To conclude, Cornwall has always been a human-scale place of small towns and buildings and family businesses and farms. Is the real answer, as MK, CASP and CoSERG have suggested, a 'local needs' housing and employment policy which limits the inflow of working-age migrants? Without such an approach, policymakers and development agencies are preoccupied in a pursuit of the unattainable, forever chasing expanding employment targets, obsessed by the need to mop-up pools of unemployment whenever and wherever they occur. Within a more modest and selective policy framework, the solutions put forward by both official and 'opposition' groups acquire a greater significance. A 'recentralisation' strategy, based upon trade with Atlantic Arc countries rather than with a 'centre' that is retreating rapidly eastwards, might not bring spectacular gains in employment. But they would be useful in a labour market which was not expanding by leaps and bounds through inward migration. Similarly the need for costly implantations of branch plants which have no real commercially-sound reason for being in Cornwall, and which therefore fade away sooner or later, would be less urgent.

In the field of energy usage, each new wind-farm, instead of merely off-setting the extra demands of one year's in-migration, would help to reduce dependence upon external supplies. Policy-makers, instead of pursuing a self-defeating quest for more and more houses, roads and jobs, could concentrate upon vital missing ingredients for economic regeneration: upmarket operations, centres of excellence that create the knowledge needed for Cornwall to grow its own industries, the pursuit of quality rather than sheer quantity in employment. Finally, a more modest set of economic objectives would fit a holistic approach built upon the interdependence of cultural, social, political and economic policies, rather than the tensions and conflicts that exist between them at the moment.

REFERENCES

1. John Blunden 'The Redevelopment of the Cornish Tin Industry' in K.J.Gregory and W.L.D Ravenshill (eds.), *Exeter Essays in Geography*, University of Exeter Press, Exeter, 1971, pp169-184; D B Barton, *A History of Tin Mining and Smelting in Cornwall*, Bradford Barton, Truro, 1967, republished Cornwall Books, Exeter, 1989; D.B.Barton, *Essays in Cornish Mining History*, 2 Vols, Bradford Barton, Truro, 1968/1970.
2. Derek Spooner 'Industrial Movement, Rural Areas and Regional Policy', Regional Development and Planning Conference, Budapest 1973 p.147; John Blunden, 1971; James Whetter, 'The Cornish Fishlng Industry' in *Cornish Essays*, CNP Publications, St Austell, 1977; South West Economic Planning Council, *A Region With a Future*, SWEPC, Bristol, 1967, and *Strategic Settlement Plan*, SWEPC, Bristol, 1973.
3. Cornwall Conservation Forum *Cornwall's Choice*, CCF, Truro, 1973; Charles Thomas, *The Importance of Being Cornish in Cornwall*, Institute of Cornish Studies, Redruth, 1973; *Cornish Nation*, No.10, 1972.
4. Cornwall County Council, *Policy Choice Consultation Document*, CCC, Truro, 1976.
5. Cornwall Industrial Development Association, *The Economy of Cornwall*, CIDA, Redruth,

1976; Ronald Perry, *The Employment Situation in Cornwall*, CIDA, Redruth, 1974.

6. Ronald Perry, *Studies in the Cornish Economy*, CIDA, Redruth, 1978.
7. Ronald Perry, *Strengthening the Small Firm Manufacturing Sector*, CIDA, Redruth, 1978.
8. Cornwall County Council, *Structure Plan*, CCC, Truro, 1980; Cornwall County Council, *Structure Plan: First Alteration*, CCC, Truro, 1987; see also County Council Discussion Papers on 'Employment' 1976 and 1985.
9. Cornish Alternatives to the Structure Plan, *Cornish Alternatives to the Structure Plan* (Submission to Examination in Public of the Structure Plan), CASP, Truro, 1989; Bernard Deacon, Andrew George, Ronald Perry, *Cornwall at the Crossroads: Living Communities or Leisure Zone?*, CoSERG, Redruth, 1988.
10. Daniel Gadbin and Malcolm MacMillan, 'The Way Ahead' in M.A.Havinden, J.Queniart, J.Stanyer (eds.), *Centre and Periphery: Brittany and Cornwall & Devon Compared*, University of Exeter Press, Exeter, 1991, p71, see also p259; Devon and Cornwall Development Company, *Cornwall: The Way Ahead*, papers presented to Conference, November 1987.
11. Perry, 1974; Robert McNabb, *Unemployment in West Cornwall*, Department of Employment, 1979; Ronald Perry, *Manufacturing Expansion and Employment Stability*, CIDA, Redruth, 1976.
12. Cornwall County Council, *Development Plan: Report of a Survey*, CCC, Truro, 1952.
13. University College of the South West, *Devon and Cornwall: A Preliminary Survey*, Wheatons, Exeter, 1947. R.A.Gibb, *The Impact of the Channel Tunnel on the Far South West*, PEP Enterprises, Plymouth, 1979, p24; British Rail, *Rail Opportunities in the South West*, 1990.
14. Cornwall County Council Highways Department, *Transport Polces and Programme*, Truro, 1989;
15. Perry, 1974; West Country Tourist Board, *Spreading Success*, WCTB, Exeter, nd, pp13,16 and 41; *Western Morning News*, 3 October 1989.
16. Cornish Social and Economic Research Group, *Roads to Superjam*, CoSERG, Redruth, 1990; Cornwall Industrial Development Association, *The Economy of Cornwall*, CIDA, Redruth, 1976.
17. Gibb, 1979, pp17,4.
18. Cornwall County Council, *A National Programme of Community Interest*, CCC, Truro, 1987; Cornwall Agricultural Group, *Priorities for Cornish Agriculture in the 1990s*, CAG, Truro, 1989.
19. Plymouth Business School, 'Cornwall/Devon and the Atlantic Arc', *South West Economic Review*, No.6, Summer 1992; Peter Wills, *Water, Water Everywhere*, CoSERG, Redruth, 1992.
20. Peter Gripaios, *The South West Economy*, Plymouth Business School, 1989 and 1991, p21.
21. Peter Newby, 'Attitudes to a Business Environment' in K.J.Gregory and W.L.D.Ravenhill (eds.), *Exeter Essays in Geography*, University of Exeter Press, Exeter, 1971.
22. Ronald Perry, *Studies of the Cornish Economy*, CIDA, Redruth, 1978; Richard Payne 'Manufacturing Investment and Macro-Economic Change' in Allan Williams and Gareth Shaw (eds.), *Economc Development and Policy in Cornwall*, South West Papers in Geography, No.2, University of Exeter, 1982.
23. Perry, 1978.
24. Newby, 1971; Perry, 1978; DCDC, 1987.
25. Ronald Perry, 'Cornwall's Small Business Sector Revisited' in *Small Business Case Studies*, Loughborough University, 1990.
26. Spooner, 1973; Peter Gripaios, *Manufacturing Industry in Devon and Cornwall*, South West Economy Unit, Plymouth, 1984.
27. Gareth Shaw and Allan Williams, *Tourism and the Economy of Cornwall*, University of Exeter, 1987; Allan Williams, 'Endogenous and Exogenous Sources of Growth' in Havinden *et al*, 1991, pp108-119; D.Phillips and A.Williams, *Development in South West England*, University of Exeter, 1987.
28. Information Technology South West, *Distance Working in the Rural Periphery*, Cornwall County Council,Truro, 1985; Ronald Perry, *Married Women and Industry*, CIDA, Redruth, 1976; Hardman Commission, *The Dispersal of Government Work form London*, HMSO, London, 1973.

29. Information Technology South West, *Enhanced Telecommunications in South West England*, Cornwall County Council, Truro, 1984.
30. Andrew Page, *Cottage Office*, Dartington Institute, Dartington, 1982; European Commission, *Model for Business and Innovation Centres*, Brussels, 1984.
31. R.W.Perry, R.A.Nichol, J.G.Newman, *Developing a New Telecoms Structure*, CIDA, Redruth, 1983.
32. L.P.S.Piper, *Cornwall College: A Short History*, Cornwall College, Redruth, 1993, p15.
33. Piper, 1993, p14.
34. Joan Vincent, in Cornwall Economic Development Office, *Economic Development Strategy 1991-92*, CCC, Truro, 1991, preface; South West Enterprise Limited in Cornwall County Council Economic and Development Committee, 1992; Devon and Cornwall Development Company, 'The New Vision' in *Towards 2000*, Autumn 1991; *West Briton*, 27 April 1989.
35. Philip Payton, *The Making of Modern Cornwall: Historical Experience and the Persistence of 'Difference'*, Dyllansow Truran, Redruth, 1992, pp167-239.

CHAPTER 4

THE AGE OF MASS TOURISM

Allan M Williams and Gareth Shaw

There is probably no topic which excites more heated exchanges in Cornwall than does tourism. The reasons for this are the strong and visible impact it has on the economy, society, culture and environment of Cornwall. As with all heated debates there is often more passion than objective analysis, and this is compounded by the absence of reliable statistical information on the industry. In this Chapter we address the available evidence on some of these issues and seek to place the post-War debate in historical perspective.

THE SHAPING OF AN INDUSTRY

In the late nineteenth century a subtle segregation of tourism destinations emerged in Britain. Resorts such as Blackpool, which had once been the preserve of the middle-classes, began to attract more working-class customers. As a consequence, there was a '. . .growing tendency for the better-off families to head for Devonshire or the continent'[1]. After the First World War there were significant improvements in personal mobility, especially for the middle-classes, as the result of a tenfold expansion of car ownership rates between 1919 and 1939. For the working-class, motor buses provided more modest gains in mobility. Pimlott writes that

> . . . by 1939, thanks largely to the motor-car and the bicycle, there was hardly a village which did not provide some facilities for holidaymakers . . . while in the hilly districts and in most of the hinterland of the coast holiday catering had become an important source of income.[2]

In a sense the infrastructure was being laid which would shape the great boom in mass tourism after the Second World War. These general trends were also evident in Cornwall, although with distinctive local colourings, and the remainder of this section examines the historical evolution of Cornish tourism up to the end of the Second World War. This sets the scene for the analysis of tourism in the second half of the twentieth century.

The early history of Cornish tourism and the change in its image from that of 'West Barbary' to Britain's 'Mediterranean' region has been well-documented.[3] The arrival of the railway in 1859 was critical and led to new hotels being constructed in established resorts such as Penzance and to the emergence of new resorts such as St Ives and Newquay. However, it was only in the early twentieth century that the full impact of railway development was experienced. The Cornish Riviera Express brought London within seven hours of Penzance and Cornwall was marketed as the 'Riviera'. St Ives was compared to Naples[4] while in an inspired piece of marketing it was argued that '. . . the lamps are alight in London before the sun sets on Newquay'.[5]

Some notion of the long term changes in Cornish tourism can be provided through examining the series of guides produced for what was, at the turn of the century, the premier resort, Penzance.[6] The 1890 *Guide to Penzance* clearly identified the attractions of the town as being 'climate extremely mild and suitable for invalids; the situation of the town is delightful and the sanitary condition perfect'.[7] Amongst the specific objects of interest mentioned were the Royal Cornwall Geological Society, the Natural History and Antiquarian Society, a heated swimming pool and a billiard club with three full size tables. In this pre-car era there was, of course, relatively little emphasis on touring from Penzance although a few sites such as St Michael's Mount are mentioned. The geographical hinterland for tourism was restricted given the reliance on cabs and carriages, although '. . . the cabmen will be found intelligent and obliging and will point out, en route, places of interest'.[8]

By 1908 there were significant changes in the presentation of the resort in *The Official Guide to Penzance*. There is considerable emphasis on improved accessibility by rail via '. . .the fastest, the smoothest running , and the most luxuriously appointed trains in the world'.[9] At the same time, the growing importance of cyclists and motorists is recognised in the claim that 'Cornish highways are quite equal to the average English country road'.[10] The attractions of the town remain essentially the same although there is more emphasis on bathing, boating, fishing, golf and other sporting forms of recreation. Penzance is still seen largely as a self-contained holiday resort but there is evidence of that changes are afoot, in the mention of the possibility of railway excursions to all the principal population centres at frequent intervals.

By the time that the *Penzance and the Land End's District* guide was produced in 1926, the balance between self-contained resort and a base for touring had changed further. There is an entire Chapter devoted to 'Penzance as a centre for touring' and '. . . by common consent, one of its most attractive features to the tourist is the advantage Penzance offers as a centre from which to make excursions'.[11] In contrast, there are few changes in the attractions offered within the town itself. By 1936 motor transport has left an indelible impression on the tourism industry. This is reflected in the title of the guide itself, *Penzance: the Holiday Centre of Cornwall's Glorious West.* According to the guide the roads have been transformed and 'hundreds of thousands of car owners'[12] use them, while AA and RAC road maps are included for the intrepid motorists. The quickening pace of tourism is to be seen in the appearance of new hotels, while - as Thornton has noted[13] - the object of 'the tourist gaze'[14] is steadily being transferred to beach activities: 'Clad only in the minimum necessary for decency, one can sprawl in the sun after one's bathe with the utmost benefit'.[15] The model for the mass tourism of the post-War period is clearly emerging. The fact that this is in Penzance, the sedate grand old lady of Cornish tourism, rather than in one of the brash new centres of the holiday industry serves only to underline the extent of the changes.

During the inter-War years, Cornish tourism was to expand further as it benefited from the rise in real incomes in the southern half of England, and from the revolution in personal mobility. This economic infusion was translated into marked demographic trends as the populations of the coastal areas rapidly outstripped that of Cornwall as a whole; between 1921 and 1931 the population of the coastal parishes grew by 3.2% and that of Cornwall by 0.7%. It was at this time that a fundamental reshaping of the tourism industry occurred. The grafting of new forms of tourism onto the old, and the emergence of new resorts and destinations produced a distinctive tourism map. This was subsequently disaggregated in a Cornwall County Council report in 1966[16] into three main components:

a) Old coastal towns and villages that had to some extent retained their original character, including Penzance, St Ives, Falmouth, Padstow and the villages of Mevagissey and Port Isaac.

b) Places where large scale tourism had fundamentally altered the character of the original settlement, as at Newquay or Bude.

c) 'New centres of the holiday industry' built during the inter-War years during a period of inadequate planning control. These were further sub-divided into four categories:

i) One or more large hotels and other tourist accommodation, together with basic facilities such as shops, eg. Carbis Bay and Carlyon Bay.
ii) Estates of holiday homes, eg. Mawgan Porth, Constantine Bay and the Plaidy Estate east of Looe.
iii) Loose groups of holiday homes on the coast, eg. Trethevy, Rock and Trebetherick.
iv) Chalet, caravan and camping sites in outlying places and often on coasts eg. Whitsand Bay and Hayle Towans.

The pressures were growing on Cornwall's environment and communities at the same time as tourism brought economic benefits in the form of jobs and incomes. The Second World War brought some respite from building but the tourism industry remained surprisingly buoyant during these years. In part this was because Cornwall was not closed to holidaymakers for security purposes as was the coast from Berwick to Dorset. By 1940, for example, Thomas Cook was still able to offer a reduced programme of holidays with a choice between Falmouth, Penzance, St Ives and Newquay. However, in retrospect the imprint of pre-War tourism would appear surprisingly light compared to the impact of mass tourism after the 1940s.

THE ARRIVAL OF MASS TOURISM

During the 1950s Wartime austerity came to an end at a time when accumulated social changes were to bring about a revolution in British domestic tourism. Growth in real incomes, combined with increased leisure time and entitlement to paid holidays, democratised the market for tourism. The result was a golden age for British seaside tourism as increasing numbers of people flocked to the coastal resorts and stayed for longer holidays. The British seaside holiday became established as one of the aspirations, even the expectations, of the working-class. At the same time, further improvements in road transport and the spread of car ownership made Cornwall more accessible to this market and ensured that it shared in the age of mass tourism. There is a lack of accurate statistics on Cornish tourism visitor numbers - a problem that persists until the present - but the most reliable estimate available suggests that numbers grew from 1.4 million in 1954 to 2.1 million in 1964, an increase of some 50% in a decade.[17]

The growth of mass tourism in Cornwall brought with it the demand for cheaper holiday accommodation. This was met by chalets, caravan and camping sites as well as by more traditional serviced accommodation. For example, there was a 310% increase in the number of chalets between 1954 and 1964. Serviced accommodation expanded more modestly but there was still a 10% increase in the number of hotels and boardinghouses between 1951 and 1961.[18] At the same time the growing reliance on personal rather than public transport meant that tourism became more spatially diffuse. The outcome was a deepening of the spatial model of tourism distribution that had emerged in the inter-War years. The older coastal resorts such as Penzance expanded at a more modest pace, and were outpaced by places such as Newquay which had effectively been transformed into leisure towns as most of their earlier functions and characters were overwhelmed by their new economic roles. Newquay alone experienced a 13.6% increase in its stock of hotels and guest houses during the decade after 1954.[19] The 'new centres of the holiday industry' also expanded rapidly. Additionally, as Malcolm Williams notes in Chapter 7, demand for 'second' or 'holiday' homes grew in attractive resort areas, while tourism also helped prompt the increasing wave of in-migration into Cornwall from outside.

The inevitable outcome was intense pressure on what was Cornwall's premier tourism attraction, the coast. As early as 1959 the Council was declaring saturation zones where further development was to be discouraged. 'Within saturation areas, no new sites or extensions to existing sites for static holiday caravans or chalets are permitted, nor are sites operated by private individuals for touring caravans, lest these sites should be used for the more profitable static caravans'.[20]

While individual car-borne tourism was to expand throughout this period, organized tours and holidays continued to be important. Thomas Cook, who had brought the first organized rail tour to Cornwall in the mid-nineteenth century continued to be active in this market throughout the 'golden age' of mass tourism. The survival of their brochures and of their magazine, *The Traveller's Gazette*,[21] provides an invaluable set of insights into how at least one segment of the domestic market was changing during these years. As early as 1946 Thomas Cook had reinstated a fairly elaborate programme of holidays in Cornwall. In addition to its tours there were ten resorts on offer, and these embraced all three of the settlement categories in the County Council classification of 1966. This underlined how well-established the new inter-War tourist resorts had already become. Figure 4.1 shows the distribution of these resorts and it is worth noting the company's comments on them:

> **Bude** is a peaceful haven on a quiet corner of the Cornish coast and has lovely walks in unspoiled countryside.
> **Carbis Bay** has summer sand gay with visitors and inland rambles through Cornish lanes luxuriant with flowers.
> **Falmouth** has an equable climate, splendid scenery and innumerable inducements to explore the surrounding countryside.
> **Fowey** is quaint hillside Fowey with an ancient harbour and tortuous streets.
> **Mullion** has striking coastal scenery and typical Cornish lanes.
> **Newquay** has abundant facilities and also 'mighty promenades in its wild and beautiful headlands framing wide bays fringed with golden sands and washed by the Atlantic rollers'.
> **Perranporth** has green hills with little hamlets and peaceful farmsteads while 'the air and scenery urge one to walk or bathe'.
> **St Agnes** has inspiring views and surfing.
> **St Ives** has a 'double life, one centering around the busy fishing harbour and the other providing endless natural pictures for artists and holiday visitors who find enchantment in the great bays and green cliffs'.
> **Trebetherick**, (one of the new centres of the holiday industry), is typically Cornish and overlooks a secluded little bay.

Putting aside the tourist writers' hyperboles and artistic embellishments, these pen portraits underline a central feature of Cornwall's tourism industry. It was never portrayed as just a series of coastal resorts or a place for superb beach holidays. Instead, even as the great post-War mass tourism boom was about to take off, Cornwall was presented as environmentally special. Whilst there were excellent beaches, these were set in superb countryside. No doubt Thomas Cook was aiming its publicity at a relatively high income market segment but, as the discussion in the final section of the paper shows, these images of Cornwall persist down to the present.

FIGURE 4.1

Resorts offered by Thomas Cook in their 1946 programme

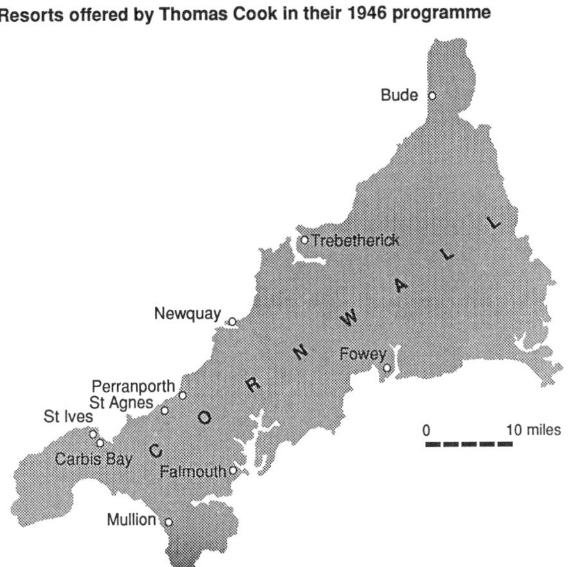

With the age of mass tourism and transport changes, Cornwall gradually became less important to Thomas Cook. As early as 1965, the number of resorts offered had fallen to just five: Penzance, Newquay, St Ives, Bude, and Falmouth. By the 1990s Thomas Cook offered no long holidays at all in Cornwall but it did have a programme of short breaks that included St Austell, Mullion, Falmouth, Penzance, and Land's End.

Thomas Cook's view of Cornwall is, inevitably, somewhat rose-tinted, and it is therefore useful to contrast its comments on individual resorts with those offered in the 1954 *Penguin Guide* to Cornwall.[22] There are complimentary remarks on all the resorts but there is also a series of telling comments:

> **Bude** has ugly houses.
> **Carbis Bay** is a very popular holiday resort with a fine beach.
> **Falmouth** has 'some good Georgian architecture but . . . for the rest . . . the casual visitor will run straight through the town'.
> **Fowey** has atmosphere and a peculiar charm.
> **Mullion** is pleasant.
> **Newquay** '. . . is nothing but a holiday resort, and like most similar places, has few special characteristics of its own, save the natural advantages of its situation and the unnatural disadvantages of careless

"development". And while it has nearly everything you would look for in the way of accommodation, it is still desolating to think that so fine a situation should have been so badly spoilt'.

Perranporth '. . . has an excellent beach, sandhills, and splendid cliffs, and is very well frequented. For the place itself, if I say that it is a 20th century seaside holiday town, that will be quite enough'.

St Agnes is barely referred to.

St Ives has grown away from old town but, nevertheless, the latter '. . . has been almost submerged. Even round the harbour the buildings are largely blotted out by signs and assorted bait for visitors'.

Trebetherick is not deemed worthy of an entry.

The *Penguin Guide* is no more objective in its assessments than the Thomas Cook brochures but it does alert us to the existence of a body of critical views which perceived the mass tourism boom as despoiling the countryside and the coast. Newquay and modern resorts such as Perranporth are particularly vilified. This raises two important questions: whether the net benefits of tourism to the local community outweigh the disadvantages and whether the growth of tourism is undermining the long term sustainability of the industry by destroying those very resources which attracted the customers in the first place. These and other related themes are considered in the final section which reviews the state of the tourism industry at the end of the present century.

TOURISM IN THE LATE TWENTIETH CENTURY

In this final section of the Chapter we address three principal themes. Firstly, the nature of the market for Cornish tourism, whether it is distinctive and the implications for economic development. Secondly, the economic structure of tourism, its contribution to the economy and the prospects for development. And, finally, we turn to the debates surrounding the relationship between tourism and the environment. In all of these areas, the analysis is constrained by a lack of a reliable statistical base. Tourism - unlike say agriculture - is not effectively covered in most UK statistical series. In part this is because of the complexity of the tourism industry. The discussion in this section therefore draws mainly upon the results of surveys undertaken in recent years, on behalf of the Cornwall Tourism Development Action Programme, the Cornwall Tourist Board and the tourism industry.

Turning first to the tourism market, the first problem to be faced is the lack of reliable data on tourist numbers. According to estimates provided by the County Council, Cornwall receives over three million tourist each year. While the absolute number of tourists must remain in question, there is broad consensus that tourist numbers have remained relatively static since the early 1980s. In contrast, there is considerable information available on the major features of the tourism market as a result of the annual surveys undertaken by the Tourism Research Group at the University of Exeter since 1987. Table 4.1 summarises the results of one of the most recent of these surveys.

TABLE 4.1
PROFILE OF CORNISH TOURISTS, 1991

Socio-economic	%
% from South East	16.8
% from South East	30.6
% Professional and Managerial	46.1
% Manual Workers	39.8
Holiday Features	
% on main holiday	69.9
% on 7 night holiday	48.1
% fast time visitors	16.1
% travelled by car	92.6
% self-catering	68.2
Perceptions of Cornwall	
% who agree there is/are:	
beautiful scenery	98.5
easy to get to	62.5
many places of interest	93.3
Holiday Activities	
% who consider activity to be important	
going to the beach	76.4
strolling in the countryside	55.5
sightseeing by car/coach	72.6
visiting historic buildings	38.5
Suggested improvements to Cornwall	
% who suggest	
protect natural beauty	31.3
improve roads	15.6

Source: Williams and Shaw

Cornwall has a distinctive tourism market. It is, in particular, a recreational playground for the South East of England, attracting almost one third of its visitors from this region. Its second most important source region is, not surprisingly, the South West. Thereafter, the Midlands, the North West and Yorkshire each provide about 8-10% each of the market. The market is equally polarised in terms of social class; whereas 46% are professional or managerial worker, 39.8% are manual workers (one half of whom are unskilled workers).

There are some differences between these social and regional groups of tourists in terms of the types of holidays they are taking, but in general they have many features in common. Cornwall is principally a destination for main holidays, particularly of one week or more; given its location it has not shared fully in the massive expansion of short break holidays during recent years. This is one reason why the tourist season has remained highly seasonal compared to some other UK regions. The vast majority of the tourist are repeat visitors, with only 16% being first-time customers. This can be interpreted in two ways. On the one hand there is the encouragement of being able to attract and hold a loyal market, but there are also concerns about the ability to draw the new visitors who are essential to replenish the market.

Most of the visitors travelled to Cornwall by car and stayed in self-catering accommodation. This is a long way removed from the early days of mass tourism when the visitors came by train and stayed in serviced accommodation. The extent of the shift to self-catering is remarkable for as recently as 1964 it was estimated that this sector only accounted for 40% of the market.[23] The reasons for this are twofold: partly the search for lower costs, and partly the demand for new types of more flexible tourism experiences.

The tourists have very distinctive perceptions of Cornwall and it is clear that these do not accord with the image of tourists as rampaging, environmental vandals. Indeed, it is the natural beauty and cultural distinctiveness of Cornwall which attracted the tourists in the first place. Most of the tourists considered that Cornwall had beautiful scenery and many places of interest. Their most important holiday activities were based on the natural environment and included going to the beach, sightseeing by car and strolling in the countryside. These were considerably more important than visiting historic houses, theme parks or other commercial attractions. And perhaps the most telling statistic of all was the reaction to the question of what improvements they would suggest for Cornwall. Unprompted, 31% stated that the first priority should be to protect natural beauty. These data suggest two conclusions. First, that tourists are attracted to Cornwall by a variety of attractions, most of which are related to its natural environment. And, secondly, that the sub-division of tourists into 'culture-lovers', 'countryside-lovers', 'beach-lovers' and so on is misleading in the case of Cornwall. There may be tourist who value some aspects of the Cornish holiday experience more highly than others, but it would seem that it is the total holiday experience, and the natural environment in general, which attracts most tourists.

Turning to the economic role of tourism, we are faced once again by the lack of reliable statistics. While official statistics are collected relating to employment in the accommodation and catering sectors, the tourism complex is constituted of a diverse range of industries which cuts across the manufacturing, transport, leisure and retailing sectors. There is, therefore, a need to rely on estimates based on input-output or multiplier analysis. The Cornish economy has never been subject to a rigorous analysis on this basis and, instead, most estimates are based on figures derived from national statistics or the results of detailed research in other regions. There are obvious limitations to such an approach given the distinctive nature of Cornish tourism, the high level of self-employment in Cornwall, and the existence of associated socio-economic issues like 'second' homes, in-migration and housing demand.

One recent set of estimates has been produced by Jeffrey[24] and, as it is broadly in line with Cornwall County Council figures, it provides the basis for the discussion in this paper. According to this study there were 33,000 jobs in tourism in Cornwall in 1987. This represented 26% of total employment in Cornwall, which underlines the contribution made by the industry to the local economy. The distribution of jobs is, of course, spatially uneven and tourism is of even greater importance in some districts (more than one third of all jobs in Penwith and Restormel) and totally dominates the labour markets in particular settlements.

While (as the history of nineteenth-century Cornwall shows) there are problems in being over-dependent on any one industry - particularly one which has a volatile level of demand - there have also been some advantages in the reliance on one of the few growth industries in the UK in recent decades. As a result, the importance of tourism as a source of employment has probably been increasing steadily throughout the post War period. For example, Lewes *et al.'s* 1970 study[25] of tourism in the mid-1960s estimated that tourism accounted 23% of all jobs at that time, a full three percentage points lower than at present. Tourism also proved to be a source of new jobs in the recessionary 1980s; for example, Jeffrey estimated that tourism employment increased by 7% between 1984 and 1987. A key question, therefore, for critics of tourism is whether, given the problems of the agriculture, fishing, mining and manufacturing sectors, there were realistic alternative sources of employment growth in Cornwall in recent decades, although any comprehensive response must also assess the effect of tourism in creating the 'imported unemployment'[26] and other features associated with in-migration (see Chapters 3 and 7).

Tourism is also criticised for the quality of the employment it provides. The term quality is of course difficult to define. In context of the debate over tourism it can be disaggregated into three different elements: incomes, seasonality and part-time work. Again the debate has been clouded by the definition of what constitutes tourism employment. Critics tend to concentrate on a narrow range of jobs in accommodation and catering. However, if a wider definition is used so as to include all those industries catering for tourism demand, then a different picture emerges. Table 4.2 gives some idea of the inter-sectoral links of the tourism industry, emphasising considerable dependence on tourism across broad areas of several local economies in Cornwall.

TABLE 4.2
TOURISM DEPENDENCY, 1986

Proportion of firms * which consider tourism to be beneficial or very beneficial:

Sector	**%**	**Total Number**
Retailing	82	83
Manufacturing	61	84
Serviced accommodation	94 **	82
Self catering	99 **	75
Public houses	72	39
Restraurants, cafes etc	100	44
Total	83	407

* Interviews undertaken in Bodmin, Callington, Helston/Porthleven, Newquay, Padstow, St Columb, Truro

** Non-holiday tourism accounts for the other responses

Source: Shaw *et al.* (1987)

Firstly, with respect to incomes, we have to admit statistical defeat for there are no reliable data on this for different industries within Cornwall, although it is known that in general terms average wages in Cornwall are amongst the lowest in the UK. Secondly, there is evidence that while tourism jobs are seasonal this is not markedly different from the pattern for the remainder of the economy. Probably the most telling evidence on this is Lewes *et al.'s* comparison of seasonality in the holiday and non-holiday trades in the

FIGURE 4.2

Seasonal variations in unemployment, 1967 (male employees only)

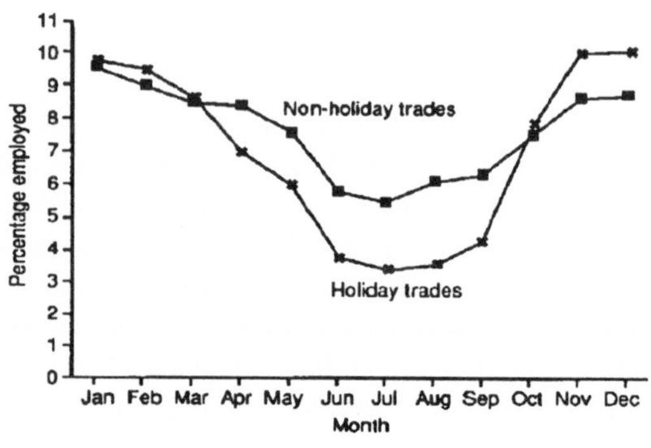

mid-1960s (Figure 4.2). Thirdly, tourism is not in essence an industry of casual or part-time employment, although both these features do apply to it.

According to Jeffrey two thirds of tourism jobs are full-time. While it is true that part time jobs were increasing more rapidly than full-time jobs in the 1980s, it must be remembered that this was a general trend in the UK economy.[27] Furthermore, there is considerable confusion in the debate over full-time jobs. The argument that the only worthwhile jobs are full-time ones is not sustainable. The argument by Dunkerley and Faerden[28] that there is a dual labour market in tourism is accepted as also is their contention that most tourism (narrowly defined) jobs are in the secondary segment which is characterised by informality, low wages and low promotion prospects. The authors also argue that seasonal workers in particular are locked into a vicious sircle of low aspirations and limited opportunities.

But part-time jobs and casual jobs can be important to individuals who wish to combine these with part-time jobs in other sectors (perhaps farming, or fishing) or with household responsibilites, particularly in the Cornish context where the development of complex 'survival strategies' by individuals and families is well-documented.[29] However, complex household survival strategies are put together not just out of economic necessity but also because of life-style preferences. This is an important debate and one which still requires empirical investigation; any such debate must adopt a comparative framework, for it is essential that tourism is not evaluated in isolation but alongside other employment opportunities in Cornwall. What is clear is that tourism has been instrumental in providing a range of jobs in the Cornwall. Whether these match the requirements of the potential (and growing) labour force is more problematical. But even if tourism does provide less full-time, year-round jobs than there is demand for, it does at least have the distinction of being one of the few industries to make a positive addition to the job market in recent years.

Finally, we turn to the question of the relationship between tourism and the environment. Mass tourism must by necessity generate pressures on the environment. This operates in two distinctive ways: the impact on the built environment and the movement of tourists (by foot or vehicle) within the area. Many of the problems relating to the first of these originated in the inter-War years when there was considerable uncontrolled and spatially diffuse construction in Cornwall, particularly in the coastal areas. This was only partly accounted for by tourism but, nevertheless, it was a contributory element. After 1947 a more effective system of development control was introduced but, by that time, significant inroads had already been made into developing previously rural areas. Therefore, when the post-War mass tourism boom occurred there was already an existing spatial framework for development, and the main effect was to increase building pressure in these areas. It was in response to these pressures that the Council in 1959 introduced its saturation areas policy in which further development of some types of tourism facilities was restricted (Figure 4.3). While the precise form of such constraints has changed over time, containment has remained the basis of public sector planning for tourism. The second direct impact of mass tourism comes via the movement of people within the region causing congestion and pollution. There is little doubt but that the shift to car-borne tourism has caused considerable difficulties in this respect.

FIGURE 4.3

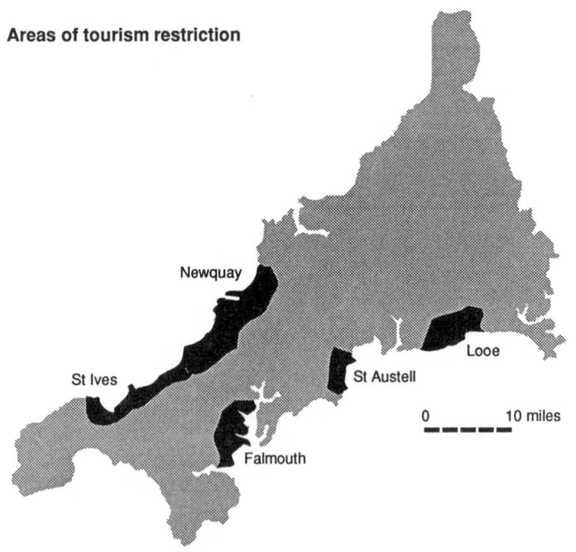

While the pressures emanating from tourism are clear, there is a need to resist any over-simplification of the problem as a clash between environment-destroying tourists and tourism entrepreneurs on the one hand, and the environmentally-conscious local community on the other hand. The visitor surveys already referred to clearly demonstrate that the natural environment is the principal tourism attraction of Cornwall. Yet tourists also complained about the lack of all-weather facilities which, to be remedied, probably implies further construction. Tourists also complained about the congested roads while suggesting that these should be improved. There is then a classic contradiction between the high value placed on the unspoilt environment and the equally high value being placed on personal mobility by car. Tourists, therefore, are a double-edged weapon in the battle to conserve the environment. At one level they are a force for conservation yet their individual consumption interests pose potential threats to this same environment. In this respect tourists are no different to the local community whose collective wish to conserve the community is also matched by individual consumption needs. This dichotomy between what economists label individual and public goods is fundamental to the way modern society is constructed. The answer lies (in Cornwall as elsewhere) not in blaming the tourists for all the ills or in a blanket constraint on new tourism developments but in an effective strategy for tourism set within context of the sometimes complementary, sometimes conflicting needs of the Cornish community.

REFERENCES

1. J.Walton, *The Blackpool Landlady: A Social History*, Manchester University Press, Manchester, 1978, p153.
2. J.A.R.Pimlott, *The Englishman's Holiday: A Social History*, Hassocks, 1976, pp256-7.
3. C.North, 'Travel in West Barbary' in J.Mattingly and J.Palmer (eds.), *From Pilgrimage to Passage Tour*, RIC, Truro, 1991.
4. P.Gilson, 'Tourism in Falmouth: From Packets to Package Tour', in Mattingly and Palmer, 1991.
5. J.Simmons, 'The Railway in Cornwall, 1835-1914', *Journal of the Royal Institution of Cornwall*, 1982.
6. P.Thornton, 'Cornwall and Changes in the Tourist Gaze', *Cornish Studies*, second series, No.1, 1993.
7. F.Rodda, *Guide to Penzance*, Penzance, 1890, p68.
8. Rodda, 1890, p68.
9. *The Official Guide to Penzance*, The Corporation, Penzance, 1908, p5.
10. The Corporation, Penzance, p7.
11. *Penzance and the Land's End District*, Homeland Association, Penzance, 1926, p18.
12. *Penzance: The Holiday Centre of Cornwall's Glorious West*, Underhill, Plymouth, 1936.
13. Thornton, 1993.
14. J.Urry, *The Tourist Gaze: Leisure and Travel in Contemporary Societies*, Sage, London, 1990.
15. *Penzance*, 1936.
16. Cornwall County Council, *Survey of the Holiday Industry*, CCC, Truro, 1966.
17. Cornwall County Council, 1966.
18. Cornwall County Council, 1966.
19. Cornwall County Council, 1966, p25.
20. Cornwall County Council, 1966, p24.
21. *The Traveller's Gazette*, Thomas Cook, London, nd.
22. J.W.Lambert, *Cornwall*, Penguin, Harmondswoth, 1954.
23. Cornwall County Council, 1966.
24. D. Jeffery, *Estimating the Level of Tourism-Related Employment by District in Cornwall: The Application of a Census-Based Non-Survey Method in 1984 and 1987*, Departmental of Environmental Science, University of Bradford, 1989.
25. F.M.M.Lewis, A.J.Culyer, G.A.Brady, *The Holiday Industry of Devon and Cornwall*, HMSO, London, 1970.
26. R.Perry, K.Dean, B.Brown, *Counterurbanisation: International Case Studies of Socio-Economic Change in Rural Areas*, Geo Books, Norwich, 1986.
27. G.Shaw, A.M.Williams, J.Greenwoood, *Tourism and the Economy of Cornwall*, Tourism Research Group, University of Exeter, Exeter, 1987.
28. D.Dunkerley and I.Faerden, 'Aspects of Seasonal Employment in Devon and Cornwall', in P.Grapaios, *The South West Economy*, Plymouth Business School, Plymouth, 1985.
29. D.Dunkerley and C.Wallace, 'Young People and Employment in the South West', *Journal of Interdisciplinary Economics*, Vol 4., 1992.

CHAPTER 5

WEALTH FROM THE GROUND: GEOLOGY AND EXTRACTIVE INDUSTRIES

Colin M. Bristow

INTRODUCTION

Geology has played a fundamental role in the development of Cornwall's scenery, mining and agriculture, with the economic development of mineral resources probably having been more significant in Cornwall than in any other region in the British Isles; even today the extractive industries still play a key role in the Cornish economy. Furthermore, some of the earliest developments in the science of geology involved aspects of Cornish geology or eminent scientists from Cornwall, and this uniqueness is further emphasised by Cornwall possessing more hard-rock Sites of Special Scientific Interest than any other county in Britain, making it a mecca for geological research and teaching. Although this Chapter will briefly review the geology of Cornwall and the historical development of its mineral resources,[1] it is mainly concerned with the development of the extractive industries since the War, together with a forward-looking analysis of possible future developments as the extractive industry evolves towards the conditions of the early twenty first century.

Academic research into the geological evolution and structure of Cornwall has made immense gains since the Second World War and Cornwall now enjoys a reputation as a showpiece for many advanced concepts in the field of geology. Cornwall is probably one of the most important areas in the whole of Britain for demonstrating complex geological structures and a wide range of igneous rocks. This is now reflected in the increasing numbers of parties of students and researchers who visit Cornwall to study the geology in the magnificent coastal sections and inland areas such as the china clay pits. There is possibly scope for further development of Cornwall's role as a huge open-air teaching laboratory for students, research scientists, and others interested in Cornish geology and mining history. The writer comes from a background of 28 years work in the china clay industry, which today is far and away Cornwall's most important industrial activity; its future therefore lies at the heart of any analysis of Cornwall's future economic prospects. With the decline of industrial activity in the western half of Cornwall caused by the closure of most of the tin mines and much manufacturing industry as well, it is clear that the china clay industry will be one of the mainstays of the Cornish economy in the foreseeable future, with the quarrying of constructional raw materials as the second most important extractive activity.

Geology and mining in Cornwall have given rise to an extensive literature, with some of the earliest works on geology anywhere in the world, such as Humphry Davy's lectures to the Royal Institution in 1805;[2] and the later publications by De la Beche (1839) and Henwood (1843)[3] providing brilliant and detailed records of the2 metalliferous mining scene in Cornwall in its heyday. Later in the century writers such as J.H. Collins (1841-1916) and W.A.E. Ussher (1849-1920) provided a prodigious output of publications on mining geology, minerals and the general geology of Cornwall, such that they almost exhausted the topic and few papers on the area appeared again until after the Second World War. By the 1950s the science of geology had advanced sufficiently to allow significant new contributions to be made, and there has been a considerable output of papers and new scientific thinking over the last three decades. Cornwall also possesses an unusually large number of learned societies, including the Royal Cornwall Polytechnic Society, the Royal Institution of Cornwall and the venerable Royal Geological Society of Cornwall, founded in 1814 and the second oldest geological society in the United Kingdom; the transactions of these societies contain many of the classic early papers on geology and mining.

CORNWALL - A PENINSULA COMPOSED OF HARDENED MUD HELD UP BY A SPINE OF GRANITE

To the geologist the peninsula west of a line from Watchet to Newton Abbot is a land full of mysterious, fascinating and difficult to understand rocks which forms a coherent unit distinctly different to any other part of the United Kingdom.[4] The geological history of Cornwall is illustrated in Figure 5.1 overleaf with a simplified geological map shown in Figure 5.2.

Throughout the Devonian and Carboniferous periods, from about 400 to 310 million years ago, most of what is present-day Cornwall lay under the sea, whose northern shore lay somewhere in the region of North Devon and the Bristol Channel. During the Devonian period, muds and sands (now slates and sandstones), with some volcanic rocks and occasional deep water cherts were deposited on the floor of this Cornish sea, at a time when the rest of the British Isles was mainly land. We can now distinguish several quite distinct parts of this sea. South and west of a line from Perranporth to Pentewan there was a relatively deep sea which, during the later part of the Devonian, was bounded on its southern side by a rising land mass, now long since submerged beneath the waters of the Bristol Channel, known to geologists as 'Normania'. North and

East Cornwall was underlain by somewhat shallower water, with some of the sediments at times within the range of wave action. There seems to have been a deeper basin in the vicinity of the Padstow estuary, which geologists call 'the Trevone Basin'.

FIGURE 5.1

A Cornish Geological Column, showing the history of the area which was to become Cornwall over the last 400 million years

CORNISH GEOLOGICAL COLUMN

AGE IN MILLION YEARS	ERA	PERIOD		MAIN EVENTS	LIFE
0		QUATERNARY		Ice Ages – Cornwall cold but not glaciated	Man, various mammals
1·64	TERTIARY	NEOGENE	Pliocene	St Erth beds – sea level slightly higher than now	Gasteropods
			Miocene	St Agnes sands and clays – sea level higher than now	Conifer forest on islands
23		PALAEOGENE	Oligocene	St Agnes clays, Dutson basin (Launceston) sands & clays	Sequoia forest.
			Eocene	Ball clays in Devon, ?Crousa & Polcrebo gravels	Some palms.
65			Palaeocene	No sediments preserved; land with deep weathering	Forest
	MESOZOIC	CRETACEOUS	Upper	Rising sea levels gradually submerge Cornwall; marine sands deposited, then some chalk.	Ammonites, belemnites, icthyosaurs, plesiosaurs in seas.
146			Lower	Cornwall probably dry land, subjected to deep tropical weathering.	Forests with Dinosaurs on land
208		JURASSIC		Cornwall probably above sea level throughout, with tropical forest and deep weathering. Atlantic ocean opens up as America drifts west and the continent of Pangaea breaks up.	Forests, primitive conifers and cycads. Dinosaurs
245		TRIASSIC		Land surface hot and dry – Cornwall probably a fairly well eroded mountain range in the centre of a supercontinent – Pangaea. Some mineralisation	Sparse or no vegetation. A few dinosaurs and primitive mammals.
290	UPPER PALAEOZOIC	PERMIAN		Land surface hot and arid, sea distant. Metalliferous mineralisation at depth. Volcanicity at Kingsand, contemporary with the intrusion of the granites. Volcanoes on top of where we see granites today.	Not much life
		CARBONIFEROUS	Upper	Sands and muds eroded from mountains rising in the south fill trough across North Cornwall.	Coal Measure vegetation, King Crabs
363			Lower	Deep marine conditions in N. Cornwall with radiolarian ooze & muds, some volcanicity, mountains begin to rise in the S. of Cornwall.	Goniatites, Trilobites, Conodonts.
		DEVONIAN	Upper	Deep water throughout Cornwall, mountains begin to rise to the south of Cornwall.	As above, plus crinoids, a few corals and shellfish.
			Middle	Deep water throughout Cornwall, shallower in mid-Cornwall, coral reefs around Plymouth.	
408			Lower U.	Most of Cornwall part of a fairly deep sea, submarine volcanoes around St. Austell.	Primitive freshwater fish in Lower Devonian.
			Lower L.	Cornwall forms part of a vast plain lying on the south side of the O.R.S. continent, with freshwater lakes. Crustal extension forms an ocean to the south, floored by oceanic crust.	
570	LOWER PALAEOZOIC	SILURIAN, ORDOVICIAN, CAMBRIAN		Represented only as fragments contained in younger rocks.	

3800 – OLDEST ROCKS IN THE WORLD – GREENLAND

© C. M. Bristow. September, 1991

FIGURE 5.2

A simplified geological map of Cornwall showing many of the features of geological structure which have been revealed by research since the Second World War. This map makes use of information from the 1:250,000 geological maps of the British Geological Survey, by permission of the Director, BGS: NERC copyright reserved.

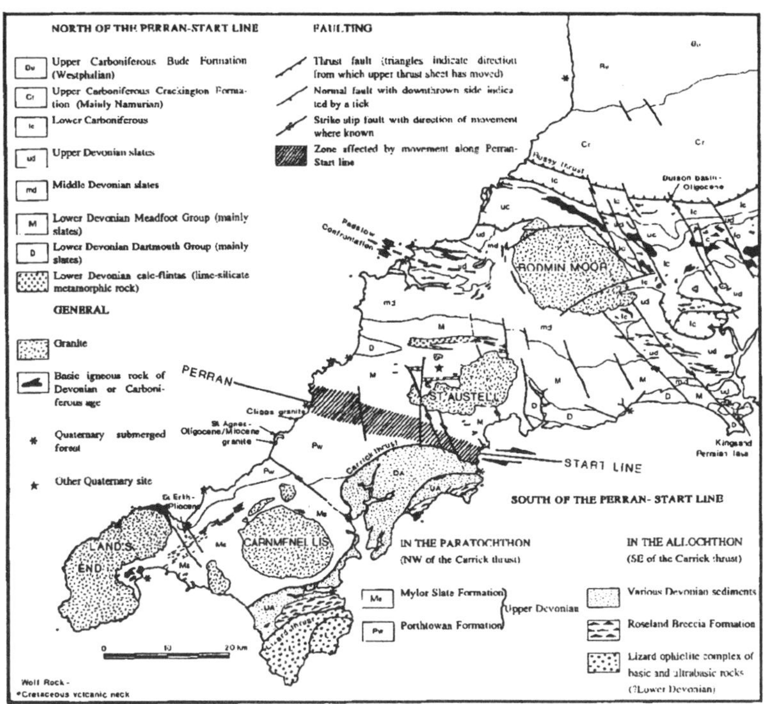

The boundary line from Perranporth to Pentewan, known to geologists as the Perran-Start line, is quite possibly the surface manifestation of some deep seated break in the earth's crust; it is one of the few features of Cornwall's geological architecture which can be picked out from space, showing up clearly on most satellite images. In the following early part of the Carboniferous period the situation is reversed, with the southern area, south of the Perran-Start line, being subjected to major earth movements and raised above sea level, and the northern area becoming deep water. Hence, most of the rocks of Carboniferous age are found in North and East Cornwall. Later on in the Carboniferous the east-west sea across Southwest Britain became more and more restricted, culminating in shallow water sediments being laid down in a lake or sea occupying part of North Cornwall and central Devon.[5]

The material which had been deposited in these Devonian and Carboniferous seas was then thrust up into a mountain range at the end of the Carboniferous period, as a result of a southern landmass colliding with the northern landmass, an event which geologists call the Variscan orogeny. The collision zone was approximately east-west and its centre is marked by an incredibly complex and controversial structure known as 'The Padstow Confrontation'. Some ocean floor was caught up in the early phases of this collision and thrust up to the surface - this now forms the Lizard, with its distinctively different topography and vegetation. Some huge masses of debris slid down from the northern slopes of Normania as it reared up during this same early phase of the collision and are now to be found along the southern coast of Cornwall in the Roseland area and westwards along the southern side of the Helford river towards Mullion - the geology of these areas has more in common with Brittany than with the rest of Britain.

Shortly after the collision reached its climax (shortly after to a geologist means about 10 million years later!), a great mass of molten granite welled up along a line from the Scillies to Dartmoor and slowly crystalised. Because granite was slightly lighter in density than the slates and sandstones forming the mountain range, it tended to bouy up the region into which it was intruded, so we may truthfully say that Cornwall is formed of hardened mud bouyed up by granite. The heat from the granite sweated out metals and minerals from both the granite itself and the rocks into which it had been intruded, which were then deposited in veins in and around the granite. The cooling of the granite was exceptionally prolonged because the content of heat producing radioactive elements in the granites of Cornwall (and Devon) is abnormally high. The heat from the atomic reaction caused water in and around the granite to circulate, thereby altering the rocks through which it passed and leaching out metals from one area and depositing them in veins in another cooler place. The slow seepage of radon at the surface is another result of the high content of radioactive elements in the granite.

The surface of Cornwall has been land for nearly all of the last 300 million years and as the Variscan mountains overlying the granite were eroded away by millions of years of erosion, the granite was bared to the elements. Rainwater soaked into the granite and was convectively circulated within the granite by the still continuing heat from radioactivity; this led to widespread alteration of the feldspars in the granite to form kaolinised granite or china clay. There were periods of heightened earthquake activity, when the peninsula was subjected to immense strains, resulting in the reactivation of old faults originally formed during the Variscan orogeny. The cracks formed by these faults assisted in the circulation of water within the granite and assisted the process of kaolinisation so that large masses of hard granite were broken down to form china clay deposits. During much of the time when Dinosaurs lived, Cornwall would probably have been a densely forested tropical island, but there are no traces from that time preserved. However, somewhat earlier, at a time shortly after the Variscan mountains had been formed, when the climate was hot and arid, we do find a small patch of sediments preserved beneath a lava flow at Kingsand. These contain burrows thought to have been made by a primitive form of reptile or amphibian. Apart from a few patches of Tertiary sediments scattered over Cornwall and more recent sediments in most of the major river valleys and estuaries formed during the period of the ice ages, there is little 'young' geology in Cornwall. During the ice ages Cornwall was not glaciated, although a floating ice shelf extending across the Irish Sea appears to have touched the Scillies and perhaps the Padstow area as well. We should not underplay the importance of the time of the ice ages, for the sudden swings in climatic conditions led to the formation of rich alluvial deposits of tin ore in the valleys of the peninsula, which were the first metalliferous deposits to be exploited by prehistoric man.

CORNWALL - A CORNUCOPIA OF MINERAL RICHES

The value of the mineral wealth obtained per unit of area in Cornwall must be one of the highest in the whole of Britain. The wealth generated from the early mining activities in the eighteenth and early nineteenth centuries, combined with the strategic value of the metals produced for the developing manufacturing industries in Britain, was one of the fundamental factors which enabled Britain to be the first state in the world to undergo an industrial revolution, with Cornwall in the vanguard. Public perception tends to associate only tin and copper with Cornwall, but, in reality, a far wider range of commodities has been exploited,[6] as demonstrated in Table 5.1 overleaf. The mineral wealth of Cornwall can be divided into:

- the metals; predominantly tin and copper
- china clay and china stone
- constructional raw materials

Whilst nearly all the metalliferous minerals and all of the china clay and china stone have originated from the Cornubian orefield; the constructional raw materials have come from a variety of sources, not all of which are part of the Cornubian orefield, and in Table 5.1 the estimated total quantity of each commodity produced from the orefield since mining began is given, which has then been multiplied by the current value of the commodity to give a notional present day value for the total amount extracted. Between 80 and 90% of the mineral value obtained from the Cornubian orefield has come from Cornwall. The production figures are partly based on figures published by Dunham *et al.*,[7] which have been updated to include production since Dunham's table was drawn up, as well as some additions and modifications in the light of other information. Some of the commodities that have been produced, such as arsenic, have no real market value today, so a purely nominal value has been assigned to them. As will be explained in greater detail below, there are grounds for believing that the tin production figure quoted by Dunham *et al.*, may have been overstated.

TABLE 5.1
MINERAL PRODUCTION FROM THE CORNUBIAN OREFIELD*

Commodity	**Total Production (tons)**	**1992 unit value (£/ton)**	**Total value (1992 prices) (millions)**
China clay	140,000,000	£90	£12,600
Tin metal	1,500,000	£3,660	£5,500
Copper metal	2,000,000	£1,300	£2,600
Lead metal	250,000	£320	£80
Zinc metal	96,500	£675	£65
Iron ore	2,000,000	£12	£24
Silver, from Pb	233	£80,000	£18
Barytes	450,000	£40	£18
Tungsten (WO)	5,600	£3,000	£17
Manganese ore	100,000	£100	£10
Silver ore	2,000	£2,000	£4
Arsenic (As O)	250,000	£15	£4
Pyrite	150,000	£12	£2
Fluorspar	10,000	£100	£1
Totals	147,000,000		£21,000

* The Cornubian orefield includes the whole of Cornwall and those mineralised areas associated with the Dartmoor granite. In addition to the commodities listed above, much granite has been quarried for constructional use and for use as china stone.

There are no records of the volume or value of constructional raw material production from Cornish quarries until relatively recently. Using the latest available figures (1991/2) the volume and value of mineral production in Cornwall is:

Commodity	**Volume**	**Value**
China clay	3,000,000t	£270 million
Tin (metal)	2,000t	£7 million
Constructional raw materials	4,000,000t	£13 million
TOTAL	7,002,000t	£290 million

(Figures from PA 1007, Minerals, published by the Business Statistics Office)

An estimate of current (late 1992) employment in the extractive industry of Cornwall shows that numbers have fallen very substantially from the peak of 36,500 quoted by Burt *et al.*.for 1854, with some 200 individuals in metalliferous extraction, 4000 in china clay and stone, and a further 1000 in constructional raw materials - making a total of 5200. It is quite possible that employment in the extractive industries in the 1950s and 1960s was at least double this figure, in spite of a lower output tonnage; continuing improvements in productivity may lead to further reductions in the numbers employed.

CORNWALL'S METALLIFEROUS MINERAL PRODUCTION

The development of metalliferous mining in Cornwall is well covered in publications such as Dines, Barton, Penhallurick, Burt, Embrey and Symes, and Payton;[8] so only a brief outline is necessary here. The distribution of the principal metalliferous lodes in Cornwall has been discussed by Hosking.[9] There is evidence of tin production and trading before the Romans came to Britain and a thriving tin mining industry was already in existence by medieval times.[10] Nearly all of the tin production up to the eighteenth century came from alluvial deposits, and most of the valleys in the granite uplands were tin streamed at one time or another. Serious exploitation of copper started in the sixteenth century; copper ore does not occur in alluvial deposits. Between 1750 and 1990 approximately 1.1 million tons of tin (metal equivalent) were produced in Cornwall, equivalent to an average rate of 4500 tpa. An above average period of production occurred from 1850-1895, which can be considered the heyday of Cornish tin mining. Production fell to a very low level from the First World War through to just after the Second World War, it then picked up to a rate of between 3000 and 5000 tpa for the period up to 1990 (Figure 5.3). The collapse of the International Tin Council agreement in 1985 meant that the price of tin fell from nearly £10,000 to between £3000 and £4000 per ton, which has resulted in four out of the five Cornish tin mines being closed, leaving only South Crofty in production.

FIGURE 5.3
CORNISH TIN PRODUCTION (METAL BASIS) 1930-1992

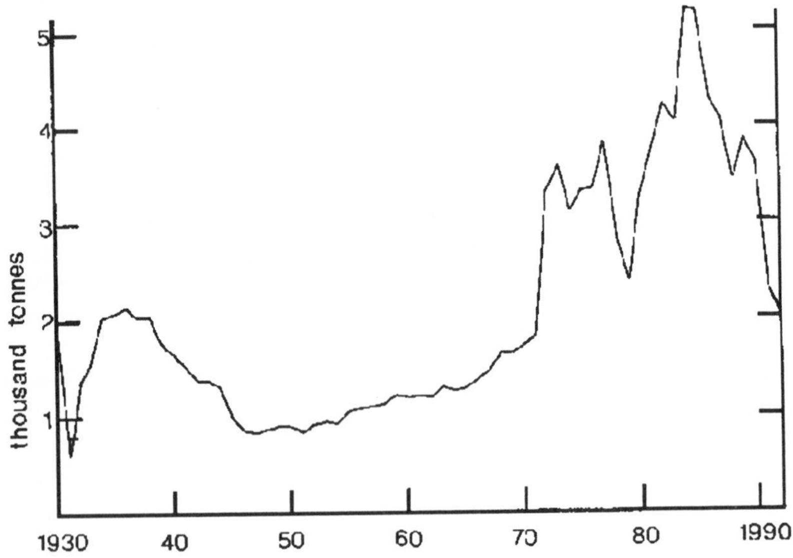

Burt *et al.*[11] published statistics for Cornish metalliferous production which appear to conflict with those put forward by Dunham *et al.*, even allowing for the shorter period covered by the Burt figures and the differences in production tonnage caused by some figures being reported in terms of the metal content and some being reported in terms of the ore (a confusion exacerbated by the Cornish practice of describing concentrate as 'ore'[12]). The main discrepancy would appear to be tin, with Dunham assigning over 2.5 million t on a metal basis, whereas Burt can only confirm production of tin ore of 0.7 million t for the period 1852-1913 , when Cornwall was in its heyday and producing 99% of Britain's tin output. In the 77 years since 1913 175,000t of tin (metal) has been produced from the Cornubian orefield,[13] and for the 100 years from 1750 to 1850 it can be inferred from De la Beche (1839)[14] that 350,000t of tin metal was produced. Therefore, over the period from 1750 to the present the total amount of tin produced from the Cornubian orefield was just over 1 million tons, which is equivalent to an average annual rate of 4500 tpa. If we accept the Dunham figure, this would mean that over 1.5 million tonnes of tin metal (60% of all tin produced to date) were produced before 1750, which does not seem reasonable, particularly bearing in mind the size of the market before 1750 for tin-containing products and the transport facilities available for such a quantity of metal. Also, Embrey and Symes[15] suggest that annual tin production was 450 tpa at the end of the fifteenth century, growing to 1500 tpa for the hundred years to 1715. The Dunham figure probably derives from a figure quoted by Collins (1912),[16] who suggested that in the seven centuries up to 1892 not less than 2 million tons of tin concentrate had been produced. Collins also estimated that half of the tin produced from the Cornubian orefield (1.1 million tons) came from alluvial sources. The writer's view is that tin metal production from the Cornubian ore field is unlikely to have exceeded 1.5 million tonnes, of which about 40% came from alluvial sources.

Tin production for the period 1930-1992 is shown in Figure 5.3.[17] From this it can be seen that there was a considerable increase in tin production after 1970 to an annual production rate of between two and five thousand tonnes of tin (metal basis). One has to go back to the period before the First World War to find comparable production levels, and back to the late nineteenth century to find levels that are substantially higher. On the eve of the Second World War Cornish production came principally from three workings: South Crofty, Geevor and East Pool & Agar.[18] By the end of the War only South Crofty remained in production, although Geevor re-opened shortly afterwards. Thereafter tin production climbed slowly towards an output of around 1500 tpa by the late sixties.

FIGURE 5.4

Locations at which the production of tin concentrate has been attempted in the period since the Second World War

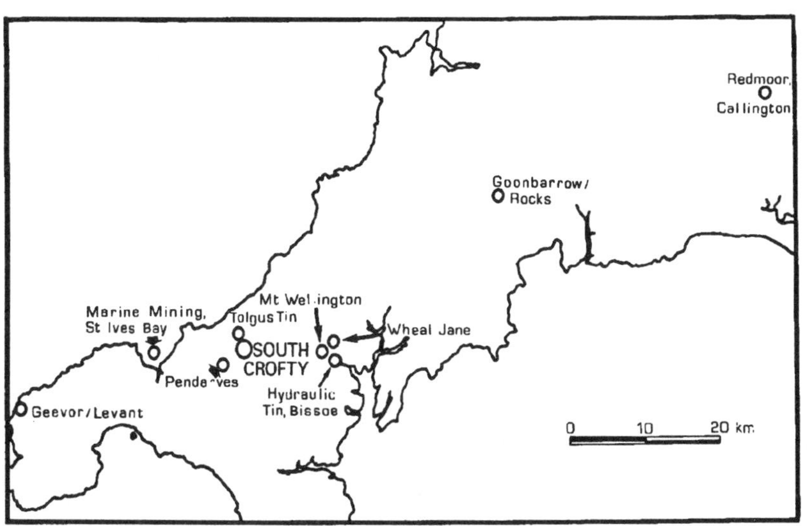

Partly as a result of research by the government-funded Warren Spring Laboratory in the sixties, a flow-sheet was developed to process the complex poly-metallic ore from Wheal Jane and, as a consequence, this mine was re-developed and a new mineral processing plant built, which was commissioned in 1971. This provided a substantial addition to Cornish tin output, which was further augmented as further new tin mines (Figure 5.4) at Wheal Pendarves (1971) and Mount Wellington (1976) were opened - the latter on an extension of the Wheal Jane orebody.[19] In addition, there was a brief working of Wheal Concord, near Blackwater, and alluvial deposits and old dumps were exploited at various locations, notably by Hydraulic Tin at Bissoe, Tolgus Tin near Redruth and Brea Tin near Carn Brea. Pilot-scale exploitation of placer tin deposits on the sea bed in St Ives Bay by Marine Mining Corporation was also attempted with a specially adapted ship.[20] Some re-processing of old mine dumps was also undertaken by these companies, as well as by the Cornish Tin Smelting Company at Roscroggan, which was originally set up to re-process old dump material but latterly became the mineral processing plant for Wheal Pendarves. Some major feats of underground mining engineering were also accomplished, with the sealing of the sea floor breach into the old Levant mine being one of the most notable. This opened up an extensive new area of mineralised ground for Geevor mine to exploit. As a result of all these developments tin production rose to just over 5000t in 1984-1985.[21] A great deal of exploration for tin was carried out by the large international mining houses and by smaller groups; some exciting (from a geological point of view) finds were made, with projects like the Redmoor mine near Callington and the Hemerdon tin/wolfram mine (across the border near Plymouth) being given serious consideration. Indeed, it is quite possible that more money has been spent on exploration for metalliferous deposits in Cornwall during the period since 1960 than the total profits from all the tin producing operations in the same period, an echo of the situation that obtained in the nineteenth century and a remarkable testament to the sanguine temperment of Cornishmen!

However, the tin price had been kept at artificially high levels during the seventies and early eighties by the activities of the International Tin Council, which ran into severe financial problems in the mid-eighties and collapsed, amidst huge debts, in 1985. As a result of this collapse, and adverse movements in the exchange rate, the price of tin metal plummeted from around £10,000 per ton to between £3000 and £4000 per ton. With the government declining to provide anything more than immediate short-term support for the Cornish mining industry, the collapse of the Tin Council led to the abandonment of Wheal Jane (where the stoppage of the pumps was to lead to the River Fal pollution scare) and Geevor, with only South Crofty remaining in production. The collapse was largely brought about by two external factors: one relating to the advent of cheaply produced tin onto world markets from new producers, principally in Brazil and China, and the other relating to the failure of tin markets to develop. Major new deposits of easily worked cassiterite were brought on stream in Rondonia Province in the Brazilian Amazon basin in the

1980s. Production of tin from Brazil reached 32,000t in 1992, which is more than ten times Cornish production in that year and also ten times Brazilian production in 1970. Chinese production has also been rising steadily and reached 45,000t in 1992. At the same time world consumption of tin has remained virtually static at around 200,000t in the years between 1972 and 1992.[22] Indeed, in developed economies such as the UK and USA, tin consumption has actually declined. Between 1988 and 1992 US apparent consumption of tin declined from 57,655t to 48,000t. Apparent consumption of tin metal in the UK fell from 28,000t in 1947 to 15,000t in 1972 and the latest available figure for 1989 is 10,000t.[23]

The main reason for this decline in consumption is that tinplate has been replaced in the manufacture of containers by glass, aluminium, plastic, plasticised cardboard and tin-free steel. Changes in food preservation, notably freezing, have also caused a further erosion of the tinplate market. The other traditional markets for tin in alloys and solders has also been under pressure, with epoxy resins replacing solder in some applications, plastics replacing bronze, plastics for bearing metals containing tin and lead and sodium for some tin chemicals. This kind of change in the markets is very much in line with the changes experienced in the markets for the other older major metals, and represents a definite long-term trend for cheaper and more cost effective non-metallic materials to replace traditional metallic material.[24] The International Tin Research Institute has carried out a considerable amount of research on new applications, but the gains through new uses have been more than outweighed by the decline in traditional markets. However, the devaluation of the pound in the autumn of 1992 has given a useful boost to the amount the Cornish tin producer receives for his tin concentrate, boosting the price from around £3000 per ton to around £4,000 per ton. This price should enable South Crofty to remain in production, but it is unlikely that any new producer could justify starting up at this price. In view of the steady decline in markets for tin, with no major new applications in sight, it has to be said that the long-term prospects for tin production in Cornwall cannot be good.

Copper is historically the next most important commodity; it was for a time in the late-eighteenth and early nineteenth centuries more important than tin in value. De la Beche[25] reported on the value of ores raised in 1837 from mines in Cornwall and Devon as follows: copper £952,855, tin £415,518, and china clay and stone £43,000. Because of the availability of cheaply won copper ore from low cost operations in South Australia, North America, Chile and Spain, Cornish copper ore production declined from around 1850, with a particularly steep decline, accompanied by the closure of many mines, in the late 1860s. The closure of many copper mines was hastened by signs of reserve exhaustion. Because of a drop in copper prices in the late nineteenth century, there has been practically no copper produced in Cornwall since before the First World War. In working the polymetallic orebody at Wheal Jane, 7000t of copper and 70,000t of zinc (metal basis) were produced in the period 1971-1990.[26] A rich diversity of other metalliferous minerals were produced from

Cornwall at various times; with significant amounts of lead, zinc, silver, wolfram and manganese being produced, mostly before the First World War. Iron ore production was, for a time, significant, but alternative cheaper sources supplanted Cornish iron ore by the mid-1880s. Most of the wolfram was extracted in the twentieth century; the Hemerdon project in Devon would have involved open-pit mining of a large orebody on the southwestern fringe of Dartmoor for wolfram and tin. Wolfram, the ore of tungsten, is notoriously sensitive to demand from the armaments industry, so in the current political and financial climate the price is likely to remain low with the Hemerdon project in abeyance.

Arsenic was another important commodity produced from the Cornubian orefield, notably in the Tamar valley; nowadays the market for arsenic is practically non-existent and little has been produced since the early part of the century. The only non-metallic vein-ore of any significance from the Cornubian orefield, apart from china clay, has been barytes, but much of this came from mines in Devon. Only small amounts of fluorspar have been produced, mostly from Cornwall, which is rather surprising in view of the high fluorine content of some of the granites; most of the fluorine tends to be locked up in the micas or the fluorine bearing mineral topaz. No topaz has ever been commercially produced, although it would be perfectly possible, from a technical standpoint, to recover it from china clay waste. None of the topaz is of gemstone quality.

The decline of the metalliferous mining industry from 1850 onwards has had huge social consequences, the 36,500 individuals employed directly in the Cornish metaliferous mines having fallen to some 7,200 by 1910 and a mere 200 or so in 1993, with the 'Great Emigration' depriving Cornwall of her ablest and most energetic offspring and their mining skills. Secondary engineering facilities, producing everything the mining industry needed, from beam engines to mineral separators, grew up and became important industries in their own right. Although the decline in mining was reflected in the demise of many engineering operations, mining-related engineering is still an important sector of the Cornish economy, with companies such as Denver-Charlestown, Compair and Mozley, whose reputations are outstanding and whose success needs every encouragement. An authentic survival of the days when Cornwall led the mining world, this sector is one of the very few where Cornish industry is internationally recognised to be of world class, and has, perhaps more than any other sector, the potential to provide increased employment opportunities in the future. The intellectual background provided by the teaching and scientific and engineering research at the world-renowned Camborne School of Mines provides an essential element in keeping the minerals engineering sector at the forefront of international trade in this sort of equipment. Thus although there may be little opportunity for the expansion of Cornish tin, mining engineering is still important to the Cornish economy, while there is possibly some potential for less conventional forms of metalliferous mineral production.

THE DEVELOPMENT OF THE CHINA CLAY & STONE INDUSTRIES

It was not until the late seventeenth century that Europeans discovered the Chinese technique of producing hard-paste porcelain from using white clay 'kao-ling' (or kaolin, as it passed into the English language) in conjunction with a rock flux. In 1745 samples of an American kaolin were shown to William Cookworthy, a Plymouth pharmacist, who was interested in porcelain-making and had himself been experimenting for a number of years.[27] Cookworthy travelled widely in Cornwall and Devon in the course of his business and first found the white clay and rock flux on Tregonning Hill, north-west of Porthleven. He subsequently identified their presence in the parishes of St Stephen and St Dennis, near St Austell.[28] In 1768 Cookworthy set up a factory in Plymouth, supplied with china clay from Carloggas, near St Stephen, and in 1770 production was transferred to a much larger factory in Bristol.[29] Once Cookworthy's patent had expired, the use of china clay and stone soon spread to the potteries, largely through the interest of Josiah Wedgwood. Thereafter, as transport improved as a result of harbours being built in Cornwall and canal and road construction in the Black Country, the industry expanded rapidly, particularly after the disruptions to trade caused by the Napoleonic Wars and the American War of Independence had been removed. By the mid-1830s, production of china clay was about 30,000 tonnes per annum (tpa) and by 1912 it had risen to a peak of some 900,000 tpa. During the First World War and the Depression of the 1930s it oscillated about a mean of about 450,000 tpa, before a severe recession to less than 200,000 tpa caused by the curtailment of the export trade during the Second World War. Thereafter, there was another period of rapid expansion and since 1970 total output has fluctuated between 2.5 and just over 3 million tpa.[30]

During the last 200 years, production methods have altered substantially in response to changing economic conditions and developing technology. A serious problem as workings grew deeper was that of pumping to recover the clay slurry from the pit bottom and to provide washing water and in the 1840s and 1850s both water-wheel and steam power (Cornish beam engines) were introduced for this purpose. Local engineering facilities such as Charlestown Engineering and West's Foundry in St Blazey provided much of the specialised equipment needed.[31] Also, about this time, coal-fired drying kilns were built, thereby accelerating what had been an obstructively slow process dependent on the vagaries of the weather. The deepening of clay pits, although causing some problems, had the advantage of providing water with a 'head' of pressure so that it became possible to wash the clay from the granite more effectively by directly attacking the working stope with water jets (monitors). Another major development during the nineteenth century was the building of local railways and roads, and the improvement of the ports of Charlestown, Pentewan, Par and Fowey.

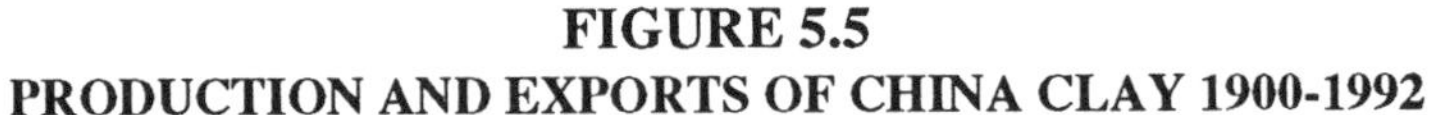

FIGURE 5.5
PRODUCTION AND EXPORTS OF CHINA CLAY 1900-1992

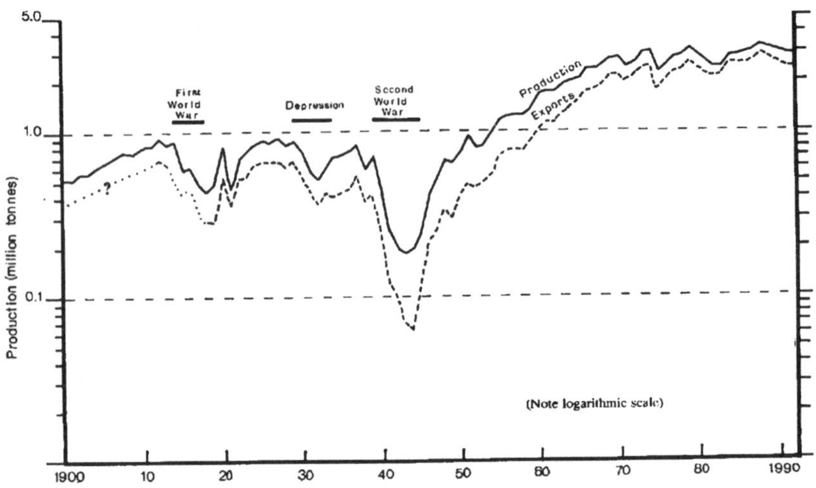

Whilst originally exploited for ceramic manufacture, in the nineteenth century china clay became increasingly used as a filler in both textiles and paper. In paper, china clay was initially used as a filler to improve the opacity and appearance of the paper, but a finer particle size product was developed just before the Second World War which could be used to coat the surface of paper and give it a smooth glossy surface for printing and writing, which was especially necessary for good quality colour printing. The social fabric of the china clay country, with its network of tight-knit villages, also developed in special ways (described by Rowse[32]) with Methodism, choirs and bands being essential features of a Celtic culture which endures to this day. From 1912 through to 1950 the industry's production averaged around 6-700,000 tpa,[33] with pronounced lows in the two world Wars, especially in the Second World War, and in the depression years of the thirties (see Figure 5.5). This period was initiated by a violent and disastrous strike in the summer of 1912 (in which riot police from Glamorgan were deployed) over wages and conditions.[34] The after effects of this strike and the departure of many men in the First World War caused many pits to close, some of which never reopened.

It was becoming clear that some form of co-operative marketing association between the producers was going to be needed, so in 1917 Associated China Clays was created for this purpose, which involved nearly all the producers then in existence. In 1919, the first of the major amalgamations took place, and the 1930s depression had a major impact on the industry which further hastened the tempo of rationalisation resulting in English China Clays becoming the dominant producer. The United States had always been the principal destination for china clay exports, but in the First World War exports of kaolin from Cornwall to the US were halved by 1918. This gave an important stimulus to the US kaolin industry in Georgia, which was then at an early stage in its development.

One of the effects of the formation of English China Clays Ltd. was that it enabled for the first time centralised research and engineering facilities to be set up, which could develop new processes and products. The full impact of this would not be felt until after the Second World War, but it has been a crucial factor in the company's post-War success. A particularly prominent figure in the post-1945 reconstruction of ECC was Sir John Keay, who not only set the china clay industry on a successful post-War course, but also developed a wide range of other activities, including quarrying, prefabricated house construction (the 'Cornish Unit' house), and the first overseas clay producing operation in Georgia. Rapidly rising demand from the paper industry, massive investment in new plant and the development of new processes and products characterised the second period of expansion from 1950 to 1974. The enormous increase in the amount of colour-printed material during this period meant that the production of the special grades of china clay required for coating paper also increased enormously. During this period china stone production declined to around 6000 t, an annual tonnage which has been maintained up to the present, due to competition from feldspar and nepheline syenite imported from Scandanavia. English China Clays built a grinding and flotation plant at Nanpean to remove fluorine bearing minerals from china stone in the early sixties, which successfully produced a 'defluorinated stone', and which operated until closure in the early seventies. Defluorination of china stone was thought to be necessary because of the production of fluorine emissions during firing in a kiln. However, nowadays most kiln gases are scrubbed anyway, so the problem is not as serious as it was.

Whilst most of the workforce and their supervisors (clay captains) were Cornish, many of the middle and senior management, engineers, scientists, salesmen and accountants in the expanding post-War industry were recruited from outside of Cornwall. With 80% of production going overseas, mainly to Europe, there was a need for extensive contact with customers from outside Britain, and English China Clays, under its Managing Director Sir Alan Dalton began an extensive programme of overseas development of mineral production, to service markets that could not be effectively reached from Cornwall. All this made the china clay industry a very cosmopolitan place to work in, with a much more international outlook than most British companies of that period.

Production increased steadily through this period from just under 750,000 tonnes in 1950 to just over 3,000,000 tonnes in 1974 (Figure 5.5). Throughout the period huge capital sums were invested in new equipment such as tanks, refiners, driers, pipelines and port facilities, most of which remains in use to this day. Pit development was put on a planned basis, with systematic geophysical and drilling programmes enabling the long-term development of the china clay resources to be properly provided for. Negotiations with the local authorities and communities enabled the pattern of roads to be rationalised so that some could be closed and new replacements built, to allow access to important new clay reserves. Many of the early pits had their sand tips right beside them on clay bearing ground, and these had to be removed. The disposal of waste began to emerge as a serious long-term problem and, following the Aberfan tragedy, new tipping rules meant that tips had to become properly engineered structures. A start was made on landscaping the tips and covering them with vegetation, following extensive botanical research by Professor Bradshaw of the University of Liverpool directed towards discovering appropriate plant communities and seeding techniques. Residues ceased to be poured into the local rivers and were pumped through a network of pipelines to large lagoons or, wherever they were available, worked-out pits.

Following the Second World War the Georgia kaolin industry in the United States began to emerge as a serious competitor not only for domestic US sales, but also in overseas markets, particularly for the lucrative paper coating clays. US kaolin exports exceeded US kaolin imports in 1963 and by 1974 three-quarters of a million tonnes of kaolin, mostly paper coating clay, was being exported; some to markets in Europe which had hitherto been the exclusive domain of clays from Cornwall. Another major challenger arose in the form of calcium carbonate. Hitherto all papermaking had been under acid conditions, but developments in papermaking technology in the late sixties allowed neutral or alkaline papermaking, thereby opening-up the possibility of using finely ground calcium carbonate derived from chalk, limestone or marble deposits. Developments in ultrafine grinding technology enabled paper coating grades to be produced at a price which was highly competitive with paper coating china clays and a significant new competitor for china clay began to emerge. Rationalisation within the industry continued after the Second World War and by the mid-seventies there were only four producers left: English China Clays (approximate capacity in Cornwall and Devon, 3,000,000 tpa), Goonvean & Restowrack (approximate capacity 120,000 tpa), Steetley (approximate capacity 80,000 tpa), and Watts, Blake and Bearne in Devon.

Since 1974 the china clay industry has ceased to expand and has maintained production within the range 2.3-3.3 million tonnes a year. Downturns in the business cycle have led to depressed sales in 1971, 1975, 1980-1, and over the last few years (Figure 5.5). The 1980-1 recession was probably the most severe of these downturns, although the recession which may now be beginning to end appears to have been the most prolonged. The pattern of sales established in the post-War years continued, with the paper industries of Finland, Germany and the Scandanavian countries being the most important export destinations.

The most significant feature of this period has been the development of intense competition in most of the markets which use Cornish china clay. The main competitors have been coating clay from Georgia in the United States and calcium carbonate based filler and coating grades from a variety of sources all over Europe and the rest of the world, as was described earlier. In 1970 practically no calcium carbonate based fillers and coatings were used in the

European paper industry, but by the early nineties between one third and one half of all the mineral matter used in paper manufacture was composed of calcium carbonate. English China Clays realised early on the future potential of calcium carbonate-based pigments and bought chalk based operations in the UK near Salisbury and Hull to enable them to offer this material. Shortly afterwards they built a plant based on scrap marble derived from dimension stone production at Carrara in Italy and opened a chalk-based plant at Precy-sur-Oise, north of Paris. Other carbonate plants in the United States, Japan, Sweden and other countries followed. Calcium carbonate based fillers and coatings from the Swiss company Pluess-Stauffer, produced at a large number of plants all over the world provided particularly aggressive competition in paper, plastics and paint markets.

Coating clays from Georgia have continued to increase their export sales and by 1990 the amount of kaolin exported from Georgia and South Carolina was the same as the amount exported from Cornwall and Devon. Domestic sales within the US were much larger than domestic sales of china clay in Britain, which meant that by 1990 the output of kaolin from Georgia and South Carolina was 9 million tonnes, as against 3 million tonnes from Cornwall and Devon. Competition for china clay (kaolin) markets has been further intensified by the appearance of entirely new producers of the lucrative paper coating kaolins in the Amazon Basin (Cadam, on the Rio Jari, 500,000 tpa) and in Queensland, Australia (Comalco, at Weipa, 150,000 tpa).[35] There are vast resources of high quality kaolin in the Amazon Basin and, at the time of writing, a further new plant on the Rio Capim is reported to be under construction. This latter plant is particularly large, at 500,000 tpa capacity, which, together with an expanded plant on the Rio Jari, means that over one million tpa of coating kaolin capacity could be available from the Amazon Basin in a few years time.

Because of the expansions in plant capacity in Georgia and the Amazon Basin in recent years, coupled with the substitution of kaolin by calcium carbonate and the effects of the recent worldwide recession on the paper industry, there now exists substantial overcapacity in the worldwide kaolin industry, making competition all the more intense. For many years price rises for china clay from Cornwall have failed to keep pace with inflation, so significant improvements in productivity have been needed to keep Cornish china clay competitive. Much of this has been obtained by changes in working practices and investment to reduce costs, principally in the form of labour. As a result the total number employed in the industry has fallen from around 6000 in the mid-seventies to approximately 4000 at present. It would be surprising if this trend did not continue. This trend is causing major social problems in the St Austell area, for ECC and the other china clay producers have been taking on very few school-leavers in recent years, drastically reducing the job opportunities for this age group in what has been seen as the traditional local employment market.

Fortunately for Cornwall, there have been two developments which have recently given the Cornish china clay industry a boost. Firstly, the devaluation of sterling has meant that, at a stroke, Cornish china clays gained a significant price advantage over most of the overseas competition. Secondly, research into the production of special grades of clay, some recovered from residues, for paper filling, has borne fruit and, as a consequence, a large number of new products have been launched in this field, which are proving to be much in demand from the paper industry, in spite of the depressed state of that industry. The china clay industry does not publish details of its mineral reserves, but statements made in recent years in the US version of English China Clays' Annual Accounts have suggested that there were at least 25 years of reserves left in the ground.

The environmental impact of the china clay industry has become a matter of increasing debate in recent years, both within the industry and in society at large in Cornwall and there are a number of issues which are worth airing in this context. In any discussion it must be remembered that china clay is the most important industrial mineral produced in Britain, by quite a wide margin, and is Britain's second most valuable mineral export after petroleum. It provides 4000 jobs in primary industry in Cornwall, which in turn, support many times that number of other jobs in secondary industries. In an area which has great difficulty in attracting inward investment to create jobs, the maintenance of this employment in the china clay industry must be of paramount importance. Mining is also a traditional Cornish industry and china clay mining forms part of a long tradition in mining stretching back for several thousand years. As a result mining is an important part of the Cornish cultural identity and most indigenous Cornish people feel that it is important to maintain mining activity in Cornwall.

As discussed earlier, the china clay industry has already made significant advances in softening the impact of its workings with the landscaping and revegetation of the tips and residue dams, and much general tidying up and planting of trees. Much progress has been made over the last 30 years, although some critics insist that in the process the distinctive 'Cornish Alps' have become over-sanitised. Indeed, a number of major issues have emerged on the environmental front, already causing considerable public debate, and it is important to look at some of these. The backfilling of china clay pits, for example, presents some quite serious problems which can only be appreciated by an understanding of the basic geometries of the three principlal types of mineral deposit. These are illustrated in Figure 5.6.

From Figure 5.6, it can be seen that the future resources of china clay always tend to lie under the pit, so premature backfilling will sterilise future resources and make them unavailable for future generations to work. A further important reason why pits cannot be backfilled is that they perform an invaluable role as water reservoirs, storing and providing the large quantities of water which are used in the production process; most of which is recirculated, using the flooded old pits as balancing reservoirs.

The cause of conservation of mineral resources is also served if more saleable mineral can be extracted from the clay matrix. Here, major advances have been made by the industry, particularly with regard to the re-processing of the residues from china clay refining. Some of these contain up to 40% coarse kaolinite, which can now be separated from the unwanted constituents of the residue by a technique known as froth flotation. Once recovered, the coarse kaolinite can be ground to produce more commercial kaolin. Some of the grades of clay which are produced by this route have been found to have valuable properties as paper fillers and for other purposes. Because of the success of these kaolins in the market-place, work has now begun on reprocessing residues in the older residue lagoons. From a conservation point of view this development is excellent news as up to 20% more clay is recovered from each ton of matrix, and some of the product is obtained from waste materials, which means that less matrix has to be mined in order to provide the same quantity of kaolin end-product. Yet another benefit is that less space is required for the disposal of residues. Research has also shown that there are small concentrations of unusual minerals in the waste residues, this aspect will be discussed in greater detail below.

Whilst some progress can be reported on the re-treatment and reduction in the quantity of mica residues produced, the same cannot be said of the vast quantities of waste sand, rock (stent) and overburden produced by the industry. About eight tons of waste are produced for every ton of china clay produced, so on the basis of an annual china clay production of three million tpa, about 24 million tons of waste material are produced. Much of this material takes the form of a coarse sand, in part gravel by particle size definition, often containing pieces of rock up to the size of a football. These rocky fragments are often of a weak partially kaolinised material which readily disintegrates on weathering. The whole question of the occurrence and utilisation of mineral and construction wastes has been considered in a report by Ove Arup and Partners on behalf of the Department of the Environment[36] and further studies by Cornwall County Council are in hand; as well as numerous internal reports by the clay producers. The total industry waste stockpile is estimated at over 600 million tonnes, with about 450 million tonnes in the St Austell area alone. In the St Austell area, Ove Arup estimated that some 1400 ha of land is covered by waste tips. The overshadowing by waste tips of some of the communities in the clay country, such as Penwithick and Bugle, is beginning to cause vociferous complaints from some sections of these communities.

The obvious use for all this sand is in the construction industries, but only a relatively small proportion, much smaller than most people realise, can be readily used as a concreting sand. This is because the sand is generally too coarse and fines-deficient for this purpose. Because of this coarseness and the presence of minerals such as mica and unkaolinised feldspar, concrete made from clay works sand can require up to 20% more cement than more conventional sands, creating a further disincentive for its use. However, as a bulk fill material for the construction of embankments and road foundations, clay works sand can be used, providing the structure is properly designed for its use.

FIGURE 5.6
TYPES OF MINERAL DEPOSIT

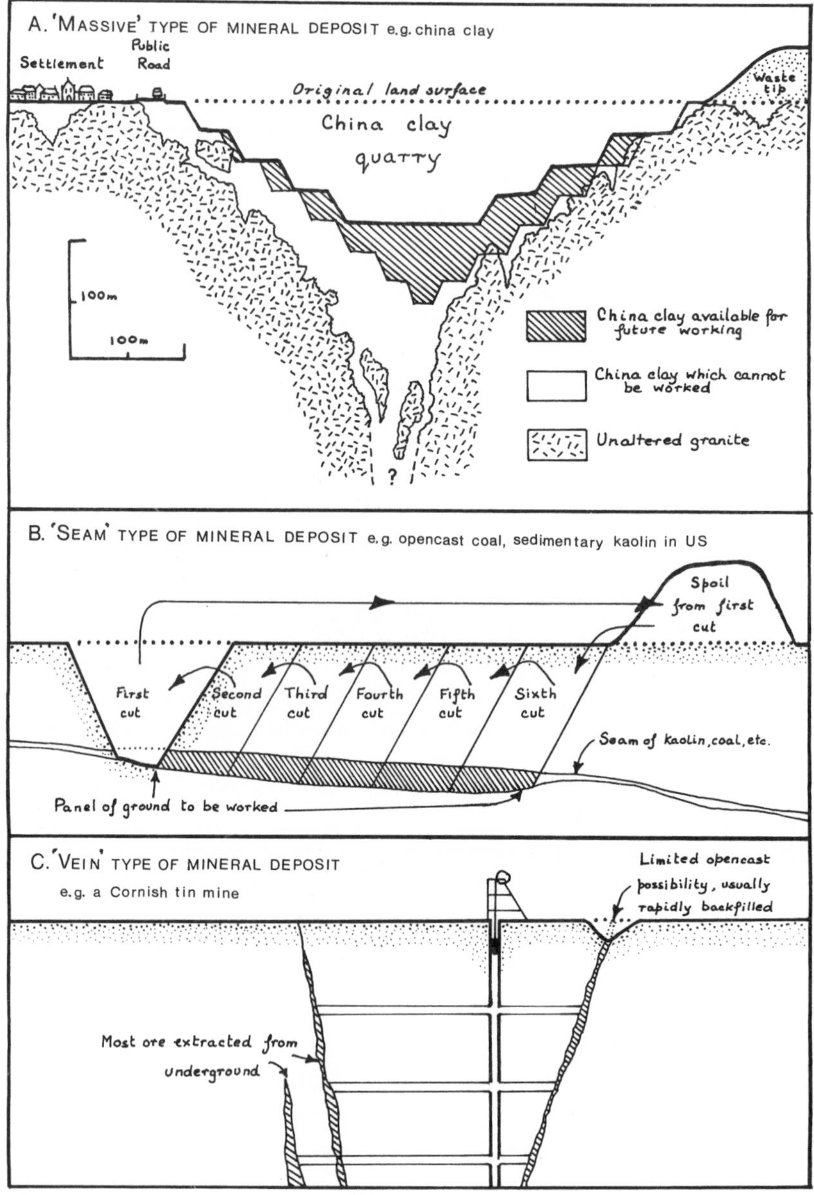
A. 'MASSIVE' TYPE OF MINERAL DEPOSIT e.g. china clay
Settlement
Public Road
Original land surface
China clay quarry
Waste tip
100m
100m
China clay available for future working
China clay which cannot be worked
Unaltered granite
?
B. 'SEAM' TYPE OF MINERAL DEPOSIT e.g. opencast coal, sedimentary kaolin in US
Spoil from first cut
First cut
Second cut
Third cut
Fourth cut
Fifth cut
Sixth cut
Seam of kaolin, coal, etc.
Panel of ground to be worked
C. 'VEIN' TYPE OF MINERAL DEPOSIT
e.g. a Cornish tin mine
Limited opencast possibility, usually rapidly backfilled
Most ore extracted from underground

COMPARISON BETWEEN THE WORKING OF CHINA CLAY AND OTHER TYPES OF MINERAL DEPOSIT

A. 'MASSIVE' TYPE OF MINERAL DEPOSIT e.g. china clay

A typical china clay deposit is funnel shaped in cross-section and is thought to have been formed by surface-derived water being drawn down into the granite on the downward limb of a hydrothermal convection cell. The maximum slope on the side of a china clay pit is governed by the engineering properties of the rocks making up the slope; in practice it is rarely steeper than that shown. Note that the main future reserves in a typical china clay pit tend to lie under the pit, particularly under the deeper part of the pit. The best quality is frequently found overlying the 'stem' of the funnel. Backfilling of any part of the pit will clearly result in some of the china clay being made impossible to work.

Note that a large tonnage on the left-hand side of the pit is unavailable for working. However, if it should prove possible to re-route the public road, then the pit edge could be moved back and a substantial additional tonnage of china clay would become available for future working, perhaps resulting in a doubling of the reserves and hence the life of the pit. Nevertheless, the small quantity of china clay under the settlement will probably never be worked because of the presence of buildings.

Other massive deposits, such as copper porphyry open mines, would demonstrate similar geometry. The main point to emphasise is that with this kind of deposit it is usually impossible to start backfilling until you are sure that all the mineral resource has been removed, otherwise resources which might have been worked by future generations will be sterilised and wasted.

B. 'SEAM' TYPE OF MINERAL DEPOSIT e.g. opencast coal or sedimentary kaolin in Georgia, USA.

In this type of operation the material to be worked, whether it be coal, sedimentary kaolin or a wide variety of other materials, occurs as a horizontal or gently dipping 'bed'. This can be 'strip-mined' by digging a deep trench down to the seam ('first cut' on the diagram) and placing the overburden at the far end of the panel of ground to be worked. Successive cuts can then be made, with the waste in each case being cast into the adjacent worked-out cut. Finally the original pile of waste is cast back into the final cut. With this method of mining the ground can be progressively re-instated as soon as the initial cut has been backfilled. Only the cut where actual mining is in progress need be open at any one time.

Very high standards of restoration are possible with this kind of mining and British Coal in this country and English China Clays in the United States will normally leave the ground in at least as good a state (sometimes better) than before they started. However, this kind of mining is only possible if there is a seam which is sub-horizontal or gently dipping.

C. 'VEIN' TYPE OF MINERAL DEPOSIT e.g. a Cornish tin mine

Underground mining is much more costly than open-pit mining. Occasionally the geological and economic circumstances will allow a 'seam' type of deposit to be mined underground, but this is rare due to the higher costs of working underground. However, where the commodity being sought is of high value, such as a non-ferrous metal, and where it occurs in narrow veins which are steeply dipping or vertical, extending down to a considerable depth, then underground mining will probably be the only option, apart from some very limited opencast working along the outcrop of the lode. Cornish tin mining is the classic example of this type of mining.

The dam wall of Colliford dam on Bodmin Moor was entirely composed of china clay sand from nearby Park china clay pit, confirming its suitability in this sort of application. Similarly, crushed rock (stent) has also been used wherever possible for road foundations, for example on the A30 Mitchell-Summercourt by-pass, the A390 Sticker by-pass and, at the time of writing, the A30 Fraddon-Indian Queens by-pass.

Local markets for sand and crushed rock in Cornwall use china clay waste materials wherever possible, so the local market can be said to be saturated; in order to use greater quantities, markets farther afield will have to be supplied. This means taking it to the larger conurbations such as the Home Counties and the Bristol area. These markets are already served from a variety of competing sources, including sand and gravel dredged from offshore, so china clay sand would have to be priced at a level no higher than these existing sources; Ove Arup state that a price somewhat lower would be needed to make up for the inherent disadvantages of china clay sand as described above.[37] The Ove Arup report shows that, using the cheapest possible method of transport (large bulk carrying ship from a terminal in St Austell Bay) the cost of transporting the sand to London would be £1.60/t more than it could possibly be sold for in the Home Counties. Transport by rail would require £3.25/t more. This is a pure transport price and allows nothing for the excavation of the sand and necessary screening to remove large rocks, and the washing and blending which would be needed to make a product which complies with construction industry specifications. One suspects that it also allows nothing for the cost of getting the sand to St Austell Bay and the cost of servicing the capital needed to build a loading jetty to load a 60,000t bulk carrier.

Let us try and put these figures in perspective and look at what this means in practice. If we assume that the object of the exercise is to try to make a start on reducing the extent of the tips in the St Austell area, then let us assume that we remove one-third of the 450 million tonnes in the existing tips over a thirty year period, while at the same time removing the entire annual output of waste (or its equivalent in already tipped material). The annual rate of waste removal then becomes 29 million tonnes a year. A quick calculation shows that moving this quantity by road is simply not feasible, because it would mean a 20t lorry every 20 seconds, 24 hours a day, every day of the week to move that amount.

Because of the enormous capital cost of the facilities in St Austell Bay needed to load 60,000t bulk carriers, let us disregard that option and use the cheapest alternative option - rail (this would mean forty 2000t trains a day). This means that the annual deficit involved in shifting this amount of sand would be well in excess of £100 million. This could be provided from the public purse, or, alternatively, if this sum was added to the china clay industry's costs it would mean that the industry would almost certainly be operating at a substantial loss (ECC's 1992 Annual Report and Accounts provides figures on the overall profitability of the industry). Bearing in mind the highly competitive situation described above for china clay sales, the effect of imposing the additional cost of transporting the sand to up-country markets would be to shut down the entire industry, so no sand would ever be moved. Clearly that is not a viable option.

On the other hand, if we say, as some of our local politicians have suggested, that public funds should be used to fund the difference, then this has the effect of requiring over £100 million to be found from somewhere. As it is people in Cornwall who seem to want it moved (assuming that people in the Home Counties are satisfied with the bulk of their supply of sand and gravel coming from the more or less limitless seabed resources in the southern North Sea), then presumably the Cornish taxpayer would be asked to pay, which would mean an annual charge on every person in Cornwall of £230 a head. Equally clearly, that is not a viable option either. The exhaustive investigations by the industry (in a number of which the writer was involved) have always come up with the same answer - it simply costs too much to transport the sand out of Cornwall to where there are sufficiently large markets to absorb it, however desirable that may be as an objective. Even the assumption that the Home Counties could absorb 29 million tonnes of sand needs to be challenged, as the total sales of land-won sand and gravel in Greater London and the whole of southeast England only amounted to 24 million tonnes in 1991, and it is inconceivable that china clay sand could claim more than a minority fraction of this total market, which is dispersed over a very wide area.[38] Taking a token amount of between two and eight million tonnes of sand from Cornwall to London, as proposed in the Ove Arup report, would make only a minor difference to the consumption of land for tipping. On a pro-rata basis it would reduce it from 30 ha a year to between 27.5 and 20 ha a year.

However, there are some interesting possibilities which may indicate a valuable future use for china clay sand. In the nineteenth and early twentieth centuries much sand found its way into the local rivers, together with large quantities of mica residue. Where the rivers and streams reached the coast, beaches of china clay sand were formed, as at Pentewan, Carlyon Bay and Par,[39] which are now some of the most popular beaches on the south Cornwall coast with the summer tourists. The beach at Carlyon Bay has remained remarkably stable, in spite of having had negligible additions of sand over the last 50 years or so. Par also appears to be stable, but Pentewan has receded somewhat since the supply of sand and mica residues to replenish it was cut off about 20 years ago. An artificial beach was created at Saltash about 25 years ago, using china clay waste, which also has apparently remained stable. China clay sand seems to be particularly suitable for beach make-up, because its coarseness and angularity of its particles ensures that it is retained on the beach. Current concerns about global warming and the consequent rise in sea levels suggest that coast protection could become a topic of major importance in the next century. Whilst many coasts can be protected by groynes, concrete walls or barriers of armourstone, one of the most cost effective ways of protecting a coast, particularly where there is an existing beach, is to simply raise the beach level by adding more sand to it. Storm energy is then dissipated by the waves pounding on the beach (as at Carlyon Bay in a southerly gale). China clay sand would appear to be the ideal material for this purpose and many of its disadvantages in concrete applications turn into advantages in sea defence applications - such as the lack of fines, which would be washed off a beach in storms.

Other useful materials may be recoverable from the waste products of the china clay industry. One of the more interesting is the lithium in the St Austell granite, which was the subject of a report by the British Geological Survey.[40] The authors point out that, using existing mineral processing technology, it should be possible to recover a mica containing 2% Li2O from mica residues and that three million tonnes of lithium are contained in the top 100m of the St Austell granite. Lithium is very much a space-age metal with established applications in aluminium metal production, aerospace, batteries, lubricants and greases and synthetic rubber production. However, the main reason why there is so much government interest in the metal is because of its predicted potential use in fusion nuclear reactors, which would require prodigious quantities of the metal. The St Austell resource is probably the largest resource of lithium in the European Union. At the present time there are adequate supplies worldwide of lithium, and a St Austell source would almost certainly not be competitive with them, but future developments might change this, particularly if a major new application like fusion power arises.

Mica has been recovered from china clay sand in several locations in Brittany for many years, and formerly was recovered from china clay waste at a plant at Lee Moor, north of Plymouth.[41] Quite apart from its use as a source of lithium, mica is an important industrial filler in its own right when ground to the correct fineness. It has the ability to convert plastics from relatively weak, easily deformed materials into engineering materials which are rigid and can withstand considerable impacts, hence its extensive use in the automotive industry. This is part of the trend for non-metallic materials to replace metal items such as bumpers on cars. Mica is also used in paints and a variety of other industrial applications, ranging from welding electrodes to drilling muds. Topaz is another mineral which may have interesting possibilities in the future; it would probably be easiest to recover from the stent. When topaz is heated to a high temperature ('calcined'), it decomposes into mullite and various gaseous fluorine compounds. The mullite is a valuable refractory material and the fluorine compounds can be used as a starting material for synthesising fluorochemicals such as the fluoride used in toothpaste. However, the fluorine chemicals given off in the calcination are rather nasty (hydrofluoric acid is one of them), so the calcination would have to be carried out in close proximity to the fluorochemical plant where they would be used. This means that one would have to persuade the fluorochemical manufacturer to change his process in order to use the topaz as a starting material, and that may not be easy.

Other minerals which could be recovered include feldspar, which could be used in the ceramics industry. In addition there are small quantities of minerals containing the rare earth metals, uranium and titanium and, at some locations, tin and wolfram minerals, all of which it is technically feasible to recover using well-established mineral processing technology. A considerable amount of research into recovering these minerals from china clay wastes was carried out in the sixties, but there has been little done in recent years. The problem is that recovering just one mineral on its own does not appear to be economic, and almost certainly many minerals would have to be recovered in a complex mineral processing operation, for there to be any chance of the whole operation being economic. The role-model for such a complex operation is in the United States, where in the Spruce Pine district of North Carolina, several large plants successfully break up a granite into all its constituent minerals and sell every last ton, with no waste heaps at all. Developing a suitable flow-sheet for china clay waste would be a considerable challenge for mineral processing engineers.

This really brings us up to the present day and from what has been said above, it can be seen that the china clay industry would appear to have a future which will take it well into the next century. The major hazard is not running out of china clay resources, but competition from alternative sources of white minerals for the paper industry, such as calcium carbonates and kaolins from the Americas. Maintaining the profitability of the china clay industry in the face of growing international competition will be a major challenge. Reprocessing of the wastes has already started, with the recovery of coarse kaolin from some of the old mica residue lagoons; it is possible that this could be developed, in the next century, into a more elaborate operation with other saleable minerals being recovered.

There is, of course, one final threat which could overwhelm the china clay industry, and that is a massive reduction in the amount of paper in use, because of a switch to electronic methods of communication and the drive by the environmental movement to reduce timber waste. Thus far, electronic communication seems to have generated more rather than less paper, but it is probably too early to forecast the longterm effect of the electronics revolution. But perhaps in one hundred years time our desendents will find the clay country a mysterious land of overgrown tips, with, here and there concrete and masonry tanks rising above the vegetation, as in some science fiction fantasy, and colossal concrete foundations of buildings, whose purpose will be endlessly debated by the future members of the Trevithick Society! No doubt the whole area will have become an extraordinarily unique ecological habitat, with all sorts of unusual plants and animals, which will be documented and conserved by future members of the Cornwall Trust for Nature Conservation and the Cornish Biological Records Unit at the Institute of Cornish Studies. A well developed heritage industry will take parties around the old area of china clay working to see preserved remnants of some of the more striking artifacts of the china clay era and perhaps view the few pits left in production for ceramic and other specialist clays. Plans to remove and re-process the tips for coastal protection or rare minerals will have been shelved because of environmental protests about destroying the unique flora and fauna on the tips, and the whole of china clay country will have becomes Britain's number one nature reserve.

Fanciful perhaps, only time will tell if such a scenario is anything like the eventual outcome!

RAW MATERIALS FOR THE CONSTRUCTION INDUSTRIES

Raw materials for the construction industry must be regarded as the Cinderella sector of the extractive industry in Cornwall, with very little ever written or said about it. Yet this sector is currently worth about twice the value of tin extracted in Cornwall and probably employs about five times as many people as metal mining. Whilst one frequently hears calls for better roads to connect Cornwall with the outside world, there is often a great deal of hostility directed towards the development of the facilities which are needed to produce the constructional raw materials to construct those roads. For instance, the construction of the long awaited A30 dual carriageway linking Launceston to Okehampton, recently opened (March, 1993), needed around a million tonnes of stone, much of which came from Greystone Quarry, near Launceston.

FIGURE 5.7
CORNISH QUARRIES

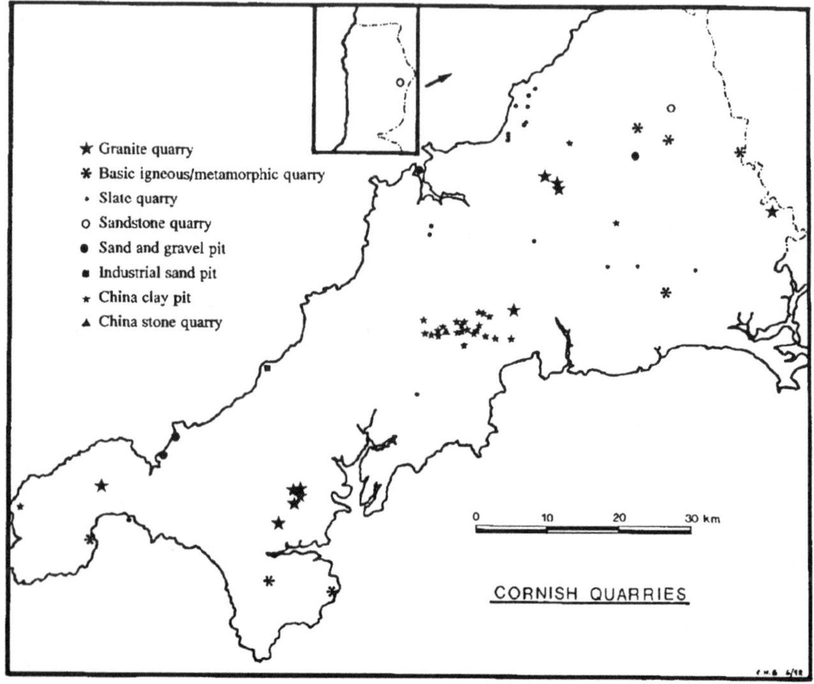

Discussion earlier in this Chapter spelt out the relative significance of this sector, and Figure 5.7 shows the location of the principal quarries in Cornwall and the types of stone produced.[42] There is little archival material describing the development of quarrying in Cornwall, the main sources are the old memoirs of the Geological Survey written at the beginning of this century. Lists of old quarries show that at the end of the nineteenth century virtually every village had its own stone quarry, most of these are now disused and filled in (much to the chagrin of the field geologist!), and the requirements for stone are met from a much smaller number of larger quarries.

Greenstone is a convenient colloquial term for a variety of basic igneous rocks. The principal greenstone quarries which are active at the moment include Greystone Quarry, near Launceston (ECC Quarries Ltd.), Dean Quarry in the Lizard (Redland Aggregates Ltd.) and Penlee Quarry near Newlyn (Penryn Granite Ltd.). There are several other smaller quarries in the Lizard and Launceston areas which also work greenstone. Greenstones, generally speaking, yield good materials for roadmaking, including the all-important wearing surface, which must use a stone with a sufficiently good polished stone value (PSV) to minimize the risk of skidding. Slightly weathered or rotted greenstone can be used for the base course of the road, whilst the freshest rock tends to be used for the wearing course. Some of the hardest and strongest greenstones known in Cornwall occur in Penlee Quarry and small tonnages have been shipped via Newlyn harbour for use in road surfacing adjacent to various English Channel ports. Formerly, there was a whole series of greenstone quarries in the quartz-dolerites occurring on both side of the valley leading from Pentewan to St Austell and Trewoon.

One of the earliest building stones used in Cornwall was Cataclews stone, which was originally obtained from a basic intrusion into Upper Devonian rocks at Cataclews Point on the North Cornwall coast about 5km west of Padstow.[43] A carbonatised picrite at Polyphant has also been worked since the 11th century for an easily carved stone, which can be used for interior work where elaborate carving is required. Many churches in East Cornwall and farther afield (including Canterbury and Exeter cathedrals) have interior features made of Polyphant stone.[44] Launceston Priory and Castle also contain much Polyphant stone, but it has not weathered well, presumably because the stone contains a substantial proportion of talc.

Large granite quarries for aggregate are worked at Hingston Down (ARC Southern), Luxulyan (ECC Quarries Ltd.), Carnsew Quarry near Falmouth (ECC Quarries Ltd.) and at Castle-an-Dinas in the Land's End granite (Penryn Granite Ltd.). There is also a large number of smaller granite quarries in the Carnmenellis granite and a few on Bodmin Moor. Crushed granite makes an excellent aggregate for general purpose use and concreting. The fine grained granite from Carnsew Quarry has a sufficiently good PSV to be extensively used for the wearing course of roads. Granite is also worked for dimension stone on the west side of Bodmin Moor at De Lank quarry (RTZ-T.W.Ward) and Hantergantick quarry (Tarmac). De Lank granite has been used for many famous lighthouses (e.g. Eddystone, Bishop Rock and Beachy Head) and bridges (e.g. Tower and Blackfriars bridges in London).[45] High quality dimension stone, renowned for its strength, was formerly also quarried from the Luxulyan area (Carbeans and Colcerrow quarries) and many famous buildings (e.g. the British Museum) and engineering structures (e.g. the old London Bridge and Plymouth breakwater) were constructed from it.[46]

Another rock of granitic composition which has been extensively used as a dimension stone for building is the famous Pentewan stone (geologically a felsite dyke), which was formerly worked in small quarries on the cliff just northeast of Pentewan and also inland in a quarry about 0.75 km north of the village. Many important buildings in Cornwall have been constructed from Pentewan stone, such as St Austell parish church and Antony House, which is an easily worked stone of excellent durability. However, much of what is nowadays called 'Pentewan stone' may well have come from other quarries in similar material at Sticker, Polgooth and Hewas Water. Similar felsitic dyke material has also been worked in the west of Cornwall for building purposes. Restoration of listed buildings composed of Pentewan stone has presented a problem in recent years because of a lack of any quarry capable of supplying new stone; a more determined attempt to create a contemporary source, by re-opening one of the old quarries, would seem to be overdue, perhaps by a conservation-oriented body such as English Heritage or the National Trust. The re-opening in 1979 by the Diocese of Exeter, using expert geological advice, of the medieval Beer stone quarries used for the building of Exeter Cathedral is a case in point.

Slate is extensively used in Cornwall for building, both for walls and roofing. It is, perhaps, the most natural material to use for building throughout most of Cornwall outside the granite areas. Delabole quarry, near Tintagel, is the largest and best known source of roofing slate, which has a pleasant pale grey colour. The large quarry at Delabole is said to have been continuously worked since Tudor times and a considerable export trade was already in existence by 1602.[47] A group of quarries in the Wadebridge area yield large quantities of slate, known as 'St Issey stone', which is used for constructing Cornish hedges alongside roads and for a variety of purposes where a natural stone finish is desired. There is a large number of other small quarries throughout Cornwall which yield slate which is locally used for walling and construction, most of these quarries are in Devonian slate. Many old quarries in the Launceston area yielded roofing and building slate from Carboniferous rocks, but these are nearly all now abandoned.

Sandstone is worked on a small scale from a few localities in North Cornwall, and was formerly worked from quarries in the Gramscatho Beds in mid-Cornwall and the Staddon Grits in South East Cornwall; its main use is as a walling stone. Limestone is almost absent from Cornwall, apart from a few pockets in the Launceston area, none of which are presently worked. In the past, this deficiency in lime-bearing rocks was overcome by using beach sands which are composed of sea-shells which have been pounded up to a fine sand on the beach by wave action. This sand, when applied to acid soils, helped to neutralise their acidity. Sands of this type are found in the Hayle and Padstow estuaries and in the Bude area. A canal was built in the early 19th century (opened 1823) from Bude to Holsworthy to take this sand to the farms of mid-Devon situated on the sour 'Culm' soils. Occasionally these Quaternary sands are cemented by calcium carbonate (e.g. Godrevy Point and Fistral Bay) and have had limited use as a building stone in some old buildings such as churches. Current requirements for agricultural lime spreading are, however, largely met from quarries in the Devonian limestones of south Devon. Sand and gravel has not been worked extensively, although, as mentioned above, the estuarine and dune sands in the Hayle and Padstow estuaries and adjoining areas are still worked as a source of fine sand for building purposes. During the sixties and seventies, when alluvial tin was being worked, sand and gravel was an important by-product, as for example Hydraulic Tin's workings at Bissoe.

Bricks have, in the past, been produced from a multitude of small brick plants, mostly working superficial clays, scattered all over Cornwall. None are now produced in Cornwall, but brickworks at Whitstone in North Cornwall and at Millbrook, near Torpoint were certainly active in the post-War period up to the late sixties. Specialist brickworks, supplying tiles for china clay pan kilns, were active in the St Austell area (e.g. Wheal Remfry brickworks) until around 1972. All bricks used in Cornwall nowadays are imported from a variety of sources all over England. One practical way of getting more china clay waste sand used would be for all the District Planning authorities in Cornwall to ban the use of bricks in all new construction, in much the same way as all new buildings in many parts of North Wales have to have slate roofs.

Waste materials from the china clay industry now represent some of the most widely used raw materials for the construction industry in Cornwall and the South West. In recent years about 1.5 million tonnes of this waste has been used in the construction industry, but the present figure will be appreciably lower due to the current recession in the building industry. The sand is used for concrete and plastering, and is the principal source of raw material for concrete block manufacture, the largest plant in Cornwall being ECC Construction Materials plant near Fraddon, in mid-Cornwall, which is capable of turning out 11 million blocks a year, which is enough to supply the entire Cornish market. Crushed stent, as noted earlier, has also been successfully used as a road foundation material on a number of trunk and main road schemes.

The latest publication from the Central Statistics Office on Minerals gives figures for the usage of constructional materials and employment in the extractive industry in Cornwall in 1991. The 2,514,000t crushed rock sold in Cornwall in 1991 comprised 175,000t coated roadstone, 308,000t roadstone for coating at remote plants, 586,000t roadstone for uncoated use, 1,123,000t fill and ballast, and 275,000t concrete aggregate. The 903,000t of sand and gravel used for construction in Cornwall in 1991 (mostly derived from china clay waste) comprised 175,000t building sand, 99,000t concreting sand, 44,000t concrete aggregate, 585,000t sand and gravel for fill. Employment in the extractive industries in Cornwall in 1991 was was some 3,150, comprising: industrial sand, seven; sand and gravel, 67; sandstone 17; igneous rock, 446; clay and shale, five; ore and other minerals, 2,606. The employment figures are a little difficult to reconcile with what one knows about the industries concerned as they only include those persons subject to the provisions of the Mines and Quarries Acts. Most probably about 2000 need to be added to the total quoted above to give a realistic view of the number directly employed in the extractive industry in Cornwall.

There has been considerable debate in recent years about the sourcing of constructional raw materials for the future needs of Britain. A document (the 'Ecotec' report) produced for the Department of the Environment by Cambridge Econometrics, which was published in 1991,[48] failed to allow for the extent of the present recession affecting the building industry and therefore their figures are unlikely to be fully realised in practice. However, the Ecotec projections caused much alarm amongst environmentalists in the limestone-producing Mendips, resurrecting discussion of the possibility of utilising china clay waste. However, rather like the suggestion that clay waste be used to construct the embankments for a second Severn Bridge, such discussions overlook the immense costs (identified above) involved. It is also worth recording some cautionary events concerning the use of unconventional raw materials in the local construction industry. One concerns the use of old metalliferous mine waste to make concrete blocks - the so-called 'mundic blocks'. Mundic means iron pyrites, and this pyrites, when exposed to a damp atmosphere, slowly oxidises, releasing sulphuric acid, which eats away at the cement, so the block eventually crumbles to dust. This process takes many years to become apparent and has only in recent years become a serious problem, with a number of properties having to be demolished and rebuilt as a consequence. A similar case of false economy in the use of raw materials is to be found just over the border in Devon, where the (original) Marsh Mills viaduct is now having to be rebuilt because the concrete which it was built with has developed 'concrete cancer'. Cases of concrete cancer also occur in Cornwall. The mechanism which causes this severe weakening of concrete is now reasonably well understood and is usually caused by a normal or high alkali cement being used in conjunction with a reactive chert in the sand or aggregate. This produces a gel which expands when wet and cracks the concrete.

A further trend we need to consider is the role of the superquarry. Already, in several parts of the developed world it is becoming apparent that opposition to the opening of new quarry sites is such that, as existing quarries run out of reserves, they are not replaced by new quarries in the same area. Production then concentrates on fewer and larger sites and, as these in turn run out of reserves, constructional raw materials are brought in from adjoining areas. Ultimately, it is argued, the only way to ensure a supply of constructional raw materials will be to open superquarries in remote situations, adjoining deep sheltered tidewater, where large ships can load and take the material to the areas without adequate operating quarries of their own. Cornwall, with its long coastline and natural harbours, has a few possible sites for a superquarry. However, environmental objections to the necessary very large quarry development, together with the costs and impact of a bulk carrier loading facility, would almost certainly be overwhelming. Penlee quarry, near Newlyn, and Dean quarry in the Lizard are the only Cornish quarries with their own shiploading facilities, but can only load relatively small ships. Some inland superquarries have been developed in England but all these have dedicated rail terminals with whole trainloads of up to 5000t at a time being despatched to major conurbations. Cornwall's distance from major markets and the limitations of its railway infrastructure probably preclude the use of super heavy mineral trains so that sort of development in Cornwall is therefore also unlikely. The conclusion must be that Cornwall's constructional raw materials industry will, in the future, mainly service markets within Cornwall, with little material either moving in or out, apart from some limited cross-border traffic with West Devon.

MINING, SCENERY & GEOLOGY - TOURISM'S 'KEENLY LODE'?

Having examined the fortunes of the extractive industries of Cornwall since the War, together with some thoughts for the future, there are two further aspects of mining and geology which merit some consideration; both of which may have appreciable potential for future development:

- The development of the 'Heritage Tourism' industry to exploit Cornwall's exceptional potential in the fields of industrial archaeological remains, geology and scenery.
- The growth since the Second World War of educational field courses to Cornwall by schools, colleges and universities, which utilise the marvellous exposures of coastal geology and scenery, and the mining activities past and present, for teaching.

Cornwall's geological importance is reflected in the fact that the county possesses more hard-rock Sites of Special Scientific Importance (SSSI) than any other, by quite a wide margin. This importance is also reflected in the fact that the Geological Conservation Review chose to make the igneous rocks of Cornwall and the South West the subject of a book in their recent series on geologically important areas in Britain.[49] In this volume 38 out of the 53 sites listed were in Cornwall. Many of the sites are of international significance, and it is possible that really important areas such as the Lizard, the north coast of the Penwith peninsula and the St Austell china clay area will qualify for placement on the 'World Heritage List' for geological sites.

What role could geology and mining play in heritage tourism? For some years it has been apparent that the traditional seaside holiday in this country has been in decline. The calamitous 1992 season in Cornwall forced the closure of many hotels and traditional tourist attractions, in spite of the strenuous efforts by many of the locally based tourism organisations to promote holidays in Cornwall. However, there has also been a steady growth in recent years of attractions which are based around relics of Cornwall's industrial and mining past; and it is clear that one of the main attractions to all types of visitor has always been the scenery, especially along the coast, yet the tourist literature very rarely makes a serious attempt to explain what elements go to make up the scenery, in terms of plants and animals, rocks, geological structures and geomorphology. Undoubtably part of the fault lies with the geological community, the scientific jargon of the GCR Review volume cited above is a perfect example of inaccessibility due to the excessive use of technical terminology. However, the writer's experience of teaching to evening classes the latest ideas concerning the geological history of Cornwall indicates that people with no previous geological training can find the subject stimulating and comprehensible. Hitherto, non-specialist presentations of Cornish geology (including, for example, the Rashleigh Gallery reopened in March 1993 at the Royal Cornwall Museum) have tended to rely on the visually dramatic quality of exhibits, but it does seem that a more analytical and explanatory approach can do much to illuminate Cornwall's unique geological history and the reason for its rich mining heritage.

At the same time there has been an enormous growth in bodies concerned with aspects of conserving the natural history, archaeology and scenery of Cornwall, many of which are backed by substantial budgets. These groups tend to draw their membership from people residing in Cornwall and several are, in fact, government or local authority quangos. Besides the National Trust we have the Countryside Services operated by Cornwall County Council, with the support of the District Councils and the Countryside Commission; and there is English Nature (an uncomfortable title for some in Cornwall; formerly it was the Nature Conservancy Council) with its special responsibility for Sites of Special Scientific Interest, both geological/ geomorphological and biological. Then there is the Cornwall Trust for Nature Conservation (CTNC), which is concerned with biological conservation and the management of nature reserves, and the Cornwall RIGS Group, which is concerned with the geological/ geomorphological conservation of non-SSSI sites. Also in the field is the Cornish Biological Records Unit (CBRU), which is part of the Institute of Cornish Studies and is concerned with the scientific recording of Cornwall's flora and fauna.

Besides the natural history organisations, there are the various groups concerned with the preservation of Cornwall's industrial and archaeological heritage. The National Trust is also very active in this area, with the recently completed Levant Engine House a prime example of the Trust's activity in this field. The Trevithick Society is concerned primarily with mining and engineering relics and has been the principal body responsible for drawing attention to Cornwall's exceptional legacy of industrial relics associated with the mining industry. A recent and highly significant initiative has been to set up the

Trevithick Trust, which is made up of representatives of Cornwall County Council, Kerrier, Penwith and Carrick District Councils, the National Trust, Kerrier Groundwork Trust, the Trevithick Society, and other bodies. This is primarily concerned with the mining, industrial and engineering sites in Cornwall, focussing initially on the Camborne-Redruth-Gwennap area but taking Geevor (recently purchased by the County Council and reopened as a tourist attraction) under its wing and forging relationships with other initiatives such as the Minions Project near Liskeard. The Mineral Tramways Project is an ambitious scheme to set up 100km of long distance trails, mainly using old tramway routes, to link together mining sites of great historical and industrial interest in the Camborne-Redruth area, with the avowed intention of attaining the status of a 'World Heritage Site' on a cultural basis (although it may, in fact, be easier to attain 'World Heritage' status on the basis of geological sites in Cornwall). In mid-Cornwall the Wheal Martyn Museum, near St Austell, is concerned with telling the story of china clay, and - with twenty years solid experience on a semi-commercial basis - it offers important experience in the development of educational roles and the attraction of both mass and more 'discerning' 'heritage' tourists. The Director of the Trevithick Trust has declared that 'The tourism and educational potential for Cornwall's industrial history is virtually limitless',[50] while Paul Thornton, Research Assistant at the Institute of Cornish Studies, has suggested that recent changes in the 'tourist gaze' (the 'unusual' that tourists expect in their holiday destinations) offers Cornwall many opportunities in the field of 'heritage' or 'cultural' tourism - should the tourist industry decide to respond to them.[51]

Another body in this general area of activity is the Cornwall Archaeological Unit, funded by the County Council, which is concerned not only with the industrial past, but also the full gamut of archaeological investigations, extending back into prehistory. A series of recent publications on the key areas of industrial interest have provided a foundation of knowledge and record for these areas.[52] Similarly, a thriving organisation, founded since the Second World War, is the Cornwall Archaeological Society, which has a lively programme of well-attended lectures and field visits and a journal of a high standard. Indeed, Cornwall is exceptionally rich in learned Societies with the Royal Institution of Cornwall in Truro, with its Royal Cornwall Museum. There is the Royal Cornwall Polytechnic Society in Falmouth, and the Cornish Gorseth must also be considered an important intellectual body. However, the most venerable of these institutions is the Royal Geological Society of Cornwall, the second oldest geological society in the UK and one of the oldest in the world, with its museum and library (recently refurbished and reopened to the public in time for the Humphry Davy celebrations in 1993) in Penzance, potentially a major all-weather tourist attraction in West Cornwall.

The emergence of 'heritage' tourism has been reflected in a noticeable growth in theme holidays based around aspects of Cornish culture, history or science, while many local residents continue to attend evening classes and field weekends organised by various bodies, including the University of Exeter, with courses on natural history, archaeology, mining, history and geology being particularly well attended. To these must be added the increasingly significant educational field parties composed of students, less affluent perhaps than normal tourists but drawn to Cornwall because its attractive features such as dramatic coastal exposures or inland exposures like china clay pits which provide superb field training opportunities. Every year large numbers of students from universities and schools in both Britain and abroad come to Cornwall for geology, geography and economic history field studies, usually staying for about a week. The peak period for these visits is the Easter vacation, with very few of the parties coming in the high season, so this business can provide a welcome way of extending the season for local hoteliers. It is difficult to estimate the total numbers involved, but estimates range from a low of 1000 up to a high of 5000. Some market research in this area would help to clarify numbers, timing and specialist requirements. Similarly, the Cornwall RIGS Group and other interested bodies will need to identify a wide and comprehensive list of sites suitable for field-work, providing supporting literature where appropriate, so that excursion leaders will have an extensive range of potential destinations and not be limited to a few, possibly over-crowded localities.

CONCLUSION

There is undoubtedly scope for increasing the numbers of both 'heritage' tourists and educational field parties visiting Cornwall, and some imaginative marketing by the tourism promotion bodies, using the expertise of the local archaeological, historical, engineering and scientific community could pay worthwhile dividends. For the residents of Cornwall, too, the mining and geological heritage should be seen increasingly as an important leisure, educational and economic amenity. But, despite the apparent lack of prospects for tin, real extractive activity - overwhelmingly, the production of china clay - will continue to make a significant contribution to the Cornish economy and will perpetuate the proud Cornish mining tradition into the twenty first century.

REFERENCES

1. Three of the best reviews are: J.H. Collins, 'Observations on the West of England Mining Region', *Transactions of the Royal Geological Society of Cornwall*, Vol.14, 1912, re-published by Cornish Mining Classics, Truro, 1988; H.G.Dines, *The Metalliferous Mining Region of South-West England*, 1956, republished British Geological Survey, London, 1988, with addenda and corrigenda by K.E. Beer; R.Burt, P.Waite, R.Burnley, *Cornish Mines: Metalliferous and Associated Minerals 1845-1913*, University of Exeter Press, Exeter, 1987.
2. See A.M. Ospovat, 'Four Hitherto Unpublished Geological Lectures Given by Sir Humphry Davy in 1805', *Transactions of the Royal Geological Society of Cornwall*, 21,; also R. Siegfried and R.H.Dott, *Humphry Davy on Geology*, University of Wisconsin Press, Wisconsin, 1980.

3. H.T.De la Beche, *Report on the Geology of Cornwall, Devon and West Somerset*, Longmans, London, 1839. W.J.Henwood, 'On the metalliferous deposits of Cornwall and Devon', *Transactions of the Royal Geological Society of Cornwall*, 5, 1-386.
4. See the *Proceedings of the Ussher Society* (1962-present) for many of the key papers describing advances in the geological understanding of Cornwall. The best introductions to Cornish geology are: E.A.Edmonds, B.J. Williams, R.T. and Taylor, *South-West England*, British Geological Survey, London, 1975, and, P.G.Embrey and R.F.Symes, *Minerals of Cornwall and Devon*, British Museum (Natural History), London, 1987.
5. The evolution of Cornwall during Devonian and Carboniferous times is beautifully depicted in the recently published *Atlas of Palaeogeography and Lithofacies*, Geological Society Memoir No 13 (eds. J.W. Cope, J.K. Ingham and P.F. Rawson) published in 1992 by the Geological Society of London.
6. J.Rowe, *Cornwall in the Age of the Industrial Revolution*, Liverpool University Press, Liverpool, 1953, republished Cornish Hillside Publications, St Austell, 1993.
7. K.Dunham, K.E.Beer, R.A.Ellis, M.J.Gallagher, M.J.C.Nutt, and B.C.Webb, 'Mineral Deposits of Europe: United Kingdom', in S.H.Bowie, A.Kvalheim, and H.W.Haslam, eds., *Mineral Deposits of Europe: Volume 1*, Institute of Mining and Metallurgy/Mineralogical Society, London, 1978, pp 263-317.
8. Dines, 1965; D.B.Barton, *A History of Tin Mining and Smelting in Cornwall*, Bradford Barton, Truro, 1965, republished Cornwall Books, Exeter, 1988, R.D.Penhallurick, *Tin in Antiquity*, Institute of Metals, London, 1986, Burt *et al.*, 1987; Embrey and Symes, 1987; P.Payton, *The Making of Modern Cornwall: Historical Experience and the Persistence of 'Difference'*, Dyllansow Truran, Redruth, 1992.
9. K.F.G.Hosking, 'Permo-Carboniferous and later Primary Mineralisation of Cornwall and South-west Devon' in K.F.G.Hosking and G.J.Shrimpton (eds.), *Present Views on the Geology of Cornwall and Devon*, Royal Cornwall Geological Society, Penzance, 1964.
10. Penhallurick, 1986.
11. Burt, 1987, ppxxxviii-l.
12. Geoffrey Blainey, *The Rush That Never Ended: A History of Australian Mining*, Melbourne University Press, Melbourne, 1963, second edition, 1969, p376.
13. Data mainly obtained from: D.Slater, *Tin Mine Dossier No9*, British Geological Survey, London, 1974, and the *United Kingdom Minerals Yearbook*, also published by the British Geological Survey.
14. De la Beche, 1839, pp588-589.
15. Embrey and Symes, 1987, p17.
16. Collins, 1912/1988, p387.
17. As per note 13.
18. See University College of the South-west, Exeter, *Devon and Cornwall: A Preliminary Survey*,Devon and Cornwall, Wheatons, Exeter, 1947, pp88-92.
19. Brief descriptions of the recent history of South Crofty, Wheal Pendarves, Wheal Jane and Mount Wellington mines will be found in: B.E.Leveridge, M.T.Holder, and A.J.J.Goode, *Geology of the Country Around Falmouth*, British Geological Survey, sheet 352, 1990, pp48-52.
20. Slater, 1974, pp36-38 and Leveridge *et al.*, 1990, p52.
21. The Annual Reports of the Cornish Mining Development Association (1975-1988) provide a useful record of the more significant exploration developments since Slater, 1974.
22. Data primarily from the US Bureau of Mines preprints on Tin.
23. Data from the *United Kingdom Minerals Yearbooks* and US Bureau of Mines preprints.
24. C.M.Bristow, 'Society's Changing Requirements for Primary Raw Materials', *Industrial Minerals*, February 1987.
25. De la Beche, 1839, p623.
26. Data from the *United Kingdom Minerals Yearbooks* and the Annual reports of Cornish Mining Development Association.
27. Most of the data obtained from two biographies: A. Douglas Selleck, *Cookworthy 1705-80 and His Circle*, Baron Jay Publishers, Plymouth, 1978, and J.Penderill-Church, *William Cookworthy 1705-1780*, Bradford Barton, Truro, 1972.

28. The early history of the china clay industry is described by: R.M.Barton, *A History of the Cornish China Clay Industry*, Bradford Barton, Truro, 1966, and J. Allen Howe, 'A Handbook to the Collection of Kaolin, China Clay and China Stone' in the *Museum of Practical Geology*, HMSO, London, 1914.
29. Selleck, 1978, pp71-83.
30. C.M.Bristow, 'Development of Kaolin Production and Future Perspectives', *Proceedings of the 10th Industrial Minerals International Congress, San Francisco*, Industrial Minerals, London, 1992, pp95-104; C.M.Bristow and C.S.Exley, 'Historical and Geological Aspects of the China Clay Industry of South-west England', *Transactions of the Royal Geological Society of Cornwall*, 21, part 5, forthcoming.
31. A history of Charlestown Engineering by Bernard Broad was published in the ECC Review for summer, 1958. A biography of William West of Tredenham was published by the Institute of Cornish Studies in 1973.
32. A.L.Rowse, *St Austell, Church, Town, and Parish*, Warne, St Austell, 1960.
33. See Barton, 1966.
34. Barton, 1966.
35. Bristow, 1992.
36. M.Whitbread, A.Marsay and C.Tunnel, *Occurance and and Utilisation of Mineral and Construction Wastes*, Report by Ove Arup and Partners on behalf of the Geological and Minerals Planning Research Programme of the Department of the Environment.
37. Whitbread *et al.*, p16.
38. Data from: Central Statistical Office, 1992, Business Monitor, PA 1007, 1991, Minerals, Table 2, pp6-7.
39. C.E.Everard, 'Mining and Shoreline Evolution near St Austell, Cornwall', *Transactions of the Royal geological Society of Cornwall*, 19, 1962, pp199-219.
40. J.R.Hawkes *et al.*, *The Lithium Potential of the St Austell Granite*, Report of the British Geological Survey, 19.
41. R.N.Crockett, *Mica*, Mineral Dossier No 15, Mineral Resources Consultative Committee, H.M.S.O., London, 1975.
42. Data to produce this map obtained from the Directory of Mines and Quarries 1991, published by the British Geological Survey.
43. C.Reid, G.Barrow and H.Dewey, *The Geology of the Country Around Padstow and Camelford*, (sheets 335 and 336), Memoir of the Geological Survey of England and Wales, p91.
44. C.Reid, G.Barrow, R.L.Sherlock, D.A.Macalister, and H.Dewey, *The Geology of the Country Arounf Tavistock and Launceston*, (sheet 337), Memoir of the Geological Survey of England and Wales, 1911, pp128-129.
45. Reid, 1910, p90.
46. W.A.E.Ussher, G. Barrow, and D.A.Macalister, *The Geology of the Country Around Bodmin and St Austell*, (sheet 347), Memoir of the Geological Survey of England and Wales, 1911, pp174-176.
47. Reid, 1910, pp91-93.
48. Cambridge Econometrics (1991) Forecasts of long-term economic growth and construction output, Department of the Environment, and; 1991 National Collation of the results of the 1989 Aggregate Minerals Survey, Department of the Environment. The Annual Reports of the South-west Regional Aggregates Working Party also contain much useful data.
49. P.A.Floyd, C.S.Exley and M.T.Styles, *Igneous Rocks of South-west England*, Geological Conservation Review Series, volume 5, Chapman and Hall, London, 1993.
50. *Western Morning News*, 8 April 1993.
51. P.Thornton, 'Cornwall and Changes in the "Tourist Gaze"', *Cornish Studies* (second series), 1, 1993.
52. For example, see P.Herring and J.Smith, *The Archaeology of the St Austell China Clay Area*, Cornwall Archaeological Unit, Truro, 1991.

CHAPTER 6

THE DEMOGRAPHIC REVOLUTION

Peter Mitchell

If we are to understand population changes in Cornwall since 1945, it is essential to see these in a longer term context. Cornwall's population history is an extremely unusual one, reflecting the development and decline of Cornwall's economy and industry, and more recently its environmental attractions as an area in which to live. As we shall see, from a population point of view, the experience of the last 30 years has been very different from what went before.[1]

THE LONG TERM CONTEXT

National Censuses of population began in 1801. Over the period of nearly two centuries which have passed since then, a number of periods stand out distinctly in terms of Cornwall's population and its history. The main features of these are outlined below.

1801-41:

These years saw rapid population growth, moving roughly parallel with British trends. In Britain generally, this growth was largely the result of the interaction of births and deaths, with improvements in medical care and public health tending to reduce mortality. The industrial revolution was moving forward apace in Cornwall as in other parts of the Britian, and Cornwall shared in the general growth.

1841-61:

In this period growth continued but Cornwall fell well below the national rate. We only have detailed information on the balance of births and deaths, and hence the net effect of migration from 1851 onwards, but it seems very probable that in the 1840s there was a continued gain with more births and deaths, but that this was partly offset by a net movement out of the Cornwall. Certainly this was the situation from 1851 onwards.

1861-1939:

By far the most striking feature of Cornwall's population history is that for the vast majority of this 80 year period Cornwall was losing people. This comes across particularly strongly if we look at migration movements alone. Over most of the 100 years 1840-1940 many more people left Cornwall than moved in. At its height (1860-80) this exodus was running at 60,000 per decade. Over the period 1841-1921 the total lost by migration was an amazing 300,000: the equivalent of almost 90% of what the population had been at the onset of this population drain.[2]

It is important to remember that we are talking here about **net** migration movements. If we assume that there were always some people moving into Cornwall - for example, because of their work or because they were marrying into Cornish families - then the actual numbers moving out must have been greater than the net figures quoted above. Deacon and Baines estimate that **gross** out migration over the 60 years 1841-1901 could have been as high as 460,000 split roughly 50/50 between those moving overseas and those moving to other parts of Britain.

One of the effects of this exodus of Cornish people (or at any rate, of people once domiciled in Cornwall) was the establishment of a substantial 'diaspora', not just in other parts of Britain but also spread around the globe. The setting-up of entire Cornish communities in Australia, South Africa and the Americas is well documented. Much of this movement to remote parts of the world was motivated by the severe problems which had arisen in the mining industry: for large numbers of Cornish miners and their families migration or emigration was the only solution to the lack of opportunity in Cornwall. It was indeed true that in many parts of the world if you found a hole in the ground, you were also likely to find at the bottom of it a Cornishman!

The effect of these changes locally was that for much of the 100 years up to the outbreak of the Second World War, not only did more people leave Cornwall than moved in, but also the population declined in absolute terms. From its high point in 1861 of 369,000 it moved downwards to a low point in 1939 of only 309,000. While Cornwall was experiencing a fall of 16%, nationally trends were moving sharply in the opposite direction: the population of England and Wales more than doubled in the same period. As Cornwall lost out in its share of national population, so its influence and importance declined, particularly when viewed from the centre. Other symptoms of the decline remain to this day. In Cornwall one will search in vain for the large swathes of 1930s suburban housing which surround many of the larger cities up-country. It could be argued too that the prevalence of old school buildings in Cornwall is also a reflection of the lack of pressure to renew these and provide new facilities over the years running up to 1939.

The immediate effect of the outbreak of War in 1939 on Cornwall's population was threefold. First, local people were conscripted and left Cornwall to serve in various capacities at home and overseas. Secondly, concern about the effect of widespread air raids on the cities led to a large-scale evacuation of children from those places thought to be at risk. This brought large numbers of evacuees to Cornwall - possibly as many as 60,000. Thirdly, a number of substantial new armed forces bases were set up in Cornwall, recognising the fact that Cornwall commands the western approaches and would thus be of especial strategic advantage in what later became known as the Battle of the Atlantic. We know that by 1949 there were 8,500 armed forces personnel stationed in Cornwall, the vast majority on bases developed since 1939. Later in the War, during the run-up to D Day in June 1944, there were large numbers of servicemen - in particular Americans - who became temporary residents in Cornwall. Cornwall's peak wartime population was 371,000, reached in 1941.

It seems likely that most of the evacuees had left Cornwall by the time War ended in 1945, but the late 1940s did see a slight continued increase in population, aided by the post-War 'bulge' in births which led to a natural increase of 4,000 or thereabouts. Over the whole period from 1939 until the next Census in 1951, population grew by 23,000 - the larger part of this being in-migration. Coastal areas seem to have been particularly favoured: Newquay grew by over 30%, Falmouth, Bude and Looe by over 15%. However, what had been Cornwall's advantages in a War situation quickly turned into disadvantages, in particular its remoteness from other part of Britain. Communications over four decades ago were far slower than today: rail services were only just beginning to recover from the pounding they had received in wartime and the accompanying lack of investment, while road construction was at a standstill. Fuel rationing had also made travel to and from Cornwall more difficult, even if families were fortunate enough to own a car.

Parts of Cornwall were declared Development Districts in the late 1940s, and some successes were scored in attracting new manufacturing companies, for example Heathcoats at Pool. Long established local firms such as Silley Cox at Falmouth and Holman Brothers at Camborne had large work forces, but the post-War boom in tourism had not yet really begun. It is interesting in this context to pause and see how the official planners viewed the prospects for Cornwall's population when they prepared the original County Development Plan for Cornwall in the early 1950s.

THE 1952 COUNTY DEVELOPMENT PLAN

The original *Development Plan* for Cornwall, prepared under the Town and Country Planning legislation of the late 1940s, was published in 1952. It was a significant document, intended to usher in the new planning system. It looked at Cornwall both in the past and as it might become in the future, and the Plan's comments and views on population matters make interesting reading. They show how the County Council at least viewed population issues, and how they thought the future might develop.

Reviewing Cornwall's past population history, the Plan attributed the persistent outward migration to a combination of chronic high unemployment and a limited choice of job opportunities. It noted that even when unemployment was less bad than it had been in the 1920s and 30s, the choice of job opportunities remained restricted. Tying this up with migration trends, it also pointed out that outward migration was greatest at the time of the onset of high unemployment (eg. the late 1920s) but was less severe in the 1930s even though unemployment continued at a very high level. This phenomenon was attributed to the fact that people were unable to move owing to poverty, and also that by this stage those unemployed who were left behind in Cornwall were generally older. The Plan noted that there had been inward migration to what it called 'amenity' areas, commenting that such migration was likely to be influenced by the cost of living and by the availability of housing in such areas.

Looking forward to 1971, the Plan made a valiant attempt to assess likely population change from 1949. Table 6.1 shows the trends thought likely to occur:

TABLE 6.1
PROJECTED POPULATION CHANGES 1949-71

	Natural Migration	Total	Change
	5,500	+14,500	9,000
	7,500	+5,500	2,000
CORNWALL	-13,000	20,500	7,000

The assumption of a net gain by migration of about 1,000 per year was broadly in line with what had been happening in the late 1940s. However, the effect of natural change was expected to reduce total growth to only 7,000 over a period of 22 years. Thus, while the planners thought that Cornwall would not continue to decline as it had done over so many years in the past, no dramatic reversal was expected and any population increases which might occur seemed likely to be limited. The Plan ended its section on population with the somewhat pompous statement that '. . . if enlightened analysis had been applied in 1931, the subsequent trends of population to 1951 could, in most cases, have been foreseen. The Second War period with the considerable temporary upheavals would only have required minor readjustments of long term trends'.

The implication seems to be that the 20 year projections to 1971 were likewise going to be fairly reliable. How far this was true we shall see later.

TRENDS IN THE 1950s

No dramatic change came about in Cornwall's population during the 1950s. The decade saw a slight excess of births over deaths (about 2,000) while migration drifted back to a position where inward and outward movements were virtually cancelling each other out an aggregate Cornish level. Within this broad balance, however, there were some interesting variations. Towns generally were showing a small amount of growth (particularly in the smaller urban areas) while rural areas were continuing to decline. However, such changes were quite small: 21 towns between them increased by only 6,000 in the 10 years, while rural areas went down by 4,000. What are now the three central Districts of Kerrier, Carrick and Restormel grew by 7,000 while the far west, and east Cornwall all lost population. Only Helston, Newquay and St Austell/St Blazey showed an increase of more than 1,000 people.

Some clues as to what was happening to the various age groups within the population can be gained by comparing the trend in each age group in Cornwall with the same trend nationally. From this analysis, two age groups stand out. The first is the 15-29 year age group where even after allowing for the fact that population growth in Cornwall was well below national average rates, there seems to have been a greater loss than that experienced at other ages. The other group which stands out from the overall trend is people aged 65-74 years: despite Cornwall'g overall stagnation, the rate of growth in this group was slightly **above** the national trend. The implication seems to be that Cornwall was experiencing a loss of young adults by migration, but that at the same time there was a net movement of retired people **into** Cornwall. This may have affected the 45-64 group as well to a lesser extent. Once again, the scale of movement was not large: possibly a net inward movement of 3,000 people aged 65-74 and perhaps 2,000 aged 45-64 . Even these figures may be over-estimates.

Small though this small net movement into Cornwall was, in the light of more recent experience it can be seen as a precursor, a 'cloud no larger than a man's hand', of the coming deluge of migration which was to come upon Cornwall. We must stress again that we are talking here about **net** migration figures. This can obscure the fact that for many years there must have been a **gross** movement of retired people into Cornwall, but this had been compensated by an outward movement. What seems to be new in the 1950s was that the numbers moving in were beginning to exceed those moving out.

Despite the hopes and forecasts of the early 1950s planners, the actual migration balance in the 1950s remained close to zero, and was indeed a good deal closer to the depressing long term picture of population stagnation or decline than it was to the admittedly modest growth which had been anticipated. By the time the early 1960s had been reached, there was a feeling that Cornwall was going to have to continue to grapple with problems of population decline, and certainly nobody had any inkling that major population growth might be about to unleash itself. There were a few areas where modest growth was occurring, but in general Cornwall seemed to have sunk back into its pre-War torpor, with a static or declining population, severe loss of young people in particular and a long term malaise intertwined with these factors and the economic situation. All this was soon to change.

THE 1960s POPULATION TURNAROUND

Against this background, it came as a shock when the Registrar General's mid-year population estimates in the early 1960s began to show Cornwall's population as increasing.[3] Could this really be true, or were the official estimates going haywire? Cornish suspicions about officials 'up-country' - even of up-country statisticians - are ever present. In fact, as the 1971 Census was to show, the statisticians in their annual estimates were actually **undercounting** the degree of net migration into Cornwall. Post 1971, the published net migration estimates needed to be increased by half as much again to get them to fit the numbers of people which the Census discovered to be living in Cornwall at the end of the decade. There is some measure of uncertainty as to just what was happening from year to year during the 1960s, but in what follows the numbers of private dwellings completed each year has been used as a guide to the probable pattern of year on year migration.

FIGURE 6.1

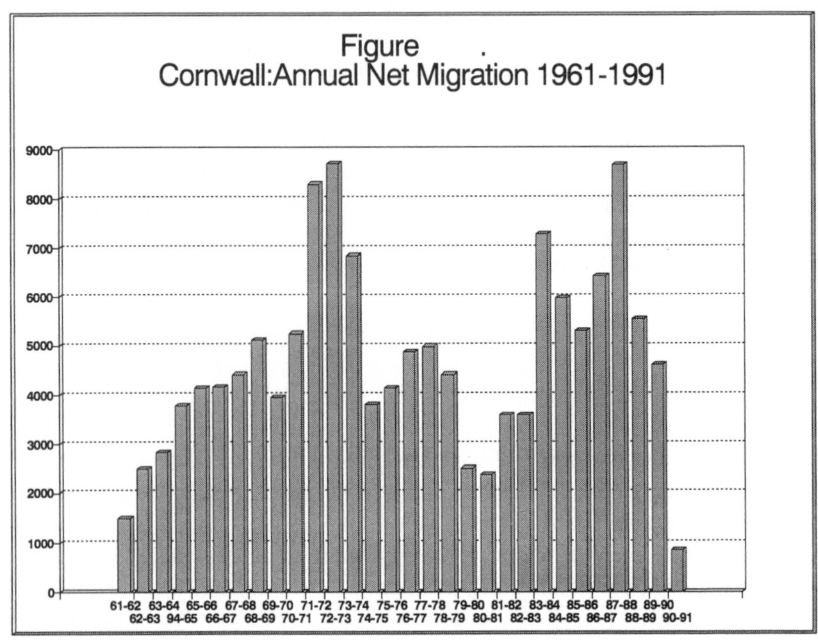

Figure 6.1. illustrates year to year trends in net migration as this affected Cornwall. The early 1960s saw a steady rise in the degree to which inward exceeded outward migration: it started at around 1500 in 1961-62 and built up to 4,000 or so by 1965-66. This rate was then sustained with very little variation from year to year through to 1971. The up-shot was that over the whole decade Cornwall gained over 35,000 people by migration, plus a further 3,000 or so by natural change. This was a dramatic turn around indeed from the experience of most of the previous 100 years!

From being an area with a strongly established pattern of population stagnation or decline, Cornwall was now seen as a location where more and more people wished to live, and by the end of the decade (taken as is usual in looking at population trends as 1971 so as to tie in with Census dates) the population of Cornwall had gone up by 11.5%. In most parts of Cornwall, the 1960s saw an abrupt upward shift in the population trend. One area which stood out even above the others was South East Cornwall: the special factor here was the opening in 1961 of the Tamar Bridge at Saltash, replacing the former road vehicle ferry, and built as a joint venture of Cornwall County and Plymouth City Councils, without the benefit of any Central Government grant. It had a major effect on South East Cornwall, opening up much of what is now Caradon District to commuters, and increasing numbers of people came to live in Cornwall while still working in Plymouth. The Caradon area moved from decline in the 1950s to rapid growth in the 1960s and this has been continuous ever since.

Although all parts of Cornwall shared in this population upturn, growth rates were far from even during the 1960s. As Table 6.2 overleaf shows, much the slowest growth was in Penwith (only 4%) while elsewhere growth rates were anything from 7% to 16%. The table also shows that towns were growing a lot more rapidly than rural areas, and although in 1961 they contained just under half of the Cornish population, they took over 70% of the growth. Natural change had become very much a secondary component of population change, reaching a loss of nearly 3% in Penwith while next door in Kerrier there was a natural increase of 3.5%. Elsewhere natural change was very small.

One of the persistent myths about migration to Cornwall has been that the net gain is largely or entirely attributable to retirement moves. How far was this true in the 1960s? The Censuses of 1966 and 1971 both asked people where they had lived five years earlier. This makes it possible to look at gross movements as well as their net effect, and broad age groups can be identified. These Census migration tables suggest that in the early 1960s Cornwall was continuing to lose young adults, but that in the latter part of the decade this was converted into a gain. The retired age groups by contrast showed a fairly even rate of gain by migration, and hence as the overall rate of growth picked up, they tended to account for a smaller share of the total. It has to be admitted, however, that alternative ways of looking at migration by comparing Census age structures in 1961 and 1971 do tell a rather different tale, and suggest that the problem of a haemorrhage of young people out of Cornwall was in fact continuing at a substantial rate in the latter part of the decade. The conclusion that migration was having less of an imbalancing effect on Cornwall's age structure as the 1960s went on seems still to be valid.

TABLE 6.2
POPULATION CHANGES BY DISTRICT 1951-91

						Turnaround at:		
		1951-61	1961-71	1971-81	1981-91	1961	1971	1981
Penwith		-2,050	+2,040	+3,500	+5,700	+4,100	+1,500	+2,200
	%	-4.1	+4.2	+6.9	+10.5	+8.3	+2.7	+3.6
Kerrier		+1,780	+10,460	+7,700	+6,000	+8,700	-2,800	-1,700
	%	+2.9	+16.7	+10.5	+7.2	+13.8	-6.2	-3.3
Carrick		+2,300	+6,740	+6,100	+8,100	+4,400	-600	+2,000
	%	+3.8	+10.7	+8.7	+10.7	+6.9	-2.0	+2.0
Restormel		+2,850	+9,750	+6,800	+9,800	+6,900	-3,000	+3,000
	%	+4.9	+16.1	+9.7	+12.5	+11.2	-6.4	+3.0
North Cornwall		-1,080	+4,850	+8,700	+9,100	+5,900	+3,900	+400
	%	-2.1	+9.5	+15.5	+13.9	+11.6	+6.0	+1.6
Caradon		-2,040	+6,650	+11,000	+9,000	+8,700	+4,400	-2,000
	%	-4.1	+13.9	+20.2	+13.1	+18.0	+6.3	-7.1
Cornwall		+1,750	+40,490	+43,800	+47,000	+38,700	+3,300	+3,900
	%	+0.5	+12.1	+11.7	+11.2	+11.6	+0.4	+0.5

THE 1970s: FROM BOOM TO RECESSION

Cornwall has always shared in British economic up and down swings, and the 1970s were no exception to this. The early years to 1974 - a British boom period - saw unprecedented growth in population, as well as in housing and the economy. In the three years from mid-1971 to mid-1974 alone, Cornwall experienced a growth of 23,000, entirely through migration. This makes a very striking contrast with the 1952 *Development Plan* forecast of 7000 growth over 22 years! Regrettably there are no sources to tell us how this extremely fast growth was distributed across the age groups, but later information on years with similarly high net migration suggests that overwhelmingly the growth is likely to have been among working age people, together with their children.

The early 1970s boom was overtaken by a moderate recession in the wake of the Yom Kippur War and swingeing oil price increases, and migration fell off from its exceptional level of 8,000 or so per year. However, despite recession, it remained at a level not very different from what had been experienced in the mid and late 1960s, averaging around 4500 each year through to 1979. At the same time, Cornwall followed UK trends with a slump in birth rates in the mid-1970s and this meant that in some years Cornwall was losing over 1000 people by natural change. This was not just a short term phenomenon, as birth numbers remained significantly less that deaths for many years and over the 12 years 1974-86 there was a significant loss amounting to over 10,000 from the excess of deaths over births. Even at the UK level there were some years when England and Wales lost out through natural change, and it is entirely understandable that Cornwall, with its slightly older age structure, tended to suffer a greater relative loss.

From 1979, a further twist of the recessionary screw affected migration severely and over the next two years the net balance dropped right back to around 2500 annually, a rate far lower than was experienced over many years preceding or subsequently. Interestingly, this falling off seems to have pre-dated the worst of the British recession, though in Cornwall there were some major economic problems early on, including the loss of 1000 jobs in the Falmouth ship repair yard in early 1979.

THE 1980s

Population and migration trends after 1981 showed continuing growth as Cornwall shook off the worst effects of the recession. Year on year trends in the 1980s were less easy to explain than in the 1970s: up to 1990 the rate of annual net migration in most years lay between 4200 and 6000, quite close to the mid/late 1960s average of 4500 which was repeated in the mid-1970s. Two exceptional years stood out: the first in 1983-84, the second 1987-88. In each of these net migration leapt up to a level of 8000 or so. The latter year is easier to explain than the former: it was the time when an upsurge in house prices began in the South East, later moving outwards in the well-documented 'ripple effect'. At the start of this phenomenon, owner occupiers in the South East found that their houses, which in the past had typically been worth 25% or so more than those in Cornwall, were now worth 70% more. This created an immediate additional motive for migration, and there is evidence in the statistics of moves from different parts of the country that more people decided to cash in on the value of their property and move to Cornwall at this time.

At the end of the decade the increasing paralysis of the housing market, together with further severe recession which unlike its predecessor 10 years earlier affected the south worse than the north, cut migration still further. Perhaps surprisingly, it seems to have been migration (in both directions) by retired people which suffered most, falling off to a greater extent than among those of working age. After 1991 there was evidence of a modest recovery in migration, but not to the typical level of the 1980s.

OVERVIEW OF MIGRATION TRENDS

Up to 1991 Cornwall's population had been rising without a break for 30 years, going from around 340,000 in 1961 to over 470,000. In as many as 19 of these years (taken from mid-year to mid-year) the rate of net migration has been surprisingly consistent, lying between 3800 and 6000, with an average of 4620 per year. There have been six years with a lower rate, three of them in the early 1960s when net inward migration was only just starting to build up, and the others in times of economic and/or housing recession. In five years the net rate of migration was above average, three of them during the early 1970s boom. The striking feature of this pattern is its consistency over time. Considering that net migration is a balance between two much larger migration flows (in the 1980s, about 17300 each year moving in and 12600 moving out) it is really quite surprising that in two years out of three since 1964 the net balance has remained within such a relatively narrow band.

If in future migration levels are to move away from this well-established pattern, it looks as though there would need to be some major shift, either in the factors which motivate people to move into and out of Cornwall, or in those which enable them to act upon this motivation. It is clear that in the early 1990s the near collapse of the housing market was severely inhibiting migration to Cornwall. If its hoped-for recovery is less than complete, then the rate of gain in Cornwall's population could be less in future than the last 25-30 years, but this is a matter of speculation - perhaps in more senses than one!

It is intriguing to speculate how far public policy might be able to influence such shifts, if the appropriate authorities were to decide through the political process that they should seek to reduce the rate of growth in the population of Cornwall. Can anything really be done to reduce pressures for population growth, and if this were to be attempted, would the side effects on local people be acceptable? The cure might be worse than the disease.

THE DISTRIBUTION OF GROWTH

Two tables summarise the geographical aspects of population changes in Cornwall since 1951.

Table 6.2 shows trends by District, Table 6.3 divides Cornwall by size of settlement. Over the whole 40 years, the population of Cornwall went up by 39%. In general, there was an east to west gradient in terms of growth rate: Penwith District grew least rapidly (+ 18%) with Caradon and Restormel in the lead with growth approaching 50%. Kerrier at 42% was a slight exception to the geographical pattern. If we look instead at the 30 year period during which substantial growth has been occurring, the east-west pattern is rather clearer: Penwith at 23% and Caradon at 55% were the extreme cases, though Kerrier exceeded Carrick's growth rate.

Over time, however, there have been some important shifts in the pattern. During the 1960s, Kerrier started out as the fastest growing District (+17% 1961-71) with Restormel close behind. By the 1970s Kerrier was losing ground as growth rates in east Cornwall picked up. In both decades Penwith had the slowest growth, though unlike the three central Districts it showed faster growth in the 1970s than it had done in the 1960s. Indeed, this continued into the 1980s when Penwith pushed Kerrier into bottom position and nearly equalled Carrick's growth rate. By the 1980s North Cornwall and Caradon had slowed down a little, but they remained the fastest growing Districts, while Restormel was catching up.

What factors lay behind this pattern of growth? Some pointers can be identified. Kerrier's early dominance was probably linked with industrial expansion but in later years recession, industrial restructuring and the collapse of mining, together with a plateauing-out of growth related to RNAS Culdrose caused population growth in Kerrier to tail off quite markedly. At the eastern end of Cornwall, the effect on Caradon of the opening of the Tamar Bridge in 1961 is clear, though its effects were not felt in full strength until the 1970s. More recently, planning authorities have been attempting to slow down the rate of growth in Caradon and this appears to have met with some success.

In the 1960s growth was generally slowest in rural areas and this naturally tended to limit the rate of growth in North Cornwall, the most rural of the Districts. However, from the 1970s onwards, the surge of rural growth together with an increasingly growth-oriented policy on the part of the District Council affected North Cornwall in particular and this has continued to the present time, giving it the fastest percentage growth of any District 1981-91. Restormel with a similar policy in recent years has experienced growth based on the china clay industry around St Austell, as well as on the tourism and residential attractions of Newquay - the latter having emerged as Cornwall's fastest growing town of the 1980s.

Somewhat of a surprise is the relatively modest rate of growth in Carrick: although Falmouth's industrial base was undermined when large numbers of jobs were lost in the shipyard both in the 1960s and again in the 1970s, one might have expected Truro to have more than counter-balanced this as it has become Cornwall's most important commercial centre, experiencing consistently low unemployment (by Cornish standards) and attracting commuters from a wide area. In the light of this, one might have expected Carrick to have shown faster population growth than has actually been the case. Perhaps commuting itself is one of the reasons for Carrick's modest growth rates: Censuses suggest that to an increasing extent people travel from neighbouring Districts to jobs in Truro. Another puzzling feature is why Penwith should have been the only District which has managed to increase its rate of growth in each decade since the 1950s.

THE URBAN TO RURAL SHIFT

As well as looking at those parts of Cornwall which have experienced lesser or greater rates of population growth, it is also interesting to look at how changes have affected urban and rural areas respectively. In 1951 the larger towns (defined as those which in 1981 had a population over 10,000) made up nearly a third of the Cornish population and rural areas just over half. Once general population growth had got moving in the 1960s, these nine 'large' towns took nearly half of the total growth while rural areas received only around a third. However, as time has gone on, this pattern has been reversed. The larger towns' share has fallen steadily to the point where in the 1980s they accounted for only a fifth of Cornwall's growth. At the same time rural areas have increased their share to over half. In smaller towns the trend has been more consistent: they had about 15% of the population in 1951 but have consistently taken 20-25% of total growth.

It has been observed at the UK scale that there has been a movement of population in recent years away from the large urban areas towards smaller towns and rural parts of Britain. This 'counter-urbanisation' is something which affects not just the UK but many countries around the world. The population movement to Cornwall can itself be seen as part of this phenomenon, but the shift from urban towards rural areas **within** Cornwall seems to suggest a parallel shift at the very local level, perhaps reflecting a change in preferences as to the kind of area in which people wish to live. From an urban-dominated growth in the 1960s, Cornwall has moved increasingly to a growth dominated by its rural areas and smaller towns. The larger towns have become less and less attractive, despite the fact that since the late 1970s a stated aim of the Cornwall Structure Plan has been to channel more growth into the towns, or failing this into only those villages which possess a decent range of community facilities.

How are we to interpret this pattern? There are two possible explanations: the first that the shift in population growth away from towns and towards rural areas represents a genuine shift in people's preferences, with more and more seeking escape from the town into the more manageable and sociable communities of villages and countryside. The second is that the urban/rural split is merely a creation of the development industry and a direct reflection of its decisions on where it wants to build houses. Very probably there is some truth in both explanations, but it must be recognised that without an underlying demand, developers could not sustain for very long a policy of building in rural areas. It is also worth reflecting that the shift towards rural growth has occurred despite the likelihood that because of its generally smaller scale, building in rural areas is less likely to offer scale economies to large developers, while at the same time it is more likely to be fraught with planning obstacles. Presumably, therefore, the customer demand to live in rural areas has been strong enough to overcome these inhibiting factors. The conclusion we are virtually forced to come to is that in the 1980s many more people were putting into action a desire to live in rural settlements and areas than was the case in the 1950s and 1960s.

TABLE 6.3.
POPULATION TRENDS IN URBAN AND RURAL AREAS 1951-91

		Large towns	Small towns	Rural areas	COUNTY
1951		106,565	50,790	182,590	339,945
Share of total		.313	.149	.537	1.000
Change 1951-61	%	+3.0	+5.8	-2.4	+0.5
1961		109,745	53,715	178,240	341,700
Share of total		.321	.157	.522	1.000
Change 1961-71	%	+17.0	+16.3	+6.1	+11.2
Share of change					
1971		128,435	62,465	189,200	380,100
Share of total		.338	.164	.498	1.000
Change 1971-81	%	+12.0	+16.0	+10.5	+11.9
Share of change					
1981		143,885	72,480	209,035	425,400
Share of total		.338	.170	.491	1.000
Change 1981-91 (Census provisional)	%	+6.1	+15.4	+11.4	+10.3
Share of change		.199	.255	.546	1.000
1991		152,595	83,660	232,920	469,175
Share of total		.325	.178	.496	1.000
Change 1961-91	Number	+42,850	+29,945	+54,680	+127,475
	%	+39.0	+55.7	+30.7	+37.3
Share of change		.336	.235	.429	1.000
Turnaround 1961	% points	+14.0	+10.5	+8.5	+10.7
Turnaround 1971	% points	-5.0	-0.3	+4.4	+0.7
Turnaround 1981	% points	-5.9	-0.6	+0.9	-1.6

Notes to Table 6.3:

(1) Large towns are those with over 10000 population in 1981, taking the continuous built up area. Towns included are Penzance, Camborne, Redruth (with Pool/Illogan), Falmouth, Truro, Newquay, St Austell, Bodmin, Saltash (nine towns).

(2) Small towns include St Ives, Hayle, Helston, Penryn, St Blazey/Par, Wadebridge, Bude, Launceston, Liskeard, Looe, Callington, Torpoint (12 towns).

(3) Rural areas include population on armed forces bases.

(4) 1991 figures are subject to revision and totals do not agree with those in Table 6.2

AGE STRUCTURE

Table 6.4 shows how the age structure of Cornwall's population has changed since 1951.

TABLE 6.4
AGE STRUCTURE 1951-91

	Population in thousands					Share of total					Change
	1951	1961	1971	1981	1991	1951	1961	1971	1981	1991	1951-91
0-14	70.0	71.9	80.4	82.6	85.3	.204	.211	.212	.195	.180	+ 21.9%
15-29	68.0	58.5	70.4	81.2	88.0	.198	.172	.186	.191	.186	29.4%
30-44	70.6	62.5	62.6	82.3	95.6	.206	.184	.165	.194	.202	35.4%
45-64	87.8	93.9	99.0	98.3	111.8	.256	.276	.261	.232	.236	27.3%
65-74	30.4	33.8	42.9	49.1	50.5	.089	.099	.113	.116	.107	66.1%
75 +	16.5	19.3	24.0	31.0	42.0	.048	.057	.063	.073	..089	154.5%
Total	343.4	340.0	379.2	424.5	473.2	1.000	1.000	1.000	1.000	1.000	+ 37.8%

Against the background of a total population increase of 38% between 1951 and 1990, there have been some important shifts in age structure. The most striking deviation from average was amongst the very elderly (those aged 75 plus) whose numbers went up to over 2.5 times their 1951 level. The 'young elderly' aged 65-74 also increased faster than average, but much less rapidly than the over 75s. In terms of their share of the total, these elderly groups advanced by six points, from 14% to 20%. Children declined as a proportion of the total, but only after 1971.

As peaks or troughs in birth rates pass through the population, there can be quite substantial variations from decade to decade in the trend in any one group and this comes out clearly in the table. It is important to understand that the rapidly growing population over 75 is not primarily the result of migration factors but rather of natural changes in the population, which Cornwall shares with the UK generally. This is borne out by the fact that between 1981 and 1991 the 'young elderly' aged 65-74 fell as a proportion of the total. Since 1961 local growth rates among the elderly have generally been closer to the UK average than is the case among working age population, underlining the fact that there really is no substance to the idea that Cornwall is becoming overrun by elderly migrants. Table 6.5 below attempts to illustrate this rather subtle point, comparing Cornwall with national rates in each decade and then standardising Cornwall's overall relation to the national trend as an index of 100. Where an age group index falls below this figure, it means that the trend in that group in Cornwall has been lower than might have been expected from Cornwall's overall performance. Conversely, an index above 100 shows that growth in that age group has been even faster than might have been expected from Cornwall's overall relationship to the national trend.

In the 1950s Cornwall was doing poorly compared with national trends, lagging behind by six points. Performance was even worse than this in the 15-29 age group especially, but with growth at 65-74 actually faster than nationally. The 1960s saw a more uniform picture and in the 1970s growth tended to favour the younger age groups rather than the elderly (though even here the 15-29s did less well than children and older working age people). The 1980s showed a less clear pattern, with growth a little more biased towards older people - though the young retired did not share in this.

TABLE 6.5

Changes by age group, Cornwall relative to England and Wales

	1951-61	1961-71	1971-81	1981-91
0-4	99	101	104	96
5-14	100	95	106	100
15-29	91	99	99	98
30-44	99	102	104	97
45-64	102	100	96	105
65-74	109	101	95	97
75 +	99	100	94	102
Total:				
actual	.940	1.052	1.138	1.086
standardised	100	100	100	100

From the mid 1970s onward, gross migration movements have been recorded via the National Health Service Central Register (NHSCR). This shows numbers of patients changing their registration from a doctor elsewhere to one in Cornwall, or vice-versa. Correction factors have been applied to the raw statistics to allow as best we can for the biases in this information, reflecting the fact that it comes from a medical source and that some age/sex groups are much more likely to register with GPs than are others. The statistics highlight the large numbers of people involved in migration movements: inward migrants have varied between 23000 and 12000 per year, while numbers moving out have been between 11000 and 15000. These ranges show very clearly that over time inward migration has varied much more than outward migration, though the two flows tend to move in parallel with each other. When conditions nationally encourage movement, this occurs in both directions, but typically numbers of inward migrants increase more than those moving out of Cornwall.

Most of the movement in both directions consists of younger people. Over the 10 years 1981-91 only 20% of those moving into Cornwall were over 55. (This makes a convenient dividing point, above which the great majority of people making long distance moves will be doing so for reasons associated with retirement). Among those moving out the proportion over 55 was even lower at 15%. The net effect was that out of a total migration gain of some 47000, less than 16000 was at ages above 55, the majority of this falling in the 55-64 age group. Over 55s accounted for just 33% of total net migration in the decade, a share very similar to their share of total population in 1981. This further demolishes the notion (if it is still standing!) that migration is responsible for causing imbalances in Cornwall's population by drawing in vast numbers of retired people above and beyond the general population growth.

Even with this very substantial net inflow of population, there was still a net loss of young adults aged 15-24. Over the 10 years Cornwall lost about 2000 from this group, and the rate of loss seems to have become worse towards the late 1980s. It was, however, greatly outweighed by gains of 10000 among children and 17000 in the 25-44 year age group.

The boom in net migration in 1987-88 has already been referred to. This was not just a Cornish phenomenon but nationally too, migration peaked at this time, rising nearly a quarter above its level of 1983-85. Since 1988, the rate of migration movements has slackened nationally and by 1990-91 these were back below their rate in 1983-85. In Cornwall out-migration followed a very similar path, especially if we allow for Cornwall's above average growth rate which over time tends to generate more out-migrants even if people's propensity to move remains the same.

Inward migration to Cornwall has been more volatile, rising much faster than nationally to 1987-88 and since then dropping more than twice as fast as in the country at large. These trends do seem to lend support to the explanation advanced earlier, that differential changes in house prices in the South East and Cornwall, together with the ripple effect of geographical movement in such prices, has influenced levels of migration to Cornwall. A geographical analysis adds further confirmation to this. Between the early 1980s and 1987-88 the South East share of in-migrants to Cornwall rose significantly, falling again by 1990-91. Conversely the rest of the UK beyond the South West lost out in the first period but then increased its share by 1990-91. These shifts occurred generally in a similar direction both for younger and older migrants but they were more pronounced among the older age group, that is those who would be influenced most purely by housing considerations in deciding on their moves to or from Cornwall. Among younger migrants, by contrast, the influence of the housing market is diluted somewhat by other considerations, notably those relating to the availability of jobs.

The tailing off in rates of gross migration since 1988 has been much more marked among the 55 plus age group than among younger migrants (though it has been significant even there). By 1991 retired people were accounting for an even smaller share of migration into and out of Cornwall than had been the case in the mid 1980s. The same kind of patterns seem to have happened nationally as well, with the increase in migration to its 1987-88 peak not all that different as between working age and retired people, but with a much sharper falling off of migration by retired people since 1988. As owner-occupation has increased, it seems likely that house prices will have exerted an ever stronger influence over people's decisions on where to live, and these migration statistics certainly seem to bear out this idea.

MIGRATION AND SOCIAL GROUPS

Cornwall is gaining many people by migration, but what kind of people? Very little information exists on this aspect of population and the way it has changed in recent years. Virtually the only source is the 1981 Census, which gave information on people moving into and out of Cornwall over a 12 month period up to April 1981. As has already been noted, the timing of this Census was unfortunate from a migration point of view, as it fell exactly at the period when migration was running at an unusually low level. It is therefore difficult to say whether its results are typical or otherwise, but the likelihood is that they are distorted.

Inward migrants 1980-81 outnumbered out-migrants by some 2100 persons. Out of this net figure, just about half were people economically active, and these can be classified into social groups. There seems to have been a distinct bias in this net migration towards the skilled and professional social groups, which accounted for about three-quarters of the net balance for all economically active persons. Nearly all of the increase in these higher social groups was accounted for by men rather than women. The semi-skilled and unskilled groups, by contrast, showed virtually no net gain by migration, with a loss among men counterbalanced by a net increase among women. Care is needed in the use of these figures, as people frequently change their occupation at the same time as making a move, and the different range of jobs available in areas of origin and destination (which may itself be a reason for the move) can easily produce such an effect. For what these figures are worth, however, it does appear that Cornwall at this time was more attractive to people in the upper social groups rather than to unskilled workers.

WHY DO PEOPLE MOVE?

The analysis of population changes and of migration thus far has tried to infer from changes over time, by age and by area what factors might have been at work to influence people in deciding to move to or from Cornwall, and conversely not to move. An alternative approach is to ask migrants directly what it was that motivated them to make a move. Various studies in the 1970s and 1980s have used this approach:

(a) Cornwall County Council 1975 migration survey - responses were obtained from 400 in-migrants, plus 200 non-migrants. These were spread across various locations in Cornwall.

(b) The 'Counter-urbanisation' survey by a group of academics, carried out in 1983 in selected wards in mid and west Cornwall[4]. This obtained 1400 responses from in-migrants and 1100 from non-migrants.

(c) The Cornwall County Council 'New Household Survey' of 1986-87, with responses from 3600 households in selected settlements across Cornwall, covering private housing estates built between 1976 and 1986. Out of the respondents, 1650 had moved from outside Cornwall direct into their existing property while a further 400 or so had come into Cornwall since 1976.

(d) A survey of out-migrants in 1987-88 by Dr. K. Dean of the College of St Mark and St John and the present author. This elicited replies from 300 people previously resident in mid and west Cornwall.

These surveys were carried out in slightly different ways and the questions used were not in a standardised form. Nevertheless they do give a valuable insight into the motivations of recent migrants, and to a remarkable degree their results tend to back each other up.

Both the 1975 and 1983 surveys found that a significant proportion of inmigrants were people who had lived in Cornwall previously. At 23%-24% these two surveys confirmed each other's results very closely on this point. We would like to know how this return migrant proportion of nearly a quarter compares with other parts of the UK, but in the absence of such comparisons it does seem to confirm the strength of the draw which Cornwall exerts, not just on the native born Cornish, but also on others who have at some time or other lived within Cornwall. If the proportion of return migrants has remained at this level over the last 10 years, then over 40000 return migrants would have come back into Cornwall in this period, though how many would have remained here is unknown.

This leads into the fascinating - and frequently posed - question of 'How much of Cornwall's population is Cornish?' A natural response to this is another question, which indeed this book does pose: 'How do you define Cornish?'. Does it mean just people born in Cornwall, even if we widen this slightly to include those whose parents are resident in Cornwall but who were unlucky enough to be born in Plymouth? What is the status of people born within Cornwall, but to non-Cornish parents? A possibly much larger group who may or may not be defined as 'Cornish' are those of the diaspora, born of Cornish stock but at one or two generations removed from Cornwall. Cornish Associations worldwide bear witness that Cornish consciousness is not dependent on Cornish birth in a geographical sense. The only piece of statistical evidence which bears on this issue comes from the early post-War period: at the 1951 Census, 69% of people enumerated in Cornwall had been born here - some 230,000 people in all. It is certain that today the proportion must be lower, but by how much remains entirely a matter of speculation, and the government Census Office - despite requests - has unfortunately declined to reinstate the Census question about County of birth or, indeed, to include to new questions which might provide a window on perceptions of Cornish ethnicity.

Going back to the migration motivation surveys, it is interesting to compare the first two in terms of the reasons given by migrants for moving to Cornwall. In interpreting and comparing these results it ghould be noted that the Cornwall County Council survey identified about a quarter of the inward migrants as retired, while the Counter-urbanisation Survey picked up about one-third retired migrants. Table 6.6 overleaf summarises the main reasons given for moving to Cornwall.

Although there are some significant differencese in the percentages quoting particular reasons as important (for example, the greater weight given to climate in the Cornwall County Council study) there is also a considerable degree of unanimity, especially if we look at the ranking, that is the **relative** importance of various factors. The outstanding feature is the prominence of non-economic factors, (what the Counter-urbanisation Study calls 'socio-environmental') in comparison with economic factors such as jobs and wages. In both surveys the most highly ranked economic factor was important for only a third of all migrants, and at best could only reach rank five. Most people moving to Cornwall seem to have been influenced by the environment or Cornwall's draw as the homeland, by climate or the desire to escape city life.

The Cornwall County Council survey explored this in another way, asking migrants to take 10 points and allocate them between economic and non-economic factors. Only a sixth of in-migrants rated economic factors at six or more out of 10, while two-thirds rated them at four or less. The average score for economic factors was only 2.75 out of 10. This confirms the picture of an environmental/social led inward migration, in which economic influences play only a rather secondary part.

TABLE 6.6
REASONS FOR MIGRATION MOVES TO CORNWALL

	CCC 1975		Counter Urbanisation 1983	
	%	Rank	%	Rank
Better/preferred environment	67	1	42	1
Near family/friends	45	4	40	2
Climate	47	3	23	7
Country life/escape rat race	49	2	39	3
Previous holidays	not asked		38	4
Housing	39	5	15	9
Return to homeland	not asked		30	6
Better for children	27	7	21	8
Sport/recreation	26	8	not asked	
Job security	32	6	not asked	
Job prospects	13	11	34	5
Better wages	15	9	3	

The New Household Survey of 1986 looked at migration, but particularly in relation to the choice of the particular property in which the household was surveyed. This slant could possibly have had some influence on the way in which people angwer the question on migration motivation. The survey also differed from the two described above in that there were no tick box answers provided: respondents had to write an open-ended reply in their own words. Undoubtedly this is the reason why the percentages quoting various reasons tend to be a good deal lower than those shown in Table 6.6 above. In descending order, the most important reasons given for moving to Cornwall were as shown in Table 6.7 overleaf.

The striking feature here, especially when looked at in comparison with previous surveys, is the high importance given to job related reasons for moving. At 35% these were a long way ahead of the next most frequently quoted, that is environmental reasons and attractions. We may speculate about the significance of this. Does it mean, for instance, that in a very short period in the early/mid 1980s there was a major shift in people's preferences and motivations for moving to Cornwall? What effects does an open-ended question have as compared with one in tick box form? Do people in filling out an open-ended question take Cornwall's environmental advantages as something understood, which do not need to be spelt out? Were the occupants of the private housing estates surveyed, who are shown by analysis of other questions in the survey to be economically relatively favoured, also more materialistic in terms of the factors which influenced them? These questions remain for discussion, and no doubt at some point for follow-up surveys.

TABLE 6.7
New Household Survey 1986: Reasons for move to Cornwall

	%	Rank
Job related	35	1
Environment	22	2
Retirement	20	3
Near family/friends	16	4
Housing related	16	4
Return to Cornwall	6	6
Escape from the city	5	7
Marriage/family circumstances	5	7

Finally we turn to the motives which lead people to move out of Cornwall. The 1987-88 survey managed to contact a sample of these via the Post Office mail redirection system. The Post Office were supplied with questionnaires which they then sent off to people on their redirection list who they knew had left Cornwall in previous months. The identity of these out-migrants was kept confidential to the Post Office. Clearly the use of a mail redirection system at once introduced a bias to the sample, probably towards the mid and upper social groups, and the survey sought as far as possible to omit armed forces personnel from its scope. It would also generally have failed to pick up individual migrants as distinct from complete households who had left Cornwall. Nevertheless it was a useful start in a previously uncharted field.

The most important reasons for leaving Cornwall, each quoted by about half of all respondents were: better job prospects, taking a better job and living near relations or friends. The last of these was overwhelmingly the most important reason (84%) for out-migration at ages over 55. Among these older migrants the next most important reason (32%) was better shopping facilities. Among working age households the motivations relating to jobs rose to 70% or so, but even in this group closeness to relatives was mentioned as important by a third of out-migrants. A similar proportion said shopping facilities were significant, while over a quarter mentioned leisure facilities and job prospects for their children.

The survey also divided out-migrants between those born in Cornwall and those born elsewhere. For most of the reasons given, there was no great difference between these two groups, though predictably more of those born outside Cornwall were moving to be near their relatives. This group also put a higher importance on shopping and health facilities than did the Cornish-born element. Also predictably, nearly half of the Cornish-born said they would like to return to Cornwall at some time in the future, while only a quarter did not wish to return. These proportions were reversed in the case of those born outside Cornwall.

The results of this survey did not spring any enormous surprises. The importance of job-related moves for working age migrants, and of family ties for the retired age group are what might have been expected. There was, however, also a significant family influence even at working ages, and those with children were substantially influenced by education opportunities and by future job opportunities for their children. The availability of shopping facilities also seems to have had a substantial influence on migrants, being quoted by nearly a third of the total.

REFERENCES

1. The principal sources employed for this Chapter are: Cornwall County Council, *Development Plan: Report of a Survey*, CCC, Truro, 1952; Cornwall County Council, *Report on New Household Survey*, CCC, Truro, 1988; *Census County Reports*, 1951, 1961, 1971, 1981, 1991.

2. Bernard Deacon, 'How Many Went?', *Devon and Cornwall Notes and Queries*, N0.36, 1986; Dudley Baines, *Migration in a Mature Economy: Emigration and Internal Migration in England and Wales, 1861-1900*, Cambridge University Press, Cambridge, 1985.

3. For a socio-economic assessment of the population 'turnaround' phenomenon, see Ronald Perry, Ken Dean, Bryan Brown, *Counterurbanisation: International Case Studies of Socio-economic Change in Rural Areas*, Geo Books, Norwich, 1986.

4. Perry *et al.*, 1986.

CHAPTER 7

HOUSING THE CORNISH

Malcolm Williams

HOMES FOR LOCALS

On the 11th May 1953 Princess Alexandra, the then Princess Royal, officially opened Penzance's largest council estate at Alverton. It was a showpiece estate consisting mainly of three and four bedroomed family houses and though its setting was perhaps leafier than many other Cornish estates of the period, it was nevertheless typical of the kind of ambitious public housing schemes completed throughout Cornwall in the decade before and the decade immediately after the Second World War. By the early 1950s virtually every local authority in Cornwall was participating fully in the government drive towards more public housing to replace the slums, to make good War damage and to provide family housing for the fifties 'baby boom'. In 1952 Cornwall County Council published its own detailed *Development Plan* which aimed to determine new demand for housing and assess the amount of re-development needed in the next 20 years.[1] Much of the projected housebuilding was to replace existing sub-standard stock and indeed the report noted that overcrowding and new households accounted for only approximately one third of total demand between 1949 and 1951.

Cornwall had suffered little bomb damage to its housing stock, although a huge percentage was considered sub-standard. At the 1951 Census 55% of the Cornish population had no access to a bath, and a staggering 33% of households lacked exclusive use of a sink (this compared to 13% in England and Wales), whilst 34% lacked piped water (17% England and Wales).[2] The projections in the *Development Plan* suggested that 4189 units would need to be replaced in the next twenty years. Post-War public housing, in Cornwall at least, was therefore mainly directed to the replacement of sub-standard housing.[3]

A large proportion of the housebuilding was local authority and of this many units were in estates of 50 plus houses.[4] Who lived on the new estates? Most of the larger ones were in or around the urban/industrial towns and villages of the west. The occupants, as elsewhere in Britain, would have been mainly skilled and semi-skilled working-class.[5] At Glasney, between Penryn and

Falmouth, dockers and their families were well represented; at Boscaswell near Pendeen anecdotal evidence suggests that more than three-quarters of the men worked in tin mining or associated trades. The mining and engineering towns of Camborne-Redruth were ringed by council estates, whilst throughout the clay district new estates of 'Cornish Units' were built in nearly every village.

Almost entirely the estates were populated by the indigenous Cornish,[6] but so were row upon row of traditional terraced granite, or slate, houses throughout Cornwall. Many of these were built in the mid-nineteenth century to house the families of miners, clay workers or farm workers. Most were damp, (in the West few had foundations let alone damp courses) and originally none had inside toilets or baths. In the mining towns there had long been a tradition of owner occupation, but nevertheless substantial numbers of traditional houses were rented. The landlords were often 'family' and rarely wealthy. Indeed, rents were low and for many landlords ownership and its responsibilities was a burden not a benefit. Young working-class married couples had two possible routes into housing (other than buying), either renting from a member of the extended family, or from someone their 'da knew'.[7] Alternatively council housing was a realistic option and a couple 'putting their names down' upon their engagement might reasonably expect to be housed within a year or so.[8]

Although unemployment was consistently higher than in much of Britain and wages lower, supply of housing pretty much equalled demand at least until the late 1960s/ early 1970s. Low wages or unemployment did not necessarily imply lack of housing opportunities whilst council houses continued to be built and houses for sale or rent, in the private sector, were accessible to most people. However, in the past twenty years there has been a shift from adequacy to crisis in the supply of houses for locals and the principal agent in the development of this crisis has been demand from outside of Cornwall. Demand has come in various forms, although the period in which the demand has grown has co-incided with the growth in popularity of Cornwall as a holiday destination and an official policy of economic diversification, which though meeting with limited success, has attracted large numbers of people to settle in Cornwall.

Economic diversification has in practice been attempts to attract external investment in the Cornish economy. This has been directly in the form of the 'branch factory',[9] or more indirectly through strategies of population-led growth.[10] Both have had implications for housing demand. Branch factories, though employing mostly local labour, also employed a number of 'key workers' from outside Cornwall, although their numbers alone would have probably made only a small difference to demand for housing. However, a level of in-migration beyond that of a few key workers was considered necessary to the creation of a viable economy. As Payton puts it, the belief of the South West Economic Planning Committee, in the 1960s, was: 'New jobs would attract new workers from outside Cornwall, which would in turn generate further demand for goods and services and thus create more economic activity'.[11]Initially this took the form of the encouragement of 'Overspill' schemes.[12] These did not receive the support of Cornish public opinion and so emphasis, particularly by Cornwall County Council, shifted toward encouraging voluntary settlement. In practice the latter policy has meant firstly an active promotion of Cornwall as an attractive place to set up a business and to live and, secondly, the prior allocation of land for house building. Again, whilst the economic benefits of this strategy have been questioned[13] it was very successful in encouraging settlement in Cornwall. Despite massive out-migration Cornwall's population increased by nearly 127,000 between 1961 and 1991.[14] However, not all of the increase in in-migration is attributable to the strategy of population led growth. Part of the increase must be seen as a direct impact of the growth of tourism.

TOURISM & THE IMPACT OF IN-MIGRATION

In the late 1940s it took, typically, a train between eight and eleven hours to reach Newquay from London or Birmingham. 'Mass tourism' of the kind commonplace twenty or so years later was only just emerging in Cornwall. For most working-class people of the South East, the Midlands and the North the nearest coastal resorts were still the most popular destinations. The tourists who came to Cornwall needed to be both patient to face the journey and a little better-off to afford it. Nevertheless they came in increasing numbers and by the early sixties substantial numbers of migrants had set-up bed and breakfasts in the seaside towns. At this stage, however, the demand was for larger (often Victorian) villas, many of these in fact having been built for the more 'elite' tourism of the Victorian and Edwardian eras.

Whilst initially in-migrants were attracted to tourist centres, later settlers moved directly into smaller towns and villages. When most small settlements under 5000 people suffered population decline, between 1951 and 1961, larger towns were experiencing population growth. Whilst some of this growth would have been attributable to internal migration within Cornwall, in towns such as St Ives, Newquay, Perranporth and Bude the population increase would mostly have been the result of in-migration. From the 1960s in-migration became geographically more dispersed. Between 1961 and 1971 settlements over 500 persons experienced growth, whilst between 1971 and 1981 and 1981 and 1991 virtually all sizes of settlement experienced some population growth.[15]

Many of those who moved to Cornwall did so specifically because, at the very least, an embryonic network of family or friends existed, who had themselves been attracted to settle in Cornwall after family holidays spent there. Perry *et al.*, in a survey of seven parishes in West and Mid Cornwall, found that 40% of their sample cited the rejoining of friends/ relatives as a reason for moving to Cornwall.[16] Networks of family and friends would have been a useful source of knowledge about available housing,[17] able to act as 'intermediaries' between the local vendor and prospective purchasers outside of Cornwall. Some evidence for this comes from a recent ethnographic study of households in the St Austell area.[18] Most of the in-migrants interviewed had family or friends in Cornwall, prior to moving and each cited friends, or relatives, already in Cornwall as sources of information/ help with housing. The respondents, in this study, who did not themselves have 'contacts' prior to moving, subsequently provided help to relatives or friends wishing to move to Cornwall.

By the mid 1980s the tourist industry itself was to a considerable extent dominated by incomers. A study by Exeter University found that 55% of 411 entrepreneurs in Cornish tourist towns in 1986/87 had moved directly from outside.[19] The 'network' extended far beyond the confines of business, catering directly to tourists, into a wider service sector. Perry *et al.* found in their study that nearly half of the heads of household of the in-migrants had moved into jobs in the service sector,[20] whilst in-migrants were also over-represented in Professional and Intermediate socio-economic groups.[21]

The earmarking of generous amounts of land for private housing development by planning authorities encouraged a great deal of speculative building in the 1960s and 1970s. It would seem then, at first sight, that the increase in housing stock must have matched the demand and that access to housing for the Cornish would have been little affected. Newcomers would simply take up the slack, as it were. For a while this was true. Unfortunately, speculative building itself created demand and the availability of inexpensive housing was itself a factor in the encouragement of in-migration during the 1960s and the 1970s. This was recognised by Cornwall County Council in 1979: 'Housing has played an important role in population growth during the 1960s and 1970s. New development in particular has had a considerable effect on the amount of inward migration by creating housing additional to the requirements of the existing population of the county.'[22]

Housing-led growth was not problematic, at least in terms of access to housing for locals, whilst sufficient houses remained available. By 1979 the Cornwall Council Survey, cited above, reported that Cornwall was building 8.4 houses per thousand of population compared to 5.4 houses per thousand in England and Wales. Throughout the sixties and much of the seventies public sector house building continued apace and as a percentage of the total housing stock increased between 1961 and 1981. However, between 1961 and 1971 privately rented accommodation in Cornwall fell from 35% of the total housing stock to 22%. In the next ten years it fell to 10.2%. Landlords owning just one or two unmodernised houses were selling off their properties as elderly tenants died or went into care. These were just the properties that young Cornish couples had hitherto moved into upon marriage and were also what the potential 'up-country' purchaser with limited means could afford. The 'speculative developments' on new estates, though generally offering cheaper properties, did not prove to be an alternative source of housing for locals. In the 1980s research by the Cornwall Planning Department found that 55% of households on the new estates had either moved there directly from outside Cornwall, or had been resident in Cornwall under ten years.[23] Although owner occupation in Cornwall increased dramatically between 1971 and 1981 much of the increase was attributable to in-migrants buying in the private sector.

Ironically, the policy of improving Cornwall's housing stock itself contributed in the long term to the lack of housing for locals. Slum clearance did not always mean demolition. Often the sub-standard properties remained *in-situ* after clearance. Individuals or larger scale speculators snapped up these properties, obtained improvement grants and either sold off the houses, after improvement, or lived there themselves. St Just Urban District Council, for example, rehoused several families from Bojewyan-Keigwin in the 1960s. The houses themselves were never demolished and are today modernised, lived in almost exclusively by families from outside of the locality. George cites the example of a coastal village, where in 1947 a landlord sold off a large number of the houses in the village. Though most occupants, after some difficulty, succeeded in buying their houses many subsequently either could not afford repayment on mortgages, or could not afford the upkeep on their houses and had them condemned. Most were rehoused in council housing and their original homes sold for improvement. Today 'natives' of the village are in a minority. Most of the inhabitants are in- migrants and many of the houses are 'second' or 'holiday' homes.[24]

House prices in Cornwall have generally been lower than much of the rest of Britain, particularly the South East. This has produced an additional benefit for in-migrants. When a house was sold 'up country' and another purchased in Cornwall there was usually a gain to be made. Owner occupiers wishing to move to Cornwall had every incentive to do so and indeed have in vast numbers. At times demand for houses from outsiders has seemed insatiable. Deacon *et al.* reported that in 1987 Millers, Cornwall's largest estate agent, admitted that in the previous twelve months 53% of house buyers were from outside of Cornwall. One year previously the Penzance estate agents Pooleys reported that 80% of properties costing £65,000 or more were purchased by those moving into the area to work or retire.[25] Although in the late 1980s house prices in Cornwall increased dramatically (thus further excluding locals from the housing market), in-migrants from elsewhere were not discouraged because price rises in other areas (notably the South East) were at least as dramatic.

A large percentage of in-migrants came to Cornwall on retirement, or with the intention of retiring in the near future. Indeed Perry *et al.*, in the study cited above, found that an average 34% of settlers were retired.[26] Whether in-migrants settled in Cornwall before or after retirement it appears that the decision to move to Cornwall emanated from Cornwall's role as a holiday destination, or its reputation as 'environmentally attractive'. Perry *et al.* found that 47% of incomers cited environmental preference as their motivation for migration and 49% cited the enjoyment of previous holidays.[27] Thus although (in the same study) better economic prospects were also important reasons for settling in Cornwall, it seems likely that Cornwall's image would have been a significant factor even for those who moved to Cornwall to work in other areas of the economy than tourism. Buck *et al.*, in the ethnographic study cited above, found that all incomers interviewed mentioned environmental factors or enjoyment of past holidays as important reasons for moving to Cornwall.[28]

In summary, we can say a number of interrelated factors led to Cornwall's population growth, but key amongst these was the growth of the popularity of Cornwall as a holiday destination. Whilst not all of those who moved to Cornwall worked in tourism, most were attracted to live in Cornwall either as a result of enjoying holidays in the past, because they considered Cornwall environmentally attractive, or they were moving to join relatives or friends. Although population growth, through in-migration, and to a lesser extent the demand for holiday accommodation, can be cited as important causal factors in Cornwall's housing shortage, mention should be made of other reasons for the decline in rented accommodation.

THE DECLINE OF THE RENTED SECTOR

Alhough it has been suggested above that the decline in private sector rented accommodation was associated with the growth of tourism, central government legislation was undoubtedly a motivating factor for many landlords to move out of long term letting. The 1965 Rent Act gave some security of tenure to tenants of unfurnished accommodation and whereas many landlords in England and Wales converted unfurnished tenancies into furnished ones, in Cornwall (and other holiday areas) there was a growing demand for furnished holiday accommodation. This kind of accommodation then has the potential for lucrative holiday letting in summer and 'winter letting' to those in need of accommodation outside of the holiday season. Winter lets have played a minor, yet important role (as have chalets and caravans) in providing accommodation for those in need for at least some of the year. Most councils have reported rises in those reporting homeless in the second quarter of each year in the past few years.[29]

Although council housing in Cornwall, as elsewhere, steadily declined from a post-War high in the late fifties and early sixties, to 19% in 1981, until the early 1980s it remained a viable housing option for many Cornish families. By 1991 only 12% of the housing stock in Cornwall was local authority. This attrition had occurred partly as a result of government imposed financial constraints on new building, and partly as a result of council house sales. Yet council housing, as George noted, is an important housing alternative in '. . . other areas of low income and housing stress'.[30] Cornwall, it will be argued below, is just such an area. In 1981 19% of the Cornish housing stock was council, compared to 82% of that of the London Borough of Tower Hamlets. 63% and 50% respectively of Glasgow and Nottingham's housing stock was also council. Thus the latter authorities, whilst experiencing similar levels of other forms of poverty to Cornwall, at least had a substantial proportion of their housing stock available for rent.

THOSE THAT STAY & THOSE THAT MOVE IN

It has been argued that housing shortage in Cornwall has been associated with high levels of in-migration in the last twenty years or so. Moreover, it has been intimated that the housing chances of the indigenous Cornish have been poorer than incomers. In order to establish whether this latter assertion is indeed the case we can contrast some aspects of the long term housing careers of those who moved into Cornwall between 1971 and 1981, with those who already lived there between those years.[31]

TABLE 7.1
MIGRATION AND TENURE

Column %	Remained in Cornwall	Not Cornwall 71 Cornwall 81	Cornwall 71 Not Cornwall 81	Outside Cornwall 71 & 81
Tenure 1971				
Owner Occupied	58	65	56	52
Council Rented	23	13	14	31
Private Rented Unfurnished*	16	15	15	14
Private Rented Furnished	3	7	14	3
100% =	2,620	825	438	396,536
Tenure 1981				
Owner Occupied	64	79	62	61
Council Rented	24	7	12	28
Private Rented Unfurnished*	11	9	16	9
Private Rented Furnished	1	4	9	2
100% =	2,625	825	438	396,760

* includes Housing Association properties
Source OPCS Longitudinal Study

Fifty eight per cent of those enumerated in Cornwall in both the Censuses of 1971 and 1981 lived in owner occupation in 1971.[32] This increased to 64% in 1981. However, of those who moved in 65% were already living in owner occupation in 1971 and by 1981, when they were enumerated in Cornwall, this figure stood at 79% (Table 7.1). Although there was an increase in owner occupation for both the indigenous Cornish and incomers between 1971 and 1981, incomers were more likely to live in owner occupation to begin with and enjoyed a greater percentage increase thereafter. Conversely, the Cornish were overepresented in council housing. Why then did the Cornish not become owner occupiers at the same rate as incomers? The answer lies in the weakness of the Cornish economy. Even in times of relative prosperity Cornwall's unemployment rates were high and wages low. Geoffrey Moorhouse, in 1964, wrote of Cornwall's relative poverty in the face of the decline in traditional industries. He pointed out that in Falmouth the unemployment rate is usually the highest in England (sic) and was usually only exceeded by Gunnislake, in East Cornwall![33]

Let us take two examples:

> In 1973 Mr T. earned £14.70 as a farmworker near Gulval, Penzance. His fiancee was unemployed, though able to earn a few pounds here and there in casual farm work. Even at that time rented property was scarce, the council waiting list growing and hopes of a mortgage, even for the cheapest property, an absurd dream. Mr T and his fiancee eventually married and moved to London where he works as a plumber.
>
> In the same year Mr and Mrs L moved from Birmingham to Penzance. They bought a small shop which was managed by Mrs L. Before moving to Cornwall they both worked and earned 'nearly £100 per week'. Additionally they made 'several thousand' profit on the sale of their house in Birmingham. Mr L quickly found a job in a local factory, where the works manager was a fellow 'Brummie'.[34]

Things have not improved for the Cornish. In 1990 George found that the mismatch between mortgage level (the average mortgage obtainable) and house prices was higher in Cornwall than anywhere else in the UK,[35] whilst Lambert *et al.* reported in 1991 that '. . .there are few properties available for less than £40,000 (in North Cornwall)'.[36] In July 1991 90% of housing applicants to North Cornwall District Council earned less than £10,000 per year, 63% had less than £6,000 and 36% relied solely on benefits. For most of these a mortgage is just as much a dream as Mr T's in 1973!

There have been few periods since the 1960s, when Moorehouse was writing, when Cornwall did not have some of the highest unemployment in Britain, or the lowest wages. Table 7.2 compares wage levels in Cornwall with Britain as a whole.

TABLE 7.2
INCOME

	Gross Weekly Earnings	
	Males	Females
Cornwall	219.2	155.4
South West	253.3	169.9
England	272.9	184.4

Source Regional Trends 25: Table 2.7

Gross weekly earnings are an average for all earners in Cornwall and given that the Cornish are underepresented in the (usually) better paid professional or management sectors, the average wage for the Cornish (if it could be calculated) would probably be considerably lower. Table 7.3 compares unemployment levels with those of the South West region. In 1991 Cornwall's unemployment was nearly twice that of its 'region' and growing faster. Though these data cannot be cross-tabulated with migration, other analyses (not shown here) using longitudinal census data show that incomers are less likely to be unemployed and more likely to live in households containing more than one wage earner.

TABLE 7.3
UNEMPLOYMENT *

	Nov 1991	March 1991	Jan 1990	Jan 1987	Oct 1985	Oct 1982
Cornwall	15.2	10.3	7.7	20.0	18.2	16.1
South West (1)	9.6	9.8	4.4	12.0	12.1	11.2

(1) Includes Cornwall
Sources Regional Trends 25 & Employment Gazette May & December 1991.
* Unemployed as a percentage of employees in employment and the unemployed.

Those who left Cornwall, or who remained in Cornwall, were more likely to have no wage earners in the family than those who moved in. Table 7.4 shows that 9.5% of those who migrated out of Cornwall between 1971 and 1981 had no earners in the household in 1971, and 50% had only one earner. 9.4% of those who remained in Cornwall had only one earner and again nearly 50% had only one earner. This compares to 6.5% and 40% respectively for England and Wales (in 1971) and 5.3% and 42.5% for those who moved into Cornwall between those years. If, in the case of incomers, households consisting wholly of retired persons were removed from the calculation then clearly the figure of 5.3% would be lower still. Of those who left Cornwall very few were retired.

TABLE 7.4
EARNERS IN THE HOUSEHOLD 1971

Column %

Number of earners in household 1971	Remained in Cornwall 81	Not Cornwall 71, Cornwall 81	Cornwall 71 Not Cornwall	Outside Cornwall 71 & 81
none	9.5	5.3	9.4	6.5
one	45.8	42.5	50.2	39.9
two	29.5	36.5	28.1	34.4
three	9.4	9.7	5.9	11.8
four or more	3.8	3.9	1.6	1.5
Total	2,625	825	438	396,760

Sources: Census, 1981; Municipal Yearbook, 1992.

In Britain, since the Second World War, housing provision has been increasingly dominated by the market. By 1991 owner occupation accounted for nearly 75% of all tenures in England and Wales (74% in Cornwall). This trend has been parallelled by a growing tendency for the rented sector, both public and private, to be occupied by the very poorest groups.[37] An individual's economic circumstances are an important indicator of their ability to compete in the housing market and their position in the housing market can determine their overall wealth and that of the next generation in their family. We have already seen that those seeking accommodation from councils are likely to lack the financial ability to purchase. Indeed, with unemployment and low wages increasingly common through two or more generations of families in Cornwall a further element in housing chances is intergenerational poverty. Those whose parents own their own home may be fortunate enough to inherit property, but this is likely to be late in their housing 'career' and many of those in greatest housing need are also the ones least likely to inherit. Nevertheless property inheritance is inevitably an important factor in determining who will be housed in the private sector in the future. A number of studies over the past twenty years has established that the wealth gap between houseowners and those with few assets of any kind (and not including a house) has grown.[38] Whilst owner occupation in Cornwall is close to the national average it remains, as elsewhere, that those who are poorest are likely to be in the rented sector. The private rented sector is virtually non-existent, the housing association sector is growing, though still accounting for only 0.7% of housing stock in 1990.[39] Furthermore, it has been criticised for catering for mainly for those retiring to Cornwall,[40] whilst council housing has shrunk dramatically in the past decade (Table 7.5). If, as seems possible, many of the indigenous Cornish are becoming 'ghettoised' in council housing then the housing situation for the next generation may be even worse. With little opportunity to move into the private sector and hardly any chance of obtaining public housing these people will increasingly be forced to leave Cornwall, live with others, or take to the streets.

TABLE 7.5
COUNCIL HOUSING IN CORNWALL

	Number of Units by year			Change 1981-91
District	1981	1986	1991	
Caradon	4676	4590	4504	-172
Carrick	5672	5173	6000	+238
Restormel	4850	4465	4057	-793
North Cornwall	4884	4493	4150	-734
Penwith	4058	4019	4109	+51
Kerrier	4382	4164	4057	-325
			Cornwall 1981-91	-1735

Sources: Census, 1981; Municipal Yearbook, 1992.

Additional evidence of better economic and housing opportunities for those who move in can be found by comparing the social class of in-migrants with out-migrants and those who have lived in Cornwall long-term. A person's social class has been shown to be a good indicator of their housing chances.[41] Those lacking housing opportunity and those living in substandard housing are more likely to be members of manual classes. Conversely, those in non-manual classes, and particularly those in professional/managerial or intermediate classes are more likely to enjoy the best housing opportunities. Table 7.6 shows the social class, in 1971, of those moving into Cornwall, those who remained and those who left. Those who remained or left are less likely to belong to managerial/professional or intermediate classes than those who moved in and anecodotal evidence suggesting that most professional and administrative posts are filled by those who have settled in Cornwall is widespread. Indeed 'unfair competition' for jobs was mentioned by several respondents in the study by Buck *et al.*.[42] We have already seen that 'entrepreneurs' are more likely to be recent settlers and that the latter are overepresented in owner occupation.

The Longitudinal Study additionally provides information on the social class of the fathers of LS members. Table 7.7 uses the Goldthorpe classification of Fathers' social class.

TABLE 7.6
Social Class* of In-migrants, Out-migrants and Long-term Residents

Class 1971	Remained in Cornwall	Not Cornwall 71, Cornwall	Cornwall 71 Not Cornwall	Outside Cornwall
Managerial/ Professional	2.6	8.6	4.8	4.9
Intermediate	23.5	29.5	26.7	17.9
Skilled non manual	9.6	12.7	13.6	10.8
Skilled manual	31.0	23.6	21.7	35.5
Semi-skilled manual	16.3	13.2	11.4	16.1
Unskilled	5.6	3.0	3.8	6.3
No class	11.2	9.3	18.1	8.5
Total	515	146	515	146

* See SSRU, (1990) for detailed soicial class definitions
Social Class 1971 is given here because it is important to determine the class of migrants (and by implication their socio-economic standing prior to migration. Analyses of social class for both 1971 and 1981 shows that those who left Cornwall were more likely to move from manual classes to non-manual classes than those who remained.

This shows that those long-terms residents in Cornwall are more likely to come from families where the father was a manual worker, and conversely those moving into Cornwall were less likely to have fathers from manual classes and more likely to have fathers from professional or self-employed classes. Assuming an association between economic position and social class, incomers are more likely to come from better off families. These 'better off' settlers, themselves the children of professionals, functionaries, or entrepreneurs, are likely to be in a position to pass on property to their own sons and daughters. When this happens many of the new generation will be some way along their housing careers and the inheritance of parental property would be a welcome source of additional capital or a holiday home.

Further generations are thus able to benefit both from the use value and exchange value of the property. The sons and daughters of council house tenants are less likely and less able to buy property and consequently unable to pass on such an asset to a further generation who are not only unable to enjoy the use value of property but also its value as a commodity for sale or rent.[43]

TABLE 7.7
Father's Goldthorpe Class 1981 Long-term Residents & In-migrants Cornwall

	Remained in Cornwall	Not Cornwall 71, Cornwall
Father's Class		
Hi Grade Professionals/Managers etc	3	13
Lo Grade Professionals/Managers etc	11	20
Non manual employees in admin/commerce	5	8
Personal service workers	1	1
Small proprietors	18	21
Farmers/smallholders	10	5
Lo Grade technicians/supervisors	7	3
Skilled manual	15	13
Semi/unskilled manual	23	14
Agricultural workers	3	1
Total	515	146

The Goldthorpe classification of father's occupation is only for a small percentage of the population, See SSRU, 1990 p283 and Goldthorpe, J H and Hope, K (1974)

If this pattern is indeed becoming established in Cornwall then we are witnessing the establishment of two housing 'classes'. The first housing class are first generation in-migrants, or the sons and daughters of in-migrants. The class is characterised by over-representation in owner occupation and sometimes individual ownership of more than one property. The second class is virtually synonymous with the indigenous Cornish population and is characterised by over-representation, through several generations, in council or other rented housing. Many of its number migrate out of Cornwall for housing-related reasons whilst others may remain and become part of a 'fringe' housing market unable to obtain public housing and reliant on 'winter lets', caravans, chalets or living in multiple occupation with other households.

HOMELESSNESS & HIDDEN HOMELESSNESS

It is only in recent years homelessness, or more correctly 'rooflessness' has become visible in Cornwall. Cornish towns, for the first time in the 1990s, began to have small colonies of mainly younger people sleeping rough. Indeed in April 1993 the BBC TV programme Spotlight South West reported that British Rail was to close off Penzance railway station at night in order to prevent rough sleepers sheltering there,[44] a measure normally associated with the larger London terminals. 'Shelter', in 1989, reported that the proportion of homelessness in Cornwall was second only to that of London.[45] Yet despite the growth in visible homelessness in Cornwall the numbers per thousand of the population reporting homeless to local authorities approximate those of neighbouring counties in South West England.[46] This discrepancy is attributable to the conflation of the concept of 'homelessness' with that of 'rooflessness'. Effectively, under the provisions of the 1977 Housing (Homeless Persons) Act and subsequent legislation, for a person to be homeless they are in effect 'roofless', in other words without access to any form of secure accommodation. The 1985 Housing Act stipulates that only the 'priority homeless' can be accepted by councils. A Cornwall Social Services Report in 1991 points out that:

> . . . on average only about half of homeless enquiries were accepted as such. This suggests up to 50% of all homeless enquiries to District Councils in Cornwall could be from such people as single homeless, couples with no dependents and/or people who are sharing over-crowded, possibly sub-standard accommodation.[47]

Bramley has argued that homelessness is more accurately seen as a continuum from a total lack of shelter to circumstances where households are 'hidden' or lack access to their own secure and minimally adequate housing space.[48] Cornwall is very much 'poorer' than neighbouring counties in South West England yet exhibits a level of visible homelessness (or rooflessness) not appreciably different to those counties and certainly not a level commensurate with an area of such high unemployment, low wages, high house prices and a very small rented sector. From this it has been argued that much of Cornwall's housing problem is 'hidden' or is dissipated through outward migration.[49] Indeed, there is some suggestion that homelessness is being 'absorbed' within existing household structures. Although statistical evidence for this is very hard to find certain types of household contain a greater 'potential' (simply because of their size and heterogeneity) for splitting into other households. These 'complex type' households can be represented through Longitudinal Study data and in 1981 accounted for 12% of all households in Cornwall. This compares to 8.5% in England and Wales.[50]

Two recent studies, those of Lambert *et al.* in North Cornwall and Buck *et al.* in the St Austell area, do, however, suggest that the social structure of the Cornish population serves to hide homelessness. Lambert reports one respondent as saying: 'If the average Cornish family rejected the notion of the extended family, then not only would North Cornwall District Council be faced with a major housing crisis, but so would Cornwall County Council and Whitehall'.[51] Nearly all of those interviewed in the St Austell study recounted living, at some time, with parents or in-laws, or having relatives to live with them. Alhough those living in 'complex type' households appeared do so as a result of constraining factors, not all expressed a desire for alternative accommodation. Such a desire may not even be manifest in those who might objectively be described as suffering hidden homelessness and does indicate the subjective nature of housing situations.

Young people are often frustrated in their efforts to set up home independently, and continue to live in the parental home, although data on their number are unavailable. This group, and adults under 30, are, however, the most likely to be homeless, or roofless, simply because they are at the beginning of their 'housing career'. Lennon suggests that up to 50% of those reporting homeless are couples with children, single people and single parent families.[52] Most of those who are more visibly homeless have been in Cornwall at least some while. The St Petroc's Society, a voluntary organisation offering hostel accommodation in Truro and Newquay, reported that in 1989 80% of those who sought accommodation at their Truro hostel and 73% who sought accommodation at Newquay, 'came from Cornwall'. Alhough it is hard to establish precise trends, it does seem likely that whilst Cornish households and migration out of Cornwall continue to absorb or dissipate homelessness the problem is becoming more 'visible' as housing options (particularly for young people) become ever more limited.

MIGRATION & THE CORNISH

The Cornish have long had the reputation of migrating, often to distant parts of the world. The past thirty years have, however, as Peter Mitchell makes clear in Chapter 6, been unusual in that the numbers leaving have been more than matched by those moving in. Between 1891 and 1939 the population of Cornwall, recorded at the Census, showed a fall from 322,600 to 310,000. Although there was an increase between 1939 and 1951 there was another fall between 1951 and 1961. However, between 1961 and 1991 Cornwall's population has increased by over a third from 343300 to 470200.[53] Since the 1950s there has been a falling birthrate in Cornwall, as elsewhere, and indeed the 1991 Census records that deaths exceeded births in the past ten years.

The massive increase in population has not then come about as a result of a 'baby boom', nor has it resulted from any large reduction in outward migration - indeed fifteen per cent of those enumerated in Cornwall in the 1971 Census had moved away by 1981.[54] Longitudinal data relating to 1991 is not yet available but it can be seen from Table 7.8 that whilst the Cornish continued to leave more than twice their number moved in. The net increase in population has served to disguise a continued outward migration from Cornwall.

TABLE 7.8
Inward and Outward Migration Cornwall 1971-1981

	Thousands
Enumerated in Cornwall 1971 & 1981: (remained in Cornwall)	262.5
Enumerated in Cornwall 1971 not 1981: (migrated out)	43
Enumerated in Cornwall 1981 not 1971: (migrated in)	82.5
Total	388

Notes
1 Figures are based upon the 1% sample of census data in the Longitudinal Study. They have been multiplied by 100. This data is unclustered and the LS has a better than 92% accuracy to census data.
2 Moves between census years are not ecorded here. Thus if someone moved out of Cornwall in 1972 and moved back in 1979, but were enumerated in Cornwall in 1971 and 1981, their move is not recorded here.
3 The institutional population is excluded.

More recent data on a smaller scale offers evidence of expectations amongst younger people about their prospects in Cornwall. In a survey of young people in Launceston in 1991, more than half either expected or hoped to move away in search of better opportunities.[55] Deacon *et al.* identified a number of factors behind individual decisions to leave Cornwall.[56] Besides housing these include education and career moves. The survey in Launceston cited above indicated that young people left for both work and housing reasons, yet work, low pay and unemployment are difficult to separate as factors in any motivation to leave. However, in Cornwall low pay or unemployment appear to be closely associated with lack of housing. Indeed, Longitudinal Study data indicates those who left Cornwall between 1971 and 1981 were more likely to have one or more members of the household seeking work, more likely to be unemployed themselves and more likely to be living in overcrowded housing conditions than those who lived in Cornwall in both years, or those who had moved in. A further indicator of lack of available housing can be found in marital status. Of those who were single in 1971 those who left Cornwall were very much more likely to marry than those who remained.[57] Availability of housing is often a crucial factor in the decision to marry.

It would be a mistake, however, to argue that those with the very worst housing chances migrated. Whilst housing and economic opportunity are often motivating factors in any decision to leave they are sufficient not necessary conditions. Many leave for educational opportunities and many stay despite poor housing chances. We can conclude only three things from migration statistics. Firstly, that outward migration has been hidden in net population figures, secondly that leaving is often associated with factors prejudicial to good housing chances, and thirdly Cornwall's present housing crisis would be very much worse had there not been substantial outward migration.

HOUSING AVAILABILITY & HOLIDAY HOMES

The economic value of housing, beyond its use value, is often cited as an important factor in the housing crisis in Cornwall. Besides the potential of larger dwellings for bed and breakfast use, many dwellings have become second or holiday homes.[58] It is notoriously difficult to estimate their numbers, although Cornwall County Council has estimated that 6.4% of household spaces are holiday homes.[59] However, this figure is now rather old (1979), yet if accurate would represent the highest figure in the UK. The same report concedes that in many villages holiday homes constituted 30% of the housing stock and in some over 50%. Griffiths, in 1989, found that '. . . these forms of residence are very significant in some areas, and even in places not usually regarded as on the tourist trail (they) played a small part in the housing market'.[60] In the twelve villages surveyed by Griffiths a third of holiday home owners that were identified, were found to come from London or the South East.

Holiday homes and second homes are big business. Most coastal towns now have at least one agency solely given over to holiday lets, whilst smaller houses coming onto the market are promoted as suitable for holiday letting. Unsurprisingly, this has caused major resentment in the communities affected. Griffiths found that this resentment was as a result of the consequences of holiday homes on the local housing market and that if sufficient housing was available at a reasonable price to meet the indigenous requirement then this problem would be transformed. The evidence is that holiday or second homes add to the pressures on the housing stock particularly in rural areas and doubtless they have generated resentment throughout Cornwall, yet the problem should be viewed in the wider context of who is able to compete in the housing market. If holiday/ second homes do represent up to ten per cent of stock this would nevertheless constitute a small proportion of the housing stock that is in the ownership of those who have moved to Cornwall. Even if in the unlikely event all of the existing holiday homes were to be put on the market tomorrow this would not help the unemployed or those on low wages. What is important is the availability of housing stock to those in housing need, and whether any particular house is a holiday home or bought by an in-migrant for permanent use is not really important whilst local people are less able to compete for its purchase. Perhaps then, with the exception of severe local effects on village communities, holiday homes in Cornwall can perhaps best be viewed as the salt in the wound.

RESPONSES TO THE CRISIS

With wages then consistently lower than the British average and unemployment as high, or higher, than the North of England, owner occupation has been increasingly beyond the reach of more and more indigenous Cornish people. Whilst there was an adequate supply of rented, either public or private housing, this was a less serious problem than of late. We have seen that the stock of council housing has dramatically reduced through the 1980s without any concomitant rise in the provision of alternative public housing, such as that provided by housing associations. At the same time private rented stock has become all but unavailable. Housing possibilities for many of those who remain in Cornwall are bleak indeed and it would appear from the foregoing that a common solution to individual housing crisis is simply to leave Cornwall.

Little officially-sponsored research has been either commissioned or conducted. Indeed, the two most recent studies conducted in North Cornwall and in twelve villages across Cornwall (both cited above) were initiated by the Rural Development Commission, while extensive local housing needs surveys have been conducted on an ad hoc parish-by-parish basis by the Cornwall Rural Community Council. Alhough councils are aware of numbers reporting homeless, information on hidden homelessness is non existent, as is the extent to which lack of housing motivates a move from Cornwall, while there are no firm statistics forthe numbers of holiday homes. For the full extent of Cornwall's lack of available housing to be known there must be some estimation and appreciation of hidden homelessness. What is perhaps more worrying is the apparent official indifference to outward migration. The view appears to be (although this is not articulated officially) that whilst Cornwall's population continues to grow there is no problem in this respect.

The housbuilding record of Cornish district councils was close to the average for 'rural' districts until the mid-1980s and, as we have seen, in the decades immediately after the War a fairly ambitious public housing programme was pursued. However, the various tranches of government legislation which have served to restrict council house building have had a dramatic effect. Since 1981, as Table 7.6 shows, only Penwith and Carrick have managed to increase their stock of houses. Some councils have initiated 'building for sale' schemes for first time local buyers. Caradon District Council, for example, has introduced a Homes for Locals policy: '. . .it indicates 75 villages where up to 10 affordable local needs dwellings could be provided'.[61]

Councils have succeeded in establishing nomination rights (in some cases of 50%) to Housing Association properties and the study by Lambert *et al.* found a '. . . supportive stance toward local housing associations, especially through the release of council owned land for new schemes'.[62] Some building for local needs has also arisen out of the Parish Surveys initiated by the Cornwall Rural Community Council. Yet such initiatives, whilst commendable, go only a small distance to addressing the problem.

The Lambert report cites further research conducted amongst 'professionals' in North Cornwall. Respondents included councillors of whom only one considered the housing problems of young people to be a councillor's concern at all! Anecdotal evidence suggests this kind of view to be widespread and an attitude of 'blaming the victim' is not uncommon. Indeed, there seems to be near universal accord amongst official bodies that housing need can and should be met by increasing the numbers of properties built for sale. And yet Cornwall County Council has for some years recognised that housing need exists and that competition from outside Cornwall is an obstacle in meeting it. The *Structure Plan* of 1980 states the objective of providing accommodation for those on low incomes and the unemployed and it stresses the importance of reducing problems created by families moving to Cornwall.[63] Despite this the Council has been criticised for accepting the market centred ethos of central government housing policy when formulating its own structure plan in the late 1980s. Warnings from a number of quarters that such housing policies, which essentially depend on a large increase in development for sale, would be environmentally disastrous and do little to ease local housing demand have mostly been disregarded.[64]

Nevertheless there is some light in all of this. Although not wholly accepted by central government the *Structure Plan Alteration* did contain a local needs policy which allowed for planning permission to be granted exceptionally to meet local housing need in rural areas. However, such developments would necessarily be small scale and, although they might possibly meet some localised rural housing need, they would do little to alleviate what is essentially an urban problem.

Since the early 1980s the government's market-led housing policy has envisaged a growing private sector demand for housing that would be met by local authorities easing planning restrictions on new development. Thus much of the housing provision in the *Structure Plan* is for houses to be sold on the open market. The supply side argument is that more houses on the market means demand is more easily satisfied and the resulting lower prices extend home ownership. Even if this argument worked in other areas, it does not work in Cornwall where there is a large 'gap' between mortgage levels available and house prices. Unfortunately, cheaper houses widen the market outside of Cornwall for Cornish properties. Those who otherwise might not have bought in Cornwall are then able to do so.

For this policy to work Deacon *et al.* maintain that 100-150,000 new properties would be needed.[65] Indeed, this amount of new properties would probably satisfy all external demand and reduce prices to a level that those who were in the position to buy (even in Cornwall) could now do so. Sadly, of course, those who are unemployed, and particularly school leavers would not be eligible. In some towns this amounts to nearly half the adult population. A 'trickle down effect' for these latter groups would have to be in the form of those who could afford to buy in the private sector vacating public housing for owner occupation. There is very little evidence from other areas of Britain, where low house prices are the norm, of this happening. Indeed, Hamnett and others have argued that there is a ceiling to the numbers in public housing who will become owner occupiers and instead of a gradual, but inexorable, shift to owner occupation tenures will become polarised with the very poorest remaining in public housing however low house prices in the private sector become.[66]

In recent years the government has made much of the need to make private sector renting easier for both landlord and tenant and, despite the lack of success of various initiatives aimed at bringing this about, it remains government policy.[67] Whatever happens elsewhere this is not a policy likely to yield benefits in Cornwall. Firstly, in holiday areas landlords can make a much more lucrative living renting out houses to summer visitors and the same houses as winter lets to locals! Secondly, in areas where holiday cottages are less common a housing market that was buoyant until quite recently has made renting hardly worthwhile.

The Lambert report lists a number of ad hoc initiatives aimed at alleviating the crisis in North Cornwall. These have ranged from a Housing Corporation allocation of £3.14 million over the next three years and sufficient to build 20 units per year, to the leasing of vacant Ministry of Defence properties. Andrew George has suggested a number of imaginative initiatives which involve the securing of development land or property at a reasonable price.[68] These include arrangements by which landowners are encouraged to donate small pieces of land to Housing Associations or Parish Councils or to sell the land with covenant preventing unsuitable development. George, and others, have also suggested a wider use Section 52 (of the Town and Country Planning Act).

RESTRICTING DEVELOPMENT TO LOCAL NEEDS

Deacon, George and Perry have discussed a number of wide ranging initiatives.[69] Several of these, such as stricter controls on developments, higher building densities or 'locals only' policies, though likely to be quite effective, suffer from the problem of vulnerability to being overruled from Westminster - even if local authorities could be convinced of their worth. Other suggestions they make, such as the creation of a two-tier housing market allowing locals to compete separately, or a tax on incoming purchasers, are without doubt imaginative and would go a long way to improving the housing chances of Cornish people. Unfortunately, at present such initiatives face insurmountable obstacles. Firstly, to attempt to implement such policies would be to encounter the same generic problem of Westminster interference - for all its claims to separate identity, Cornwall is not a Jersey or a Guernsey and - just like any other county -can only operate within the limits prescribed by the central government. Secondly, many of these potential solutions are aimed at increasing the local share of owner occupation, but those people on the very lowest incomes, or the unemployed, would still not be able to compete even in this more equitable market and would be reliant on public or private sector renting. Finally, it is a 'chicken and egg' situation. For many years a variety of organisations in Cornwall have argued for a greater level of local self-determination in order to tackle problems such as lack of housing.[70] In the absence of solutions from outside of Cornwall, they maintain, initiatives must come from the inside. Yet these initiatives cannot come from inside Cornwall without the legislative powers to enable them, and such powers are hardly likely to be granted by a central government all too willing to overturn Section 52 agreements!

The housing situation in Cornwall is unusual in Britain with parallels only in North Wales and the Lake District. Rarely is an area afflicted by both unemployment/low wages and high house prices. It is not a convergence of these factors that has produced the current housing crisis in Cornwall, rather it is the emergence of the second as a problem relative to the first. In other words, it is low incomes that make house prices appear high in Cornwall - for those outside Cornwall house prices are not especially high. It is for this reason that a housing-led approach to the crisis will only ever be a palliative. An increase in availability of houses for sale will undoubtedly benefit some, but will do nothing for those in the direst need. An increase in public housing (either council or housing association) will simply legitimate and intensify the 'housing class' divide with the indigenous Cornish population increasingly concentrated in public housing and in-migrants further strengthening their hold on the private sector.

Housing problems are a symptom of individual and community economic malaise. In this the Cornish and Cornwall are no exception. Economic policies based on population-led growth and the service sector as a principle employer, have had unfortunate consequences for housing in Cornwall. The problem of housing need alone suggests the need for planners to consider alternative economic strategies.

REFERENCES

1. Cornwall County Council, *Development Plan - Report of Survey*, Truro, 1952.
2. OPCS, *Census, 1951 County Report - Cornwall*, HMSO, London, 1952.
3. G.Barrington, in 1970, reports 'As regards the amount of accommodation for residents, the study area (West Cornwall) is rather better served than England and Wales and the South West Region: As regards quality however the housing stock of the study area is inferior to national and regional standards'. G. Barrington, *West Cornwall Study*, Cornwall County Council, Truro, 1970.
4. The *Development Plan* of 1952 reports 3494 completions between 1949-51.
5. S.Merrett, *State Housing in Britain*, Routledge & Kegan Paul, London, 1979.
6. In the immediate post War years and probably for some time after, the majority of the

population of Cornwall would have been Cornish - however defined. The 1952 Census records that 68.9% of those enumerated in Cornwall were born there and a further 6.7% were born in Devon. The usage of the term 'Cornish' in this Chapter then has a statistical basis. The Cornish are defined as those who were born in Cornwall or had lived there long enough to share the statistical likelihood of having the same housing characteristics. Thus in linked longitudinal comparisons of 1971 and 1981 census data those who were enumerated in Cornwall in both years are taken to be the Cornish. Inevitably some will not have been born in Cornwall or lived there much before 1971 and some of those who moved into Cornwall between those years will in fact be returned exiles.

7. Evidence from middle-aged and older people suggests that a 'cousin' network (of close to quite distant relatives) was very important in the resolution of housing need up until fairly recently. Help within the closer family continues to be important, but dissipation of communities (amongst other factors) makes this less common now. These findings are tentative and from a pilot study. See: M.Buck, L.Bryant and M.Williams, *Housing and Households in Cornwall - A Pilot Study of Cornish Families*, University of Plymouth, Occasional Papers in Social Science, Plymouth, 1993.
8. Anecdotal evidence for this practice is widespread, though little documentation concerning allocation policies is available from pre 1974 Cornish local authorities. Indeed the topic is a sensitive one even today.
9. R.Perry, K.Dean and B.Brown, *Counterurbanisation - Case Studies of Urban to Rural Movement*, Geo Books, Norwich, 1986.
10. Perry, 1986, pp.66-79.
11. P.Payton, *The Making of Modern Cornwall*, Dyllansow Truran, Redruth, 1992, p.182.
12. Payton, 1992.
13. See B.Deacon, A.George and R.Perry, *Cornwall at the Crossroads*, CoSERG, Redruth, 1988.
14. OPCS, *1991 Census - County Monitor, Cornwall and the Isles of Scilly*, Office of Population Census and Survey, Government Statistical Service, London, 1992.
15. OPCS, *County Reports*, Office of Population Census and Survey, Government Statistical Service, HMSO, London, 1971, 1981.
16. Perry *et al.*, 1986, p.93.
17. Buck *et al.*, 1993, pp.47-48.
18. Buck *et al.*, 1993, pp.47-48.
19. Cited in Deacon *et al.*, 1988.
20. Perry *et al.*, 1986, pp.113-114. This category is described as Other Services (including tourism).
21. Perry *et al.*, 1986.
22. Cornwall County Council, *County Structure Plan - Report of Survey*, Truro, 1979.
23. Report by Mrs E.J.Vincent, Chair of Cornwall County Council Planning and Economic Development Committee, to *Meeting Local Housing Need*, Conference organised by Cornwall Rural Community Council (CRCC), Truro, 9th November 1990.
24. A.George, *Homes for Locals in Cornwall - Chyow rag Genesygyon ys Kernow*, Cornwall Rural Community Council, Truro, 1987.
25. Deacon, George, Perry, 1988.
26. Perry *et al.*, 1986, p.90.
27. Perry *et al.*, 1986, p.93.
28. Buck *et al.*, 1993.
29. Department of the Environment, *Local Housing Statistics*, DoE, London, 1988, 1989.
30. A.George, reporting to the CRCC Conference cited above.
31. This data is taken from analyses in the OPCS Longitudinal Study (LS). The LS is a 1% linked sample of census records from 1971 and 1981. In 1993 data from the 1991 Census will be added thus allowing longitudinal analysis of records from time points over 30 years. The data is unclustered and has a better than 92% accuracy with Census data. See: SSRU, *OPCS Longitudinal Study User Manual*, Social Statistics Research Unit, City University, London, 1990.
32. Longitudinal Study members (See above).
33. G.Moorhouse, *The Other England*, Penguin, Harmondsworth, 1964.

34. M.Williams, *Housing Deprivation in Urban and Rural Areas*, unpublished manuscript, Polytechnic of North London, 1989. Quotes are taken from housing case histories based on six depth interviews. These consisted of interviews with:
    2 out migrants
    2 in migrants
    2 long-term residents
35. A.George, *Review of the Current Situation in Cornwall and the Isles of Scilly*, Report to the Meeting Housing Need Conference, 1990.
36. C.Lambert, S.Jeffers, P.Burton, G.Bramley, *Homelessness in Rural Areas - A report on research for the Rural Development Commission by the School for Advanced Urban Studies, University of Bristol*, Rural Development Commission, Salisbury, 1992.
37. See for example: J.Morris, M.Winn, *Housing and Social Inequality*, Hilary Shipman, London, 1990.
38. A.Murie, *Housing Inequality and Deprivation*, Heinemann, London, 1983.
39. George, 1990.
40. Cornish Social and Economic Research Group, *Reclaiming our Destiny*, CoSERG, Redruth, 1987.
41. See for example Morris & Winn.
42. Buck *et al.*, 1993, p.38.
43. S.Merrett with F.Gray, , *Owner Occupation in Britain*, Routledge & Kegan Paul, London, 1982.
44. BBC TV 'Spotlight South West', 22nd April 1993.
45. George, 1990.
46. DoE, Local Housing Statistics 1990, 1991.
47. J.Lennon, *The Homeless in Cornwall*, Cornwall Social Services, Truro, 1991, p.4.
48. G.Bramley, *The Definition and Measurement of Homelessness* in G.Bramley, K.Doogan, P.Leather, A.Murie, E.Watson, *Homelessness and the London Housing Market*, School for Advanced Urban Studies, University of Bristol, Bristol, 1988.
49. See Buck *et al.*, 1993; Lambert *et al.*
50. Buck *et al.*, Table 1, 1993, p.6.
51. Lambert *et al.*, 1992, p.56.
52. Lennon, 1991, p.4.
53. Office of Population Census and Survey, *1991 Census, County Monitor, Cornwall and the Isles of Scilly*, Government Statistical Service, London, 1992.
54. This is based on the 1% Longitudinal Study sample. 85% of LS Members enumerated in Cornwall, in 1971, were enumerated there ten years later and 15% outside of Cornwall.
55. Lambert *et al.*, 1992.
56. Deacon, George & Perry, 1988, pp.89-97.
57. Longitudinal Study.
58. George, 1987; Lambert *et al.*, 1992.
59. Cornwall County Council, *Report of Survey*, Truro, 1979.
60 A.Griffiths, *Change in the Countryside - The Cornish Perspective. A Study of Twelve Rural Parishes In Cornwall*, Exeter, 1989.
61. S.Foster, *The Role of Local Planning Authorities*, Meeting Local Housing Need Conference, 1990.
62. Lambert, 1992.
63. Cornwall County Council, *Structure Plan*, Cornwall County Council, Truro, 1981.
64. Several organisations and individuals including the Cornish Economic and Social Research Group (CoSERG) and Cornwall Against the Structure Plan (CASP) to the Examination in Public, of the Structure Plan, by the Department of the Environment in March 1989. Points made at the hearing were that there is no evidence that in-migration helped the jlocal economy and that in-migrants enjoyed advantages in housing over locals. See: DoE *Cornwall County Council - Structure Plan, First Alteration. Examination in public, Report of Panel*, Department of the Environment, London, 1989.
65. Deacon, George, Perry, 1988, p.33.

66. C.Hamnett, *Housing the two Nations - Socio-tenurial polarization in England and Wales, 1961-1981*, *Urban Studies*, Vol.21, 1984.
67. Shelter, *Roof*, Vol.12, No 2, 1992.
68. George, 1987.
69. Deacon, George, Perry, 1981, pp.141-148.
70. Since the early 1950s a number of organisations have pressed the claim for some level of one or other form of political or economic 'self determination' in Cornwall. These have ranged from the autonomist/nationalist demands of Mebyon Kernow to recent support for a Cornish Development board by Liberal Democrat MPs. See, for example, Payton, 1992.

CHAPTER 8

THE CORNISH FAMILY

Lyn Bryant

INTRODUCTION

Rosser and Harris, writing about families in Wales,[1] argued that in studying one's own society it is very difficult to develop enough detachment to stand apart from, and view objectively, the familiar and taken-for-granted aspects of social behaviour. It is especially hard to be dispassionate when thinking or writing about the family as personal experiences tend to intrude in this area almost more than in any other and it is sometimes hard to separate out individual experiences from shared behaviour and values. This makes it especially important to place any discussion of contemporary family life in an historical context. In order to understand the relationships and structures of the present we need to develop a clear understanding of the processes and pressures that have led up to the current situation.

An historical perspective is particularly important in considering Cornish families since much of the existing academic literature points to apparent overall similarities in cultural experiences in family life throughout England even if Scottish and Welsh experiences are recognised as distinctive. Many theorists argue that family structures and identities, while varied, do not display systematic regional differences and, furthermore, that all families underwent similar transformations during the process of industrialisation. In fact, however, the experiences of Cornish families provide striking illumination of the theses put forward by those sociologists and historians who dispute such views and point to the variability of family and kinship forms both pre- and post-industrialisation. Equally there is evidence of specific Cornish experiences in the recent past which might lead us to expect to observe a number of contemporary differences.

Many Cornish people are clear about the special nature of Cornish life both now and in the past. Both oral history accounts and autobiographies point to a sense of felt Cornish identity and give evidence of a unique culture. A.L. Rowse,[2] for example, gives an account of his own childhood which, even from his perspective as an academic historian, he saw as being in some ways different from alternative childhoods that he might have lived in England. He experienced, he said, '. . . the age-long routine of Cornish life still unbroken . . . the continuity of custom . . .'.[2] In particular, '. . . there was one thing of interest to the social historian . . . the families, the family names which for generations and even for centuries had belonged to some particular spot . . . there were always Jenkinses at Phernyssick, Pascoes at Holmbush, Tretheweys at Roche; Kellows, Blameys, Rowses at Tregonnissey'.[3]

To this was added the fact '. . . that to be Cornish is a very different thing from being English . . . we Cornish are very different'.[4] The family as a vehicle for separate identity was also emphasised by Winifred Hawkey: 'I am very proud of being completely Cornish on both sides of my family. Why shouldn't I be?'[5] Similarly, Mary Lakeman recalled her childhood at Mevagissey, '. . . a closely-knit classless society where ties of blood, of interdependence, of shared fear of death and joy-in-life were as strong as any human connections could ever be', a tight community in which one could always spot those '. . . of foreign extraction and by that I mean English, not Cornish'.[6]

There is also much anecdotal evidence about the persistence of family loyalties and family care in Cornwall in the present. Community health professionals, for instance, recognise the willingness of family members to provide nursing care, and neighbours speak pityingly of the newcomers who have no kin to turn to in times of illness and distress. But there are few empirical studies to back up assertions about this sense of present family difference, and much current writing about families in the United Kingdom as a whole points to diminishing regional differences, both in cultural and structural terms. In this Chapter the perspectives and literature which point to the growing similarities of family experiences and identities in industrialised societies will be considered and the extent to which Cornwall's distinctive past has left a present which it can be claimed is 'different' will be examined. Little in-depth research has been carried out on Cornish families specifically and much of what appears here is therefore speculative. The major conclusion must be that what is needed is further systematic study, and yet even this preliminary sweep of the evidence (scant as it is) poses intriguing questions about the nature of the Cornish family.

FAMILIES AND INDUSTRIALISATION: THE BROAD SWEEP OF CHANGE

In order to examine the contention that Cornish experiences are indeed in some way different, it is important first to look at the conflicting arguments that have been made about the nature of change in family structures and processes during industrialisation generally. The situation for Cornwall can then be seen in a comparative perspective. Sociologists and social commentators have constantly debated the ways in which families have changed in the past and are still changing in the present. Much of the debate has revolved around the extent to which the processes of industrialisation and urbanisation affected both the structure, or form, of the family and the functions carried out by families, both for their members and for society at large.

Many commentators[7] have argued that in the past the most dominant family form was that of the extended family. Parents, children, grandparents and frequently other kin, it is claimed, lived together working on the land or in domestic industry. The large numbers of people of different ages and responsibilities living together meant that all the needs of family members from the cradle to the grave could be met within that family. A number of factors were seen to have intervened to change this rural idyll. From the middle of the eighteenth century the onset of industrialisation and urbanisation together with rapid population growth contributed to increased rates of geographical and social mobility and to a much more complex division of labour. These in turn, it is claimed, meant that a nuclear family form (parent(s) and dependent child(ren)) living a more separate and independent life was much more suited to the needs of both individuals and the state.

In some ways it is quite clearly a truism to say that change in the family inevitably accompanies change in the economy, but the somewhat simplified view of events just described has been challenged by a number of writers who, examining both past and present evidence, argue that family structures and household composition varied in the past just as they do now. Diana Gittins for example, points out that; 'Prior to industrialism most people lived in relatively small households - the average being about 4.75 persons. Most of these households . . . correspond to nuclear families, a substantial proportion of people never married at all and either lived with other kin or with other single people or, in some cases, alone'.[8] Additionally, parish records indicate that in the countryside families were certainly likely to live near kin, but in separate households.[9] Extended families living under the same roof were fairly rare and geographical mobility more common than the available modes of transport might have led one to suspect. Many households also contained lodgers or apprentices. The pattern of lodging has been used by some commentators to support the view that at least in its early stages the process of industrialisation in terms of factory growth was aided by family members who lived in the growing towns providing accommodation for relatives from rural areas.[10]

Families then, have been seen to change in a variety of ways, and the evidence from the past indicates that ordinary families were unlikely to have lived in extended groups in common households. Families were frequently split by death and the relatively short expectation of life meant that three generations of a family all being alive at one time would have been a much rarer event, even in the nineteenth century, than it is now.[11] It is also evident that the lives of ordinary people were much harsher in the past and that the conditions of the poor must have frequently been intolerable. A life of labour and exploitation was the common lot of many children, and family life for the poor and a large proportion of ordinary working people was lived out in conditions that could hardly be described as comfortable.[12]

The picture of the large extended family in the past providing care and comfort in a way that is not possible in contemporary families has, then, increasingly been seen as a distortion. The debates centring on the effects of industrial change have not, however, just been focussed on the relatively distant past, they were also enriched in the 1950s and 60s by the 'discovery' of networks of extended kin in long settled city areas as well as in the countryside. Increasing evidence was accumulated which demonstrated the variability of family relationships both in the past and in the present, as was some evidence indicating regional variations in the exact nature of both kin and community relationships.[13]

Studies of particular communities, indeed, demonstrated the presence of kinship networks and extended family care. Perhaps one of the most famous studies was that of Wilmott and Young in Bethnal Green.[14] They found that family members preferred to live close to one another, with mothers helping their daughters to care for their young children, who in turn, looked after their parents and grandparents in old age.

Rosser and Harris[15] in Swansea similarly found the wider kinship group to be important, with the key relationships being, wife's mother-wife-husband-husband's mother. Certainly they found a great deal of diversity in wider family ties, but reported that only rarely did they meet with elementary families entirely isolated from kin. Of considerable significance are the major functions that they found to be performed by extended families. Firstly, social identification and secondly social support in need or crisis. They found only slight differences in the organisation of Welsh and non-Welsh families, and further came to the conclusion that extended kin networks were changing to become more loosely knit and more adjusted to a mobile society. They also commented that the women were becoming 'less domesticated'.

Rural communities[16] were also found to contain close kin ties, especially among farming families, where sons frequently inherited farms from their fathers. Families in rural areas have been shown, too, to place great importance on both 'sides' of the family (cognatic kin recognition) with male and female relationships being important in the giving and receiving of help. Strong community ties and close kinship network also typified mining areas. Dennis, Henriques and Slaughter[17] described the comradeship and mutual dependency of the miners and the reliance of the women on their female relations in the village of 'Ashton'. The strength of mining communities has been seen to reside both in the shared occupational conditions and in the family and friendship networks that grow up around the life of the pit.

The kinship networks documented in the 1950s and 60s also show family patterns varying according to the social class[18] of the residents and the type of community. Mother and daughter ties tended to dominate in long settled working-class areas, with both father-son ties and cognatic kin being important in rural areas. Middle class families were also likely to keep in touch with both sides of the family, even if at a distance, with support often being in terms of money and valuable gifts as well as in the form of practical assistance at times of illness and crisis.[19]

CORNISH FAMILIES: LOOKING AT THE PAST

Because it was involved at a very early stage in the processes of industrialisation, Cornwall, and its families, might be expected to have been in the vanguard of any changes related to these processes. Cornish history does indeed, in many ways, provide a 'case study' of kin variability and household patterns. However, a closer examination reveals some crucial differences from the general pattern.

Looking back at the nineteenth century, the 1851 Census records for Cornwall show little evidence of the existence of extended kin groups living under one roof, but ***do*** show working-class households enlarged by the presence of lodgers, craftsmen's households enlarged by apprentices and the households of farmers and landowners enlarged by servants and/ or agricultural labourers. The parish of St Minver, for example, shows the presence of only two three generation families, but a multiplicity of households enlarged by people who are not members of the immediate nuclear family. What is also clear from the Census is that in many of the predominantly rural areas quite a large proportion of people lived in or near their places of birth. The migrants tended to be either house servants, miners or, to a lesser extent, skilled workers.

The picture for the parishes in which mining and industrial growth were evident is of a much more mobile population with more incomers from other parts of Cornwall. Bernard Deacon[20] has demonstrated both the movement of miners within Cornwall and the extent of local recruitment. Movements in to the mining parishes, it must be emphasised, were most often from other parts of Cornwall, so that while the mobile members of the population might not have been exactly local, most of them were Cornish. Industrial development in Cornwall itself took place on the basis of relatively small settlements and factory growth was not huge. Mining already provided a heavy industry base in many of the areas which developed manufacturing and the manufacture was generally of the machines that formed the basis of other manufacturing processes, rather than the growth of large mass production factories churning out cloth or items for mass consumption. (The production of engines and mining machinery at Camborne and Hayle may be seen as a examples of this). The general environment was in fact more rural that was the case in many other industrial areas.

Looking at household and family patterns in Cornwall in the nineteenth century, there is evidence of a variety of factors at play. There is evidence of the persistence of traditional rural kinship patterns and in the mining areas the pattern of lodging was similar to that of many industrialising areas with mobility being based largely upon kinship links. In St Minver, for example, a rural area but with some mining activity in the locality, there is evidence that men moving up to work in the mines there came from specific areas in West Cornwall, so that family members and friends probably helped each other in finding work and housing. While some household servants had come from outside Cornwall, those living-in were mainly of local birth and so would have had kin living nearby.

Thus while kinship and household patterns, and mobility in to industrial areas, show similarities to national patterns, mobility related to industrial development in Cornwall seems usually to have taken place *within* the county. Movements out of Cornwall were likely to have been movements to mining areas abroad for Cornish miners. Both these factors have effects upon family patterns and relationships.

The role of women in Cornish families again shows both similarities with other regions and important differences. In mining areas generally women tend to stay in close contact with their female kin and exchange help both at times of crisis and in the everyday problems involved with child care.[21] High male death rates occasioned by dangerous work, such as mining, also tend to pull the women of the family together into self-help groups. Such kinship links have also been shown to be particularly important when husbands are absent through work or their presence at home is 'unreliable'[22] Relationships with kin, then, would have been doubly important for many Cornish women.

Of significance, too, is that Cornish women in mining areas, like the pit brow lasses in Yorkshire,[23] but unlike their counterparts in many other areas, maintained a presence in the surface work of the mines right through the nineteenth century. They were also more successful than the Yorkshire women in sustaining a presence in the early part of this century. Thus women in the mining areas had a double commitment to work and community. They maintained the home in cases where the husbands worked abroad, they - like other women in mining areas - shared the women's' networks and participated in the shared understandings surrounding mining, but they were also linked more closely to the occupation because women were, far longer than in other regions of Britain, part of the surface workforce. Thus family ties and shared identity were potentially very strong. In fishing communities, too, Cornish women occupied an important position. Like the bal-maidens, they had often a specific occupational role as 'fish-jowsters' (fishwives or fish-sellers), and also they played a major role in the family and the community when the men-folk were away for extended periods in dangerous conditions. In rural communities women have always played a vital role in the work of the farm and smallholding and have worked as day labourers at harvest and other times of the year. In some mining areas of Cornwall and in the china clay area, the men's wages were frequently supplemented by rearing animals or carrying out horticulture on a small scale. In these areas the women's labour was crucial in keeping the enterprise going. The link between home and work, family and occupation would once again have been strong and capable of helping to underpin supportive and enduring family structures.

Towards the end of the nineteenth century the fluctuating fortunes of Cornish mining and the pull of the mines in countries like Australia and South Africa meant that many men frequently moved between Cornwall and other countries. Often they travelled on their own with the intention of earning money to send home and, eventually, to return with a 'fortune'. Others made frequent trips abroad while having a settled base in Cornwall. Whole families also went off together sometimes to settle, although sometimes finding the pull of their Cornish homeland to great to resist.[24] Farming families and other workers too spread out over the globe, but once again the available evidence points to the maintaining of strong links with home.[25] The strength of kin and community links was overlaid by a strong sense of Cornish identity, rooted in the memory of a separate language and shared cultural expectations. Cornish miners and farmers maintained strong links with their homeland when they went abroad to work or settle. They founded Cornish Associations in most of the places into which they moved, maintaining a distinctive presence and spreading kinship and community links out over the globe. Miners catching the train at Camborne on a Thursday to journey to Southampton and then on to South Africa could travel safe in the knowledge that if they stood on a certain corner in 'Jo'burg' sooner or later another Cornishman would come along to offer help with work or accommodation:[26]

> ... if it meant aching hearts at home, many separations and much grief, there was also much fun, the enjoyment of camaraderie, the sticking together of Cornish folk, Cousin Jacks, out there. There were fights and quarrels and jealousies; but there was also the helping hand, the close-knit ties of friendship in a strange country. There was much coming and going to and fro between South Africa and home. Out there, there were in time Cornish Societies and Associations which welcomed the newcomers. These still exist, and a good many contacts continue though the flow of emigration has stopped. At home people knew what was going on in South Africa often rather better than what was happening 'up-country'.[27]

Cornwall's past, then, has elements of similarity to and difference from, other regions of Britain. In other regions the presence of mining and rurality have been found to produce strong kinship ties and specific cultural norms.[28] Cornwall, because of its rurality, the presence of mining and fishing, and its particular pattern of industrial growth and activity, has a history containing elements which, at the very least, *allow* the development of a strong sense of difference from the outside world together with a strong sense of obligation to members of the immediate family and the wider kin group.

RECENT CHANGE

Writers in the post-War period, then, had dispelled the notion of the general emergence of isolated nuclear families as the norm. Extended families had been found to be relatively common and in Cornwall it can be argued that internationally extended kin groups were not uncommon. However, more recent commentaries on family life have argued that the rate of change has accelerated and even Peter Wilmott, who sees British kinship as very resilient, has argued that the kinship systems described in the 1960s were coming to an end. In reviewing more recent changes in family and community patterns he argues that '. . . the research of the 1950s and 1960s was describing something that was coming to the end of its reign.'[29] His view of the change that was taking place was mainly based upon the post-War studies of inner-city areas where sociological research had found that in long settled, especially working-class, districts close knit communities, based on kinship networks, were common. Geographical mobility, re-development and wives going out to work, thus reducing contacts with their mothers, he argued, had broken the 'old order'. Community life was becoming more individualistic with nuclear families growing more independent.

Rosser and Harris[30] also argued that kin ties in Swansea were becoming more dispersed with residents of areas undergoing 'slum' clearance often being regretful of what they felt was a loss of community. These sentiments have been echoed in other studies and residents of the 'Island' in east London, for example, write regretfully of the loss of past closeness in the community and the development of more 'distant' social relationships.[31] Thus while writers of the 1950s and 60s disputed early theories which postulated that industrialisation and urbanisation had produced a largely isolated nuclear family, their commentaries in the 1970s and 1980s seemed to be describing further family change. They described a sense of loss of community and a growing independence of nuclear families. It is important to note, however, that it is not being argued that kin relationships are totally disintegrating but more that they are adapting to become looser and more dispersed.

There are certainly demographic trends which are being reflected in changing household structures. Falling death and birth rates have given rise to an increasingly ageing population, a trend which has had helped to affect household composition in a number of ways. Firstly, there has been an increase in the number of households consisting only of an elderly couple. There has also been an increase in the number of older people, especially women as increased life expectancy has benefitted them to a slightly greater extent than men, living on their own after the death of a partner. The percentage of households made up of one person over retirement rose from 7% of the total in 1961 to 16% in 1987. During the same period the proportion of households made up of single people under retirement age rose from 4% to 9%, and the number of households composed of two or more families declined from 3% to 1% of the total.[32]

With couples tending to have fewer children there has also been a decrease in household size generally. Over the period 1961 to 1987 the average household size fell slightly from 3.09 to 2.55 people and the proportion of households made up of married couples with dependent children fell from 38% to 28%. The general trend is for households to be smaller and for the different generations of families to be separately housed. For people aged 65 and over 11% live with children (7%) or other relatives but of those aged 80 or more 26%

live with children (21%) or other relatives. In spite of this trend to separate housing The Family Policy Studies Unit[33] sees care as still being provided by extended family members. Elderly people do receive help from their families and grandmothers are most likely to be the carers of children whose mothers are in full time employment. Other trends noted in family life are the increase in lone parent families - 14% of the total by 1987 and the greater numbers of reconstituted families because of the increasing rates of divorce and re-marriage. There is also a decreasing likelihood of younger family members being in full time employment. The proportion of 16 year old school leavers in full time 'traditional' employment had fallen from 60% in 1975 to under 20% in 1988. This is likely to mean that children will be dependent upon their parents for a longer period of time and in some cases, it has been argued, is resulting in young people being made homeless if their parents are unable to support them or there has been a family quarrel. Older people too, are less likely to be in employment after they have reached retirement age.

The Policy Studies document argues that in the future households are likely to be smaller and there is likely to be considerable diversity in their composition. The trend towards a greater number of single person households is likely to continue, as are the proportions of lone parent and married couple only households. In considering current family structures many commentators have also pointed to the lack of regional variations. The Family Policy Studies Centre, for example, states '. . . there is very little difference in the household composition of of different regions in the United Kingdom.'[34] Janet Finch in an extensive study of family obligations is more cautious and observes that in looking at extended kin relationships regional differences have proved the most difficult to uncover. She notes that it is difficult to be certain that any observed variations '...can be attributed to, say, peoples' views about family responsibilities being different in the north-east of England from the prevailing norms of the south-west'.[35] Her general advice is that we should remain 'agnostic' about regional variations until more studies are carried out, although she does add that there does appear to be evidence for certain similarities in family behaviour.

For many commentators it would appear that the situation for families is changing from one in which there were few differences in kinship patterns to one in which there are even fewer. In recent years, too, some theorists have postulated even greater changes than those that have been associated with the first processes of industrialisation. The rapid rate of change facilitated by technological developments is seen as ushering in a new era, with families becoming less important in bestowing and maintaining identity.

FAMILIES IN CORNWALL TODAY

Cornish families have obviously not been untouched by the economic and social changes taking place and we have seen that many writers have argued that family life and kinship ties have become very similar everywhere. Others have postulated that Cornish identity has been submerged by a flood of incomers and the onslaught of the mass media.[36] The remnants of Cornish identity are thus seen as somewhat self-conscious and under threat of further dilution. Attitudes towards family and kinship obligations it might be argued have become much the same in Cornwall as in Hertfordshire. But Cornwall's past would suggest the possibility of a distinctive present and while there have been few studies which have concerned themselves with Cornish family life, there is evidence of at least some structural and attitudinal differences.

It is probably important to begin the discussion of families in Cornwall today by looking at some of the arguments that would see Cornwall as having been exposed to particular as well as general pressures that would lead to an erosion of cultural differences. Taking a general perspective first, current postmodernist writers[37] tend to see family life as subject to pressures which are liable to precipitate a decline in the importance of families as sources of individual identity. Changes such as the 'media saturation' of society and the breakdown of the distinction between culture and society are seen as having encouraged the fragmentation of traditional cultures and an increasing emphasis on style and form rather than substance and structure. Traditional values, it is argued, are eroded and structural variations become less important in the creation of identity.

Evidence for these changes has been sought by tracing patterns of change in consumption, media presentations, music and the plastic arts, including architecture. Less detailed scrutiny has been afforded to family life. But the emphasis on style, the sense that time and space have become confused and less stable and comprehensible and that traditional points of reference decline are seen to have an impact on family relationships and values. The authority of older family members in such circumstances are undermined and traditional values rendered less important. The large scale changes identified by postmodernist writers as taking place currently might, it could be argued, destroy the last flowerings of any specifically Cornish ways of family life. Another pressure within Cornwall which could be seen as likely to militate against specifically Cornish family identities is illustrated in Chapter 7 by Malcolm Williams. He demonstrates the extent of recent in-migration to Cornwall. While some of these migrants may be returners to Cornwall, there are many new settlers. These new settlers, while they may be sympathetic to Cornwall and its traditions are often, partly because of their educational and economic backgrounds, relatively cosmopolitan in outlook and liable to be selective about the cultural elements that they adopt. Return migrants as Perry *et al.*[38] have shown certainly may be returning to their homeland (78% of survey respondents cited this as one of the main reasons for re-settling in Cornwall) but those studied did differ from the long-settled local population. Like the new settlers they tended to be more 'middle-aged' and more 'middle-class'. These return migrants, then, may have been subject to educational and occupational processes which emphasise general rather than particularistic (local) values.

An adherence to generalised national cultural values may also be the case for professional workers, even those whose lives, apart perhaps from temporary absences in institutions of higher education, have been spent in Cornwall. Because of the lack of higher education opportunities most Cornish children have to leave the county if they wish to pursue graduate or post graduate studies. As higher education was opened up during the 1960s increasing numbers of would-be students made the educational journey out of Cornwall. The process of education, is among other things, a process of socialisation: of shaping and developing social and personal identities. Researchers like Jackson and Marsden[39] have documented the ways in which working-class children in higher education 'grew away' from their families - a process graphically described by a mature student 'Its as if one of us has moved on while the other stood still'.[40] Thus returning migrants and returning students may have, in spite of a sense of being 'repatriated,' changed in a number of ways that distance them from their local, family roots. If postmodernist views are taken seriously, these changes may be in the direction of changes in sources of personal identity and loss of a sense of the importance of locality. Factors which may militate against the continuance of family tradition and the sense of belonging to a particular area (as well as belonging to do particular things). The lack of ethnofractional movements mentioned by Deacon in Chapter 9 may also mean that there is a lack of focus for the maintenance and renewal of local values and behaviours.

In spite of these general and particular pressures, for some observers the sense of Cornish difference remains stubbornly present. Philip Payton,[41] for example, argues cogently for the persistence of separateness in spite of the pressures for conformity. The difference he sees as being largely due to the centre-periphery power relationship remaining unbroken. Taking issue with Perry's conclusion that the middle-class, middle-aged, middle-browed in-migrants have 'urbanised' Cornwall, Payton agrees with Grafton and Bolton that the centre-periphery relationship has remained in place and sees Cornwall as having entered the era of 'Third Peripheralism'. Drawing on a number of studies he argues that Cornwall is '. . . still different in terms of culture, society, economics and, perhaps particularly, politics'.[42] The separation from the centre or core is seen as the root cause of identity difference. This difference is manifested particularly in political behaviour. Payton goes on to note that concern about the demise of Cornish identity paradoxically demonstrates its survival. Certainly, there is a recognition of Cornish identity, both by the Cornish and others as Deacon has pointed out. Obviously in a world of fast moving communications and multinational corporations differences in social and occupational behaviour have diminished, but the significance of felt differences, and structural situation, for individuals and groups, should not be underestimated even if the behavioural outcomes seem to be small. Perhaps the importance is best summed up by Goffman, 'Our status is backed by the solid buildings of the world, while our sense of identity often resides in the cracks'.[43]

Rosser and Harris[44] pointed out in their Swansea study that one of the important functions carried out by kin groups was the providing of identification for their members. Families, in fact, are crucial in passing on identities and 'felt differences' during the processes of both adult and childhood socialisation in which we learn the ways of the group both through deliberate teaching and through day to day interaction with those around us. In families our early learning takes place with people who are of an earlier generation. Grandparents and parents teach us ideas and behaviour which are often some years 'out of date'. Thus in our families we are touched by a lived experience of the recent past and may also be exposed to a rich vein of more distant memories and feelings which may have a deep influence upon the way we feel about ourselves and the places in which we live. Thus children and young people will be exposed to ideas, values, beliefs and an 'oral history' which owes much to the recent past and carries in it knowledge of the experience of grandparents and great grandparents.

Without further systematic study it is difficult to either quantify or qualify the elements that go to make up the sense of Cornish family identity. From both autobiography and oral history accounts it is clear that part of the identification is linked to shared behaviour surrounding occupational activities which are not merely occupations, but are related to 'ways of life', for example, mining, farming and fishing. These activities in Cornwall, as has been argued elsewhere,[45] were associated with fairly independent ways of working, but on the basis of a strong, and extended, family network. Methodism, too, which became a strong influence, encourages a similar attitude of self-responsibility within a set of shared beliefs and accepted behaviour. Cornwall's geographical situation also fostered a sense of separateness, and sometimes hostility to the outside world, remarked upon by generations of travellers.[46]It is perhaps this sense of separateness, as much as the customs that have been handed down from past generations, that is a crucial part of Cornish family identity today. Cornish people's expectations related to their industrial inheritance may have been changed but have, nevertheless, influenced current attitudes.

From observation it is apparent that there are in Cornwall differences in culture and belief that continue to permeate family relationships. In the past and perhaps to a lesser extent currently, the importance of cognatic kin and women's family background were recognised in daily life, possibly a recognition of the central role played by women occupationally as well as in domestic life. One small example of this is that married women, perhaps particularly in rural areas, would continue to be referred to by their maiden names. So, for instance, Marie Pearce having married Ernie Bryant would continue to be referred to as Marie Pearce, or more familiarly, as maid Pearce. Another example of family recognition through names is that sons working locally are sometimes called by their father's names. When Ernie and Marie's son started work, for example, he was immediately dubbed 'Ernie'.

The assumption of shared understandings is also clear in everyday conversation and in terms of address.[47] Outsiders frequently feel excluded from conversations and some Cornish people have commented on their awareness of their ability to exclude the non-Cornish both in intended and unintended ways.

Studies of rural areas have reported the importance of what Frankenberg has called 'redundancy' in social interaction.[48] By this he means the inclusion of a number of items of conversation that are not strictly pertinent to the business in hand, but serve to oil the social wheels. It has been suggested that family anecdotes make up a major proportion of Cornish social redundancy[49]. This suggestion needs to be systematically tested although there is some evidence[50] that talk about the past, especially family connections and community life perform an important role in reinforcing a sense of shared identity. While in-migrants would certainly dilute this activity to an extent, their presence could also serve to strengthen the sense of family and kinship solidarity in areas where these are still present. As Erikson has suggested,[51] the presence of people who are different may serve to reinforce the norms of an in-group.

The strength of family sentiment and attachment to family roots and identity is also evidenced by the thriving Cornwall Family History Society. 'Cornish people' from all over the world belong to the Society, but, importantly, there is a large membership in Cornwall itself. Extended family networks also, as in the past, continue to be world wide. Family members who have never seen each other keep relationships alive over time and in spite of distance.[52] The sense of family membership is very strong and frequently extends to fairly distant cousins. Significantly, far from declining with the passage of time, the sense of an international Cornish identity - and with it global family connections - has increased markedly in the post-War era. An awareness of Cornish culture manifested in the intimacy of family life is also evidenced by the continued (and increasing) use of specifically Cornish first names, for example, Perran, Gawen, and Trystan, Loveday, Tamsyn and Lowena, which may be particularly important in enhancing cultural identity when it is linked with an increased interest in the Cornish language and an appreciation both of Cornwall's more distant past and its recent history. While it may be claimed that such manifestations are both over self-conscious and, at least in part, products of the mass media, useful mainly in helping Cornwall to 'turn an honest buck' from tourists, the presence of a separate language, folklore and names bear witness to the existence of *real* differences which have real effects, especially in supporting a sense of separation from outsiders.

Cornish family behaviour also differs in a further important way. In Chapter 7 Malcolm Williams points out that in 1951 the majority of the population in Cornwall might be defined as Cornish and that their housing characteristics were similar to those of other long settled areas - housing often being acquired via family members or someone their 'da' knew. By the time of the 1981 Census he notes that 10% of the Cornish population lived in houses containing more than one potential household and he considers that lack of housing was becoming a factor in out-migration. Many young people are frustrated in their efforts to set up home and continue to live in the parental home, but trying to move out. Widespread unemployment and low incomes together with the tendency for second homes and holiday lets to force up house prices have certainly disadvantaged young Cornish people in their search for independent housing. However, even taking this into consideration the proportion of complex households, which are largely made up of two or more families is still relatively high in Cornwall. The OPCS(LS)[53] data show that at the time of the 1981 Census, of people resident in Cornwall both in 1971 and 1981, 9.8% were living in complex households compared with 7.8% of the rest of the population. Further, people moving out of Cornwall between 1971 and 1981 were more likely to live in complex households and people moving into Cornwall during the same period were less likely to do so. Both permanent residents of Cornwall and those moving out of Cornwall were more likely to live in complex households comprised of two or more families.

Family relationships, then, more often than in England, include the sharing of a home. While the differences may seem small the numbers of people involved are significant and may well be indicative of important differences in attitudes towards family obligations. In other respects demographic changes and household composition show similar trends to those described by the Family Policy unit, with an increasing number of single parent and 're-constituted' families. Cornwall also has a slightly higher proportion of elderly people living alone and also a higher proportion of elderly couples than the total IPCS sample. The extent and nature of family contacts for elderly people and the differences, if any, between long term residents and in-comers really needs further investigation.

Other evidence has come from studies of young people in the South West. For example, a survey by Dunkerley and Wallace[54] indicated that young people in Cornwall, especially in rural areas, were very frequently involved in family enterprises. Clearly this is very likely to be the case in farming where youngsters may be able to keep stock on their own account - courtesy of mother or father - and this indeed was found to be the case. However, Dunkerley and Wallace also found that together with a high rate of self-employment in Cornwall there was also a high rate of children's involvement in parents' enterprises. This may indicate not just economic necessity but also closeness, and continuing involvement could allow the child to gain independence and adulthood within the family rather than outside it.

CONCLUSION

Much of the argument for the special nature of Cornish family links has been based upon unsystematic data, evidence from discussions and snippets of information gleaned from a variety of sources. The hard data employed has come mainly from Census data and from a small number of surveys. However, in spite of the weight of scholarly opinion as to the increasing similarity of family and kinship structures and behaviour, it would seem reasonable to argue that there is, both from the Census data and the more qualitative studies, evidence of somewhat stronger kinship links and distinctive identities rooted in the family in Cornwall. Cornwall's history has certainly laid the foundations for some differences in family recognition and behaviour. Current economic differences, unemployment, the effects of de-industrialisation and rural poverty, may be seen to make the continuance of family support and identity a necessity. At the present time it is difficult to ascertain whether the difference in household composition and the sense of belonging to specifically Cornish families is merely the result of 'cultural lag' and economic necessity which will disappear with the next generation. However, the 'persistence of difference' in contemporary Cornwall that Philip Payton has identified,[55] suggests that the continuing differences are not merely residual but reflect an enduring dymanic in Cornish life.

REFERENCES:

1. C.Rosser and C.C.Harris, *The Family and Social Change: A Study of Family and Kinship in a South Wales Town*, Routledge & Kegan Paul, London, 1966.
2. A.L.Rowse, *A Cornish Childhood*, Jonathan Cape, London, 1942, republished Cardinal, London, 1975, p7.
3. Rowse, 1975, pp7-8; see also Chapter 3, 'The Family'.
4. Rowse, 1975, p61.
5. Winifred Hawkey, *Memoirs of a Redruth Childhood*, Dyllansow Truran, Redruth, 1987, p50.
6. Mary Lakeman, *Early Tide: A Mevagissey Childhood*, William Kimber, London, 1978, republished Dyllansow Truran, Redruth, 1987, pp29 and 32.
7. This argument is made strongly by many functionalist writers, the foundations for such arguments were very clearly set out by R.M.MacIver and C.Page, *Society*, Macmillan, London, 1957, Chapter 11.
8. D. Gittins, *The Family in Question*, Macmillan, London, 1985, p6.
9. See, for example, P.Laslett & R.Wall (eds.), *Household and Family in Past Times*, Cambridge University Press, Cambridge, 1972.
10. Gittins, 1985, Chapter 1.
11. In 1860-61, for example, average life expectancy at birth was 42.3 for men and 46.2 for women in England and Wales and 7.5% of the population was aged 60 or over. By 1991 people aged 65 or over made up 15.8% of the population and life expectancy at birth had reached the mid 70s for both sexes.
12. See, for example, the account by D. George, *England in Transition*, Penguin, London, 1953.
13. R.Frankenberg, *Communities in Britain*, Penguin, London, 1977.
14. M.Young and P. Willmott, *Family and Kinship in East London*, Penguin, London, 1957.
15. Rosser and Harris, 1966.
16. See, for example the studies reported in R. Frankenberg, 1977.
17. N.Dennis, F.M.Henriques and C. Slaughter, *Coal Is Our Life*, Eyre & Spottiswoode, London, 1957.
18. See, for example, P.Willmott and M.Young, *Family and Class in a London Suburb*, Routledge and Kegan Paul, London, 1960.
19. C.R.Bell, *Middle Class Families*, Routledge and Kegan Paul, London, 1968.
20. B.Deacon, *Migration and the Mining Industry in East Cornwall in the Mid-Nineteenth Century*, Project on Deindustrialisation in the South-West, University of Exeter, 1985.
21. See, for example Dennis *et al.*, 1957.
22. Dennis *et al.*, 1957.
23. A.John, *By the Sweat of their Brow: Women Workers at Victorian Coal Mines*, Croom Helm, London, 1980.
24. There are many written and anecdotal accounts of both 'long distance commuting' and movements away from and back to Cornwall. Stephen Thomas from Redruth, for example,

went abroad to get together enough money to marry his sweetheart, subsequently did marry her and over the years spent a number of periods working abroad both with and without his family. The literature on Cornish emigration is extensive; for example, see A.C.Todd, *The Cornish Miner in America*, Bradford Barton, Truro, 1967, A.L.Rowse, *The Cornish in America*, Macmillan, London, 1969, republished Dyllansow Truran, Redruth, 1991, John Rowe, *The Hard-rock Men: Cornish Immigrants and the North American MIning Frontier*, Liverpool University Press, Liverpool, 1974, Philip Payton, *Pictorial History of Australia's Little Cornwall*, Rigby, Adelaide, 1978, Philip Payton, *The Cornish Miner in Australia*, Dyllansow Truran, Redruth, 1984, Philip Payton, *The Cornish Farmer in Australia*, Dyllansow Truran, Redruth, 1987, A.C.Todd, *The Search For Silver: Cornish Miners in Mexico, 1824-1947*, Lodenek Press, Padstow, 1977, Graham B.Dickason, *Cornish Immigrants to South Africa*, Balkema, Cape Town, 1978.

25. See, for example, the account in A.C.Todd and D.James, *Ever Westward the Land*, University of Exeter Press, Exeter, 1986.
26. Taken from conversations with S.Thomas.
27. Rowse, 1975, pp34-35.
28. See Dennis *et al.*, 1957.
29. P.Willmott, *Kinship and Urban Communities: Past and Present*, The Ninth H J Dyos Memorial Lecture, 1987.
30. Rosser and Harris, 1966.
31. Centerprise Trust Ltd, *The Island: The Life and Death of a London Community 1870- 1970*, Centerprise, London, 1979.
32. Figures taken from *Social Trends* 17/18/19.
33. K.Kiernan and M. Wicks, *Family Change and Future Policy*, Published in association with the Family Policy Studies Centre by the Joseph Rowntree Memorial Trust, 1990.
34. Family Policy Studies Centre, Fact Sheet 1, 1985, p9.
35. J.Finch, *Family Obligations and Social Change*, Polity Press, Cambridge, 1989.
36. R.Perry, K.Dean and B.Brown, *Counterurbanisation: International Case Studies of Socio-Economic change in Rural Areas*, Geo Books, Norwich, 1986.
37. See, for example, S. Connor, *Postmodernist Culture*, Basil Blackwell, Oxford, 1989, or D. Harvey, *The Condition of Post-modernity*, Basil Blackwell, Oxford, 1989,
38. Perry *et al.*, 1986.
39. J.Jackson and K.Marsden, *Education and the Working class*, Penguin, London, 1966.
40. L.Bryant and S.Stupple, *Mature Students at Plymouth Polytechnic*, Department of Social & Political Studies, Plymouth Polytechnic, 1966.
41. P.Payton, *The Making of Modern Cornwall: Historical Experience and the Persistence of 'Difference'*, Dyllansow Truran, Redruth, 1992, Chapter 8.
42. Payton, 1992, Chapter 8.
43. E.Goffman, *Asylums*, Anchor Books, Doubleday & Co, 1961.
44. Rosser and Harris, 1966.
45. See, for example, Payton, 1992.
46. Although there are a number of accounts an early, and interesting, one comes from William Borlase in the eighteenth century in his *The Natural History of Cornwall*.
47. Many counties have specific dialect words and forms. Cornwall's, however, are also based to some extent upon a separate language. Interviews with both Cornish residents and newcomers have confirmed the persistence of felt differences, see M.Buck, L.Bryant and M. Williams, *Housing and Households in Cornwall: A Pilot Study of Cornish Families*, University of Plymouth, 1993.
48. For a discussion of the concept of social redundancy see R.Frankenberg, *Communities in Britain*, Penguin, London, 1969, especially Chapter 11.
49. This idea came about in a conversation and while it does need systematic investigation a number of people with whom it has been discussed consider it to be worth further study.
50. Buck *et al.*, 1993.
51. K.Erikson, *Wayward Puritans*, Wiley, London, 1966.
52. The author has spoken to a large number of people who continue to correspond with cousins

and other family members in the United States, Australia and South Africa. With some they exchange visits, but some they have never actually met. In the author's own (Cornish) family letters, cards and presents are exchanged with 'never-seen' cousins.

53. Data from the Office of Population Censuses and Surveys, Longitudinal Survey, 1971/1981.
54. D.Dunkerley D. and C. Wallace, 'Young People and Employment in the South West', *Journal of Interdisciplinary Economics*, Vol 4, 1992.
55. Payton, 1992, p187.

PART THREE:

A RE-DEFINING IDENTITY

CHAPTER 9

AND SHALL TRELAWNY DIE? THE CORNISH IDENTITY

Bernard Deacon

In 1992 Mr Ernest Nute of Ponsanooth pleaded 'not guilty' to a charge of failing to make a Census return. Mr Nute's defence was that '. . . completion of this form would be for me to state I am English. Our people are not descended from the Angles and Saxons, so therefore, identically with the Welsh, we are most certainly not English'.[1] Mr Nute clearly had a sense of Cornish identity. He was not alone - a few days after his court appearance over 40,000 Cornish men and women travelled eastwards to Twickenham to support the Cornish rugby team in the final of the County Championship, a competition virtually ignored by the media, rugby officianados and the public alike east of the Tamar.

These events seem to indicate that there is a continuing, indeed even increasingly self-assertive, popular sense of 'being Cornish'. Many in Cornwall would argue that this is based on a recognisable Cornish culture and a persisting sense of 'difference'. For example, Cornwall County Council in 1980 could go so far as to claim that Cornwall '. . . has maintained much of its identity in traditions and culture'.[2] This sense of identity was sufficiently distinct to give rise to a cultural nationalism in the 1920s and a small, but persistent, political nationalist movement which appeared in the early 1950s. However, academic studies of Cornwall may deny the significance of this Cornish identity: '. . . arguments based on the existence of an ethnic identity have a plausibility which is totally lacking in the far south-west'.[3] It is also easy to find others who claim that everyday life in Cornwall seems to be much the same as everywhere else in the UK and that '. . . the culture enjoyed by the great majority of Cornish people differs hardly one jot from that of the overwhelming majority living elsewhere in our developed, industrial world'.[4] And finally, the political nationalism that emerged has not achieved lasting and permanent electoral success.

It seems, therefore, that the Cornish identity is beset by paradoxes. In this Chapter we will ask what Cornish identity is and look at the nature of Cornish culture. After discussing some structural changes we will explain the relatively limited political consequences of the Cornish identity and briefly speculate on the future of the identity.

WHAT IS THE CORNISH IDENTITY?

As individuals we gain a sense of who we are from a variety of factors, which can include occupation or class, age, or gender. Place is another powerful source of identity, giving rise to local, regional and national identities. The Cornish identity is a regional (to some a national) identity, a sense of self based on association with a particular place.

However, identities are not static. They are produced and reproduced socially over time. Although there is continuity each generation can re-make its identity.[5] Identities are about ideas and representations, representations about who we are or ideas about the boundaries between that group which shares our identity and those groups which do not. For identities are a form of 'collective representation' that persuade people they are part of a wider group with characteristic attitudes and a certain kind of unity.[6] Cohen, from an anthropological perspective, stresses the imaginary aspect of group identities. Boundaries between groups, he suggests, are purely mental constructs.[7] These points, that identities change over time and that they are mental constructs, need to be grounded on a third point: identities are linked to a context. The context is usually seen as the culture that gives rise to the shared meanings and values that underpin group identities.[8] The source of a regional identity is therefore the regional culture.

But this still does not really help us to explain how regional identities are formed or why they differ, some giving rise to vigorous political movements, others not. For assistance in this we can turn to the work of a Finnish geographer, Anssi Paasi, who has provided an explanation for the formation of regional identities.[9] Paasi sees regional identity as linking the objective, material aspects of everyday life - the culture and economics of the people - to the subjective representations of individuals and groups. But it is not just a matter of imagination or mental constructs in a vacuum. Regional identities have institutional forms and are produced and reproduced by social institutions, both formal (e.g.media, churches, political parties) or informal (e.g. families, feast day crowds). These institutions can be powerful (the state) or less powerful (the Cornish Gorseth).

Paasi further distinguishes between the regional consciousness of the inhabitants themselves and the more general 'identity of the region'. The former is linked to notions of community and ideas about belonging as well as the way the inhabitants interpret the past and their region's place in it. The latter is linked to images of the region and of its inhabitants. These images may be created and held either by 'insiders' or 'outsiders' but are generated in a political and social structure and in a context of ideas and classifications of the region by academics. The images will also affect the self-awareness of the inhabitants, and this self-awareness may well in turn feed back into both internal and external images. But the regional identity is the product of both factors - the regional consciousness and the identity of the region. This may perhaps be best illustrated by a diagram applying Paasi's model to the Cornish identity.

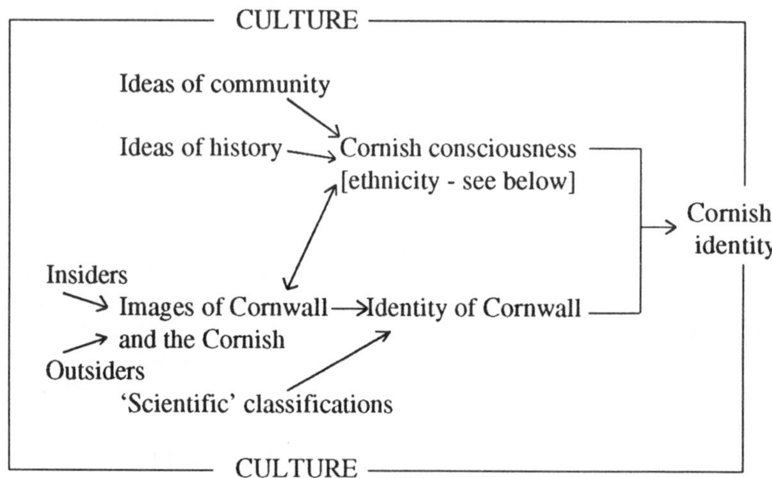

Regional identity is thus not reduced to a distinctive regional culture, although the culture is the arena within which ideas and images are constructed. Regional identities also do not arise directly from the everyday practices of the inhabitants. They are mediated by ideas about those practices and about the history of the region. This helps explain why an accountant or an estate agent could feel as 'Cornish' as a miner or a fisherman. The above model provides a loose framework for understanding the different dimensions of Cornish identity.

CORNISH CONSCIOUSNESS

So who, or what, are the Cornish and what is the nature of their consciousness of 'being Cornish'? When people become aware of shared ties of residence, descent, language or customs then they are described as an 'ethnic group'. According to Anthony Smith, '. . . an ethnic community . . . may . . . be defined as a named human population, possessing a myth of common descent, common historical memories, elements of shared culture, an association with a particular territory, a sense of solidarity'.[10] Elsewhere he adds the criterion of one or more '. . . distinct characteristics and some sense of collective solidarity'.[11] Let's apply Smith's criteria to Cornwall.

Mary McArthur has provided the only survey of Cornish ethnicity to date which is based on an actual sample.[12] The sample is, admittedly, a small one of just 18 informants but her work does provide some clues as to the nature of the modern identity. The notion of common origins of a spreading kinship group was strong among her informants and may also be reflected in the phenomenal interest in family history shown both in Cornwall and by descendants of Cornish emigrants to North America and Australasia. Similarly, '. . . not all informants were concerned with the Celtic past as being particularly relevant, but all were aware of it, even when specific details of Cornwall's history were unknown'.[13] The past may be interpreted in many different ways but there appears to be a shared idea of a common past. We are on less sure ground when we come to Smith's 'one or more distinct characteristics'. Objectively, 'distinctiveness' may be less obvious at first glance. There is no sizeable community speaking a non-English language or worshipping in a different church. Subjectively however, Cornish people will perceive a whole host of attributes as being 'distinctive', from the subtle differences of Cornish rugby or brass bands or the Cornish sense of humour to the more obvious elements of dialect and the even more obvious Cornish language placenames or personal names that still abound. In any case, whether or not cultural practices are seen as 'distinctive' would seem to be itself dependent on Smith's criterion, the sense of collective solidarity.

McArthur concluded from her informants that the Cornish do have a '. . . self-awareness (albeit of differing degrees) of a separate identity, being long established in a well-defined territory, and . . . do qualify for the label 'ethnic group' or 'ethnic community'.[14] This is supported both by the readiness of Cornish people generally to self-identify as 'Cornish', and by the collective expressions of this identification through such celebratory events as the trips to Twickenham to support the rugby team or at occasions like Camborne's Trevithick Day. The historical accident that results in Cornwall being, administratively, a county of England may lead observers to see Cornish regional identity as a local form of a more general 'county' identity (albeit well-developed, like that of Yorkshire). However, a more considered observation of this identity would seem to suggest that it is on a different dimension to a mere 'county' local allegiance. The Cornish identity is subjectively both perceived as stronger and as different from English county allegiances. Indeed many will, like the Mr Nute cited at the beginning of this Chapter, define themselves as Cornish or as belonging to a Cornish nation in preference to self-defining as English.[15] Clearly, not everyone will do this, and there are '. . . differing degrees of Cornishness in day to day life, consciousness of ethnic difference can range from being non-existent on the part of both Cornish and English to being very important'.[16] But Smith makes the point that not all members of an ethnic group will have the same level of solidarity and that this does not negate the existence of that ethnic group.[17]

The fact that the non-Cornish are also aware of this 'difference' is important. Rex points out how ethnic groups can be defined by others.[18] Helped by its attraction as a place for visitors and tourists since the eighteenth century and the spawning of a guide book industry, the Cornish have been seen as a named group with certain characteristics for some time. The Cornish, we are assured, '. . . remain as they always were . . . dour and difficult . . . permeated with romanticism . . . totally removed from the pragmatism of the English . . . dominated by superstition'.[19] All this may be glorious nonsense but the sheer weight of the production of this type of imagery reinforces the sense of the Cornish as a named group apart from others.

So the Cornish can be said to comprise a self-aware ethnic group with a sense of shared roots, common history and some notion of a distinctive culture. The Cornish identity finds its resources in its culture. It is also here that we find the images and ideas that give rise to the identity of Cornwall and its people. So let's now turn to that culture.

VIEWS OF CORNISH CULTURE

Intent on identifying obvious and distinctive cultural content such as language or religion, the sparse literature on Cornish culture raises doubts about its very existence.[20] However, people in Cornwall did and do believe that such a thing as Cornish culture exists and that it is more than just culture in Cornwall. In 1949, in the first issue of the *Cornish Review,* the very first article was on the subject of 'Cornish culture'. Written by the Revivalist Robert Morton Nance, it stated that '. . . there is a difference between Culture in Cornwall and Cornish Culture'. The former concerned drama, music and art but the latter was '. . .a continuity of culture that is natively Cornish'.[21] More recently, Ronald Perry *et.al.*, in their study of migration into Cornwall in 1984, found that 60 % of in-migrants to Redruth felt there was a distinctive local culture.[22]

Focusing on the nature of local culture leads observers to pessimistic conclusions about '. . . the erosion of what it is fashionable to call our cultural identity'.[23] And yet at the same time such conclusions will be vigorously contested by those who defend the existence of 'Cornish culture'. Part of the confusion rests on adopting different definitions of culture, with some confining Cornish culture to 'Celtic' culture and others taking it to mean the culture of local people. Similarly, some concentrate on culture as the arts and literature and others see it as a way of life.

However, culture is more than an objective 'way of life' that can be measured, tabulated and dissected. Cultures have objective content, e.g. pasties, but a focus on this content will miss an important point; cultures also carry values and meanings about their content. It is not the existence of a pasty as a mixture of meat, potatoes and turnips enclosed in a pastry covering that is important. It is the symbolism of that article of diet for a certain group. Pasties may have a particular meaning inside Cornish culture but they will have other meanings or no other meanings at all when viewed from within other cultures. Cultures therefore have at their heart a symbolic dimension. This view of 'culture' stresses what cultures do rather than what they are, their practices rather than their content.[24]

THE PRODUCTION OF CORNISH CULTURE

What is now popularly called 'Cornish' culture is the product of three waves of cultural production, which all added aspects to the symbolic repertoire that identity draws on. These three waves can be classified as industrial culture, guide book service culture and Revivalist culture. They do not follow each other neatly in a procession through history, but overlap and interact in a complex fashion.[25] Each wave of cultural reproduction added its own content to the modern Cornish cultural complex.

There were two phases in the production of the industrial culture. In the first phase, before the 1870s, it was a dynamic, confident and outward-looking culture of mine and chapel overlaid and combined with a pre-industrial culture of feast days, customs such as the Padstow Obby Oss and Helston's Furry Day or popular recreations such as wrestling. By the mid-nineteenth century an expressive regional industrial culture had been forged and it was this culture that left us symbols like the pasty, saffron bun and engine house. But, in the economic re-structuring that followed the 1860s the process of modernisation faltered, lost its internal dynamism and was fossilised. A new round of capital investment, or in this case dis-investment, combined after the 1870s with an opening up to newer influences from across the Tamar to restructure the industrial culture. In this second phase of the industrial culture new symbols were grafted on to 'Cornish' culture. These included forms from English and Welsh working-class culture after the 1870s. Brass bands, male voice choirs and a spectator sport in the form of rugby football all found a ready appeal, especially in the west. These merged with the older Methodist-mining culture to produce an industrial culture by the 1900s closer in form to that in South Wales and parts of Northern England.

However, whereas these latter regions were still dynamic in the later nineteenth century, the Cornish people were forced to come to terms with a declining industrial base. Under-employment and economic insecurity led to a culture of 'making-do' as heroism in the face of grinding day to day hardship became a social virtue.[26] This in turn produced a fatalistic edge to the local culture by the later 1890s, reflected in the regional literature of the time.[27] An inward-looking, more austere attitude to life accompanied this mood as the culture was re-structured away from a confident assertiveness towards dependency.[28] It was perhaps this phase that produced the '. . . familial and communal support networks which have been developed by Padstonians in the face of adversity' that Gilligan noted in his study of post-War Padstow. McArthur also suggests that close kinship networks '. . . do seem noticeable among Cornish people, forming a "society within a society"'.[29]

Meanwhile, as Cornish culture shifted towards dependency, the older culture of mining-Methodist communities had been exported across the globe. Mass emigration resulted in the short-lived phenomenon of a global Cornish culture, particularly evident in such places as South Australia.[30] Emigration in turn had further local effects such as reinforcing the emerging myth of individualism and in producing a new sexual division of labour, although one in which women, because of the absence of their men for shorter or longer periods, retained a relative autonomy and independence, at least in the domestic sphere.[31]

Despite the experiences of the later nineteenth century Cornwall, 'Cornishness' could still be collectively and vigorously expressed in the Edwardian period, but this time, significantly enough, through support for the Cornish rugby team rather than through the 'Cornish' version of religious revivalism. By the early twentieth century this popular Cornish industrial culture had become primarily associated with the working-class. Twentieth century Cornish popular culture was a class culture but, significantly, a class culture without class politics, as levels of trade unionisation and Labour Party support remained low. Meanwhile, some of the Cornish middle-classes were exploring other forms of 'Cornish' culture, forms which comprise the second and third waves of cultural production and which were to play their part in creating late twentieth century Cornish culture.

One wave of culture production rested on the expansion of tourism. John Urry has suggested how tourism, by emphasising the 'difference' of a particular place in order to sell it, can add to the 'symbolic repertoire' of locality, re-emphasising and articulating existing differences.[32] This role for tourism was certainly present in Cornwall, but with a significant difference. Tourism and the associated outpouring of guide book literature on Cornwall did not in the main re-emphasise existing differences but created new differences and new myths often revolving around aspects of the landscape and a sense of 'mystery'.[33] There were few immediate links between these outsider images of Cornwall and the popular, indigenous view, based on the experience of nineteenth century industrialisation. And yet the new aspects of 'difference' gradually, as the twentieth century progressed, fed back into local notions of Cornish culture. This was partly because the guide book view of a timeless, mysterious Cornwall, a place of seascape and escape, was part of that dominant service-class culture based on the South East of England. This culture was in turn spread both by the emerging mass communication networks of post-War Britain and by the growing numbers of new middle-class residents after the 1950s who brought their own images of Cornwall with them.[34]

In contrast, the third wave of cultural production, while sharing similar roots as the guide book wave in the broad romantic movement, unashamedly appealed to indigenous Cornish 'difference'. This was the Cornish Revival, emerging in the late nineteenth century and taking organisational form in the inter-War period. The Revivalists looked to the more distant past in order to rebuild the cultural identity. Surrounded by the relics of a failed industrialism, they preferred to return to the pre-Reformation era when Cornwall was more indisputably 'Cornish' and non-English and a Celtic vernacular was the majority language. They set to with a will to create and recreate all the symbols and paraphernalia of a Celtic nationality - the Cornish language, the flag, a Gorseth modelled on Wales and Brittany, even kilts and a Cornish tartan. Much of their effort in the 1950s was expended in trying to popularise these.

All three of these waves of cultural production, despite their apparent exclusiveness, appear to have converged and, to some extent, merged since the 1970s to produce a rich complex of Cornish culture from which the contemporary identity draws. This was most noticeable in the late 1980s and early 1990s when the pilgrimages to Twickenham marked a new, qualitatively different 'style' of Cornishness. A new cultural synthesis was being constructed as symbols were borrowed in an eclectic and unselfconscious fashion from the various streams that make up the stock of Cornish cultural resources. Singing 'The Song of the Western Men', better known as 'Trelawny', the symbolic hanging of a pasty from the goalposts, or the parading of an Obby Oss all have deep roots in popular Cornish culture. But these were supplemented by St Piran's flags, tartan kilts and other aspects of the Revivalist culture, along with an enthusiastic adoption of symbols from other cultures such as the 'Mexican wave'! At last, the gulf between popular and Revivalist culture seemed to have been bridged with this co-mingling of cultural symbols. Popular culture, Celticity and history were merging.

This observation is reinforced by comparing the pre-match messages in 1991 of the Presidents of the Cornwall and the Yorkshire Rugby Football Unions. While the Yorkshireman saw 'county' rugby mainly as a stepping stone to 'English rugby', this emphasis was entirely missing from the Cornish President's address. Instead, he referred to Bishop Trelawny's imprisonment and the legendary events of the seventeenth century and argued that '. . . the Cornish have the additional motivation of a Celtic people striving to preserve an identity'.[35]

This emphasises our earlier point that the actual form of the cultural complex is far less important than the meanings given to it. This helps us resolve one aspect of the Cornish paradox. Cornish culture, seen from the outside, is not obviously distinguishable from wider 'British' culture. After all there is no commonly spoken Celtic language as in Wales nor distinct administrative-legal forms as in Scotland. Academics search in vain for those distinct and objective cultural markers of difference that are instrumental rather than 'merely' affective symbols. And yet there remains a surprisingly persistent identity. The Cornish people continue to define themselves as somehow 'different'. Such an apparent paradox can only be explained if we stop seeing identity as being reduced to and defined by culture. The relationship may in fact be the other way around. As McArthur argues, the debate over whether Cornish culture is indistinguishable from wider English culture is immaterial. The perception of difference is what is important.[36] This is not to argue that there is no relation between culture and the strength of ethnic identity. Clearly there is. However, the point is that culture does not have a rigid determining effect. Cultures can and do change but ethnic identities remain, as the experience of Eastern Europe and Central Asia attests. In any case, the conclusion has to be that Cornish culture has sufficient distinguishing features which, together with a distinct image of Cornwall, provide resources for the Cornish identity.

STRUCTURAL CHANGES & THE CORNISH IDENTITY

How has the identity been affected by the major economic and demographic changes in Cornwall since 1945? The Cornish economy since the War has moved steadily away from its former base of farming, extractive industries and engineering. There has been a parallel rise of service employment and a growth of tourism which have both helped to attract a mobile new population. This has led, outside the clay district, to a break-up of traditional communities based on occupational homogeneity and solidarity. The arrival of a new population, attracted by environmental considerations, and the rise of second home ownership has had its effect on the housing market and helped exacerbate housing problems for the indigenous population. Since the 1970s the population-led growth that has occurred has added its own developmental pressures as Cornwall experiences some of the fastest growth rates in the UK. Grief at loss of environment combines with the disappearance of the former social networks and community solidarities to result in what are seen as 'threats' to the identity.[37]

Demographic growth is perceived as the biggest threat in this broad process of change. Immigration is often seen as 'submerging' a Cornish way of life. McArthur found that her informants, especially the older ones, saw incomers as 'basically materialistic' and as having more class-ridden values. They tended to contrast the 'greedy and competitive' attitudes being brought in with the 'indigenous attitude of sufficient is enough' (more than a hint here of the 'making-do' culture referred to above).[38] This popular and fatalist reaction has been mirrored by the Cornish intelligentsia. Professor Charles Thomas wrote in 1973 that '. . . there are not many real Cornish left and there is not all that much left of the real Cornwall'.[39] Perry has also drawn a bleak picture of a 'Cornwall swamped by a flood of middle-class, middle-aged, middle-browed city-dwellers who effectively imposed their standards upon local society. Integration and assimilation was a one-way process - of "urbanisation" rather than "ruralisation"'.[40] This '. . . invasion by functionaries of the dominant consumer culture of southern England combined with other forces to erode local identity'.[41]

The scale of demographic change since the 1960s should of course not be underestimated, although, interestingly enough, it is often exaggerated, both in popular comments and by the local media.[42] It appears from the rather scattered evidence on the numbers of Cornish-born (not necessarily the same, it should be noted, as the numbers claiming to be Cornish) that the proportion in the early 1990s was probably between 50 and 55%, with less in rural, and especially rural-coastal areas and the commuter belt near Plymouth, and a higher proportion in the towns and the remaining rural-industrial parishes of mid-Cornwall. This proportion has fallen from between 70-75% in the space of one generation, clearly a fairly large social change.[43]

However, while Perry and Thomas, along with much popular sentiment, conclude that this has had a negative effect on the local cultural identity, the actual effect was in fact the complete reverse. Analysis that focuses on 'erosion' of culture and 'submergence' of the Cornish seems to co-exist oddly with the other evidence already noted about the persistence of a sense of regional identity. For example, McArthur notes the '... sharpening of ethnic sentiment among many Cornish people ...' in the 1980s and points out that while, in the past, people had been '...brought up to feel inferior about being Cornish' there was now a reaction against this and '... younger people were said to be more explicitly aware of their ethnicity than their parents had been'.[44]

More spectacular evidence for the strengthening of Cornish ethnic consciousness in the 1980s and early 1990s was provided by the upsurge of displays of Cornish allegiance ('Trelawny's Army') that accompanied the trips of the Cornish rugby team to Twickenham in 1989, 1991 and 1992. Success in the County Championship provided a catalyst for ethnic assertion. This was less to do with rugby and more to do with celebrating Cornishness. Twickenham provided the location for a celebration of Cornish ethnicity. It was carnival on a large scale, an unashamed collective display of Cornish pride. The symbolism of Twickenham echoed through smaller scale carnivals in communities across Cornwall in the early 1990s.[45]

So we have the apparent paradox of a vigorous ethnic consciousness finding expression in social and communal terms together with rapid social and cultural change. This puzzle is explained by suggesting that the demographic and social changes themselves were a key factor in strengthening ethnic identity during the years since the 1960s. For evidence of this we can turn to Herman Gilligan's work on social change in Padstow. He found that the economic and social changes in the 1960s associated with the appearance of a better-off incoming population attracted via tourism in fact enhanced '... the cultural significance of what it meant to be "local", and engendered an almost exaggerated sense of Padstonian communal solidarity'.[46] It was no coincidence that Padstow figured prominently among the first successful electoral interventions of MK (Mebyon Kernow) in the mid-1960s. This renewed sense of 'difference' was heightened by a reaction to social change rather than submerged by it. Local 'Cornish' culture had sufficient resilience and vitality to restructure itself as a bulwark against social change, a restructuring that revitalised the identity. In the 1970s and 1980s, with continuing high levels of in-migration to all parts of Cornwall, this reaction was generalised and led to an enhanced sense of identity, at one and the same time nostalgic and defensive and yet also assertive and forward-looking. This is not a phenomenon confined to Cornwall. Savage has noted that, instead of the spread of mass society having eradicated the sense of place and local culture as was predicted by many in the 1950s, what has happened since the 1960s is that people have a greater identification with their imagined community.[47] An increased perception and awareness of local 'difference' co-exists with a growing uniformity of leisure pursuits, shopping practices or consumption patterns. Cohen reiterates this;

> ... the strength of local culture thus does not necessarily

> diminish as the locality becomes increasingly precarious: quite often the reverse seems to be the case, when the maintenance of the culture becomes the effective *raison d'etre* of the peripheral community.[48]

The apparent paradox of Cornwall - a renewed sense of identity along with a reduction in cultural isolation - is thus explained.

To sum up thus far, we have seen how a particular history has helped produce an ethnic consciousness among the Cornish. This has interacted with changing images of Cornwall to produce a distinct regional identity. However, regional and national identities can also act as possible sites of resistance and give rise to their own ideas of the 'good society'.[49] In the Cornish case this aspect has been much more limited.

THE POLITICS OF THE CORNISH IDENTITY

In Cornwall the heightened sense of identification with a locality is able to tap into an existing sense of Cornishness that has, as we have seen, deep historical roots. However, a more assertive sense of social identity has not been transformed into an active political ethnonationalism. As McArthur notes, the social changes of the post-1950 period have produced 'ongoing grumbles', but not '. . . nationalist political mobilisation'.[50] Cornish popular identity was not, of itself, able to transform resentment at social change into a demand for political change, and preferred to take refuge in fatalism and nostalgia:

> The population is practically new and is increasing. The few old residents who parade the streets at times to do their shopping must not expect to meet any of their old friends but must be content to mix with a crowd of strangers as if they were walking the streets of London . . . Do we old residents like it? No, we don't, but what can we do about it . . . .[51]

Cornish ethnicity has only sporadically been mobilised in a political way and then in what were essentially reactive campaigns. Clearly, if one focuses on political aspects of identity rather than social aspects then the strength of the Cornish identity is more questionable. Indeed, the tendency by political scientists has been to equate regional identity with support for ethnonationalist movements. Levels of ethnic consciousness are simply read off from the numbers voting for political nationalist movements.[52] In the British state, this means votes in General Elections. However, this approach is far too narrow. Even in the electoral sphere, a concentration on Westminister elections underestimates the strength of voting for MK. In the 1979 Euro-election, when it scored its biggest electoral success, it won 6% of the vote. In fact, because of the combined constituency, this must have represented a far bigger proportion

- perhaps as much as 9.5% - of the vote in Cornwall, or (it might be argued) up to 17% of the ethnic Cornish vote. The consistently respectable votes achieved by MK at Cornish local elections are also ignored.[53] For example, in the 1993 Cornwall County Council elections MK - as well as retaining its seat at Penzance - was able to beat Labour into fourth place in one ward and the mean vote of its seven candidates, at 19.0%, compared well with Labour at 22.4%, the six Liberals on 15.3% and the four Green Party candidates who averaged 5.4%.

In fact there is no necessary correlation between the strength of a cultural identity and the support for political groups and parties. Oddly enough, this is sometimes recognised for places other than Cornwall at the same time as the failure of a Cornish nationalist electoral breakthrough is seen as reason to deny the existence of a Cornish identity. While writing-off Cornish ethnonationalism as 'miniscule' (although its very presence would seem to distinguish Cornwall from its neighbours to the east) Jeffrey Stanyer *et al.* argue that the sense of cultural identity is '. . .one of the strongest sources of difference between [Cornwall/Devon and Brittany]'.[54] Brittany is thus invested with a strong sense of cultural identity, in contrast to Cornwall. And yet the level of support for Breton political nationalist parties has been no higher than that for Cornish nationalists during the past 20 years. In the 1992 French Regional elections Breton nationalist/regionalist lists won only from 1.7% of the votes in Loire Atlantique to 3.8% in Cotes d'Armor.[55] This was no higher than the Cornish nationalist share of the poll in West Cornwall (i.e. 3-4%) in the 1979 General Election, despite the first past the post system in Britain which has a built-in bias against minor parties.

Although the relative weakness of Cornish ethnonationalism would therefore seem to be exaggerated by its detractors from east of the Tamar, we still need to explain the absence of a strong ethnonationalist movement. There are three broad types of factors that could be cited. First, structural factors could militate against political mobilisation on ethnic grounds. Second, one could turn to the nature of Cornish culture itself. The weakness of ethnonationalism could be linked to the absence of those cultural elements strong enough to underpin political mobilisation.[56] Finally, we could look to the role of the Cornish intelligentsia for our explanation.

We have already seen suggestions that the Cornish identity has been 'submerged' by the structural changes of the past 30 years. Perry *et al.*, for example, argued that '. . . whereas the century-long intrusions of artists, craftworkers, traders and visitors had barely disturbed the traditional core of Cornish life . . . the bourgeois invasion of the 1960s and 1970s, along with technological and economic changes, destroyed it!'[57] But the economic changes that have transformed Cornwall can be interpreted quite differently. For example, Colin Williams has set out three preconditions for ethnic mobilisation. First, there is 'regional structural decline' leading to economic dependency and marginalisation; second, a cultural division of labour exists, with the higher status posts in the economy occupied by non-indigenous people; finally, state policies or local entrepreneurs are unable to redress the balance.[58] All three of these are surely applicable to Cornwall.

First, the emergence of a 'branch-plant economy' and the continuation of a 'dependent, relatively weak regional economy' has been well documented.[59] Second, McArthur offers the qualitative observation that '... in local government administration, teaching establishments, the health authority, and the professions generally, far more incomers are employed at intermediate and higher levels than are Cornish people'[60] and this cultural division of labour may be extended to management of local business. Quantitatively, this impression is reinforced by the survey carried out by Ronald Perry and others in the early 1980s. They found that 49% of 'new settlers' were located in the two highest socio-economic groups, whereas only 23% of 'locals' were in these groups.[61] Finally, state policies, both at Westminister and locally, have failed to solve the chronic economic problems of high unemployment and low wage levels. So, following Williams' criteria, Cornwall should if anything have a strong ethnonationalist movement, and not a weak one. The structural pre-conditions are there but the reasons for a weak ethnonationalism must be sought elsewhere.

CULTURAL CORE VALUES

Daniele Conversi argues that certain core values in an ethnic culture can be prompted for the purposes of ethnic mobilisation. These core values are certain symbols and images, '... pivots around which the whole social and identificational system of the group is organised'.[62] Conversi suggests the key values that can be used for mobilisation are religion (as for Serbs and Croats), family (secular Jews, Italians), race (Chinese), language (Welsh), or territory (Australian aborigines). One of these tends to be stressed as symbolic of the group and its membership, although the choice of core values can change over time.

In Cornwall, religion was an important differentiating factor in the early nineteenth century; Methodism '... came to serve as a badge of regionalism, and as a buttress to Cornish "nationalism" in the face of encroaching forces and influences from "up-country" England'.[63] However, although Cornwall still has a far higher proportion of Methodists amongst its church attenders - 48% in 1979 compared to only 18% in Devon - the general decline of religious attendance, down to around 12% of the adult Cornish population in 1979, indicates a less central role for religion.[64]

We have already seen how family links have been cited as an important element of Cornish culture, a factor emphasised by Lyn Bryant in Chapter 8. However, it is unlikely that family can fill the role of a core value, differentiating the Cornish from other groups. In a similar way, 'race' presents problems. While McArthur found that her informants often mentioned such factors as 'blood' she argues that '... familial descent seemed to provide a much stronger basis for Cornishness than reference to "race", or its associated communal "blood"'.[65] But there is no commonly accepted popular definition of who should be regarded as 'Cornish' according to descent criteria. In any case, appeals to a core value of 'race' has certain problems, particularly in a polyethnic society such as Cornwall as large numbers will be excluded.[66] As Conversi puts it, '. . .it is always possible to learn a new language. It is never possible to change one's forefathers'.[67] This and the difficulties of definition may be why appeals to race have not been strikingly successful in Cornwall.[68]

A far more universal core value for ethnicity in the modern world is language. It is no coincidence that one of the first tasks of the Cornish Revivalists of the 'Celto-Cornish Movement' in the early 1900s was to persuade Henry Jenner to write his *Handbook of the Cornish Language*. The revival of the Cornish language has been a central symbolic aspiration of the broad Cornish Revival movement. The difficulty facing this project is, however, that the Cornish language presents certain (insuperable?) problems in becoming a core value for ethnicity. First and foremost, it is not an instrumental part of people's lives; it is not a community vernacular in any part of Cornwall and all there is to show for the efforts of Revivalists over almost half a century is a handful of bi-lingual children and maybe 200 relatively competent speakers. While an important affective symbol of Cornishness, the language is unlikely to mobilise large numbers of people in its defence. With its demise too close in time to be ignored by the Revivalists but too far in the past to be captured (as was Manx) by tape recorders and modern linguists the language is also prone to fragmentation and dispute over its revived basis.[69] Its ghost walks uneasily among the modern Cornish, present in place and personal names but nevertheless elusive. Attempts to replace the Cornish language by Cornish dialect/accent as a core value also run up against the problem that there are two (at least) accents in Cornwall, the one in the east being close to the accent of English spoken in West Devon. Indeed, the Cornish dialect has rarely been used for purposes of political mobilisation.[70] All these factors - religion, family, race, language - therefore play a part in Cornish cultural identity and can mean something to an individual Cornish person. However, none of them seems to qualify as a 'core value' and this may help to explain the relative absence of mobilisation along ethnic lines in Cornwall.

Those examples of mobilisation that have occurred have been in response to threats to the integrity of Cornwall. The physical land of Cornwall itself has become something of an ethnic symbol, the 'border question' which mobilised the Cornish population more than any other.[71] The local government proposals of 1969-72 which threatened a 'Tamarside' county centred on Plymouth led to a widespread campaign to defend the territorial integrity of Cornwall. This, Payton argues, was '. . . a demonstration of the extent to which the politicised objective to defend and promote the Cornish identity had permeated Cornish society'.[72] This broad based (and successful) campaign in defence of the territory in that period was succeeded in the 1980s by the campaign for a separate Cornish constituency for the European Parliament. The strength of feeling against the boundary recommendations of 1978 that joined Cornwall to Plymouth was illustrated by the objections received from 76 parish councils in Cornwall compared to the mere 18 parish council objections to the proposed constituency boundaries for the whole of England. Similarly, in 1983 and 1988, Cornish objections forced Boundary Commission inquiries, the Campaign for a Cornish Constituency bringing together objections from a wide range of bodies, including Cornwall County Council, all the District Councils, and a majority of the local M.P.s, despite four of the five of them being government supporters.[73]

However, a core value of territory does not easily lend itself to political mobilisation, as it only reacts to perceived threats to that territory. Therefore, in part, the weakness of Cornish ethnonationalism may be explained by the legacy of Cornish culture and the absence of religion or language as core values. But this does not entirely explain the weakness as it is possible for popular culture to be re-moulded and new images made more central in the pursuit of ethnic political ends. If the group gives meaning to the cultural attributes then why have not the Cornish been able to give a political meaning to Cornish culture?

THE ROLE OF THE INTELLIGENTSIA

Anthony Smith has outlined another explanation of ethnic mobilisation. He argues that the role of the intelligentsia, such as teachers, journalists, ministers, writers, poets, is crucial in the articulation of an ethnic identity. If this intelligentsia finds its opportunities blocked it will turn to its ethnic roots, first spearheading a cultural renaissance and then leading political movements demanding autonomy.[74] It is certainly true that these groups - especially teachers - played an important role in both the cultural Revival in the pre-War period and in the formation and early years of MK in the 1950s and 1960s.

The precise role of the ethnic intellectuals (as the producers of ideas) is, according to Smith, to provide maps and moralities for the people. This takes two forms - 'poetic spaces', whereby history is 'naturalised' through the integration of monuments and landscape, and 'golden ages', where an ethnic past is re-created through a historiography that authentically belongs to that group. In Cornwall the 'poetic spaces' are more apparent than the 'golden ages'! Standing stones, quoits, even ruined engine houses and clay burrows, have been integrated into the landscape and have become quintessentially 'part' of Cornwall. Yet a distinct Cornish historiography is less visible. And the role of the Cornish intelligentsia has been limited and ambiguous in the post-War period. Because of this, political mobilisation has also been limited and partial.

The reasons for this are four-fold: ideological, historical, economic and social. Ideologically, there was, in the early pre-War period, a lack of harmonisation between the leaders of the Cornish Revival and the Cornish people. Early twentieth century Revivalism had bequeathed to the post-War generations a Celtic project. Henry Jenner and his contemporaries had returned to an idealised pre-industrial, Catholic, Cornish speaking past for their inspiration.

To the early Revivalists what was 'most Celtic' was 'most Cornish'.[75] However, the problem with this vision of Celtic purity was that it lacked a harmony and continuity with the more immediate past.[76] As we have seen, the culture of the Cornish people had been forged by their experience of, first, industrialisation and, then, de-industrialisation. It was predominantly Methodist, Liberal in its politics, with leisure pursuits drawn from the nineteenth century. As a consequence it always required a conscious effort of will to identify with the vision of the Revivalists.[77] Attempts to synthesise the Revival and popular culture, most notable in the Old Cornwall movement begun in the 1920s, foundered on the difficulties of bridging the gap between a politically limited but socially still vibrant Cornish popular identity and a politically more aware (in the broadest sense) but socially irrelevant Revivalism.

Hindsight can, however, make us too critical of those early Revivalists. There were also major objective problems posed by Cornish history. These were essentially the problems of de-industrialisation. While Cornish popular identity was moulded by its industrial experience, that industrial experience had palpably collapsed. Living amongst the ruins of Cornwall's industrial past - in the early twentieth century - Cornish intellectuals had difficulties coming to terms with it. Payton has pointed out how they were torn between contrasting visions (or ideologies) of Cornwall's past.[78] Some looked to the achievements of the industrial period, when Cornwall led the world in deep mining technology. The problem was that, with the collapse of mining and the stagnation and dependence of the Cornish economy, this view of an industrial golden age became pure nostalgia as each glimmer of economic recovery proved a false dawn and it became ever plainer that the classic age of industrial prowess would not return. Others, as we have seen, returned to a golden age more securely lost in the past, but, in doing so, ignored the facts of modern Cornish history. The failures of the period of 'paralysis' were therefore either glorified or ignored. Neither was a satisfactory strategic response for articulating a view of the past that could form a basis of mobilisation for the future. In addition, the presence of those contrasting visions also meant that there was no generally accepted consensus of values uniting the intelligentsia.

The third and fourth factors are more important for explaining the constraints on the growth of a self-confident Cornish intelligentsia. The dependence of the Cornish economy results in a relatively low level of administrative and professional jobs, so those Cornish people with qualifications have left in search of jobs. The stunted higher education infrastructure in Cornwall, with only specialised institutions like the Camborne School of Mines and Falmouth School of Art present, has a similar effect. The absence of a generalised Higher Education institution in Cornwall means that the research and development that accompanies it is also missing, together with the associated employment opportunities, so those who leave find it difficult to return. Other developments reinforced the constraints on the emergence of a powerful indigenous middle-class. The UK-wide labour market for middle-class jobs after 1945 combined with the increasing relative environmental attractiveness of Cornwall, in turn resting on rising mobility and holidaymaking, to guarantee growing competition for such jobs in Cornwall. Environmental attractions and the labour market thus provide limits to the production of a 'Cornish' middle-class.

Socially also, the indigenous intelligentsia would require a rational reason for adopting ethnic politics. Two points are relevant in explaining the absence of such a rationality and both relate back to the nature of Cornish culture. First, there was no obvious ethnic basis for enhanced life-chances. Unlike in Wales, where the Welsh language provides opportunities for a bi-lingual middle-class, there was nothing similar for an indigenous Cornish middle-class to aim at. Second, the Cornish intelligentsia did not find their opportunities blocked as long as they were prepared to leave Cornwall. There were no cultural barriers to their advancement in England (except perhaps an unduly pronounced Cornish accent). It is significant in this respect that the upsurges in Cornish political nationalism both at the end of the 1940s and again in the 1970s coincided with the presence of an increased number of qualified people who were demanding, for a variety of reasons, the right to live in Cornwall but who, in Cornwall, *did* find their opportunities blocked by the way the labour market worked.

As a result of these factors Cornwall has tended to look outside for its intelligentsia.[79] These come in two types. First, there is that class of modernising intelligentsia that occupy local government bureaucracies or business offices. These do little to establish an ideological reservoir of 'difference'. Quite the contrary, as their presence helps tie Cornwall into policies and processes devised elsewhere and denies the 'differentness' of Cornwall, at least in 'practical' policy terms. But the effects of such 'career-transient' migrants are leavened by those among their colleagues who move for more or less explicit environmental reasons. Moreover, there has been a movement since the late nineteenth century of a second kind of intelligentsia -the artists, attracted to the reputation of first Newlyn, and then St Ives as art colonies. Their role in helping to create a romantic image of Cornwall's 'difference', an image which interacted with the guide book writers of the tourist industry, needs exploring.[80]

We can suggest that the art colonies played a role, given the relative weakness of the indigenous intelligentsia, in extending the base of cultural resources to buttress people's ethnic identity. McArthur has pointed out that '. . . the romantic images of Cornwall were felt to be so powerful, that many Cornish people were said to "believe" in them'.[81] The nature of the myth created by the art colonisers provided a particular form of 'poetic space' while ignoring 'golden ages'. In this form it was not just the monuments that were 'naturalised'. If Cornwall had a '. . . hidden force, this strange, brooding, compelling quality', then so did the Cornish people, who were '. . . like their land, an old and knowing race, withdrawn to strangers, living as much in the past as the present; without, as has been said, much creative inspiration yet with a quick response to things of that nature'.[82] This view was not so far removed from the nostalgia for the disappeared days of glory induced by the socio-economic paralysis of the early twentieth century or the associated defeatism and fatalism that permeated the 'making-do' culture of the people. In fact, it provided that dependent culture with an air of mystery, to some extent legitimising it in the process. The artistic intelligentsia thus helped to maintain the stock of ethnic cultural resources through the period of paralysis into the 1950s and 1960s and, from yet another direction, reassured the Cornish that they were indeed 'different'. These were 'outsider' images that became, to some extent, 'insider' images. But these romantic images did not politicise - indeed may even have helped de-politicise - the regional identity.

The nature of the Cornish Revival, the problems of coping with a recent history of de-industrialisation, the economic and social structures that limited the growth of an indigenous middle class and replaced it in part by an incoming one, all help to explain the limited emergence of a confident and self-assertive Cornish intelligentsia before the 1980s.[83] However, again there were some signs in the 1980s that this was changing, some glimmerings of an intellectual renaissance in Cornwall. Elements of both the Cornish and the incoming middle-class found common ground in the later 1980s in opposition to the environmental effects of large scale 'developments' and a massive road building programme linked to a continued high rate of population growth. Green protest in Cornwall had a cultural dimension. A more confident articulation of a Cornish identity in the late 1980s in turn drew from and paralleled the growing confidence of the popular identity. Generational changes in the Cornish working-class and the increased educational mobility of the 1960s and 1970s had brought popular culture and the Cornish middle-classes closer together again. Just as the Cornish popular culture drew strength from the sporadic articulation of identity in the local media (the appearance of Radio Cornwall in 1982 was a significant factor in this) so too did the new Cornish intelligentsia draw inspiration from, and join in, the activities of popular culture.

Artistically too, the late 1980s saw a minor flowering of theatre groups, Cornish dancing and musical activities. 'Cornish' artistic culture is probably as vigorous as at any time since 1945. Even in the field of literature - as John Hurst notes in Chapter 13 - the 1980s saw the emergence of a 'new wave' of indigenous novelists. These, while still containing elements of the fatalism that marked the work of Jack Clemo in the 1940s, show a lively indigenous re-working of both older themes and the influences popularised by the guide-book writers.[84]

CORNISH ETHNICITY INTO THE TWENTY FIRST CENTURY

What is the future of the Cornish identity in the next century? There are probably three main interrelated perceived 'threats' to Cornish identity. The first is the broad process of 'development' based on large-scale population growth. The 'development' paradigm in Cornwall, driven by global forces and centralist political structures, appears to imply a 'denial of separateness' and poses an immediate and visible physical threat to Cornwall's 'poetic spaces' and, by implication, the Cornish identity. And yet it was this same threat which, in the 1980s, helped to stimulate the emergence of greater resistance to the dominant development paradigm and precipitate a more articulate Cornish-based anti-metropolitan alternative.

The second threat is the general process of globalisation. This appears to lead to a cultural uniformity as people across the globe consume the same package of cultural products constructed by (typically) American-based transnational media corporations and transmitted via global TV networks based on satellite broadcasting technology. In the spirit of post-Cold War triumphalism a new culture of bland consumerism is being imposed, eroding differences between peoples. Or is it? Just as ethnic allegiances appear to have survived, indeed strengthened, during the move to a mass consumer society based on Fordist production methods, so they may well survive the globalised mass society version of the 'post-Fordist' era. Smith has pointed to the pastiche of cultural styles and the common 'scientific/technical' discourse that marks the 'global' culture. But he also notes how the cultural artefacts are ripped from national cultures. Without the cultural resource of these national cultures the global culture could have no existence. It is, he argues, only through people's identification with a particular place that cultures take on meanings and he rejects the possibility of a homogenous 'global' culture.[85]

The third threat to the Cornish identity is the more local process leading to 'Devonwall', the amalgamation of Devon and Cornwall for administrative and business purposes. This is an example of a changing scientific classification of the region (see Paasi's model above) linked to institutions that are engaged in a project to re-form regional identities . The years since the late 1960s have seen the gradual construction of Devon-and-Cornwall institutions - for example, the police authority, privatised monopolies like water, gas and electricity, business organisations like the CBI, chambers of commerce, political parties (the Cornwall Young Conservatives merged with their colleagues in Devon in 1992) - culminating in the formation of the Devon and Cornwall TEC.

The results of this process have been the removal of administration and employment from Cornwall and the blurring of any case for special treatment that policy makers in Cornwall might want to make. Indeed, local policy makers seem to follow a twin-track policy on Devonwall. Publically, moves to form 'Tamarside' counties are opposed or the demand for a Cornish only Euro-constituency supported. Privately, co-operation with planners and policy-makers in Devon has proceeded within an increasingly institutionalised Devonwall framework since the formation of the Devon and Cornwall Joint Committee in 1974. Culturally, however, the Cornish identity is a problem for the Devonwall-builders. This was recognised in 1974 when Cornwall County Council's planners saw one role of the Devon and Cornwall Joint Committee as establishing '. . . a regional identity for Devon and Cornwall comparable to that of other peripheral regions'.[86] Clearly, there is a conflict between the social engineering of a Devonwall identity (of which it must be said there is precious little evidence in Cornwall, despite the generally uncritically Devonwall assumptions of media, higher education bodies such as the Plymouth Business School, and the state) and the persistence of a specifically Cornish identity. Given the salience of territory as a core value of the Cornish identity, cultural Devonwall could only be built on the ashes of that identity. There is thus a clear contradiction between the Cornish identity and the Devonwall project.

However, there are also opportunities for the Cornish identity as it nears the end of the century. The move into Europe has had the result of shifting attention back to a regional level. Local authorities in the UK now lobby Europe and meet with other European regions independently of London (as in the Atlantic Arc). At the same time the emergence of a European level of governmental institutions has combined with the renewed emphasis on regions to downgrade the importance of the traditional nation-state. While this can be exaggerated, perhaps especially so in respect of the relatively conservative and centralist British state structures, it does provide more potential autonomy for regional level initiatives. Additionally, the Cornish identity has received re-assurance and moral support from Brussels and Strasbourg in a manner that has never been possible with Westminster and Whitehall, Cornish culture having received recognition in the European Parliament's *Laroni* and draft *Killillea* reports, and with the Cornish Bureau for European Relations forging links with the Parliament's Inter-Group on Minority Languages and Cultures. Similarly, the Council of Europe has responded enthusiastically to European expressions of Cornish identity, with the Council sponsoring the opening of the 'St Michael's Way' pilgrimage route in Cornwall in May 1994.

Furthermore, it has been proposed that so-called 'post-industrialism' brings with it new post-materialist values, such as concern with the quality of life and the need for 'belonging'. Studler and McAllister argue that, among life-style issues that will mark the political debates of the post-industrial world, ethnicity will be a major one.[87] While there may be some problems with this thesis, not the least of which is that those societies with the greatest ethnic cleavages - in Eastern Europe and Central Asia - do not seem to be the most 'post-industrial', the enhanced need to 'belong' and to have 'roots' in an otherwise anonymous, privatised society dominated by the unpredictabilities of market relations may well lead to a greater level of ethnic identification over time.

CONCLUSION

The question we are left with for the twenty first century is whether the Cornish cultural renaissance will remain on a purely popular and socio-cultural level, an interesting element to be co-opted by the next generation of guide book writers, or whether the social identity will find lasting political aspirations. At present we are living in somewhat ambiguous and confusing times. There is a revitalised and strengthened Cornish identity in the cultural and social sphere, but despite the emergence of a strongly anti-metropolitan political culture reflected in political behaviour often distinct from that of England, there is a seemingly inexorable movement towards Devonwall institutions in the political and economic arena. There is, however, evidence of a renewed concern for territory and identity within the planning process in Cornwall.[88] Only time will show how these contradictions will be resolved, but historical experience suggests the resiliance of Cornish ethnicity.

REFERENCES

1. *West Briton*, 16 April 1992.
2. Cornwall County Council, *Cornwall Structure Plan*, Truro, 1980, p11.
3. Michel Denis, Jean Pihan and Jeffrey Stanyer, 'The Peripheries Today', in Michael Havinden, J.Queniart, J.Stanyer, *Centre and Periphery : Brittany and Cornwall and Devon Compared*, University of Exeter Press, Exeter, 1991, p38; see pp70-71 and Chapter 17 of the same book for what appears to be evidence for marked differences between Cornwall and Devon.
4. *Cornish Times*, 20 March 1987.
5. Philip Abrams, *Historical Sociology*, Shepton Mallet, 1982, p230.
6. Kenneth Thompson, 'Religion, Values and Ideology', in Robert Bocock and Kenneth Thompson (eds.), *Social and Cultural Forms of Modernity*, Polity Press, Cambridge, 1992, pp230-268.
7. Anthony P.Cohen (ed.), *Symbolising Boundaries: Identity and Diversity in British Cultures*, Manchester University Press, Manchester, 1986, p17.
8. Nigel Thrift, 'For a new Regional Geography', *Progress in Human Geography*, 15, 4, 1991; Robert Bocock, 'The cultural formations of modern society', in Stuart Hall and Bram Gieben (eds.), *Formations of Modernity*, Polity Press, Cambridge, 1992, pp230-268.
9. Anssi Paasi, 'The Institutionalization of Regions: A Theoretical Framework for Understanding the Emergence of Regions and the Constitution of Regional Identity', *Fennia*, 164, 1, 1986, pp105-146.
10. Anthony D.Smith, 'The Myth of the "Modern Nation" and the Myths of Nations', *Ethnic and Racial Studies*, 11, 1, 1988.
11. Anthony D.Smith, *The Ethnic Revival in the Modern World*, Cambridge, 1981, p70; note that this is a far wider definition than the view that equates ethnic identity only with political nationalism.
12. Mary McArthur, 'The Cornish: a Case Study in Ethnicity', unpublished MSc thesis, University of Bristol, 1988.
13. McArthur, 1988, p77.
14. McArthur, 1988, p81.
15. See also McArthur, 1988, pp.58-59 and the letters columns of the *Cornish Times* in June/July 1988.
16. McArthur, 1988, p.96.
17. Anthony D.Smith, *National Identity*, Penguin, London, 1991, p59.
18. John Rex, *Race and Ethnicity*, Open University Press, Milton Keynes, 1986.
19. Denys Val Baker, *The Spirit of Cornwall*, W.H.Allen, London, 1980, pp18 and 26.
20. For references to Cornish culture that emphasise its 'weakness' see Michael Hechter, *Internal Colonialism: The Celtic Fringe in British National Development*, Routledge and Kegan Paul, London, 1975, pp.64-65 and 101; Ken Shaw, 'Elements in the Notion of Peripheral Identity', in Michael Havinden *et al.* (eds.), 1991, pp224-227; Ronald Perry, Ken Dean, Bryan Brown, *Counterurbanisation: International Case Studies of Socio-Economic Change in Rural Areas*, Geo Books, Norwich, 1986, p.65.

21. Robert Morton Nance, 'Cornish Culture', *Cornish Review*, Spring 1949.
22. Perry *et al.*, 1986, p107.
23. *West Briton*, 5 May 1987.
24. See Bocock, 1992, pp.232-233; Raymond Williams, *Culture*, Fontana, London, 1981, pp10-11 and 13; Nigel Thrift, 'Images of Social Change', in Chris Hamnett *et al.* (eds.), *The Changing Social Structure*, Sage, London, 1989, pp12-42.
25. For a review of the history of cultural change in Cornwall see Philip Payton, *The Making of Modern Cornwall: Historical Experience and the Persistence of 'Difference'*, Dyllansow Truran, Redruth, 1992, pp55-65, 89-94, 128-135; see also Bernard Deacon and Philip Payton, 'Re-inventing Cornwall: Culture Change on the European Periphery', *Cornish Studies*, second series, 1, 1993.
26. For a comparative 'making-do' culture see Pauline Barner, 'Culture, Capital and Class Conflicts in the Political Economy of Cape Breton', *Journal of Historical Sociology*, 3, 4, 1980.
27. See Henry Harris, *The Luck of Wheal Vor*, Joseph Pollard, Truro, 1901 or H.D.Lowry, *Wreckers and Methodists*, Heinemann, London, 1893.
28. Payton, 1992, p114.
29. J.Herman Gilligan, 'The Rural Labour Process: A Case Study of a Cornish Town', in Tony Bradley and Philip Lowe (eds.), *Locality and Rurality: Economy and Society in Rural Regions*, Geo Books, Norwich, 1984, p102 and McArthur, 1988, p71.
30. See Philip Payton, 'The Cornish - a Global Identity?', *Kernowyon dres all an bys/Cornish Worldwide*, 6, 1992.
31. A.K.Hamilton Jenkin, *Cornwall and its People*, 1932-34, republished David and Charles, Newton Abbot, 1983; Gill Burke, 'The Cornish Miner and the Cornish Mining Industry, 1870-1921', unpublished PhD thesis, University of London, 1981, pp288ff and 331ff.
32. John Urry, *Holidaymaking, Cultural Change and the Seaside*, Lancaster Regional Group Working Paper No.22, 1987.
33. See Daphne du Maurier, *Vanishing Cornwall*, Gollancz, London, 1967; Denys Val Baker, *The Timeless Land*, Adams and Dart, Bath, 1973; also see Peter Stanier, *Cornwall's Literary Heritage*, Twelveheads Press, Truro, 1992, especially p2 and pp8-9, for other examples of this genre.
34. The 1980s emphasis on 'heritage' has provided new opportunities for the guide book culture to articulate with the classical, industrial culture in Cornwall. However, this project is by no means uncontested. For a vigorous critique of the heritage industry in Cornwall see Clive Carter, 'The Heritage Game', *Newsletter of the Trevithick Society*, 64, 1989.
35. *The Packet*, 13 April 1991.
36. McArthur, 1988, p81; also see D.H.Luker, 'Cornish Methodism, Revivalism and Popular Belief c.1780-1870', unpublished D.Phil thesis, University of Oxford, 1987, chapters 7 and 9 for the argument that the Cornish moulded early nineteenth century Methodism to make local Methodism distinctively 'Cornish'.
37. For this type of approach see Bernard Deacon, Andrew George, Ronald Perry, *Cornwall at the Crossroads*, CoSERG, Redruth, 1988 or Ronald Perry *et al.*, 1986.
38. McArthur, 1988, pp58, 75 and 89-90.
39. Charles Thomas, *The Importance of Being Cornish*, University of Exeter, 1973, p21.
40. Perry *et al*, 1986, p129.
41. Ronald Perry, 'Self-image, External Perceptions and Development Strategy in Cornwall', in Havinden *et al.* (eds.), 1991, pp230-232.
42. For example Radio Cornwall pronounced on opening in the early 1980s that only 40% of the population of Cornwall were Cornish - despite no evidence to support this assertion.
43. Bernard Deacon, 'We are not alone', *Carn*, 43, 1983; Perry *et al.*, 1986, Andrew Griffiths, *Change in the Countryside - the Cornish Perspective*, University of Exeter, Exeter, 1989, p121; information from Mr Peter Wills, 1992.
44. McArthur, 1988, p98.
45. See also the books that soon emerged to celebrate the Twickenham success of 1991 - Jerry Clarke and Terry Harry, *Tales of Twickenham*, Harry and Clarke, Redruth, 1991, and Colin

Gregory, *Cornwall: Rugby Champions*, Partridge Press, London, 1991.
46. Gilligan, 1984, p108.
47. Mike Savage, 'Spatial Differences in Modern Britain', in Hamnett *et al.* (eds.), 1989, pp244-268.
48. Anthony P.Cohen, 'Belonging: the Experience of Culture', in Cohen (ed.), *Belonging: Identity and Social Organisation in British Rural Cultures*, Manchester University Press, Manchester, 1982, p7.
49. John Borland, Ralph Fevre and David Denny, 'Nationalism and Community in North West Wales', *The Sociological Review*, 1992.
50. McArthur, 1988, p75.
51. Tom Tremewan, *A Builder's Life in Perranporth*, Oscar Blackford, Truro, 1974, pp103-104.
52. See Derek Hearl et al., 'Politics and Government in the Far South West', in Havinden *et al.* (eds.), 1991, p211.
53. Bernard Deacon, 'The Electoral Impact of Cornish Nationalism', in Cathal O Luain (ed.), *For a Celtic Future*, The Celtic League, Dublin, 1983, pp243-252.
54. Denis *et al.*, 1991, p38.
55. *Le Figaro*, 24 March 1992.
56. See Ken Shaw, 1991, pp224-227.
57. Perry *et al*, 1986, p66.
58. Colin H.Williams, 'Ideology and the Interpretation of Minority Cultures', *Political Geography Quarterly*, 3.2, 1984.
59. See for example Ronald Perry, 'The Role of the Small Manufacturing Business in Cornwall's Economic Development', in Gareth Shaw and Allan M.Williams (eds.), *Economic Development and Policy in Cornwall*, Plymouth Polytechnic, Plymouth, 1982, pp30-42 or D.Grafton and N.Bolton, 'Planning Policy and Economic Development in Devon and Cornwall 1945-84', in Peter Gripaios (ed.), *The Economy of Devon and Cornwall*, Plymouth Polytechnic, Plymouth, 1984, pp3-11.
60. McArthur, 1988, p81, and see Thomas, 1973, p13.
61. Perry *et al.*, 1986, p89.
62. Daniele Conversi, 'Language or Race?: The Choice of Core Values in the Development of Catalan and Basque Nationalisms', *Ethnic and Racial Studies*, 13, 1, 1990.
63. Luker, 1987, pxi.
64. Grace Davie and Derek Hearl, 'Religion and Politics in Cornwall and Devon', in Havinden *et al.* (eds.), 1991, pp223.
65. McArthur, 1988, p80.
66. c.f. Borland *et al*, 1992, for notions of 'community' in North West Wales.
67. Conversi, 1990, p68.
68. For examples see James Whetter, *A Celtic Tomorrow*, CNP Publications, St Austell, 1977, p79 and pp87-88 or *An Kenethlor*.
69. See also Chapter 10.
70. For an example of dialect being used in the 1885 Mining Division election see Bernard Deacon, 'Conybeare for ever!', in *Old Redruth*, Redruth Old Cornwall Society, Redruth, 1992, pp37-43.
71. McArthur, 1988, pp67 and 89.
72. Payton, 1992, p212.
73. See Philip Payton, 'Territory, Identity and Development: Cornish Politics in the Eighties', paper presented to COBER Conference, St Austell, 1991, p12.
74. See Anthony D.Smith, National Identity, Penquin, London, 1991, p.141.
75. Morton Nance, 1949.
76. c.f. Anthony D.Smith, 'The Supersession of Nationalism?', *International Journal of Comparative Sociology*, xxxi, 1-2, 1990.
77. For one Cornishman's struggle with this effort and then rejection of it see Jack Clemo, *Confessions of a Rebel*, Chatto and Windus, London, 1949, pp88-90.
78. Payton, 1992, pp.129-130.
79. See Perry, 1991, pp230-232.
80. So far, studies have focused on the art colonies as producers of art rather than on them as

producers of ideas; see Tom Cross, *Painting the Warmth of the Sun: St Ives artists 1939-75*, Penzance, 1984.

81. McArthur, 1988, p60.
82. Denys Val Baker, *Britain's Art Colony by the Sea*, Ronald, London, 1959, pp10-11.
83. For a comparative study that emphasises a similar paradox between a renewed social identity and a quiescent political identity, and also suggests a critical role for the local intelligentsia, see Richard Prentice, '"The Manxness of Mann": Renewed Immigration to the Isle of Man and the Nationalist Response', *Scottish Geographical Magazine*, 106, 2, 1990, pp75-88.
84. See N.R.Phillips, *The Saffron Eaters*, Devon Books, Exeter, 1987; Myrna Combellack, *The Playing Place*, Dyllansow Truran, Redruth, 1989; Alan M.Kent, *Clay*, Amigo Books, Launceston, 1991, and compare Jack Clemo, *Wilding Graft*, Chatto and Windus, London, 1948. Unfortunately, the 'Cornish novel' still awaits a full historical and comparative analysis but for the post-War context see Chapter 13.
85. Anthony D.Smith, 1990.
86. Cornwall County Council Planning Committee Agenda, 6 September 1988. And this project to re-construct regional identities was echoed in Havinden *et al.* (eds.), 1991.
87. Donley T.Studlar and Ian McAllister, 'Nationalism in Scotland and Wales: A Post-Industrial Phenomenon?', *Ethnic and Racial Studies*, 11, 1, 1988, pp168-191.
88. Cornwall County Council, *Cornwall - A Land Apart: Issues for the Structure Plan*, CCC, Truro, 1993.

CHAPTER 10

TERRITORY AND IDENTITY

Philip Payton

Taking his cue from the work of Daniele Conversi,[1] Bernard Deacon has argued (see Chapter 9) that in Cornwall the relative weakness of the ethnonational movement and its general failure to achieve ethnic mobilisation has rested in part upon the paucity of 'core values' around which ethnic solidarity can be built. Unlike other regions in Europe (for example, the Basque Country or the various components of the former Yugoslavia), typical 'core value' factors such as religion, family, 'race' and language have not been pervasive or coherent enough to precipitate ethnic mobilisation. Although Methodism, kinship ties (not least the enthusiasm for family history), perceptions of 'Celtic descent', and the phenomenon of language revival are each notable elements of contemporary Cornish identity, none has been an over-riding imperative in the determination of Cornish behaviour in the years since 1945.

The one hint of a unifying 'core value', argues Deacon, is that of territory. Although sporadic and generally reactive or defensive, and not leading to a sustained ethnic mobilisation, a general concern for the territorial integrity of Cornwall has become increasingly significant since the War. This concern has been to a considerable extent a function of the new anti-metropolitanism that came to characterise Cornish politics after 1945, a sentiment by no means confined to the nationalist groups (Mebyon Kernow and the Cornish Nationalist Party) and affecting the broad range of political opinion, its principal territorial objectives being to defend the Tamar border and to prevent the loss of Cornish decision-making powers to 'regional' loci beyond the territory of Cornwall at Plymouth, Exeter or Bristol.[2]

Phrases such as 'border blurring' and 'creeping regionalisation' were well established in the vocabulary of Cornish anti-metropolitanism by the 1960s and 1970s. By the 1970s and 80s the concern for the territorial integrity of Cornwall had developed not only into limited discussion of Cornish claims for devolution (at the same time that the devolution issue was in vogue in Scotland and Wales) but also to a renewed interest in the extent to which the Duchy of Cornwall and Stannary Law afforded contemporary Cornwall a separate constitutional-territorial identity, together with an increasing advocacy of Cornwall-wide strategies to deal with socio-economic issues. By the late 80s and 1990s the enhanced popular territorial consciousness that had accompanied the growth of anti-metropolitanism had found an important cultural expression in rugby football, support for the Cornwall team in the County Championship expressed through territorial symbolism such as St Piran's flag (which also flies at County Hall), the wearing of black-and-gold (the traditional Cornish colours), the singing of 'Trelawny' (with its overt references to the territory of Cornwall), and even use of the word 'Kernow'. Similarly, the extreme degree of listener loyalty generated by BBC Radio Cornwall (the most popular BBC local station in mainland Britain, and the only element of the communications media to match exactly the geographical extent of Cornwall) and the sustained support for the 'Cornwall Air Ambulance' were perhaps measures of this popular territorial consciousness. To McArthur these were remarkable developments, demonstrating that it was '. . . the land of Cornwall itself which has proved to be a powerful focus of ethnic mobilisation'.[3]

The purpose of this Chapter is to examine further the issue of territory in post-War Cornwall. It will be argued briefly that, given the antiquity of Cornwall's territorial identity, it is no surprise that notions of territory have been often fundamental to expressions of 'Cornishness', with a popular territorial consciousness observable at key stages in Cornwall's history. After all, as Peter Taylor has pointed out, at root concepts of identity are linked inextricably to the facts of territory.[4] However, it also will be argued (in rather more detail) that after 1945 the 'core value' of territory became increasingly important - partly for internal reasons, reflecting the changing nature of Cornish political culture, and partly as a result of external pressures in which increasingly interventionist central government regional development and other policies appeared to take little or no notice of Cornish territorial sensibilities.

TERRITORY & TAMAR - AN ENDURING POPULAR CONSCIOUSNESS

Cornwall is amongst the oldest geo-political entities in Western Europe, and so it is no surprise that territory has featured as an important element of Cornish identity. Charles Thomas has suggested that Cornwall was probably a 'pagus' or administrative sub-division during the Roman occupation of Britain, while Peter Berresford Ellis has postulated (less convincingly) that the kingdom of Kernow remained independent of the post-Roman Celtic realm of Dumnonia that emerged after the departure of the legions.[5] Certainly, by the tenth century the territorial extent of modern Cornwall had been established, the Athelstan settlement setting the River Tamar as the divide between Celt and Saxon and investing the territory of Cornwall with an enduring constitutional identity which would be reflected later in the distinctive institutions of Earldom, Duchy and Stannaries. Even in the nineteenth century, with the emergence of modern local government in England and Wales in which Cornwall acquired a status ostensibly identical to that of other adminstrative counties, the Duchy was moved to assert its constitutional authority in Cornwall[6] while the High Sheriff continued (in marked contrast to every other English and Welsh county) to be appointed by the Duke of Cornwall and not the Crown.

Cognisance of Cornwall as a distinct entity entered European tradition at an early stage (not least via the Arthurian cycles which became integral parts of Medieval European romance and yet continued to reflect the territorial significance of Cornwall in the 'Matter of Britain'[7]), with many European languages soon developing their own words for 'Cornwall'. Within Cornwall itself, there is evidence of a popular territorial consciousness in the Cornish rebellions of 1497 and 1549, and again in the Civil War. This popular consciousness was further enhanced in the nineteenth century as the copper and tin industries expanded to embrace almost the entire geographical extent of Cornwall (the exhaustive investigations of A.K. Hamilton Jenkin have shown that virtually no Cornish parish was left untouched by the mining boom at its zenith [8]), the new pride in Cornish technological prowess expressed in part in identification with the territory of Cornwall. Mining was Cornwall, and Cornwall was mining. Indeed, such was the strength of this identity that the sense of place and territory spilled across the Tamar, the Cornish stamp of the Bible Christian religion extending its influence into the wild expanses of North Devon, and the Tamar itself - with its ceaseless mineral traffic - becoming momentarily a unifying rather than dividing factor as for a time the neighbourhood of Tavistock became to all intents and purposes an eastward extension of the Cornish mining district. This identification was still further enhanced by the 'Great Emigration', with Cornish communities in Australia, North America and elsewhere expressing allegiance 'to Cornwall' and developing a cultural perspective in which the territory of Cornwall became all-important as a source and focus of identity. At home, the enormous enthusiasm that attended the foundation of Truro Cathedral and the establishment of a Cornish Diocese in 1877 was in part an expression of this heightened territorial awareness.[9]

Central to the fabric of Cornwall's territorial identity, and in particular to the enduring popular territorial consciousness descibed above, has been (and is) the status of the River Tamar. For Cornish folk it has been perceived as a *ne plus ultra*, a physical and psychological (and therefore cultural) barrier of timeless significance. In 1602 Richard Carew, for example, acknowledged the significance of the Tamar to Cornwall, insisting that it be considered exclusively a Cornish river, for 'Now though this haven thus bound both shires, yet doth the jurisdiction of the water wholly appertain to the Duchy of Cornwall, and may therefore be claimed as part of that county'.[10] In other words, the territory of Cornwall extended to the east bank of the Tamar. Almost four hundred years on this perspective had changed little, with post-War contemporary popular literature still insisting upon the importance of the Tamar. Martin Lister in 1988 pondered '. . . the Tamar as it winds its magic course between Cornwall and England',[11] while for A.L. Rowse 'The Tamar is a decisive boundary such as no other county possesses - but, then, Cornwall is not an ordinary county, it is a "Little Land" of its own'.[12] As Donald R. Rawe added, 'The Tamar . . . is . . . the traditional frontier of Cornwall . . . even today, as the CORNWALL-KERNOW signboards on the bridges announce, west of the Tamar is another people, another little world'.[13] Even Havinden *et al.* had to admit in their 1991 study that 'The River Tamar is still to some extent an historic boundary between "Celtic" Britain and "Saxon" England'.[14] As John Fleet had explained, the physical act of 'crossing the Tamar' was for Cornish people still something of a ritual: '. . . the Tamar has come to acquire a symbolic, almost mystical significance . . . the place of parting or return, the end or the beginning of home'.[15]

Reflecting this all-important status, a continuing preocuupation for Cornish folk pondering their territorial integrity has been the various territorial anomolies along the Tamar border. Until 1844 part of the parish of Maker in 'Cornwall's Forgotten Corner' was considered (for strategic reasons associated with the tenth-century Athelstan settlement) part of Devon,[16] and in the post-1945 era Cornish concern was for the status of the parishes of Werrington and North Petherwin. Again for ancient historic reasons (partly to do with the influence of Tavistock Abbey, and partly - as placenames attest - a reflection of early English intrusion) these two parishes were administered as part of Devon, despite their geographic situation west of the Tamar.[17] This anomoly was at last rectified as recently as 1966 when Cornwall viewed with quiet satisfaction the 'restoration' of Werrington and North Petherwin and thus the confirmation of the Tamar border. There were, however, as Sarah Foot observed, occasional individuals in those marcher parishes who resented this acquisition of Cornish identity ('I was born in Devon, and I want to die in Devon'[18]), for:

> It has always mattered enormously to people whether they are from Cornwall or Devon. And people living on the banks of the Tamar will be all the more staunchly Devonian or Cornish than those living further into the counties, not wanting to lose their identity.[19]

Indeed, in 1988 Cornwall County Council could muse that 'Culturally the River Tamar is a national boundary . . .',[20] while in 1989, reflecting upon both the territorial rationalisations noted above and the defeat of Plymouth's expansionary designs in the 1970s, the Council could observe with pleasure that Cornwall '. . . retains most of the Tamar as the barrier to invasion from England'.[21]

INDEPENDENT AMBASSADORS & THE DUAL POLITY

These confident assertions belied a more complex process, however, for while the Tamar and the territory of Cornwall have enjoyed an enduring significance, the years between 1945 and the 1980s and 90s witnessed a considerable change in the function of territory as a focus and determinant of political behaviour. As Ronald Perry notes in Chapter 2, Cornwall in the immediate post-War era, although still a 'tight little island' with a general if rather unconscious sense of 'Cornishness', was politically a land of 'city states' which guarded their interests, independence and identities with considerable jealousy. There was rivalry between Truro and Bodmin (competing as they were for the status of 'County Town'), Torpoint and Saltash were adamant that they were not suburbs of Plymouth, and towns such as Camelford, Bude, Launceston, Liskeard, St Austell, and Helston basked in their roles as local centres of importance. The passing of the era of industrial prowess meant that mining was no longer a territorially unifying factor, and the fragmentation of overseas Cornish communities meant that Cornwall as a territorial focus of international identity had diminished.

Although attempts by Plymouth in the mid-1940s to expand into South East Cornwall led to a vociferous and successful defence of the Tamar border, reminding observers that the popular sense of territorial identity had by no means disappeared, expressions of territory *per se* were rare. Rather, the 'city states' were concerned principally with their own rural hinterlands, the capital in distant Truro seen often as a remote and unwelcome influence in local affairs. In such a climate, as Adrian Lee notes in Chapter 12, County Councillors went to Truro mainly as local 'ambassadors', coming up from Penzance or down from Bude to fight their local corners, with little sense of a need to develop Cornwall-wide strategies.

This 'ambassadorial' role, and the consequent inability to devise strategic territorial perspectives, was to a considerable degree a reflection of the 'Independent' tradition in Cornish politics. This, in turn, reflected the development of Cornish political culture in Cornwall's era of 'paralysis' (broadly, from the late-nineteenth to mid-twentieth centuries) in which Cornwall had failed to participate in the great Labour-Conservative 'alignment' occurring elsewhere, and where the 'dual polity' described by Jim Bulpitt had had a limiting effect on local government.[22] Bulpitt has argued that the period of social and political modernisation in Britain from 1870 to 1926 (in which Cornwall, paradoxically, failed to participate) had had a conservative impact on territorial politics. Consequently, the period 1926-1960 was characterised by a 'dual polity' in which national (or 'high') and local (or 'low') politics were systematically divorced from one another. Contacts between the national and the local were generally bureaucratic and de-politicised, national government being the preserve of 'high' politics such as foreign policy or economic management, and local government concerned with apolitical issues such as the provision of services like street-lights or refuse collection.

In Cornwall, experiencing as it was its own political 'fossilisation' and an increasing marginalisation from the mainstream of British politics, the emergence of this 'dual polity' led to an extraordinary level of de-politicisation in local government. From its very first meeting in 1889, Cornwall County

Council had tried to establish an apolitical balance, with local elections fought on a non-partisan basis and with candidates offering themselves as 'Independents'. In Cornwall local politics were seen as divorced from and irrelevant to national politics, and it was a matter of pride from 1889 through to even the 1970s and 80s that 'high' politics were kept out of local debate. Indeed, such was the level of de-politicisation achieved that habitually a majority of local government seats went uncontested, with candidates (drawn usually from the ranks of the local 'great and good'; ideal 'ambassadors' to send to Truro) having already gained some form of local concensus and being returned unopposed.

This state of affairs survived well into the post-War era. In 1973, in the first elections fought within the reformed local government structure, Cornwall was one of only five counties (three of the others were in Wales) to fall under the control of Independents, while even in 1977 a full 55% of seats on Cornwall County Council were filled through unopposed returns.[23] However, by the 1970s there were already important and noticeable changes in Cornish political culture. Rapid socio-economic change, in particular high levels of in-migration, had triggered a territorial response in Cornwall, with a new anti-metropolitanism emerging which insisted that Cornwall as a cultural-territorial entity was under threat. The 'Overspill' schemes of the 1960s, in which Londoners were to be re-housed in Cornwall, proved an important catalyst in this process and precipitated the emergence of anti-metropolitanism in County Council politics. Interestingly, this first challenge to the apolitical Independent hegemony came from Mebyon Kernow as it moved towards defining its own party-political role, its candidate Colin Murley in 1967 winning the St Day seat on Cornwall County Council with an 'anti-Overspill' campaign.

The Liberal Party, however, had also been affected by the new anti-metropolitanism. Having survived the lengthy era of Cornish political 'fossilisation', preserved 'in aspic' as the radical party in Cornwall, it began to respond to socio-economic change and the mood of anti-metropolitanism by adopting a new Cornish agenda. In 1964 Peter Bessell won the Parliamentary seat of Bodmin for the Liberals, and in 1966 he held Bodmin while his colleague John Pardoe won neighbouring North Cornwall. Both men joined Mebyon Kernow, an indication of their anti-metropolitan credentials, in 1967 asserting that '. . . the Cornish people have the same right to control their country, its economy and its political future, as the other Celtic peoples of Scotland and Wales'.[24] Territorial strategies were at last emerging but in so doing exposed an increasing tension between the new Cornish agenda of the Liberal Parliamentarians and the continuing apolitical Independent tradition (only partially dented by the Mebyon Kernow intervention) at County Council level.

Writing in the immediate aftermath of the 1973 County Council elections, John Pardoe served notice that the 'ambasssadorial', apolitical Independents were now under threat. The sustained attack would come not from Mebyon Kernow but from the Liberal Party, building a network of grass-roots activity and articulating anti-metropolitan policies which would reflect the new Cornish agenda. Pardoe warned that 'The county elections have numbered the days of the Independents'. He criticised the fact that of 79 seats only 42 had been contested, and complained that 'Almost without exception the candidates for Cornwall County Council were drawn from that class of society that has got time to spare'. Of 138 candidates seeking election, 42 were retired, 17 were farmers, and 24 company directors or self-employed business people. He claimed that '. . . the elections in Cornwall were not an excercise in democracy but a charade by which the local establishment retained the reigns of power . . .'. Significantly, he dismissed the vacuous election leaflets produced by many of the candidates; they said '. . . nothing of what they stood for, nothing about the sort of Cornwall they wanted to build'.[25]

As Pardoe had forecast, after 1973 the position of the Independents was progressively eroded, although the process proved to be lengthy. In the retiring County Council in 1989 there were still 26 Independents, and in the new Council elected that year their numbers had fallen to 24, with the Council being run (ironically) by a loose alliance of Independents and Liberals (or Liberal Democrats as they had by then become). In the 1993 elections the Liberal Democrats at last won overall control of Cornwall County Council, the number of Independents being reduced to 21.

To some observers this historic moment was merely part of a wider swing to the Liberal Democrats across the whole of the South West (they also won Somerset and Dorset, and became the largest single group in Devon), the electorate passing judgement on John Major's unpopular Conservative government, but closer scrutiny revealed deeper structural changes within Cornwall. In the 1989 County Council elections the Liberal Democrats had continued their steady progress in Cornwall, in contrast to neighbouring Devon and Somerset where their performance was lacklustre and the Conservatives had won control. In the 1989 European Parliamentary elections the Liberal Democrats performed badly in many areas (including Devon, where they trailed a poor third behind the Greens) while in Cornwall (and Plymouth) they achieved their best result in Britain.[26]

Thus while the 1993 result in Devon, Somerset and Dorset might indeed have reflected in large measure disatisfaction with Major's regime, in Cornwall it also represented the latest stage of a long-established trend. In Cornwall, as Pardoe had predicted, there had been a sea change in political culture and behaviour. Significantly, the other parties in Cornwall had by this time become alive to the electoral opportunities of anti-metropolitanism, with Conservatives especially (as in the notable Parliamentary careers of David Mudd and Robert Hicks) often attempting to steal the Liberal Democrat (and Mebyon Kernow) thunder. Ironically, the final triumph of the Liberal Democrats - the victory of grass-roots democracy over the local establishment, as Pardoe would have seen it - came at a time when the powers of local government were diminishing and when the local establishment was re-asserting its local influence by new means. The *Western Morning News* exposed 'The great and the good who rule us by decree',[27] pointing to the Devon and Cornwall Training and Enterprise Council (TEC) with its annual budget of £42 million and its leadership by a government-appointee (Cornwall County Council had requested a Cornwall-only TEC, but was unsuccessful), noting also that the chairman of the Health Trust was appointed centrally by the Health Secretary. Indeed, to return to Bulpitt's perspective, these developments represented the central government's response to the disturbance of the 'dual polity' after 1960 (not least the emergence of anti-metropolitanism in Scotland, Wales, Northern Ireland - and, of course, Cornwall, as well as later in certain English local authorities such as Liverpool or the Greater London Council), the centre eroding the influence of potentially 'difficult' local politicians by the key appointment of placemen in new positions of authority.

THE SOUTH WEST PLANNING PARADIGM

At the same time that anti-metropolitanism was emerging as a central feature of Cornish political culture, allowing the development of new Cornish strategic territorial perspectives but sounding the death knell of the old 'ambassadorial' style of local politics, so external pressures were beginning to impinge upon the territorial identity of Cornwall. Principal amongst these was the emergence in the 1960s of the standard regional planning areas, in which Cornwall was merely part of a much wider region (with an extent greater than that of Wales) also comprising Devon, Somerset, Dorset, Wiltshire, Gloucestershire and (later) Avon. Although this development stood potentially to marginalise any claims to separate regional status that Cornwall might harbour, the language and ideology of the new anti-metropolitanism were increasingly well-equipped to deal with this 'threat'. Thus political debate in Cornwall became more and more focussed on territorial issues, the ever-impinging 'regionalisation' matched by the growing sophistication of the anti-metropolitan activists.

A South West Economic Planning Council (SWEPC) was set-up to devise a socio-economic plan for the new 'Region', in 1967 publishing its *A Region With A Future: A Draft Strategy for the South West*. This was, for Cornwall, a significant document which set the model and established the paradigm in which Cornwall was thereafter constrained to act. The plan admitted the inherent diversity, even artificiality of the 'South West', recognising that the distance from Lands End to the northern tip of Gloucestershire was the same as that of Manchester and Leeds from Brighton, adding that '. . . it is not physically all of a piece'.[28] However, there was no attempt to articulate a separate Cornish identity within this diversity. Although noting briefly (but without any specific reference to Cornwall!) that historically a '. . . notable activity was the working of minerals - iron, lead, china clay, copper, tin, and coal',[29] the plan's main emphasis was on the belief that '. . . the land is free from the ugliness produced in other parts of the country by 19th-century industrialisation':[30] although enthusiasts for Cornish industrial archaeology might have agreed with the aesthetic element of this assessment, they would have been dismayed by the implication that there was little industrial dereliction in Cornwall. Instead, the plan sought to emphasise:

> The Region's splendid countryside throughout, its 700 miles of largely unspolied coastline, and its gentle climate (which) make it a most agreeable place to work in, the country's main holiday area and a favourite resort for people when they retire.[31]

Thus the image was formed and the planners' agenda set. But more than this, the plan also sought to express the diversity of the Region in socio-economic terms, pointing to 'The marked contrasts between the remote south west and the parts of the Region in close contact with the West Midlands and South East . . .'.[32] In this was born the enduring concept of the 'remote' or 'far south west' (in a practice a euphemism for Devon and Cornwall) which would inform the activities of many planners, politicians, academics and others in the years ahead,[33] and which also led SWEPC to devise a bewildering set of sub-regions which ignored traditional territorial boundaries (including the Tamar) and created a plethora of 'Economic Planning and Administrative Divisions'. A 'Western Sub-Region' was created which included the two Divisions of 'West Cornwall' and 'Bodmin-Exmoor' and, while excluding South East Cornwall, stretched from Lands End almost to Burnham-on-Sea in Somerset. Amongst the several other sub-regions was the 'Southern Sub-Region'. This included the 'Plymouth Area' Division, a large part of which was South East Cornwall stretching as far as the Fowey estuary. This was, *par excellence*, functional planning without regard to territory and identity.

Formulated beyond the Tamar, SWEPC's approach drew criticism from within Cornwall - not from Cornwall County Council (still locked in its apolitical 'ambassadorial' tradition) but, initially, from Mebyon Kernow and soon after from new pressure groups which were formed in response to the new 'regional' planning process - a further expression of the emerging anti-metropolitanism. The Cornwall Conservation Forum, formed in 1972, aimed much of its activity at SWEPC, in 1974 issuing a firm critique of SWEPC's *A Strategic Settlement Pattern for the South West* (the latter having called for regional aid/population growth led development). It also questioned the wider assumptions of central government regional aid policies, fearing that these would lead to a 'begging bowl' and 'branch factory' economy in Cornwall, a view echoed by the Cornwall Industrial Development Association (formed in 1974) which was similarly critical of regional planning.[34] Here, significantly, was an indication that the politics of territory and identity in Cornwall would often go hand-in-hand with the 'opposition' economic critiques that emerged in the 1970s and 80s (discussed by Ronald Perry in Chapter 3). Indeed, at times it was almost impossible for observers to disentangle territorial politics from 'opposition' economics, particularly in the activities of pressure groups in the 1980s such as Cornish Alternatives to the Structure Plan (CASP) and the Cornish Social and Economic Research Group (CoSERG).

DEVONWALL

In January 1993 the *Western Morning News* carried a triumphant article, 'It's best in the West, and now it's official'. Drawing upon recently released statistics it exclaimed that 'New government figures on the health, wealth and life-style of the nation show that the Westcountry really is the place to live'.[35] To the low-wage earners, unemployed or homeless in Cornwall, such an extravagant claim might have seemed unduly unrealistic but the statistics upon which the article was based were for the South West Region as a whole, including such relatively affluent spots as Bristol, Bath, Cheltenham, Swindon and Bournemouth. When Cornish figures were disaggregated from the whole, a much different picture emerged - as *The Times* noted, for example, when Census data showed '. . . clearly that chronic ill health is linked closely with poverty' and that '. . . in the North, inner cities and *Cornwall*, over a quarter of households contain at least one person suffering from long term illness'.[36] *The Western Morning News*, tripped-up perhaps by its own use of its favourite but geographically and culturally imprecise term 'Westcountry', had fallen foul of the old trap of 'statistical invisibility' of which even SWEPC had been aware in 1967.

But, despite conflicting interpretations of what this amorphous 'Westcountry' might be, this article was unusual in that the *Western Morning News* was in fact normally well aware of the problem of 'statistical invisibility'. However, its solution was not to disaggregate for the benefit of Cornwall but rather, following suit with other agencies such as the Devon and Cornwall TEC and taking its cue from the notion of the 'far south west', to argue for the assertion of a Devon-and-Cornwall sub-region. This, indeed, reflected a conventional wisdom that had emerged strongly in the 1970s and 80s, shared both by central government and some local (mainly Devon) business and political interests. Again, the approach was principally one of functional planning, although laboured attempts to create a Devon-and-Cornwall identity (mainly by co-opting elements of Cornish culture) had some limited external success, as evidenced by 'English Heritage's' uncomfortable and not entirely self-assured suggestion that:

> **Devon** and, more particularly, **Cornwall** are distinct from the rest of England and provide glimpses of a foreign land. For centuries the region's social and economic basis was different from most English counties, in the Celtic origins of many of its institutions, the survival of the Cornish language into the 18th century, and tin mining, with its tinners' parliaments and stannary towns.[37]

('English Heritage', indeed, became a *bete noir* for more extreme Cornish nationalists, the prefix 'English' on its plaques being painted-out by vandals not only in a prime spot in Liskeard town centre but also invariably at more remote locations such as Trethevy Quoit and Carn Euny).

To its detractors in Cornwall, the Devon-and-Cornwall sub-regional model was known as 'Devonwall', a pejorative and rather derogatory term which nonetheless soon passed into popular parlance. Although opposition to Devonwall came from across the political spectrum (it was, for example, the cause of some dissension and confusion within the Liberal Democrat ranks), the clearest case against the model was that articulated by CoSERG. CoSERG singled out the Devon and Cornwall TEC for particular criticism, claiming that 'It appears that the Devonwall TEC is making policy for Cornwall rather than Cornwall Council'.[38] And as well as attacking the economic assumptions of Devonwall, arguing that it weakened the Cornish case for grant aid by linking it statistically to better-off Devon and also focussed investment on Plymouth, CoSERG insisted that the model prevented Cornwall from deploying its '... great strengths - its sense of identity and its heritage'.[39] The uncompromising conclusion was that

> Our future is being hi-jacked by a business led agenda that refuses to recognise Cornwall's territorial integrity. Instead of producing a sustainable economy this locks the Cornish economy into a dependent and peripheral relationship with the rest of the European economy.[40]

Here again was the link between territorial politics and 'opposition' economics. Across the Tamar, however, the perspective was entirely different, with the Plymouth Business School emerging as an enthusiastic supporter of the Devon-and-Cornwall model.[41] Indeed, in April 1992 the School went so far as to demand a devolutionary regional government for the 'South West' (by which it meant Devon-and-Cornwall; Bristol and its hinterland were firmly excluded from this Plymouth-centric model), a view that was also supported in following issues of the School's *South West: The Economic Review*.[42]

In the same month, an article in the *Western Morning News* examined the success of Wales (with its Welsh Development Agency) compared to the relatively poor performance of Devon-and-Cornwall in attracting support and funding from central government. Seeking to explain this contrast, the article concluded that 'The simple answer is politics. Wales has its own Government department and its own cabinet minister . . . There is also a distinct Welsh nationality . . .'.[43] Ignoring the obvious but inconvenient fact that, like Wales, Cornwall had its own Celtic identity that could also be mobilised as a political force, the article went on to opine that '. . . although politicians and local agencies believe that Devon and Cornwall must work together to develop the regional economy, animosity between the two counties has held the region back'.[44] The coded message was clear - concern for the territorial integrity and identity of Cornwall was getting in the way of functional regional planning.

The debate over the Devon-and-Cornwall sub-regional model came to a head in 1992/93 in two separate events - the application to the European

Community for regional grants, and the foundation of the Westcountry Development Corporation. In both of these Cornwall County Council found itself in an unenviable position, its instinct being to promote the territorial identity of Cornwall as a political and economic asset but with the dictates of central government constraining it to act within the sub-regional model. The Council's solution was to adopt an aggressively pragmatic approach, attempting where possible for Cornwall to take the lead in sub-regional initiatives (a sort of 'if you cant beat 'em, join 'em' policy) but also constructing a reserve Cornish position, retaining the right (as far as might be allowed) to articulate Cornish interests separately. This was not always an easy balance to achieve, and the sometimes Janus-like approach that followed led to what were for some uncomfortable decisions. For example, in May 1992 the Council announced that its European Community policy was 'To retain the Council's status and voice directly in Europe as a region'.[45] However, the 'as a region' caveat was quietly dropped soon after, while the Council's 'Cornwall Office' in Brussels - run energetically by a young, talented and highly successful team - was expanded into a 'Cornwall and Devon Office'.

As part of this aggressive pragmatism, Cornwall County Council took the initiative in hosting in November 1992 at St Mellion (on the Cornish bank of the Tamar) a conference to discuss a joint economic strategy and joint sub-regional bid to the European Community for 'Cornwall and Devon' (a telling inversion of nomenclature!). A subsequent document, *Towards an Economic Strategy for Cornwall and Devon*, drew together the several strands of the conference, but with commentaries that were sometimes contrasting rather than complementary. Thus an observation that 'Many still see Cornwall as having a distinct "national" identity' was followed by the view that 'There is some history of collective action across both Counties, but the region's problems have tended only to be recognised after tremendous efforts'.[46] Additionally, to bolster its separate position, Cornwall produced its own supporting document, entitled *Cornwall Towards 2000: Our Need for EC Funding*, '. . . presented in order to highlight the particular characteristics of Cornwall',[47] with a further document - *5b for Cornwall: 1994-99*[48] - produced later as a direct Cornish appeal to Europe.

Oddly, at the same time that the sub-regional strategy was being presented, the central government determined upon its own bid to the European Community for 'Objective 1' status (a category reserved for the very poorest regions of Europe but attracting a high level of grant aid) for Merseyside, the Highlands and Islands, and Devon-and-Cornwall. Not surprisingly, while the Merseyside and Highlands bids were to come ultimately to fruition, the Devon-and-Cornwall case failed. The criteria for Objective 1 status was notionally 75% of average European Community Gross Domestic Product. Merseyside and the Highlands were slightly high at 79% each but Cornwall was closer at 76%. Devon-and-Cornwall together, however, produced an unfortunately high figure of 83%. Cornish Liberal Democrat MPs (Matthew Taylor and Paul Tyler) were furious, accusing Michael Heseltine (the architect of the bid) of 'bias or blunder',[49] and Cornish businessman Peter Fitzgerald - chairman of the recently-formed Cornwall Economic Forum - wrote that 'Cornwall should be allowed to obtain Brussels grants directly and additionally obtain the same level of assistance from the Government as would be given to Scotland and Wales'.[50] This expression of Cornish anti-metropolitanism was even echoed in the editorial page of the *Western Morning News*, with a candid admission that there was a '. . . case for Cornwall to be treated differently to its neighbour across the Tamar. The Government has the power to insist the rules are changed to allow the EC to judge Cornwall's special needs separately. They should use them'.[51]

However, despite the apparent shortcomings of a sub-regional approach in a European Community context, at home the model was applied with increasing vigour. As the Devon and Cornwall Development Company faltered and finally expired during 1992 (since 1987 it had been the business sector's expression of the Devon-and-Cornwall model), discussion focussed on the need (or otherwise) for a successor body. During the General Election of April 1992 Liberal Democrat candidates in Cornwall (together with the Conservative Seb Coe) had called for the establishment of a Cornish Development Agency, arguing strongly that Cornwall's territorial identity should be mobilised as an economic and political force in both Britain and Europe. However, in the election's aftermath proposals emerged (prompted by the Devon and Cornwall TEC) for a Westcountry (Devon-and-Cornwall) Development Corporation, business interests in which would be respresented by a South West Enterprise Limited, with local authorities participating in a Strategic Forum for the sub-region.

In Cornwall the proposal was at first treated with some caution, the *Western Morning News* noting that 'Many in Cornwall want a separate Development Agency for the county . . . ',[52] and with Cornwall County Councillors - in their mood of aggressive pragmatism - being prepared to go along with the idea but not wanting to prejudice the efforts of Cornish MPs in attempting to secure a Cornish agency.[53] Again reflecting its pragmatic but sometimes Janus-like stance, Cornwall County Council also initiated, as a direct counterbalance to the 'Westcountry' scheme, a Cornwall Economic Forum. It was explained that 'Cornish business and political leaders say it is necessary to have their own voice for Cornish concerns in the corridors of power in Whitehall and Brussels',[54] a view that was strongly criticised by the Devon and Cornwall TEC. But by this time the call for a Cornish Development Agency had more or less disappeared from the active political agenda, and in September 1993 the Westcountry Development Corporation was at last born, stressing the need for a 'unified voice' for the sub-region and wishing to construct an 'overall vision' for Devon-and-Cornwall.[55]

To opponents of the Devonwall model much of this made depressing news, but the insistence that the territorial identity of Cornwall had a positive role to play and that the planning process should take account of questions of territory and identity, had not fallen entirely on deaf ears. At the wider 'Regional' level, the 'South West Regional Planning Conference' (the spiritual successor to the old SWEPC, and covering the same geographic area) had noted that the South West was not a coherent unit and that its diversity should be reflected in sub-regional policies. However, in marked contrast to the determinedly functional approach of SWEPC, the Conference - in seeking responses to its ideas - had accepted that 'A particular point stressed by a number of respondents was the need to recognise the distinct cultural heritage and geographical position of Cornwall'.[56] It also recorded

> ... strong views on the separate and distinct identity of Cornwall. Some felt that it had little to do with the rest of the South West while others believed that its relative remoteness meant that it was too easily ignored by a centralised administration.[57]

Similarly, Cornwall County Council in June 1993 signalled the continuing importance of territory and identity to its planning process in its consultative document *Cornwall: A Land Apart - Issues for the New Structure Plan*. Here the premise was that 'Cornwall is different . . . surrounded on three sides by sea and separated from its only neighbour, Devon, by the River Tamar, still a significant physical and cultural divide'.[58] And, in seeking a vision for Cornwall into the next century, it considered that 'The County's environment, its way of life, its culture and heritage can all be seen as resources that are tied up with Cornwall's future and its social and economic well being'.[59] This seemed at odds, perhaps, with the alternative Devon-and-Cornwall 'overall vision' being articulated elsewhere, but - like some of the Janus-like postures that Cornwall had been forced to adopt - it revealed that the wider tensions and debates were far from resolved. Almost thirty years after the emergence of SWEPC, it was still by no means clear how the concern for territory and identity in Cornwall was to be reconciled with a top-down functional approach to 'Regional' planning.

FROM HEALTH CARE TO EURO-CONSTITUENCY

Against this wider backdrop of the tension between territory and identity on the one hand and 'Regional' planning on the other, occurred a multiplicity of events which reflected the relationship between the new anti-metropolitanism and the enhanced popular territorial consciousness of the Cornish. The increasing tendency to organise public (and later privatised) services and utilities on a Devon-and-Cornwall or South West basis (or in a manner that simply ignored the Tamar) came in for constant criticism. Mebyon Kernow attacked '. . . the amalgamation of Cornish authorities with those of Devon - notably the police and water authorites . . .',[60] while plans in the early 1970s by the South Western Electricity Board to bring South East Cornwall under the control of its Plymouth area met stiff opposition. Although the Cornish critics were not able to get SWEB to engage in a strategic re-think, they did at least persuade the organisation to name the newly-expanded area 'Plymouth and East Cornwall' rather than the unwelcome 'Tamarside'.[61] Likewise, the Post Office drew Cornish ire when, with the introduction of Post Codes, it decided that East Cornwall should be allocated PL (Plymouth) codes while the North-East received EX (Exeter) codes. Later, plans to combine the Cornwall Ambulance Service with those of Devon and Somerset were also attacked,[62] while in 1993 'A major campaign to prevent control of Cornish courts being moved out of the county has been started by magistrates, MPs and lawyers'.[63] The Lord Chancellor wished the Cornish courts to be merged with those of Devon but '. . . ministers fail to understand the distance between Penzance and Exeter . . . and show no concern for the historic identity of Cornwall'.[64]

The territorial dimension of health service provision was a recurring theme. In 1984 the Cornwall Community Health Council undertook a survey of 1,000 Cornish mothers. A major concern in East Cornwall was the lack of maternity provision, with Cornish babies having to be born across the border at Plymouth. A mother from St Germans commented, '. . . having to have my babies at Freedom Fields (Plymouth) I was therefore unable to have them registered in Cornwall, and being Cornish myself felt very disappointed about this . . .'.[65] Similarly, a mother from St Ive said 'I'd like to see more Cornish babies born in their own county. Perhaps small units at some of the county's smaller hospitals like Liskeard, Saltash and Launceston'.[66] Five years later, in 1989, the *Cornish Guardian* expressed similar concerns, criticising the division of health care provision in Cornwall between authorities in Cornwall, Plymouth and North Devon. Cornwall east of Bodmin had become a 'Gaza Strip', falling between the several stools and suffering as a consequence, with the *Cornish Guardian* calling for the rationalisation of all Cornish health services under one Cornish authority and further arguing for the territorial expression of utilities and services:

> This is not Cornish nationalism . . . just plain common sense, a commodity that appears to have been eroded in the process of centralisation. And why should it stop at health care? Ask anyone in Cornwall (Cornish-born or not) if they would prefer a Cornwall Police Force rather than the existing Devon and Cornwall Police, and most would say a firm yes. A Plymouth-Cornwall Euro MP is another example of a remote bureaucratic decision that does not make sense for Cornwall. The Fire Brigade seems to operate perfectly well as a single county body. Why not the rest?[67]

A major territorial innovation in the 1980s, one which seemed to buck the sub-regional trend and was widely welcomed in Cornwall, was the creation of 'Cornish Railways' in November 1983. The magazine *Rail Enthusiast* announced 'Cornish Railways -A New Deal for the Duchy',[68] explaining that Cornish Railways was now a semi-independent area within British Rail. The changes were not merely cosmetic for the Truro-based management now had the power to make decisions which would otherwise have been made at Paddington or Swindon. As well as introducing a Cornish Railcard, re-timing branch trains to make better connections with the mainline, and adjusting local fares, Cornish Railways adopted its own logo (incorporating St Piran's flag and the Cornish Arms) which was featured on station nameboards, locomotives, uniform ties and promotional literature. The name 'Kernow' was also used, and there was even talk of the possibility of introducing bi-lingual Cornish-English timetables. The judicious use of Cornish territorial symbolism was therefore an important part of the Cornish Railways marketing strategy. And, although the experiment in managerial devolution was relatively short-lived (it was dismantled from 1987), the Cornish symbolism remained. However, the ensuing reorganisation of British Rail led to the creation of Regional Railways, of which the Cornish system was one small part. Anxious to impress its own corporate identity, the Cornish symbolism was progressively replaced by Regional Railways, culminating in the summary removal from Penzance station of a bi-lingual 'welcome' sign that had been negotiated and paid for by the Cornish Gorseth. This precipitated widespread criticism of Regional Railways from the Cornish public, and in 1993 a rather bewildered Regional Railways management tried to make ammends by erecting at Penzance a massive granite carn engraved with a 'welcome' message in Cornish and English. Honour was satisfied, but many in Cornwall regretted the passing of the territorial symbolism and territorial self-government that Cornish Railways had embodied.

Although the major conceptual-ideological challenge to the perspective that emphasised territory and identity came from models of regional planning, in practice the principal physical threat to the territorial integrity of Cornwall after 1945 came from the expansionist plans of Plymouth City Council. An attempt by Plymouth in 1946 to absorb parts of South East Cornwall was beaten off by the County Council, under the energetic leadership of Colonel Sir Edward Bolitho, but some twenty years later the issue resurfaced under the guise of local government reform. This time, the Redcliffe-Maude Commission was sympathetic to Plymothian claims, and recommended the creation of Plymouth as a 'unitary authority' with territory drawn from both South East Cornwall and South West Devon. Cornish opinion was horrified, with Mebyon Kernow fearing that 'In the years ahead the strategies of Plymouth City Council - the Moloch across the Tamar - will have to be fought with great care and skill', the movement's Chairman exclaiming:

> Saltash, Torpoint, Cremyll, Crafthole, Millbrook, Kingsand and Cawsand, Portwrinkle, Tregantle, Polbathic - each a name dear to Cornishmen everywhere and each charged with the magic of the Rame Peninsula, the Tamar and the Lynher - but who plans their future? Our Cornish Council of course - and may it ever be so. But who schemes to grab, control, and exploit them for their own interest? - why, Alderman Pattinson and his Plymouth City Council.[69]

FIGURE 10.1
Cornish opposition to Plymouth expansion depicted in *Cornish Nation* Vol.2, No.1, September 1970

'KING ARTHUR IS NOT DEAD !'

The General Election of 1970 (which saw Mebyon Kernow member David Mudd elected as Conservative MP for Falmouth and Camborne) led to a change of Government, and the incoming Conservatives carried out their own assessment of local government needs - a process which confirmed the territorial integrity of Cornwall, with the Tamar continuing as the border. A determined rearguard action by Plymouth, advocating the creation of a 'Tamarside' authority, was defeated by Cornwall County Council with its leader - Alderman K.G. Foster - co-ordinating the opposition of a wide range of Cornish organisations.

Thereafter, Cornish activists did continue to watch Plymouth closely, so that in 1973 they co-ordinated the efforts which led to the defeat of the City's plan to build an airport at Winstone Beacon, near Saltash.[70] Similarly, in the 1990s proposals that a second Tamar Bridge be constructed led to widespread alarm in South East Cornwall. Tambrig (the Tamar Bridge Information Group) warned that a second bridge would be 'an environmental disaster',[71] while others feared that it would transform the South East into merely a suburb of Plymouth, at the same time further concentrating resources and services in the City at the expense of places like Liskeard and Callington. In the 1993 County elections there was something of a sensation when the Conservative candidate in the St Germans seat was defeated by an Independent standing on an anti-second bridge ticket.

After the episode of Redcliffe-Maud and Tamarside, however, the principal concern with regard to Plymouth was the establishment in 1978 of the

European Parliamentary Constituency (EPC) for Cornwall & Plymouth.[72] Coming so soon after the defeat of Plymouth's expansionary aspirations, the creation of the joint EPC seemed singularly insensitive to many people in Cornwall. However, the Boundary Commission had been instructed to draw EPC boundaries with a fundamental regard for electoral parity between constituencies, and so Cornwall had been judged 'too small' to have its own EPC. Notwithstanding this explanation, Cornwall County Council, all six District Councils, the Cornish MPs, 76 Parish/Town Councils, and scores of other Cornish organisations and individuals objected formally to the Boundary Commission's plans. These were over-ridden, however, and in the ensuing Euro-election in 1979 Mebyon Kernow secured almost 10% of the Cornish vote in the Cornwall & Plymouth EPC, in part a measure of Cornish disatisfaction with the new Euro-constituency. In 1983 a general mobilisation of Cornish opinion again demanded a Cornish EPC consistent with the territorial extent of Cornwall, and again the request was rejected by the Boundary Commission.

In 1988 the strength and continuity of Cornish opinion was demonstrated when a Campaign for A Cornish Constituency emerged to co-ordinate yet another round of Cornish representations to the Boundary Commission. At a Public Inquiry at Bodmin the Boundary Commission was told by Cornwall County Council that 'It seems anomalous that such a community (as Cornwall) should not have its own separate voice in the European Parliament'.[73] Other objectors argued that although the electorate of a Cornwall-only EPC would be lower than the electoral quota set as the criterion, it would nonetheless be comparable with the electorates that elected one MEP for the Highlands & Islands of Scotland and three MEPs for Northern Ireland. Indeed, it was noted that under the terms of the enabling legislation the Boundary Commission was in fact empowered to recommend the creation of EPCs with electorates lower than the quota, should there be appropriate 'special geographical considerations'. Presenting an array of physical, economic, historical and political 'special geographical considerations', with an opinion that the oft-expressed democratic will of the Cornish people was itself one such consideration, Cornish objectors insisted that Cornwall should thus attract special attention. The Assistant Commissioner who presided at the Bodmin Inquiry did agree, remarakably, that there were certain 'special geographical relations' with regard to Cornwall but - within the terms of the Act - he did not feel it 'appropriate' to act upon them. Thus the joint EPC was perpetuated.

In 1992, as part of the Maastricht deal agreed at Edinburgh, it was announced that the United Kingdom was to have six additional seats in the European Parliament. To Cornwall County Council and others in Cornwall, this seemed to be the opportunity that the Boundary Commission needed to acquiesce to demands for a Cornish EPC. Indeed, the Council and other bodies presented submissions (including a petition with some 2000 signatures) to the Boundary Commission even before the Commission announced its recommendations for the new EPCs in September 1993. But when the Boundary Commission did present its proposals, there was considerable dismay in

Cornwall that the opportunity had been not been taken (Doris Ansari, Chairman of the Council's Policy Committee, retorted 'I don't see where the argument is against Cornwall having its own seat'[74]). Instead, a reconstituted Cornwall & West Plymouth EPC had been created, with a dismissive observation from the Boundary Commission '. . . that Cornwall did not warrant being a separate constituency as, with an electorate of 372,382, the deviation from the electoral quota would amount to 27%'[75] (the same, incidently, as that for the Highlands & Islands). Despite the judgement of the Assistant Commissioner after the Bodmin Inquiry of 1988, there was in 1993 no many mention of any 'special geographical considerations' relating to Cornwall (not even a mention of the Tamar), despite the fact that 'The Committee had regard to special geographical considerations . . . in concluding that there should not be a constituency crossing the Pennines or the Thames Estuary . . .'.[78] 'Geographical', it seemed, had been interpreted in a strictly limited, physical manner: rather like the SWEPC approach to regional planning, issues of territory and identity had no place in this purely functional exercise.

DEVOLUTION & THE DUCHY

As noted earlier, and as evidenced at length above, the articulation of territorial issues in Cornwall was often sporadic and generally defensive or reactive, even in major political battles such as the containment of Plymouth or the campaign for a Cornwall EPC. However, the growth of anti-metropolitan sentiment did allow the development of Cornwall-wide strategic perspectives, manifested in the policies of groups such as Mebyon Kernow and the Liberal Party and, later, CoSERG and CASP. To a considerable degree these were socio-economic in character, formulated in response to the rapid change that Cornwall had experienced, and they informed the development of the 'opposition' economics discussed in Chapter 3. However, hand-in-hand with these socio-economic critiques went a constitutional perspective which argued for the renewed 'accommodation' of Cornwall - that is, for the recognition or construction of a distinct Cornish territorial-constitutional status and identity.

Of course, the insistence upon a special status for the River Tamar and the demand for a Cornwall EPC were part of this drive for 'accommodation', as were campaigns for a Cornish postage stamp and a brief initiative to secure a 'Minister for Cornwall'. But more than this, during the period in which the devolution issue was enjoying extensive debate in the United Kingdom as a whole, the issue of 'home rule' for Cornwall received serious if limited discussion - not only amongst the nationalist groups but in the mainstream political parties too, with several prominent political figures in Cornwall advocating a degree of self-government.[77] The Crowther (later Kilbrandon) Commission received substantional submissions from several Cornish groups (but went no further west than Exeter in its regional consultative visits!), with Mebyon Kernow explaining that '. . . we stated that we sought recognition for

Kernow as a member nation of a British federation. The fact that we are a nation should be written into the constitution and the Tamar border guarenteed by statute'.[78] In fact, the Kilbrandon Commission, when it reported, did not recommend a devolutionary assembly for Cornwall but it did urge that greater use be made of the title 'Duchy of Cornwall' to emphasise Cornwall's constitutional status, as well as acknowledging the need to recognise the general concern for Cornish territorial integrity.[79] However, unlike the situations in Scotland and Wales, there was no congruency between these suggestions and the wider designs of regional planning, and so the Kilbrandon proposals for Cornwall received no more than cursory attention at official levels.

Nonetheless, Kilbrandon served to further inform the development of Cornish anti-metropolitanism, particularly with regard to the status of the Duchy of Cornwall and its constitutional relationship with the County and territory of Cornwall. Hitherto, the conventional wisdom (and indeed the practice of the Duchy of Cornwall as an institution) had been to emphasise that the relationship was only incidental.[80] Despite some residual constitutional eccentricities, such as the appointment of the High Sherrif by the Duke of Cornwall instead of the Crown, the Duchy of Cornwall was a landed estate (with more property outside of Cornwall than within) managed as the source of income for the Heir Apparent. The County of Cornwall was, by contrast, the physical territory of Cornwall, while Cornwall County Council was the local authority empowered to govern within that territory. The description of Cornwall as 'the Duchy' (encouraged at the turn of the century by literary figures such as Sir Arthur Quiller-Couch) was charming, romantic, harmless but inaccurate. Accepting this analysis, most Cornish activists were thus critical of the Duchy of Cornwall, seeing it as an historical anachronism with little relevance to contemporary Cornwall and indeed milking off the surplus value of an already impoverished land.

Although in 1972 Ian Soulsby remarked that '. . . those who oppose the office of the duke of Cornwall might remember that this is Cornwall's only claim to separate constitutional status',[81] it was the publication of the Kilbrandon proposals in the following year that alerted proponents of Cornish anti-metropolitanism to the significance of the Duchy. Thereafter, demands for political 'accommodation' or assertions of territorial identity invariably alluded to the constitutional status lent Cornwall by the Duchy. Coincidently, new research indicated that as recently as the mid-nineteenth century the Duchy of Cornwall itself had carefully analysed the original Duchy Charters, offering a surprising set of conclusions which stated that the Duchy and County were, after all, co-terminous, that the Duchy was the ultimate source of governmental authority in Cornwall wherein the Duke was quasi-sovereign, and that Cornwall was constituionally distinct from England.[82] These ideas were presented neatly by Jim Pengelly in a Cowethas Flamank publication *The Detectable Duchy*[83] (the title itself a neat play on words) in 1986. Later, in 1992, Tim Saunders re-examined the Duchy's self-analysis of 1855-56 (undertaken by Sir George Harrison, then the Duchy's Attorney-General), concluding that '. . .this authoritative statement by no less exalted a Duchy official than the Attorney-General completely invalidates the erroneous notion that the Duchy of Cornwall is just a glorified esate office, having no connection but its name with Cornwall'.[84] Similarly, in an article discussing the constitutional nature of the Duchy, Kit Hawkins alleged that:

> An attempt has been made to separate the Duchy of Cornwall, which is not subject to English tax legislation, from the territory of Cornwall, the argument being that the Duchy has a separate existence to the geographical area of Cornwall and holds property outside of that area. The argument is spurious and flies in the face of the Duchy case of 1856.[85]

Interestingly, the Assistant Commissioner who presided at the 1988 Bodmin Euro-constituency Inquiry was impressed by such arguments, noting a 'de facto, if not de jure joinder with England',[86] although not all Cornish activists approved of this 'rehabilitation' of the Duchy. Writing in the mid-1980s, Royston Green reminded his readers that the Duchy of Cornwall as an institution still received very substantial income directly from possessions and activities in Cornwall, including the property of those in Cornwall who died without heirs (*bona vacantia*). To Green, the Duchy was 'A feudal estate run like big business . . . Nothing to do with Cornwall's ancient and distinct tradition'. And yet, in a moment of anguished confusion, he conceded that

> Deep within the Duchy's greedy possession is the territorial patrimony of the Cornish kings. The Duchy is part of the monstrous atavistic medieval humbug maintained with English monarchism. It is a changeleing, albeit not with full success, for the residual political memory that Cornwall, being not English, was once a separate state.[88]

Co-incident with this debate regarding the status of the Duchy of Cornwall was renewed interest in Cornish Stannary Law, prompted in part by Pennington's scholarly survey of the subject in 1973 in which he concluded that the ancient Stannary Convocation or Parliament '. . . had legislative powers . . . which equalled those of the national Parliament in Westminster . . . stannary law is still formally part of the law of England'.[88] The Stannary system was, of course, an integral part of the Duchy of Cornwall, and amongst existing Duchy officials was (and is) the formal position of Lord Warden of the Stannaries. Again, proponents of anti-metropolitanism in Cornwall siezed upon this apparent further evidence of Cornish constitutional 'difference', arguing (as indeed had the Duchy in 1855-56) that the extent of the Stannary system's legislative and judicial powers extended beyond the traditional mining areas (Foweymore, Blackmore, Tywarnhaile, Penwith-and-Kerrier) to encompass the entire territory of Cornwall. Indeed, for a small band of activists, this

Stannary status was not merely another piece of ammunition in the armoury of Cornish 'difference' but was actually a device by which Cornish self-government might be achieved.

As Brian Hambly emphasised in 1974, they believed '. . . that the long-disused and dormant Convocation of Cornwall . . . was the basic unit upon which internal self-government could be rapidly built'.[89] He explained how those seeking the recall of the Convocation (which had last met in 1752) had circularised, as required by Stannary Law, the Cornish mining industry to seek signatures to petition the Lord Warden of the Stannaries. Some signatures were indeed forthcoming, and the town clerks of the six Stannary towns were then contacted and advised of their alleged duty to elect six Stannators each. 'The Duchy, however, immediately became obstructive, asking various questions and deliberately disuading the Stannary towns from participating'.[90] Suitably enraged, the Stannary enthusiasts decided to reconvene the Parliament unilaterally, a step they took amidst considerable publicity on 20th May 1974.

Thereafter, the reconvened Stannary Parliament was often in the news. As well as arousing media curiosity it also attracted the attention of legal practitioners. One of these, Paul Laity, a lawyer and judge (and a Cornishman), informed observers that the Stannary system had been an important element of constitutional-territorial 'accommodation' as late as the first half of the nineteenth century, its legal powers vibrant and intact. As an amusing but telling example, he cited a case of 14th May 1825 in which the Counsel for the Plaintiff complained:

> The Plaintiff, being a native of Northumberland, was therefore denominated a foreigner in Cornwall, and they were determined to get rid of a foreigner. When a person heard the people of Cornwall talking of getting rid of a foreigner, he would naturally ask the question, 'What, have you an Aliens Act?' 'Oh! No', the Cornishmen would reply, 'but we'll soon make Cornwall too hot for him; we'll Stannary him'.[91]

Laity's sympathy for the legal case presented by the Stannary Parliament was also apparent in an article in which, remininding readers that the Stannary system was an integral part of the organs of the Duchy of Cornwall, he concluded that 'The concept of the Duchy rests on the existence of a separate and ancient territory of Cornwall. That separate territory has never been assimilated formally into England'. Given that the Duchy had all its instruments of government in place - a Duchy Council, a Chancellor, an Attorney General, a Lord Warden of the Stannaries - but declined to use them in the way the latter-day Stannators desired, the implication was that as '. . . the Duchy officials appear to have abdicated all of their constitutional functions',[92] its was legitimate for the reconvened Stannary Parliament to have acted in its unilateral fashion.

However, in the late 1980s and early 1990s the main media focus was not on the niceties of legal debate but rather on the manner in which the Stannary Parliament had become embroiled in the anti-Community Charge campaign. Arguing initially that the 'Poll Tax' was illegal in Cornwall (because it had not been ratified by the Stannary Parliament), a more ingenius position soon emerged in which the Parliament alleged that anyone who was a 'Cornish tinner' was automatically (under the privileges afforded tinners by the Charter of Pardon of 1508) exempt from the Community Charge. Offering shares in a Royal Cornish Consols United Tin Mines Cost Book Company as a device by which anyone anywhere in the United Kingdom could become a 'Cornish tinner', the Stannary Parliament became an important player in the anti-Community Charge battle not only in Cornwall but in Britain as a whole.[93] In December 1991, for example, it was reported that individuals in Basingstoke were still refusing to pay their 'Poll Tax' on the grounds that they were 'Cornish tinners'![94]

Although this activity brought the Stannary Parliament to a much wider public in Britain, critics within the movement felt it had moved the Parliament's concerns uncomfortably far from the issues of Cornish constitutional identity. Perhaps, even, the Stannary movement had allowed itself to be used or hi-jacked by other forces with very different aims. Certainly, rifts appeared within the Stannary movement, so that by 1993 there were in fact two separate organisations claiming to be the Cornish Stannary Parliament. Taking the initiative, those who had been unhappy with the movement's direction and had broken away, in October 1993 published *The Constitution of Cornwall or Kernow: The Country of the West Britons*.[95] Styled 'An Official Publication of the Stannary Parliament of the Cornish People', the booklet proved a remarkably comprehensive review of the constitutional, legal and historical background of the status the Stannary Parliament claimed.

However, to outside observers the setting-up of a breakaway Stannary Parliament (the original itself being a unilateral creation) had more than a hint of the absurd. The *West Briton* felt that 'The spectacle of two groups in Cornwall each claiming to be the true inheritors of the Stannary Parliament is unedifying'.[96] Instead of using archaic language and tortuous legal arguments rooted in the medieval period, the Stannators should (the paper thought) be concentrating on real, contemporary issues such as jobs, affordable housing, and the future of the Cornish railway system. Unity of purpose and not divisive behaviour was the way ahead, the *West Briton* inevitably making comparison with the Cornish solidarity generated by rugby football: 'It may be called the county championship, but when the boys in black and gold trot out the fans are cheering on a national side'.[97] From this perspective, the Stannary movement had become not so much a serious exponent of Cornish concerns as a bit of a laugh, perhaps rather like the three Cornish people who in 1992 travelled through five European countries on souvenir 'Cornish Passports' that they had purchased at their local cornershop.[98]

LOCAL GOVERNMENT REFORM - THE ABOLITION OF CORNWALL?

Interesting though the squabbles within the Stannary movement might be, far more serious for the future territorial integrity of Cornwall was the prospect of local government reform. When in early 1991 the government announced its then forthcoming review of local government, the signals were conflicting. On the one hand there was talk of respecting (even resurrecting) traditional boundaries, while also taking into account the aspirations of local communities, but on the other there was a strong hint that in the desire for rationalisation and efficiency there would be a reduction in the number of tiers in local government. Inevitably, this appeared to be a threat to County Councils, the likelihood being that they would be replaced by territorially smaller unitary authorities, but there was also a broad hint that in one or two areas it would be appropriate for the County structure to survive. One of these, it was suggested, might be Cornwall. The fact that Sir John Banham (an adopted Cornishman who had even requested 'Trelawny' as a 'Desert Island Discs' choice) was appointed to lead the review was interpreted in Cornwall as a positive sign.

Although there seemed to be a general air of disbelief that Cornwall as an administrative entity might be abolished (it would be an act of unspeakable malice against an historic territory and the people that inhabited it), the potential threat was taken seriously by some observers. Pondering the enhanced popular territorial consciousness that had characterised the recent decades, the *West Briton* considered that:

> Cornish feelings would be understandably outraged if the county disappeared at a time when claims for increased recognition are being pressed . . . though few would wish to travel too far down the road of separatism, there would be widespread relief if . . . Cornwall will continue to have a distinctive identity and speak with a single voice . . . the county council, far from disappearing, could scale new heights. As the unitary authority for the whole county it would have greater powers and more functions than ever before.[99]

The County Council itself pledged that 'Cornwall County Council will fight to the last should the Government make any attempt to abolish it',[100] with the then Chairman, David Roberts, insisting that 'It is essential that we should fight for, and keep, our identity'.[101] Contemplating the possibility of abolition, Doris Ansari, for the Liberal Democrats, commented 'I do not think people would accept it'.[102] John Daniel, leader of the County Council's Conservative group, promised that if there was any threat to the Council he would be '. . . out in front shouting to keep it'.[103] Godfrey Smale, the Labour leader, added that the Labour Party in Cornwall was in favour of the Council's survival. In the House of Lords, Viscount Falmouth - the Lord Lieutenant of Cornwall -

outlined the case for Cornwall. The *Western Morning News* considered that 'There would be widespread anger if the county council - Cornwall's only single voice - were abolished'.[104] The only prominent dissenting voice appeared to be that of Robert Hicks, MP for South East Cornwall, who tentatively suggested that the division of Cornwall into three unitary authorities might be a preferred solution, so long as the Tamar border was preserved.[105] But even within his constituency there was immediate and strong reaction, Councillors Barbara Spring (Liberal Democrat, Saltash) and Jim Maddever (Independent, Menheniot) refusing to countenance the territorial sub-division of Cornwall,[106] the latter arguing that 'It would weaken Cornwall's identity both in the country and in Europe . . .'.[107]

Despite the declared Labour position within Cornwall, the party locally experienced some embarrassment when in July 1991 the Labour Party centrally announced its own proposals for regional government. Here the Devon-and-Cornwall model was adhered to with precision, the party calling for the creation of a super-county region covering the two territories. Even the *Western Morning News* was taken-aback by the bald audacity of the plan, protesting that although it favoured a very much closer level of co-operation between Cornwall and Devon, Cornwall would never be coerced into some new constitutional structure against its will. Labour's proposals were the unacceptable face of Devonwall, 'For the first principle of government is consent. And rightly or wrongly the people of Cornwall, including many born and bred elsewhere who have chosen to live there, are not going to agree to lose their county identity'.[108] Needless to say, Cornish reaction to Labour's plan was one of hostility, with David Blunkett admitting hastily that 'We have a real difficulty with the South West... We are very open to persuasion on... the question of whether Cornwall should provide a unitary authority in its own right . . .'.[109] Concidently, Adrian Lee, in an ingenious investigation of 'English Regions: Political and Electoral Possibilities', showed that in fact the creation of a Cornwall-only region (in the wider context of the implemention by Labour of regional government) would be in Labour's electoral favour: 'South of the Severn-Wash line, Conservative predominance could be reduced by giving regional status to Cornwall . . .'.[110] However, such speculation remained purely hypothetical, for the Conservatives won the General Election of 1992, perpetuating their own local government review.

CONCLUSION

Although the thorny question of whether the District Councils in Cornwall should survive or disappear did not attract an early local consensus, the near unaninimity of opinion regarding the County Council and the desire to preserve a level of government consistent with the territorial extent of Cornwall was a remarkable demonstration of the importance of territory and identity in contemporary Cornwall. The rise of anti-metropolitanism and a more dynamic political culture, together with the experience of the myriad 'Tamarside', Kilbrandon, Euro-constituency, 'Devonwall', Stannary and other campaigns, had raised the level of territorial consciousness to a degree which led Cornish popular opinion to call for '... not only the retention of a Cornish administrative unit but for further powers to be devolved to it'.[111] This was, perhaps, something like the 'core value' factor described by Conversi and Deacon, an indication of a degree of ethnic mobilisation in response to a perceived threat to the most fundamental political expression of the territory and identity of Cornwall - the County Council itself. The question remained, however, as to the extent to which this strength and unanimity of opinion would be effective in appealing to a central administration that was traditionally unresponsive to territorial demands and wedded to top-down functional approaches to planning.

REFERENCES

1. Daniele Conversi, 'Language or Race? The choice of core values in the Development of Catalan and Basque Nationalisms', *Ethnic and Racial Studies*, Vol.13, No.1, 1990.
2. Philip Payton, *The Making of Modern Cornwall: Historical Experience and the Persistence of 'Difference'*, Dyllansow Truran, Redruth, 1992, Chapter 10.
3. Mary McArthur, 'The Cornish: A Case Study in Ethnicity', unpublished MSc thesis, University of Bristol, 1988, pp66-67.
4. Peter J.Taylor, 'The meaning of the North: England's "foreign country" within', *Political Geography*, Vol.12, N0.2, March 1993.
5. Charles Thomas, *The Importance of Being Cornish in Cornwall*, Institute of Cornish Studies, 1973, p5; Peter Berresford Ellis, *Celt and Saxon: The Struggle for Britain AD 410-937*, Constable, London, 1993, pp71-73.
6. The Duchy of Cornwall, *Preliminary Statement Showing the Grounds on Which is Founded the Right of the Duchy of Cornwall to the Tidal Estuaries, Foreshore, and Under-Sea Minerals Within and Around the Coasts of the County of Cornwall*, Duchy of Cornwall, London, 1855; The Duchy of Cornwall, *The Tidal Estuaries, Foreshore, And Under-Sea Minerals Within and Around the Coast of the County of Cornwall*, Duchy of Cornwall, London, 1857.
7. For example, the territorial existence and significance of Cornwall is made plain in Malory's *Le Morte d'Arthur*; see Michael Senior (ed.), *Sir Thomas Malory's Tales of King Arthur*, Guild Publishing, London, 1980, p29.
8. A.K.Hamilton Jenkin, *Mines and Miners of Cornwall*, 16 Vols., Bradford Barton/Federation of Old Cornwall Societies, Truro/Penzance, 1961-70.
9. A.L.Rowse, *The Little Land of Cornwall*, Sutton, Gloucester, 1986, p278.
10. F.E.Halliday (ed.), Richard Carew of Antony's *The Survey of Cornwall*, Melrose, London, 1953, p164.
11. Martin Lister, *Cornish Times Reflected*, Tamara, Saltash, 1988, p32.
12. A.L.Rowse, *A.L.Rowse's Cornwall*, Weidenfeld & Nicolson, 1988, p160.
13. Donald R.Rawe, *A Prospect for Cornwall*, Robert Hales, London, 1986, p38.
14. M.A.Havinden, J.Queniart, J.Stanyer, *Centre and Periphery: Brittany and Cornwall & Devon Compared*, University of Exeter Press, Exeter, 1991, p259.
15. John Fleet, 'The Cornish Border, 1969-1972', in F.G.Thompson, *The Celtic Experience*, Celtic League, Dublin, 1972, p118.
16. W.G.Hoskins, 'Celt, Saxon and Norman in the Rame Peninsula', unpublished paper held in MSS collection *Essays and Notes on Rame Peninsula* in Torpoint Public Library; see also Tony Carne, *Cornwall's Forgotten Corner*, Lodenek Press, Padstow, 1985, p9, and Philip Payton, *Tregantle and Scraesdon: Their Forts and Railway*, Dyllansow Truran, Redruth, 1987, pp1-2.

17. H.P.R.Finberg, 'The Early History of Werrington', *English Historical Review*, Vol.LIX, 1944.
18. Sarah Foot, *Following the Tamar*, Bossiney Books, 1980, pp16-17.
19. Sarah Foot, 1980, p17.
20. Ivan Rabey (ed.), *Cornwall: An Official Guide*, Cornwall County Council/British Publishing Co., Gloucester, nd c.1988, p31.
21. A.L.Dennis (ed.), *Cornwall County Council 1889-1989: A History of 100 Years of County*, Cornwall County Council, 1989, p1.
22. Jim Bulpitt, *Territory and Power in the United Kingdom*, Manchester University Press, Manchester, 1993.
23. Wyn Grant, *Independent Local Politics in England and Wales*, Saxon House, Farnborough, 1977, p2.
24. *Western Morning News*, February 1967.
25. *Sunday Independent*, 22 April 1973; see also *Cornish Nation*, June 1973.
26. Payton, 1992, p230.
27. *Western Morning News*, 4 April 1993; see also *Guardian* 30 December 1992.
28. South West Economic Planning Council, *A Region with a Future: A Draft Strategy for the South West*, HMSO, London, 1967, p1.
29. SWEPC, 1967, pp1-2.
30. SWEPC, 1967, p1.
31. SWEPC, 1967, p1.
32. SWEPC, 1967, p1.
33. for example, see Havinden *et al*, 1991.
34. Payton, 1992, pp219-220.
35. *Western Morning News*, 28 January 1993.
36. *The Times*, 10 August 1993.
37. Andrew Saunders, *Exploring England's Heritage: Devon and Cornwall*, English Heriatge/HMSO, London, 1991, dustcover notes.
38. Cornish Social and Economic Research Group, *A Strategic Forum for Devon and Cornwall? Not a SWEL Idea*, CoSERG, Redruth, 1992.
39. Cornish Social and Economic Research Group, *Devonwall: Some Preliminary Background Information*, CoSERG, Redruth, 1992.
40. CoSERG, *Devonwall*, 1992.
41. *Western Morning News*, 26 November 1992.
42. *Western Morning News*, 1 April 1992; *South West: The Economic Review*, No.7, Winter 1992; No.8, Summer 1993.
43. *Western Morning News*, 4 September 1992.
44. *Western Morning News*, 4 September 1992.
45. Policy statement summary supplied to Institute of Cornish Studies by Cornwall Economic Development Office, May 1992.
46. Cornwall County Council, Devon County Council, Plymouth City Council, *Towards an Economic Strategy for Cornwall and Devon*, Exeter, 1992, pp14-15.
47. Cornwall County Council, *Cornwall Towards 2000: Our Need for EC Funding*, Truro, 1993.
48. Cornwall County Coucil, *5b for Cornwall: 1994-99*, Truro, 1993.
49. *Western Morning News*, 25 February 1993.
50. *Western Morning News*, 27 February 1993.
51. *Western Morning News*, 25 February 1993.
52. *Western Morning News*, 8 July 1992.
53. *Western Morning News*, 29 July 1992.
54. *Western Morning News*, 3 December 1992; see also *Western Morning News*, 21 October 1992.
55. *Western Morning News*, 30 September 1993.
56. South West Regional Planning Conference, *Towards a Regional Strategy: Key Elements of the Response*, SWRPC, Taunton, 1992.
57. SWRPC, 1992.
58. Cornwall County Council, *Cornwall - A Land Apart: Issues for the Structure Plan*, Truro, 1993, p1.
59. Cornwall County Council, *Cornwall*, 1993, p47.

60. *Cornish Nation*, Vol.2, No.8, December 1974.
61. *Cornish Nation*, Vol.2, No.11, March 1973.
62. *Western Morning News*, 13 November 1991; 31 July 1992.
63. *West Briton*, 26 August 1993.
64. *West Briton*, 26 August 1993, according to Matthew Taylor MP.
65. *Cornish Times*, cited in *Cornish Banner*, November 1984.
66. *Cornish Banner*, November 1984.
67. *Cornish Guardian*, 16 November 1989.
68. *Rail Enthusiast*, September 1984.
69. *Cornish Nation*, Vol.2, No.1, September 1970.
70. *Cornish Nation*, Vol.2, No.14, December 1973.
71. *Western Morning News*, 12 March 1993.
72. Payton, 1992, pp213-216.
73. Cornwall County Council, *European Parliamentary Elections Act 1978 (as amended): Representations to the Boundary Commission for England on Their Provisional Recommendations Published 17th March 1988*, 1988.
74. *Western Morning News*, 5 October 1993.
75. European Parliamentary Constituency Committee for England, *News Release No.2*, September 1993.
76. European Parliamentary Constituency Committee, September 1993.
77. Payton, 1992, pp238-242.
78. *Cornish Nation*, Vol.2, No.5, September 1971.
79. *Royal Commission on the Constitution*, Cmnd 5460, Report Volume 1, HMSO, London, 1973, paragraphs 221, 329, 1211.
80. For example, see Crispin Gill (ed.), *The Duchy of Cornwall*, David & Charles, Newton Abbot, 1987.
81. Ian Soulsby, 'A Millenium of Cornish Society', in Thompson, 1972, p112.
82. Payton, 1992, pp47-49.
83. E.J.Pengelly, *The Detectable Duchy*, Cowethas Flamank, Redruth, 1986.
84. *Peninsula Voice*, September 1992.
85. *Kernow*, April-May 1990.
86. Boundary Commission for England, *The Report by Mr Assistant Commissioner G.D.Flather, QC upon the Local Inquiry held by him on 12 and 13 July in Bodmin, Cornwall, into the proposed Cornwall and Plymouth and Devon European Parliamentary Constituencies*, 1988.
87. Royston Green, *What is the Duchy of Cornwall?*, Cornwall Branch - Communist Party of Great Britain, Redruth, c.1985, pp6-7.
88. Robert R.Pennington, *Stannary Law: A History of the Mining Law of Cornwall and Devon*, David & Charles, Newton Abbot, 1973, p7. and p9.
89. *Cornish Nation*, Vol.2, No.8, December 1974.
90. *Cornish Nation*, Vol.2, No.8, December 1974.
91. Paul Laity, 'The Cornish Stannary and its Institutions', unpublished paper, 1989.
92. *Kernow*, August-September 1989.
93. *Western Morning News*, 14 June 1989.
94. *Western Morning News*, 7 December 1991.
95. The Stannary Parliament of the Cornish People, *The Constitution of Cornwall or Kernow: The Country of the West Britons*, Stannary Parliament, Truro, 1993.
96. *West Briton*, 14 October 1993.
97. *West Briton*, 14 October 1993.
98. *Western Morning News*, 20 January 1993.
99. *West Briton*, 21 March 1993.
100. *West Briton*, 21 March 1993.
101. *West Briton*, 21 March 1993.
102. *West Briton*, 21 March 1993.
103. *West Briton*, 21 March 1993.
104. *Western Morning News*, 26 November 1991.
105. *Western Morning News*, 13 November 1991.

106. *Western Morning News*, 15 November 1991; 19 November 1991; see also *Western Morning News*, 14 November 1991.
107. *Western Morning News*, 19 November 1991.
108. *Western Morning News*, 6 July 1991.
109. Letter from David Blunkett MP to Philip Payton, 18 July 1991.
110. Adrian Lee, 'English Regions: Political and Electoral Possibilities', unpublished paper presented at PSA UK Politics Workgroup Conference, Newcastle-upon-Tyne Polytechnic, September 1991.
111. *Western Morning News*, 20 January 1992; according to Robin Teverson.

CHAPTER 11

POLITICAL PARTIES AND ELECTIONS

Adrian Lee

The central aim of this Chapter is to examine the proposition that Cornwall's continuing difference from the rest of the United Kingdom finds expression through electoral behaviour, and to demonstrate the significance of the consequent variations. Variations and divergences in electoral behaviour in particular regions or areas are frequently lost in the mass of aggregate statistics which electoral studies and elections themselves produce. The measurement of variation is often difficult, and its explanation more so. This Chapter's conclusions are therefore tentative, and more suggestive of paths of future investigation than of firm generalisation.

CORNWALL, REGIONAL DIVERSITY & THE UNITED KINGDOM

In a general political sense, the status of Cornwall as a social and economic periphery of the United Kingdom is by now well established and widely accepted.[1] This view corresponds with contemporary interpretations and views of the United Kingdom as a relatively heterogenous collection of territories, and of the state itself as the product of a series of amalgamations, conquests and Unions, rather than as some sort of 'natural' political entity.[2] Cornwall's political integration into what was to become the United Kingdom was, like that of other territories, a partial one. Indeed, its experience reflects the general pattern of 'union without uniformity' in several significant respects. The absence of a general project of centre-directed national integration to create a single overarching United Kingdom identity analogous to the Jacobin-inspired attempt to create the 'one and indivisible' French Republic meant that political integration within the United Kingdom was, by modern standards, incomplete. Examples of the absence of uniformity in political structures abound, as do instances of the differing strategies employed by the centre for the management of the 'UK estate' throughout the political system's existence. The result of this unique pattern of historical development has been that lack of political integration has continued to find political, and especially electoral expression. Electorally, the constituent parts of the United Kingdom diverge in their behaviour, and continue to do so, despite the presence of strong 'nationalising' influences. Is Cornwall a divergent case? Are intensified or new patterns of divergence emerging?

The case for Cornwall's divergence can be made through an examination of post-War electoral behaviour in respect of both parliamentary and local elections. The reasons for difference can be tentatively suggested, and the evidence for continuing divergence assessed through a closer examination of electoral data which is often submerged in aggregate statewide studies.

To take 1945 as a starting point for this examination may seem somewhat arbitrary, if conventional. A cursory survey of parliamentary election results for the Cornish constituencies since that date apparently provides little meriting more detailed comment, and most general studies of the British electoral system used to restrict themeselves to the occasional aside about Liberal performance in an undifferentiated and imprecise 'Celtic fringe'.[3] The bald facts that since 1945 seven elections have seen Conservatives hold four of the five Cornish constituencies, and in the other seven three; that Labour held one of the seats until 1970; and that latterly Liberals held either one or two seats, does not seem to be too far removed from the electoral experience of other remote rural areas. Both in particular elections and in the trend over time, the behaviour of the Cornish electorate seemed to reproduce the pattern, albeit with a few 'local' differences in the extent of support for particular parties, common in rural England.

However, if elections in Cornwall since 1945 are examined from a rather different perspective and in more detail, a somewhat different picture emerges. If the conventional commonplaces about the largely integrated and homogeneous behaviour of the British electorate are put aside in favour of an approach which focusses upon the differences between and within the various parts of the United Kingdom, then a different light is thrown upon electoral behaviour in Cornwall. This means discarding the conventional view, not of the politically integrative effects of a statewide party system *per se*, but on the extent of these effects. The history of the British party system has been overwhelmingly written from a 'central perspective', looking at the system as a whole. Most significantly, it was assumed on the basis of experience until the mid 1960s that the statewide party system had emerged from its period of transition in the 1920s and 1930s as a system embodying uniformity of competition across the territory of the United Kingdom (with the partial exception of Northern Ireland, which was usually, and conveniently, ignored in most studies). At the risk of over-summarising, the view that emerged assumed that a 'modern' party system existed as the framework for electoral choice across the UK as a whole. It was seen as a successful component of political integration, producing uniform political competition throughout Britain, to which the electorate responded by behaving in a uniform manner. The swing of opinion between the two major parties was seen as a uniform phenomenon operating across the entire territory, produced by the assumed fact that class was the basis of British politics. To paraphrase Pulzer, other influences on the vote were relegated to embellishment and detail.[4] Regional effects were thus seen as minimal: either they were 'explained' by the class basis of electoral behaviour, or they were the expression of relict regional isolation. If the latter, the tide of modernisation and the 'nationalisation of politics' could be expected to dispose of them in time.[5]

This latter assumption is central to our present concern, and reflects a widely held view of the process through which mass politics emerged in modern states, and particularly in the United Kingdom. The clear emphasis in this view was upon the party system as a whole, which was not only seen as uniform, but which was assumed to have developed and to be changing uniformly and equally across the whole territory of at least Great Britain. This was a powerful view, encapsulated in the textbook concepts of the 'two-party system', or even, later, of the 'two and a half party system', both of which implied uniformity. So did the conventional historical view, which saw the 'age of alignment' of the 1920s and 1930s as having produced a statewide replacement of the Liberal Party by Labour as the main party of opposition to the Conservatives.[6] Hence from this statewide or centre perspective, various attempts were made to identify the 'watershed' election at which this shift was finally confirmed. Whatever the result of these enquiries, the landslide Labour victory of 1945 was taken to be the final registration of the death of the Liberal Party as a significant political force at the very moment that Labour first attained its majority.

What was true at an aggregate level, or at a regional level in particular parts of England, was not necessarily true everywhere. Aggregate electoral data, coupled with the assumptions discussed above, effectively obscured the amount of real variation and non-uniformity which the electoral and party systems displayed. As a consequence, studies with these bases failed to capture both the complexity of the variation in electoral behaviour and the varying patterns of party competition and contestation that existed, and exists, in the various parts of the United Kingdom. If the assumptions are discarded, and an alternative 'bottom-up' approach is taken to the data, rather than one which starts with the aggregate, then the variety of patterns of electoral politics may be discerned, and the distinctive place of regions such as Cornwall in the operation of the system more adequately assessed. Moreover, such an approach is much more suited to handling the problems posed by recent changes at the aggregate level, such as the much-noted phenomenon of electoral volatility, which aggregate approaches have again sometimes assumed to be uniform volatility, and the declining share of the total vote amassed by the two major statewide parties in recent elections.[7]

A simple point illustrates the diversity that lies behind aggregate electoral outcomes, whether the measure is share of the vote or seats. Contrary to widespread belief, in no post-War election has every elector everywhere been presented with the same electoral choice. The choice between parties facing electors has not been uniform, and indeed the variation has increased in the latter part of the period under discussion. The product of the system may appear uniform and party competition may appear to be uniform, but only at an aggregate level. It is quite possible for established three or four party systems, or regionally dominant single parties to exist within an overall 'two party' or 'two and a half party' system. Equally, it is possible for a third party at the aggregate level to achieve in a particular region the level of support normally associated with the definition of a major party.

More significantly, this approach immediately casts doubt on the conventional view of the development of the party system itself. It may not be what it at first sight seems to be. In place of a uniform statewide system we see diversity of electoral competition, or put another way, an imperfect nationalisation of British politics. The system did not achieve uniformity as a two party system; the major parties did not penetrate all areas of the United Kingdom in the 'age of alignment'; in particular, the Labour Party failed to achieve the mobilisation of its presumed natural constituency everywhere; and the great loser of the aggregate game, the Liberal Party, did not disappear from the contest everywhere. Add to these observations the later development of self-sustaining substate parties in Scotland and Wales - the development of parties independently of the central party system - and the picture of imperfect nationalisation is complete. All of these features have major implications for any attempt to understand the development and operation of electoral politics in Cornwall.

1945 - THE 'ALIGNMENT' ARRIVES IN CORNWALL?

In the light of the features identified above we may embark on a necessarily brief survey of the Cornish political scene in the post-War years, to determine whether or not it represents a significantly divergent case. The General Election of 1945 seemed to indicate that at last the 'alignment' had arrived in Cornwall, demonstrating Cornwall's full integration into a truly national party system. The Labour landslide was represented by the party at last taking Penryn and Falmouth from the Conservatives and its near miss in Camborne, where the sitting Conservative held on by a mere 1.8% of the vote. Correspondence with the statewide pattern of two party competition appeared nearly complete. There was but one exception in Cornwall. In the Northern division, T.L.Horabin held the seat for the Liberals, becoming one of that party's twelve MPs, and in the process achieving a share of the vote 7.4% higher than that of his Conservative opponent. His victory could be dismissed as an aberration: he was one of the few candidates to face no official Labour opposition. In any event, Horabin soon left the party and joined Labour. The election was completed with the Conservatives holding Isaac Foot's old seat of Bodmin, and the National Liberal (of course without Conservative opposition) holding St.Ives.[8]

This apparent normality and congruence with national trends concealed a number of significant differences between the election in Cornwall and that in England in particular. Firstly, the Liberal Party contested only 52% of all

English seats, but fought all five in Cornwall. This was to continue through the subsequent years of the Liberal Party's decline as a national political force. Its presence ensured that three party competition became the norm in all the Cornish constuencies, with the sole exception of Truro in 1951, when no Liberal stood. In other words, of the 71 parliamentary contests in Cornwall between 1945 and 1992, 69 saw a minimum of three candidates standing. The vote they attracted was also significant and divergent from the English norm, with the average vote per candidate consistently higher in Cornwall than in the rural English seats that the party did contest in the 1950s, demonstrating a continuing strength that had only been partially eroded by the effect of the Conservative-Labour polarisation.

The overall pattern since 1945 obscures another important feature. In contrast to experience in much of rural England, it was only in the post-War period that Labour became a regular and consistent contender for parliamentary seats in Cornwall. In the 72 constituency contests between 1918 and 1935 Labour candidiates appeared in only 18. Moreover, first Labour contests in Cornish constituencies were late in comparison with those in England, excepting the candidatures in Camborne and St Ives in 1918, and sporadic. Bodmin saw a Labour candidate twice in the period, the first time in 1929, and again in 1935. Penryn and Falmouth was fought more consistently, on five out of a possible seven occasions, with A.L.Rowse as the standard bearer on two of these. Along with Bodmin, the Northern division also saw only two Labour candidates, and in St lves nine contests (including two by-elections) produced four Labour candidates. On this evidence, Labour's late emergence onto the Cornish political scene made its establishment as a significant contender difficult and allowed the Liberal Party to continue as the main repository for the anti-Conservative vote long beyond its loss of that function in other rural areas.

This may be to put the point too negatively. It may be argued that the 'age of alignment' as experienced in Cornwall was itself very different from the process that took place in much of England. Usually seen as the process by which Labour replaced the Liberals as the main party of opposition to the Conservatives, in Cornwall it was somewhat different. Here, the 1920s and 1930s saw the beginning of a process which was to reach its climax in the 1950s, but it was one in which the Conservatives, in the absence of effective Labour opposition, made major inroads into what had been before the First World War an area dominated by the Liberal Party. The scale of this dominance, as Pelling and Pugh note, was considerable. In the elections between 1885 and December 1910 only four Conservative victories can be identified, all in the Penryn and Falmouth constituency, together with thirteen Liberal Unionist wins, out of a total of 63 electoral occasions. Despite the fact that in Cornwall Liberal Unionism was properly 'Liberalism with a Unionist face' the erstwhile vote clearly formed the basis for subsequent Conservative penetration, and although the evidence is sparse, the Conservatives were clearly able to attract a proportion of newly-enfranchised electors to their camp, as well as making inroads into the Liberal vote. Nevertheless, a pattern that has persisted to this day was established, namely that the Conservative Party, despite its post-War electoral dominance in Cornwall, has never polled at the level that would be expected, given the social and economic structure of the Cornish constituencies. The party's vote has been consistently below the level achieved in comparable English rural constituencies, but unsurprisingly above its performance levels in England as a whole.

Clearly, Cornish politics entered the post-War period in a significantly different cast to that obtaining elsewhere, and some major features of the pattern were to be maintained and develop towards greater divergence. Nevertheless, the years following the War seemed at first sight to show that Cornwall was following the normal rural English pattern. Only consistent Liberal contestation seemed to be unusual. In the 1950s four Conservatives, including one National Liberal, and one Labour member were regularly returned to Westminster. Later Liberal revivals nationwide seemed to find their echo in Cornwall: even in this respect integration into a statewide party system appeared complete. Against this view can be set the simple historical view, stressing the lateness of Cornwall's integration. This would suggest that a related combination of Liberal survival and late Labour penetration meant that the latter's rise to the role of providing the major opposition to the Conservatives never occurred in Cornwall. The easy conclusion that the nineteenth century statewide pattern of politics persisted in Cornwall, preserved in isolation from the mainstream in a form of 'Celtic aspic', can be reached. However, this would be too simple: it ignores, among other factors, the historic dominance of Liberalism, the question over the nature of subsequent Conservative electoral dominance, and the reasons why Labour found Cornwall to be such inhospitable territory.[9]

These straightforward observations of the basis for difference require consideration in more detail. In particular, the question of how divergent Cornish politics as a whole have been and are from the patterns obtaining statewide needs to be addressed. A simple comparison of the percentage shares of the vote obtained by a party or parties in one area with that gained in another does not allow for overall comparison. Similarly, an average calculated over a number of separate elections does not allow the general pattern of movement over time to be discerned. An effective answer to the first problem is provided by Miller's 'MD formula', which seeks to measure the difference between the multiparty electoral outcome in one area with that in another.[10] The measure produces a minimum score of zero when each area has an identical pattern of party competition and electoral behaviour. Conversely, the higher the score, the greater the deviation between the two patterns of politics under comparison. As an example, Miller's calculation of the measure of deviation (%MD) for the 1979 General Election for Wales, Scotland and Northern Ireland, gave scores of 15, 17, and 74 respectively, the latter of course reflecting the significantly different pattern of party competition in the province.

The measure also allows comparison in time, and when applied to post-War elections in Cornwall produces:

Election	Cornwall-England %MD
1945	23.32
1950	24.41
1951	22.02
1955	18.12
1959	20.76
1964	23.34
1966	29.03
1970	20.44
1974F	18.83
19740	18.80
1979	19.04
1983	16.23
1987	16.37
1992	21.30

While making the necessary caveat that an exaggerative effect is introduced by the small number of constituencies in the Cornish case, the remarkable features of this gross measure of deviation are firstly its size and secondly its remarkable consistency over time. The variation ranges from 16.23% in 1983 to 24.41% in 1950. In both size and consistency the deviations compare with those calculated by Miller for a selection of general elections in Wales. In no year does the figure for Cornwall fall below the Welsh, and from 1959 to 1966 it is substantially above. The measure reveals a startling consistency in the patterns of party contestation and electoral behaviour in Cornwall. From 1945 to 1970 the %MD is over 20 for all elections save that of 1955, and largely accounted for by the presence of Liberal candidates garnering respectable levels of support in all the Cornish constituencies, as compared with the party's less than universal presence in England. Similarly, the decreased variations from February 1974 to 1987, and particularly those for 1983 and 1987 reflect wider contestation by and increased support for Liberal and subsequently Alliance candidates in English constituencies. In the two latter elections, the Alliance's displacement of Labour as the second party in a large number of these seats briefly created a pattern of competition, particularly in southern and rural England, which mirrored that which had obtained throughout the post-War period in Cornwall. The apparently temporary nature of this phenomenon is illustrated by the 1992 figure, which registers the fallback of the Liberal Democrat vote in these selfsame areas, coupled with an increase in the party's share of the vote in Cornwall.

A further note on the relative distinctiveness of the pattern of party competition and electoral behaviour which the measure expresses should be added. If the measure is calculated for the four South Western counties as a whole (Cornwall, Devon, Dorset and Somerset), then the deviation is much less. If however the two, and sometimes three, northernmost and westernmost seats in Devon (excluding Plymouth) are added to the Cornish totals as a base for the measurement, then the resulting measure varies hardly at all from that calculated for Cornwall. This indicates a number of similarities, and also that these geographically contiguous areas share a number of social and economic features and some aspects of political development with their Cornish neighbours. While the label of 'Greater Cornwall' may be eschewed as offensive to many, it is apparent that these constituencies continue to show more political similarity with those to their west than they do with those to their south and east.

CORNISH VOTERS - MARCHING TO A DIFFERENT DRUM?

The consistency of political distinctiveness requires more comment. Are changes in party fortunes statewide followed by comparable change in Cornwall - are Cornish electors in step, or are they marching to a different drum? More precisely, if a particular party gains at the expense of others statewide, is this trend followed in Cornwall, or do Cornish electors move to a different extent or in different directions?

TABLE 11.1
VOTE CHANGE ENGLAND-CORNWALL

	Conservative		Labour		Liberal	
	England	Cornwall	England	Cornwall	England	Cornwall
1945	-14.3	-4.7	10	9.4	3.1	-4.4
1950	3.6	2.4	-2.3	3.7	0	-6
1951	5	6.1	2.6	3.6	-7.1	-9.6
1955	1.6	-1.9	-2	-2.8	0.3	4.6
1959	-0.4	-4.5	-3.2	-3.3	3.7	7.8
1964	-5.9	-2.9	-0.1	-1.4	5.8	4.1
1966	-1.4	0.2	4.5	1.7	-3.1	-1.7
1970	5.6	6.5	-4.6	-3	-1.1	-4
1974F	-8.1	-6.1	-5.8	-4.8	13.4	11
1974O	-1.3	1.9	2.5	0.5	-1.1	2.4
1979	8.3	7.5	-3.4	-6.7	-5.3	-3.3
1983	-1.2	-1.9	-9.7	-3	11.4	7.2
1987	0.2	-2.1	2.6	3.8	-2.6	-0.5
1992	0.8	-4.6	4.4	1.1	-4.6	1.9

A partial answer to these questions can be gained by comparing the movement in the parties' shares of the vote, again for the post-War general elections. Table 11.1 shows the gain or loss by each party at each election, and expresses the difference in vote share between one election and the next. For example, the Conservative share of the vote in Cornwall in 1987 was 47.3% and in 1992 42.7% (-4.6% of total votes cast). In four elections (1955, 1966, October 1974 and 1987) the Conservative share of the vote in Cornwall moved in a direction opposite to its movement in England. In only one election (1950) did the Labour vote do the same. In four elections (1945, 1950, October 1974 and 1992) the Liberal vote moved in an opposite direction. However, the table does not clearly show the relationship between one party's gains and losses over time, or the pattern of movement of all parties in relation to the English average. These features can best be demonstrated graphically, as in Figure 11.1.

FIGURE 11.1

Losses and gains by Political Parties in General Elections in Cornwall

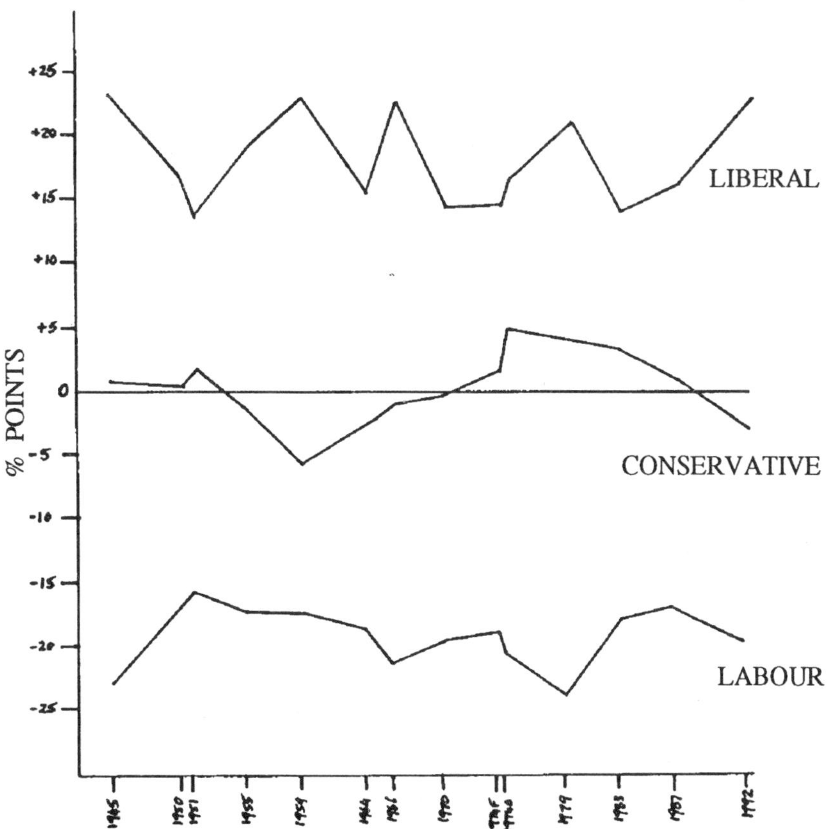

The central line '0' represents the average vote share that each party gained in England at each of the post-War elections. The line for each party shows the extent to which that party's vote in Cornwall varied from the English average. Therefore, a consistent performance below line '0' indicates the extent to which a party underperformed in comparison to its achievement in England, while a performance above indicates the opposite. The graph also shows the extent to which the votes of the parties in Cornwall vary in relation to one another, providing a visual representation of change in the party system. It demonstrates that the Liberal and Labour votes have been and continue to be the most divergent from the English pattern, and secondly that the most immediately apparent direct relationship is between the Conservative vote and that for the Liberals.

The basic shape of this party system, and the ways in which it has changed since 1945 are now clear. In effect, Cornwall has a ' two and a half' party system, with Conservatives and Liberals as the two, and Labour the half. In terms of the share of the vote, the Conservatives have never slipped below 41%, and only twice, in 1951 and 1979, has their share exceeded 50%. The Liberal share of the vote has never exceeded that gained by the Conservatives in the post-War period, although in 1992 the two parties were separated by a single percentage point, with the Conservatives on 42.7% and the Liberal Democrats on 41.7%, the closest the two parties had approached each other. The overall consistency of the relationship between the votes for the two parties is striking. Liberal recovery after the 1951 General Election and throughout the 1950s in Cornwall as a whole was largely at the Conservatives' expense, although the gradual squeeze which the party was able to place on the Labour vote in particular constituencies was a marked feature of these years. The general rule that when the Liberal vote increases that for the Conservatives declines, and vice versa, has held true in all post-War general elections save for two, those of 1945 and October 1974. In the first, both suffered loss, in the second both gained. Although this relationship between the vote for the two parties is the most prominent feature, Labour's long decline in the Liberals' favour is also noteworthy. In comparison with the development of this phenomenon in English rural seats, its appearance in Cornwall was both much earlier and much more strongly sustained. The Liberals had displaced Labour from its temporary position as the second party in Cornwall by 1959. Since then, Labour's decline as a significant force in parliamentary elections in Cornwall was both steady and sustained until it reached its nadir of a 9.0% share of the vote in 1983. The subsequent recovery to 12.8% in 1987 and 13.9% in 1992 represented a climb back to only half the level of support the party had achieved in the 1950s and early 1960s.[11]

That these patterns represent a series of distinctive variations on the general theme of English electoral behaviour is demonstrable. However, it must not be thought that electoral politics in Cornwall is *sui generis* and a wholly independent phenomenon. The impact of statewide political developments is visible: a major shift in the fortunes of a party statewide is reflected in particular elections. For example, the Conservative victory of 1979 saw the party's vote in Cornwall rise to its highest post-War figure of 51.3%, and Labour's 1983 debacle produced the 9.0% already mentioned. In fact Labour, as the smallest statewide party in Cornwall, is the party whose vote most closely reflects statewide trends. In the fourteen elections, Labour has only seen its share of the vote move in an opposite direction to the national trend on one occasion, in 1950. In seven other elections, the movement was less than that in England, and in the remaining six, more. The corresponding figures for the Conservatives are five opposite, five less, and four greater, and for the Liberals four opposite, six less, and four greater.

Broader developments at a statewide level have similarly had a variable and generally lesser impact on the pattern of party competition and electoral behaviour in Cornwall. The Liberal revivals from the late 1950s onwards are a case in point. Although in rural, suburban, and later urban England these episodes can properly be seen as revivals of a party that had reached a virtually moribund state, with Liberal candidiates making a reappearance after, in some cases, two decades of non-contestation, this was certainly not the case in Cornwall. Here the Liberal Party, though depleted, had never dropped out from the electoral battle. The rapid revivals experienced elsewhere therefore did not take place: the increase in the party's share of the vote started earlier in Cornwall and lasted longer: 'Bodmin man' was a somewhat more substantial figure than 'Orpington man' ever was. A similar muted effect can be detected in the impact of the formation, meteoric rise, and subsequent collapse of the Liberal-SDP Alliance in the 1980s. Its impact in Cornwall was limited. In the allocation of parliamentary seats to fight, the newly formed Social Democratic Party was given St lves and Falmouth and Camborne, where the Liberals had registered their worst performances in the post-War period. The apparent effect was to raise the Alliance to a position of real contention in both, but it must be considered, in terms of the general shift in voting allegiance in Cornwall at this period, that both constituencies still had reasonably large Labour votes that were vulnerable to the squeeze in 1983 and 1987. Would a Liberal candidate have fared any worse than the SDP contenders did? The evidence from the 1992 General Election suggests not. With the Liberal Democrats now fighting both seats, the St.lves result pushed the seat into the ultra-marginal category. Falmouth and Camborne will go into the next general election as that *rara avis*, a three-way marginal, given the locally-specific recovery by Labour into a position of contention.

One feature of the Cornish electoral scene is however unique. Cornwall is the only territory formally part of England to have given rise to occasional electoral contestation by sub-state nationalist/autonomist parties. As Payton notes, the electoral impact of Mebyon Kernow and the Cornish Nationalist Party has been minimal for various reasons, including the Liberals' embracing of anti-metropolitan stances and devolutionist policies, and their occasional echo by the other parties in Cornwall and their candidates. Consequently, their ability to detach and convert voters from the main parties at general elections on the issue of Cornwall's status has been very limited.[12] There has in fact been only one electoral occasion, that of the first direct elections to the European Parliament in 1979, when a Mebyon Kernow candidate obtained 5.9% of the vote in the Cornwall and Plymouth constituency. A recalculation results in an estimate that this represented over 9% of the poll in Cornwall. In any case, it was the highest minor party vote in any United Kingdom constituency. Building on Cornish resentment at the attachment to Plymouth for European purposes, the MK campaign benefited, in the aftermath of that year's General Election, from probably the most lacklustre Liberal campaign in Cornwall in recent memory. The Liberals came in a poor third behind Labour, with 13.5% of the vote. Nationalists' subsequent incursions into the electoral process have met with scant success, for the reasons outlined above and detailed elsewhere.[13]

At the level of parliamentary elections, then, Cornwall exhibits a distinctive pattern of electoral politics which does not match the English pattern. Occasional similarities with English rural areas can be detected, but the whole package is unique. Constituency by constituency comparisons may throw up some similarities, but taken together, the Cornish constituencies exhibit considerable divergence from assumed norms, and find their place in the general and growing diversity of the United Kingdom electoral and party system. However, to complete the picture of political distinctiveness, another aspect, that of local politics, must be considered.

THE DISTINCTIVE PATTERN OF LOCAL POLITICS

Until recently, the study of local elections and the electoral behaviour associated with them has been relatively neglected in Britain, with the result that generalisations about the operation of local political systems have either been based on relatively few and largely urban case studies or have been restricted to the aggregate level. Various trends, such as the growing party presence in local electoral contests in the post-War period; the decline of Independents; the relationship between electors' behaviour in parliamentary and local elections; and the question of turnout have been subjected to more detailed study. However, the amount of investigation undertaken to date in no way matches the attention that has been paid to parliamentary elections. Comparing the pattern of local politics in Cornwall with that obtaining elsewhere is therefore difficult, and consequently statements about its distinctiveness must be more conditional.

While one element of the distinctive patterns of party competition and electoral behaviour exhibited in parliamentary elections in Cornwall is their consistency over time, it might be expected that this would also obtain at the local level. In fact, the position is more complex. What is at first sight unusual about the pattern of local politics in Cornwall is its apparent resistance to change until very recently. Furthermore, the changes that have taken place, particularly in the 1980s, seem to show that, far from an emerging pattern of local politics identical to the rural English norm, Cornish developments point to the stabilisation of a very different system. For example, we might expect based on experience elsewhere, that the partisanisation of Cornish local politics would have taken place more rapidly than it has, and would result in a more or less uniform pattern of contestation between the parties dominant in parliamentary elections and reflecting their strengths at that level. In Cornwall, neither of these conditions has obtained, and there are at present few signs that it will.

Apart from the social, cultural and economic explanations covered elsewhere, two major reasons can be adduced for this position, before the operation of local politics is discussed in more detail. Firstly, there is an element of longstanding political attitude and belief, which stems from the late nineteenth century, and combines with attitudes which value local identity within Cornwall. Payton describes the development of an 'Independent' tradition in which local politics were seen as divorced from and irrelevant to statewide politics, and its correspondence with Bulpitt's 'dual polity' explanation of the structure of central-local relations in the first part of the twentieth century. Specifically, this localist tradition was connected to the very inception of County government in Cornwall. Dennis describes how a conflict-reducing mechanism was introduced after the first County Council elections of 1889. The first chairman was a Liberal Unionist, but the vice-chairman was a Liberal. The organisation of committees followed a similar pattern, contributing towards the development and preservation of the exclusion of partisan conflict, both within the Council itself and increasingly in elections to it. A form of extreme localism thus became embedded, and to some extent remains. As late as 1990 some County Councillors, mostly Independents, but including some elected with a party label, tended still to define their primary role as that of 'ambassador to Truro' for their localities.[14]

The second reason is essentially a political structural one. The reform of local government areas produced by the 1972 Act had a relatively minimal effect on the structure of local politics in Cornwall, particularly at County level. In common with rural areas in Wales, Cornwall was one of the few new Counties which did not find substantial urban areas included within it. The absence of this feature was significant for the preservation of the by now distinctive pattern of contestation and local politics. For example, after 1974, neighbouring Devon saw its pattern of party competition, both within the County Council and electorally, irrevocably changed by the inclusion of the three county boroughs of Plymouth, Exeter, and Torbay, with their developed urban patterns of party competition. A full party system was in effect imported into the new County Council, and quickly served to assist the fall of Independents from their previous position of electoral and political dominance in the rural areas. No such phenomenon occurred in Cornwall. Indeed, at the first county elections under the reformed system in 1973, Cornwall shared the distinction of Independent control with only four other counties - Dyfed, Gwynedd, Powys, and the Isle of Wight.

The Independent tradition and localism combined to produce that other notable phenomenon of Cornish local politics in the post-War period, the prevalence of the unopposed return, particularly in County Council elections. Since 1973, unopposed returns in Cornwall have not been the isolated phenomena that they are elsewhere, where they usually result from the absence of even ritual contestation by a party in areas where their opponents have overwhelming strength, such as in a few of the heavily Conservative divisions of Dorset. Unopposed returns took place for 55% of Cornwall County Council seats in 1977, representing a significant change from the position in the mid 1950s. In 1955, the extreme example, there were a mere 78 candidates for the 72 seats. Although the number of candidates increased at subsequent elections, this meant that the vast majority of Cornish electors never had the chance to vote in a County election before 1973. By 1985, the figure was still at 21%, and at the following election in 1989 the proportion dropped to 10%. This decline reflects the corresponding decline of the Independent tradition represented by fewer Independent candidates, fewer Independents elected, and the increasing partisanisation of local politics in Cornwall. The broad picture of the trends can be discerned from the following table. It should be noted that from 1946 - 1970 72 seats were at stake, and that after reorganisation in 1973 the number increased to 79.[16]

TABLE 11.2
Number of Candidates standing in Cornwall County Elections

	Seats	Total Candidates	CON	LAB	LIB	Ratepayer	IND	GRN	Nationalist	Others
1946	72	102	0	5	0	0	97	0	0	0
1949	72	107	2	10	0	0	95	0	0	0
1952	72	85	0	6	0	0	79	0	0	0
1955	72	78	0	5	0	0	73	0	0	0
1958	72	86	0	4	0	0	82	0	0	0
1961	72	92	1	4	0	0	87	0	0	0
1964	72	94	0	2	0	0	92	0	0	0
1967	72	95	0	2	0	0	92	0	1	0
1970	72	96	2	2	1	0	86	0	5	0
1973	79	135	9	11	1	0	114	0	0	0
1977	79	153	16	12	3	3	101	4	8	6
1981	79	170	31	24	25	1	73	1	14	1
1985	79	173	41	23	43	2	54	1	5	4
1989	79	179	62	19	49	2	38	0	3	6
1993	79	210	54	39	58	2	43	4	6	4

The incidence of contestation revealed shows both the strength and decline of the Independent tradition. It also reveals the relatively small impact of reform on the pattern of contestation in Cornwall. The increase in the number of Independent candidates in 1973 may be explained by the number of displaced councillors from previous borough and urban and rural district councils now seeking County seats, but the increase in candidates with a party label was far lower than was the case in other rural Counties. Although from the mid-1970s the Liberals in particular had aspired to greater intervention, it was not until 1981 that partisanisation intensified in earnest. In that year the numbers of both Conservative and Labour candidates doubled, and Liberal candidatures increased eightfold. The year of the largest Nationalist intervention to date saw their candidates increase to 14. As the reverse of this process, Independent candidacies declined by some 25%, and by 1989 stood at just over a third of the 1977 figure.[17]

The table gives a broad hint that the extent of party contestation should not be overestimated. To date, no party has contested every division in Cornwall at a County election. Labour's highpoint was in 1985, when it ran candidates in 30% of the seats, while that for both the Liberal Democrats and the Conservatives was in 1993 - the year that the Liberal Democrats won overall control of the Council. The result is that County elections in Cornwall display the greatest variety of patterns of contestation to be found anywhere in the United Kingdom. For example, of the 42 types of contest (CON v LAB; CON v LAB v LIB; CON v LAB v LIB v IND; etc) theoretically possible in 1985, Cornwall had no fewer than 28. Of the contests in Cornwall, only three were of the 'standard' CON v LAB v LIB type so prevalent in parts of England. At County level, therefore, Cornish electors do not face a uniform choice. Moreover, the choice from one election to another in the same division is unlikely to be the same, making generalisations about changes over time in local electoral behaviour somewhat hazardous to say the least. Relating shares of the vote obtained by parties and groups to seats won reveals little: an increase in a party's overall share of the vote is just as likely to reflect an increase in the number of divisions contested as is to register standing in public esteem. Add these features to the survival of the localist ad hominem support for particular candidates, irrespective of party, and conventional interpretations of election results can become deeply flawed. The overall results from the 1981 increase in partisan activity to 1993 must therefore be treated with extreme care (Table 11.3 overleaf).

An investigation of electoral behaviour at District level faces many of the same problems, but many of the same trends that are apparent in county elections have been replicated. The 1950s generally displayed similar levels of unopposed returns to those seen in County elections of the period, except for the Camborne-Redruth Urban District Council, where local Labour activity made itself felt. However, even this tailed off in the early 1960s, and in no election in the post-War period did Labour contest all the seats. The striking feature that emerged later, in the context of the generally increasing partisanisation of local politics, was again that of variety from one district to another. If patterns of contestation, of electoral allegiance and of local party strengths are considered, no two districts in Cornwall exhibited an identical system. Instead, considerable variation was the order of the day. By 1991, North Cornwall was at one extreme, with Independents holding 31 of the 38 council seats, the next largest group being four Liberal Democrats. At the other was Carrick, where the Conservatives' 27 out of 45 seats in 1979 had been reduced to 8 in the face of a Liberal Democrat total of 24, with Independents also reduced to 8. These variations conceal one major trend: the Independent decline in the districts has been just as swift as at County level, and in some cases more severe. Even in North Cornwall, 1973 to 1991 saw Independent representation drop by 10 seats.

TABLE 11.3
% of Votes and Number of Seats won in Cornwall County Elections

	Conservative		Labour		Liberal		Independent		Others	
	Vote%	Seats	Vote%	Seats	Vote%	Seats	Vote%	Seats	Vote%	Seats
1981	16.8	13	11.4	5	21.7	13	44	48	6.1	0
1985	24.6	16	9.1	5	32.3	30	30.3	27	3.6	1
1989	32.3	14	8.9	8	35.2	31	18.6	23	5.1	3
1993	22.4	6	12.3	8	41.5	41	19.5	21	4.2	3

As well as by the impact of partisanisation, this trend has been produced by a marked drop in candidature on the part of avowed Independents. In the 1973 District Council elections, the five districts saw a total of 420 Independent candidates, again swollen by displaced councillors from previous authorities. By 1976, the total was down to 281, starting a steady decline to reach 175 in 1991. Over the same period, Conservative candidacies increased from 13 in 1973 to 123 in 1991, Liberal from nine to 116, and Labour more slowly from 31 to 63. However, with 246 seats at stake in each electoral round (if the seats in Penwith, the only Council to elect by thirds, are consolidated into the total for each main electoral year) it is apparent that the pattern of contestation from one ward to another is just as diverse as in the County electoral divisions. Unopposed returns have declined from their post reorganisation peak of 96 in 1979 to 31 in 1991, at the latter date half of the total being accounted for by North Cornwall, with a further six in Caradon.

Similarities between the distribution of support for the parties in district and County elections began to emerge clearly in the mid-1980s. The dominance of the Liberal Democrats in Carrick and Restormel, of the Independents in North Cornwall, Labour's pockets of support in Camborne-Redruth, and the Conservative presence in Penwith and parts of Carrick and Caradon all showed at both levels of election. The phenomenon of Cornwall marching to a different electoral drum also began to show through the local electoral process with a degree of clarity. For example, with hindsight the Conservative Party ought to have been more worried about the implications of the 1989 County Council election result in Cornwall for the subsequent general election than it appeared to be at the time. In 1989, the newly formed Liberal Democrats lost heavily in terms of seats and votes both statewide and in the South West region. The fall of 7.1% in their share of the vote from the Alliance total for 1985 in Somerset was not untypical. In Cornwall, precisely the reverse happened, with the Conservatives suffering a loss of 7.9% from 1985, and the Liberal Democrats increasing their share by 2.9%. In general, while repeating the caveats entered above, many other instances of such divergence from statewide trends on the part of the Cornish electorate when it is voting locally can be identified, adding another dimension to the patterns of divergence and difference discerned in voting behaviour in parliamentary elections.

CONCLUSION

This survey of elections and electoral behaviour in Cornwall has been necessarily brief, and has focussed on the major points of difference and divergence which give Cornish politics its particular flavour. Of necessity, much has been omitted, particularly from the treatment of the local scene. Consideration of the impact of many socio-economic factors has been kept to a minimum, with the result that fascinating questions remain. The political impact of the considerable in-migration to Cornwall since the 1960s is a case in point, although it may be an instance of a dog that did not bark in the night, given that at first sight its expected effect of adding to the strengths of both Conservative and Labour has not materialised. Other instances, such as the impact of anti-metropolitanism, the development of an enhanced Cornish consciousness, and the movement of Cornish society and economy from the 'Second' to a 'Third' stage of Peripheralism identified by Payton, stand as producers of the political changes discussed above.

What does emerge from this survey is, first and foremost, that electoral politics in Cornwall is a distinctive phenomenon. The differences identified are not simply being eroded by statewide developments - in this respect politics in Cornwall is not being observably 'nationalised'. In comparison with England, Cornish electoral politics are divergent. Electoral trends in the former are not necessarily replicated in the latter, and indeed the patterns of development discerned seem likely to stabilise in a form which shows considerable and consistent variation from the English, and specifically the rural English case.

REFERENCES

1. See especially P.Payton, *The Making of Modern Cornwall: Historical Experience and the Persistence of 'Difference'*, Dyllansow Truran, Redruth, 1992.
2. For examples see: J.Bulpitt, *Territory and Power in the United Kingdom : An Interpretation*, Manchester University Press, Manchester, 1983; Rose, R. *Understanding the United Kingdom*, Longman, London, 1982; D.Urwin, 'Territorial Structures and Political Developments in the

United Kingdom' in S. Rokkan and D.Urwin (eds.), *The Politics of Territorial Identity: Studies in European Regionalism,* Sage, London, 1982; and M.Keating, *State and Regional Nationalism: Territorial Politics and the European State,* Harvester Wheatsheaf, Hemel Hempstead, 1988.

3. P.Pulzer, *Political Representation and Elections in Britain*, Allen & Unwin, London, 1975 pp112-20, provides an example.
4. Pulzer, 1975.
5. For an example see D.E.Butler and D.Stokes, *Political Change in Britain : Forces Shaping Electoral Choice,* Macmillan, London, 1974, pp121-30.
6. C.Cook, *The Age of Alignment: Electoral Politics in Britain, 1922-29,* Macmillan, London, 1975.
7. For discussion of volatility see *inter alia*, A. Heath, R. Jowell, and J.Curtice, *How Britain Votes*, Pergamon, Oxford, 1985.
8. Data for parliamentary elections from F.W.S.Craig, *Britain Parliamentary Election results 1918-1949,* Parliamentary Reference Publications, Chichester, 1977, and F.W.S Craig, *British Parliamentary Election Results 1950-1970.,* Parliamentary Reference Publications, Chichester, 1979.
9. For a further discussion see A.N.Lee, 'The Persistence of Difference? Electoral Change in Cornwal', paper presented at PSA Annual Conference, Plymouth, 1988, and Payton, 1992, pp207-234.
10. W.Miller, 'Variations in Electoral Behaviour in the United Kingdom' in P.Madgwick and R.Rose, (eds.) *The Territorial Dimension in United Kingdom Politics,* Macmillan, London, 1982, pp225-50.
11. See D.Butler and D.Kavanagh, *The British General Election of 1983, The British General Election of 1987, The British General Election of 1992,* Macmillan, London, 1984, 1988, 1992.
12. Payton, 1992, pp227-8.
13. For the 1979 election, see D.Butler and D.Marquand, *European Elections and British Politics,* Longman, London, 1981. For 1989 see M.Burgess and A.N.Lee, 'The United Kingdom' in J.Lodge, *The 1989 Election to the European Parliament,* Macmillan, London, 1990.
14. Information supplied to the author.
15. W.Grant, *Independent Local Politics in England and Wales,* Saxon House, Farnborough, 1977 pp2-3.
16. Information supplied by Local Government Chronicle Elections Centre, University Of Plymouth, and by Bernard Deacon.
17. All information on local elections has been calculated from data supplied by Bernard Deacon for the period 1945-1973, by the local Government Chronicle Elections Centre, University of Plymouth for 1973 onwards, and C.Rallings and M.Thrasher, *The 1985 County Council Election Results; The 1989 Local Election Handbook*; and Local Government Chronicle Elections Centre, University of Plymouth 1985, 1989, and 1991.

CHAPTER 12

THE IDEOLOGY OF LANGUAGE REVIVAL

Philip Payton and Bernard Deacon

The Cornish language, and the twentieth century movement to revive it, pose problems for observers of modern Cornwall. For those who write from within the 'Cornwall as part of the South West' school the persistence, even the existence, of a long-established revival movement based on a non-English language is difficult to explain.[1] Similarly, for those writing from the very different perspective of Celtic nationalism, the failure of the Cornish language revival to become a mass movement raises equal problems.[2]

Although the great majority of Cornish place-names are of Cornish derivation[3] and the Cornish language still lives in dialect words and personal surnames, it is not used on a day-to-day instrumental basis by more than a handful of people. Its ghostly remains may still stalk the territory west of the Tamar but they are, for most people, remains. Outside the small band of Cornish speakers people carry on their affairs in English, English is the dominant language of a mainly monoglot Cornish population. Thus the Cornish language movement could be viewed as a marginal element of modern Cornish life, the plaything of a few romantics. However, the language and the movement to revive it is an important theme of study for two reasons.

Firstly, Cornish still has resonance on a symbolic level. As Chapter 9 has shown, the language is one symbol of a separate identity. This was echoed by the words of Professor Charles Thomas in 1973; '. . . the knowledge of the existence of a separate language, as distinct from a full knowledge of that language itself, is probably sufficient. . ...to foster a sense of otherness'.[4] The enthusiastic adoption of a few words of Cornish, notably 'Kernow', during the 1980s within popular Cornish culture, illustrates this interaction between the language as symbol and the popular identity.

Secondly, the Revivalist movement itself and its persistence is worthy of study for the very reason that its task - to revive a language that had apparently 'died' as a colloquial vernacular around 1800 - would appear to be so ambitious.[5] There have not been many examples of language 'death' in modern Europe, and even fewer examples of successful language revivals, so the case of an attempted language resuscitation has wider comparative interest.

Surprisingly, there have been no studies of the Cornish language movement and its internal dynamics by historians and social scientists. Instead work on it has been dominated by linguists. In this Chapter we set out to remedy that gap by providing a preliminary analysis of the language movement, concentratlng on the years since 1945. Because of the small scale of the subject to some extent we will have to focus on the micro-level. However, analysis cannot and will not be confined to that level. Even the Cornish language movement is situated within broader structures. In its own way the movement has had to adapt to, and can be explained by, factors external to the movement itself - a point sometimes lost by lts participants. Ideological positions adopted by Cornish language practitioners relate not only to purely linguistic issues or even the practical mechanics of revival but also reflect wider debates about the basis, nature and purpose of the broader 'Cornish Revival'.

UNIFIED CORNISH - THE INTER-WAR LEGACY

The Cornish Revival has its roots in the years at the end of the nineteenth century. This in turn was an echo of the more general cultural and linguistic revival taking place in the other Celtic countries. Henry Jenner's *A Handbook of the Cornish Language* in 1904 marked the real beginnings of the revival of Cornish as a written and spoken medium.[6] But it was to be the efforts of Robert Morton Nance ('Mordon'), with the able assistance of other enthusiasts such as A.S.D.Smith ('Caradar'), that led to the full-scale reconstruction of the language.

Nance's 'Unified' Cornish was based principally upon the surviving literary texts of Middle Cornish, the language of the fourteenth to early sixteenth centuries contained in the Miracle Plays and Passion Poem. Although these texts were agreeably medieval in ambience (an important consideration for those looking back to the culture of pre-industrial Cornwall) and provided a wealth of linguistic material to facilitate the process of reconstruction, there were gaps in the knowledge that they afforded. Consequently, in building his 'Unified' system Nance was obliged to employ techniques of internal analogy and to use evidence from later periods of wrltten Cornish, as well as drawing comparisons with other Celtic languages.[7] This assisted in the construction of parts of verbs not actually found in the texts, and led to vocabulary borrowings from Welsh and Breton. As there were no apparent means of gauging accurately how Middle Cornish might have been spoken, phonology remained problematical although Nance insisted in 1929 that '. . . the vowel sounds of Cornish as last spoken can still be heard from the inhabitants of West Cornwall'.[8] 'Unified' Cornish, therefore, presented in its written and spoken expressions an alliance of Middle Cornish orthography and Late Cornish phonology (or at least Nance's perceptions thereof), with various assumptions, additions and accretions decided at Nance's discretion.

Thus constituted 'Unified' Cornish proved the vehicle for language revival in the years before the Second World War. Nance's *Cornish for All*, published in 1929, Smith's *Lessons In Spoken Cornish* (1931) and *Cornish Simplified* (1939), plus the appearance of English-Cornish and Cornish-English dictionaries in the same decade, provided a basic infrastructure for those wanting to learn this revived 'Unified' Cornish. It was embraced enthusiastically by those whose romantic vision saw it as both a window to an older Celtic-Catholic Cornwall for which they yearned and as a means of recreating such a culture within contemporary Cornwall. In this sense the language Revival can be seen as a response to the identity crisis that accompanied the industrial collapse and socio-economic paralysis of later nineteenth century Cornwall.[9] The inter-War Revivalists preferred to take refuge from the ugly realities of modern Cornwall by returning to a past when Cornwall was 'purely Cornish'. To attempt this, however, they had to undertake an enormous effort of imagination in ignoring four hundred years of Cornish history that included the experience of industrialisation. As Quiller-Couch had percipiently noted, if the medieval miracle plays were to be revived as Jenner wished then '. . . the audience would have to be play-acting even more strenuously than the actors'.[10]

Of course, one consequence of basing the language Revival so firmly on the medieval period was to distance it from the culture of contemporary Cornish people. This, predominantly Methodist in religion and Liberal in politics, had precious few points of connection with the medieval nostalgia and Bardic symbolism of the Revivalists.[11] Although a Cornish language pressure group - Tyr ha Tavas - had been formed in 1933, most of its founder members lived in London and Surrey.[12] It was middle-class Cornish emigres who were most active in the pre-War Cornish language movement and the pages of the Cornish language periodical *Kernow*, which appeared in the mid-1930s, give few indications that Cornwall itself was languishing in deep economic depression during those years.

THE POST-WAR YEARS

The War, however, had a dislocating effect, and in 1946 J.J.Parry - an American observer of the Revival - wondered if and how it would be possible to draw the Cornish language movement together again and revive its vigour.[13] But Smith, for one, had no doubts about the inherent strength of the language and its future direction, writing confidently in the following year that '. . . we have a compact medieval language. . .and (it is) little likely to undergo any further change'.[14] In his estimation, 'Unified' Cornish fitted perfectly the aspirations of the Revivalists, while the Revival itself - having survived the intrusions of War - could simply pick up from where it had left off beforehand.

However, in the years after 1945 the Cornish Revival changed in response to new conditions in a a manner that neither Smith nor his inter-War contemporaries could have anticipated. Cornwall was disturbed at length from her 'paralysis', with the intervention of new socio-economic trends associated with central government regional development policies and other manifestations of post-War economic management. Cornwall became a land of branch factories and of tourism, and in time a process of counter-urbanisation led to a reversal of the century-long experience of emigration and an unprecedented wave of in-migration from across the Tamar.[15] Partly in response to these changes, a new spirit of anti-metropolitanism had become apparent in Cornish political behaviour by the 1960s. Prefiguring this was the birth of political nationalism in Cornwall; Mebyon Kernow (Sons of Cornwall) was formed as early as 1951. Although it proved far readier than the pre-War revivalists had ever been in coming to terms with the reality of Cornwall's parlous socio-economic condition (producing as it did a range of policies to address these problems), it nonetheless grew out of the Cornish Revival and thus shared many of its assumptions and aspirations. Inevitably, therefore, despite the new concern for socio-economic issues, questions of language revival were central to the preocupations of Mebyon Kernow and Cornish nationalists in the 1950s and 60s, and even into the 1970s.

FIGURE 12.1
The ideology of language revival articulated in *Cornish Nation* Vol.2, No.4, June 1971

SELF-UNDERSTANDING TO WORLD UNDERSTANDING

For example, a principal aim was to promote the study of Cornish in schools. Richard Gendall wrote in the journal *New Cornwall* in June 1968 that the language was '. . . an inalienable part of Cornwall's heritage - and should be put within reach of Cornwall's children'. There was an element of cultural conservation in this, for '. . . few sensitive people question the good sense of attempting to save rare animals and plant life from extinction. . .'[16] (and the same rules should therefore be applied to Cornish). James Whetter offered a more fundamental motivation for children (and others) to learn Cornish: '. . . because they are in Kernow, and language is the summation of the Cornish identity'.[17] That such dogmatic insistence could be effective was evidenced in the response of at least one youngster, who in the pages of *New Cornwall* argued with teenage passion that the revival of the language to the point of official bi-lingualism was '. . . an absolute necessity for our growth and development as a nation separate from England'.[18]

However, such unquestioning acceptance of language as a central plank of the Cornish national movement's ideology and programme was progressively eroded after the mid 1960s. By 1976 Tim Saunders - while still protesting that he wrote in Cornish because '. . .the Cornish nation is fast approaching its greatest crisis. . .' - reminded observers that '. . .it is not the verbal inflexions and the spirant mutations we fight for, but for the working masses'.[19] In other words, for Saunders and others like him, the language was not so much important in its own right but rather as a symbol of Cornish 'difference', perhaps even as a weapon with which to defend or even mobilise the Cornish people.

By this time, the Cornish political movement was further maturing in the face of continuing rapid socio-economic change. While Mebyon Kernow's attempts to break through in the party-political arena in the later 70s and early 80s proved largely unsuccessful, its role was then increasingly usurped by highly-articulate and well-informed pressure groups such as the Cornwall Conservation Forum, Cornish Alternatives to the Structure Plan, the Campaign for a Cornish (Euro) Constituency, and the Cornish Social and Economic Research Group. For each of these organisations the Cornish language still had a role to perform, as a marker of Cornish 'difference' and a 'card' to be played as necessary to reinforce claims to separate identity, but increasingly their concern was for the condition of modern Cornwall. CoSERG's polemic, *Cornwall at the Crossroads*, published at the end of 1988, epitomised a newer strand within the Cornish movement, with its emphasis upon problems of planning, development, housing, the environment, and with consideration of the language subsumed in a wider and more complex concern for ethnic identity.[20] Similarly, academic assessments of the nature of modern Cornwall sought explanations for a wide variety of socio-economic, political and cultural behaviour where the Cornish experience was often distinct from that which obtained east of the Tamar, but where language revival was seen in context as merely one index of 'difference' in 'post-industrial' Cornwall.[21]

Although this approach disturbed Peter Berresford Ellis, who continued to insist upon a 'linguistic criterion' for Cornwall's claim to national or regional status (with a warning that '. . .unless the language is restored, unless one recognises what one is tossing aside, it will be future generations who will cease to be Celtic'),[22] Gregor had in 1980 voiced in his comparative study of Celtic languages a more general consensus that '. . . the awareness of a Cornish identity finds expression also in other than linguistic fields'.[23] Language remained a powerful symbol of 'difference', and the early post-War Revivalists had themselves been instrumental in precipitating the politics of anti-metropolitanism, but, by the 1980s, the promotion of Cornish was no longer central to the new politics of the periphery that had emerged in Cornwall. The Cornish language had, in that sense, effectively been de-politicised.

THE YEARS OF EXPANSION: 1967-87

This removal of the language Revival from its overt role in the politics of anti-metropolitanism (disturbed only occasionally by political demands for bi-lingual road signs) made it easier for bodies such as the Federation of Old Cornwall Societies and the Cornish Gorseth to insist that the language movement was itself apolitical and that learning the language was by no means a political act.[24] Certainly, by 1979 Myrna Combellack was able to look back on *Twelve Year's Progress in Unified Cornish* and review with satisfaction a period of rapid growth.[25] Before 1967 there had been only a handful of Cornish language classes, organised informally. In addition, '. . .publications were printed and distributed in a primitlve way. . .'[26] and the only teaching of Cornish to children was in a private school. But in 1967 the language movement was restructured when the Gorseth and the Federation of Old Cornwall Societies came together, along with other interested bodies, to set up the Cornish Language Board to provide a framework for the development of 'Unified' Cornish.

The expansion of interest that took place in the years after 1973 is reflected in the steep rise in the numbers of candidates for the Cornish Language Board's annual examinations in the mid-1970s (see Table 12.1 below). In addition, by 1978 Cornish was being taught as a Certificate of Secondary Education subject to pupils in five state schools. By that year, there were three magazines devoted entirely to Cornish - *An Gannas*, *An Lef Kernewek*, founded in the early 1950s, and *Eythen*, a short-lived satirical magazine. Many more accessible text-books had appeared, notably Richard Gendall's popular *Kernewek Bew*, far removed from the dry 'Latin primer' style of previous Cornish language teaching aids.[27]

Further additions to the language movement infrastructure in the late 1970s accompanied this new wave of Cornish learners. Cowethas an Yeth Kernewek (the Cornish Language Fellowship) was formed in 1979 to link the Cornish Language Board to a wider constituency of Cornish users and to '. . . encourage the development and use of our language in everyday use'.[28] Similarly, late 1979 saw the formation of the group Dalleth with the aim of publishing children's books and giving support to those families that were using the Cornish language as a means of communication in the home - a new phenomenon of the late 1970s.[29] It is perhaps not surprising, in the light of these developments, that an air of triumphalism emerged in language movement publications. The editorial comments in *An Gannas* in the years from 1977 to 1980 hammer home the theme of a steadily expanding language movement.

'Yma omsaf an yeth ow tevy moy uskys ages bythqueth kens ha defnydhyes yu hy moy menough'[30] (The language movement is growing faster than ever before and it (Cornish) is used more often).

TABLE 12.1
Candidates for the Cornish Language Board exams, 1968-91

	total sitting exams	total successful
1968	20	n/a
1969	25	n/a
1970	26	n/a
1971	24	n/a
1972	20	n/a
1973	24	n/a
1974	48	n/a
1975	71	n/a
1976	71	n/a
1977	58	51
1978	85	n/a
1979	67	55
1980	90	77
1981	93	n/a
1982	61	47
1983	59	53
1984	80	71
1985	82	73
1986	72	61
1987	n/a	47
1988	n/a	n/a
1989	n/a	n/a
1990	n/a	36
1991	n/a	36

(Sources: *Report on the state of the language*, Cowethas an Yeth Kernewek, 1984 and *An Gannas*).

In one way these developments can be viewed in terms of a generational change, as one generation of language users gave way to a younger generatlon in the 1970s. This new generation put more emphasis on spoken Cornish rather than written and did more to turn the aims of the early Revivalists into reality, attempting to use the language in more domains, as in the 'Yeth an Weryn' meetings (get-togethers of Cornish speakers) that sprang up during the later 1970s. Gradually the new generation ousted the old and, by the mid-1980s, this transfer of power was completed by a further restructuring of the Cornish

Language Board. The previous rather clumsy structure whereby the Language Board was dominated by the Gorseth and the Federation of Old Cornwall Societies, bodies where Cornish speakers were by no means in a majority, was replaced at the end of 1985 by a new Cornish Language Board constitution whereby the majority of the twenty Cornish Language Board members was chosen directly by the Cowethas an Yeth Kernewek,[31] wedding the Board more closely to a particular constituency of Cornish speakers.

PORTENTS OF CHANGE: THE REFORMS OF THE MID-1980s

However, by this time, the confidence of the late 1970s was giving way to renewed doubts. Back in 1947 Smith had pointed out that the Cornish Revival '... has not yet produced many speakers of Cornish. More are badly needed'.[32] But in 1981 it was still estimated that no more than '... deugans a wor clappya yn freth hepken'[33] (only forty know how to talk fluently), and this despite there being around a thousand people alive who had attended some kind of Cornish class. To some people this seemed a poor return for the effort of almost two generations of Revivalists. Some critics had already raised questions about the form of the teaching - 'Y predersyn bos an classow noswyth ow tysky re vur a Gernewek scryfys ha lyes studhyor a as an class wosa un vledhen hep an gallos a gewsel an yeth man'[34] (we thought that the evening classes were teaching too much written Cornish and many students leave the class after one year without the ability to talk the language at all). Despite the regular pronouncements of the Cornish Language Board and Cowethas that the number of speakers was growing each year, the painfully slow generation of fluent speakers remained an underlying cause for concern in some quarters. For example, in Penwith in 1984 it was estimated that '... nyns yu sa(w) pymp po whegh cowsor a yl synsy kescows a hes'[35] (there are only five or six speakers who can hold a lengthy conversation).

By the early 1980s, therefore, questions were increasingly being raised about the direction of the Revival. But how do we explain the timing of this? Partly it was a response to the less favourable external environment of those years. In 1980 Cornwall County Council cut back on evening classes and the number of official Cornish classes plummetted to a mere five.[36] Although the evening class situation had recovered by 1985, the numbers attempting the Cornish Language Board exams were not to reach their 1980/81 peak again. It seemed that the growth of the late 70s had run out of steam. Despite the apolitical pronouncements of the Language Board and others, the expansion of the 70s had in fact accompanied a rising interest in Cornish political nationalism, itself stimulated partly by the successes of Welsh and Scottish nationalism in the late 60s and early 70s. In the very different climate of the 80s, political nationalism in Cornwall fragmented and the language movement could no longer count on a source of recruits from this direction. Indeed, the depoliticisation of the language was apparently not leading to a new and more numerous wave of learners. Moreover, the unfavourable environment of the early 80s gave the opportunity for deeper internal criticisms of the form of the Revival to come into the open.

In 1984 Ken George wrote that '. . . until very recently, the subject of spelling has been almost taboo in Cornish-speaking circles'.[37] Yet there had been several earlier critics despite this apparent 'taboo'. In the mid-70s Tim Saunders was expressing increasing dissatisfaction with the literature of the Revival, with Cornish language composition seemingly still locked in the romantic Celtic-Catholic vision of the early Revivalists. He criticised 'Nance's and Jenner's pseudo-archaism, and the kind of vague pantheism especially associated with E.Chirgwin',[38] and regretted the influence that this inheritance (the 'Nancean synthesis',[39] as he was later to call it) had had upon contemporary Cornish writing. But Saunders' criticisms went further than literature. He argued that 'Unified' Cornish was an insufficiently robust vehicle for language revival, unscientiflc and haphazard in its construction, and went on to evolve his own 'scientific' spelling system based on '. . . a modern linguistic analysis of the language'.[40] However Saunders, who lived in Wales, could be easily marginalised by the 'Unified' Cornish establishment in Cornwall. Others, such as Richard Gendall, who was increaslngly dissatisfied with the form of 'Unified' Cornish, took another route ln the 1970s and withdrew from active involvement in the movement.

It was the pressures of relative success in the late 1970s surge that sowed the seeds for change in the 80s. Frustrated by apparent growth but a continuing relatively small number of language Bards who actually spoke the language, some, like Rod Lyon, made forthright criticisms of the language establishment.[41] Those who struggled through three years of study and then never used the language seemed to epitomlse the continuing failure of the language movement to produce a large body of fluent speakers. Lyon, and others such as Chris Jeffery, began to raise the possibility of re-founding the Revival on the ('Late') Cornish spoken in the seventeenth and eighteenth centuries, a project that Henry Jenner had first attempted but was dropped by Nance.[42]

But the impasse was broken not by those who wanted to base Cornish upon its Late phase but by those who, instead, preferred to found it more securely on its medieval base. Moreover, this was a reaction as much to external criticism as to the failure to meet the expectations aroused in the boom of the 70s. The problem, as Charles Thomas explained to a conference of the Celtic Congress in 1963, was that '. . .serious criticisms come from the rarified world of Celtic scholarship. . .' and that '. . . modern Celticists, from Professor Kenneth Jackson downwards, unite in ignoring any of Nance's or Smith's work, and almost all of Jenner's. . .'.[43] Indeed, in 1958 Profesor C.L.Wrenn had dismissed Nance's 1938 Cornish-English dictionary with the view that it '. . .displays that scarcely scientific revivalist local patriotism which is still so commonly associated with Cornish studies'.[44]

The success of the Language Board after 1967 did little to ameliorate these academic objections to 'Unified' Cornish, and in a sustained attack in

1984 Profesor Glanville Price condemned the language as 'pseudo-Cornish' and a mutant 'Cornic', insisting that '... the old Celtic speech of Cornwall died out two centuries ago. It is still dead, and will evermore remain so'.[45] The Revivalists were promoting '...a type of language that is partially derived from the old Celtic speech of Cornwall, but is also partially invented. . .'.[46] These inventions were the devices employed by Nance to overcome the deficiencies in the grammar, vocabulary and even consistency of the Middle Cornish texts, and which led to the construction of his 'Unified' system. Price also attacked the inconsistency between orthography and phonology, arguing that even if the intonation and pronunciation of Late Cornish could be detected in the accent of West Cornwall, '. . .what is preserved is the sounds of Cornish in its last stages. . .whereas written Cornic is based on Middle Cornish'.[47] His damning conclusion was that '...Cornic is to a considerable extent a nineteenth and, more especially, a twentieth-century invention, in its orthography, its pronunciation, its vocabulary, and even its grammar'.[48]

To these uncompromising assaults were added new doubts about the cherished belief that the accent and dialect of the far-west held clues to the sounds of Late Cornish, with Wakelin asserting that the speech of West Penwith '. . .is at the present time of no use whatever to the student of Cornish, and it is my opinion that it never was',[49] and with North agreeing that '... there is no need to turn to Cornish... to explain any feature of Anglo-Cornish phonology'[50] - even in the far-west. Recognising that 'Unified' was more or less under continuous academic fire, the Language Board had even at its inception in 1967 admitted that ' . . . it considers that Unified Cornish as now in use provides an acceptable base for spelling modern writings in the language, but recognises that it has little significance for more advanced linguistic studies'.[51]

Although Charles Thomas readily accepted the criticisms of the Celticists, writing in 1972 that 'Unified' Cornish, '. . .as to its spelling, an increasing part of its vocabulary, and most of its pronunciation, cannot be regarded as genuine. . .',[52] he was perhaps less inhibited than the Language Board in defending and explaining the significance of language Revival in modern Cornwall. Thomas recognised that the real success of the Revival had been '. . .the establishment of a sense of Cornishness, of national consciousness . . .',[53] insisting upon a distinction '. . .between the Cornish language as it actually was (a linguistic phenomenon), and Cornish as Nance to some extent re-modelled it (a vehicle for extending national consciousness)'.[54] In a sense, therefore, not only had the Revivalists been wrong in their attempts to 'de-politicise' the language (depriving it in part of its *raison d'etre*), but also they had been looking to the wrong set of academics for scholarly approval. Given their disciplinary training, interests and perspectives, Celticists such as Wrenn or Price could never look favourably upon 'Unified' but observers elsewhere in the academic world - historians and social scientists, with their interests in human behaviour - would come to recognise that the Revival of Cornish and the impact that this had had spoke volumes about the nature of modern Cornwall.[55] By focusing upon their own alleged academic shortcomings, the

Revivalists had in fact underestimated their contribution to contemporary Cornish life.

Curiously, the language Revivalists seemed only dimly aware of this. Even those who sought to defend 'Unified' did so for what P.A.S.Pool called 'practical' and 'sentimental' reasons, arguing that 'Unified' - whatever its shortcomings - had served the mechanics of revival well and that it was after all a living memorial to Robert Morton Nance, the man who had dedicated his life's work to the rebirth of Cornish.[56] Thomas himself had declared in 1963 that there was '. . . no objection to unified Cornish. . .' as a tool of language Revival and that, indeed, its use was '. . . essential to create any wide public interest in the language. . .'.[57] Given that codification, standardisation and synthesis were necessary to any process of language revival, Nance had done a competent job and the result was certainly less 'objectionable' than Manx orthography '. . . which is merely a laboured attempt to reproduce a Gaelic speech in a kind of phonetic convention'.[58] However, Thomas' reassuring words did not entirely remove the self-doubts of Cornish practitioners, and in 1984 Wella Brown, in the introduction to his book on Cornish grammar, explained carefully the origins of 'Unified' orthography but went on to admit that the phonology was rather more uncertain. This was, however, a theoretical rather than practical problem, for '. . . speakers of any language are not required to converse with the past and some uncertainty as to how former generations of Cornish people actually spoke does not hinder communication in Cornish today'.[59] Others, however, were not so convinced, and at about the same time Ken George - in a doctoral thesis joining the ranks of academic detractors - was stating in unequivocal and uncompromising tones that '. . ."Unified" Cornish is unsatisfactory because it does not have a firm phonological base'.[60]

Indeed, George's criticisms, coming as they did from within the heart of the language Revival, proved far more traumatic than the periodic sniping of outside observers or internal critics had ever been. As George admitted, after many years of criticism from external academics, '. . . now the whole basis of . . . Revived Cornish is being called into question by Cornish speakers from within the language movement'.[61] Moreover, he considered that '. . . if Revived Cornish is to gain any respectability in the academic world, it is is essential that the reconstruction be seen to be as accurate as possible'.[62] For George, the 'academic world' was that of the Celticists, while the accurate 'reconstruction' that he sought was essentially phonological - so much so, that the spelling changes that he was to advocate were driven almost entirely by phonological considerations. As he explained in the introduction to his thesis, '. . . the inspiration of the work is not so much the investigation of how Cornish was traditionally spoken, as the desire to improve the pronunciation of Revived Cornish'.[63]

In developing his criticism of 'Unified', George considered that Nance's syntax, based on Middle Cornish and Middle Breton, was largely satisfactory. Revision, therefore, could safely concentrate upon the phonological problem. Like others before him, George pointed to the apparent inconsistency of Middle

Cornish spelling and Late Cornish pronunciation inherent in 'Unified'. In doing so he attacked Gendall's attempts to consolidate Late Cornish pronunciation through the medium of *Kernewek Bew* with the view that '...this automatically introduced a three hundred year difference between the spelling and the pronunciation'.[64] Likewise, although avoiding the dismissive manner of Wakelin or North, George largely accepted '...the view that the English dialect of West Penwith is a development of the standard English of the late seventeenth-century rather than of Late Cornish'.[65] Consequently, he believed that '...the dialect of the early twentieth century natives of West Penwith, representing perhaps the eighth generation of English speakers, may owe as much to the development of English during the two hundred year interval as to Late Cornish'.[66] In other words, 'Unified' adherents were not only wrong in adopting a Late Cornish pronunciation, but their estimation of that pronunciation was probably also flawed.

In constructing his new phonological base, George employed a complex computer analysis to derive an approximate phonology of Middle Cornish. To improve the pronunciation of Revived Cornish, George argued that this base should be employed to make the language as 'phonemic' as possible. This would be an aid to learning as well as pronunciation (most people learned Cornish from books), although care would be needed not to mask the etymology of words or their relationships with Breton and Welsh. The resultant 'phonemic' orthography should also not be so different in appearance from 'Unified' '... as to be rejected by users of Cornish'.[67] In 1986 George placed these ideas before the Cornish Language Board, recommending that Middle Cornish continue to be used as the basis for Revived Cornish and that, specifically, the phonology of the revived language be based upon his detailed estimation of the pronunciation of Cornish as it was circa 1500. Most importantly, he advocated that the revived '...orthography be modified so as to fit the phonological base and form a system which aspires to phonemic perfection'.[68] He claimed that his proposed system meant that Revived Cornish was now 95% 'correct' rather than 70%. Perhaps anticipating the objections of those who might point out that his revised 'phonemic' orthography was also 'invented', he added that '...invention is not of itself a bad thing, provided that the sources and reasoning behind the inventions are clarified',[69] reminding potentially sceptical Celticists that their field was comparative philology while he was in the business of language planning.

FRAGMENTATION OR FLOWERING? THE LANGUAGE MOVEMENT FROM 1987

George's *Pronunciation and Spelling of the Cornish Language* had brought his ideas to a wider audience within the language movement in 1986 and the ensuing debate reached a head in the summer of 1987 when the Cornish Language Board embraced George's proposals with enthusiasm and set a programme and timetable for adopting his new 'phonemic' Cornish.[70] The Language Board, although recognising that '. . . y fyth an chanj . . . completh y gowlwul'[71] (the change will be difficult to complete), envisaged a relatively smooth change-over phased in over a three year transitional period. However, things would not prove to be so simple and the Revivalists underestimated the problems.

Predictably, those wedded to the Nancean tradition were horrified by this decision, with Pool and others lamenting the loss of general agreement on spelling and pronunciation after sixty years or more of apparent consensus and progress. According to Pool, '. . . the revival of Cornish has become a triumphant success, verging at times almost on the miraculous', but now all this was jeopardised '. . .and there is a real danger that the revival will fail'.[72] The public at large would be perplexed, and those who had learnt or were learning the language would feel confused, even betrayed, for students '. . .are entitled to expect unanimity among their teachers. . .'.[73] More than this, the 'phonemic' revisions were a '. . . virtual repudiation of the work of Robert Morton Nance, our Grand Bard without compare'.[74]

Following the Cowethas an Yeth elections to the Cornish Language Board in early 1989, when explicit supporters of 'Unified' Cornish found themselves at the bottom of the poll,[75] a meeting at Truro in May 1989 brought together opponents of the change. Under the auspices of Agan Tavas, a group originally formed to stimulate the use of spoken Cornish, these appealed to '...all those who support traditionally developed Cornish and not computerised hypotheses' and expressed concern '. . .at the way Unified Cornish was being cast aside in favour of the newly devised Phonemic system. . .'.[76] Membership of Agan Tavas included senior figures of the Cornish language Revival (some of whom had known Nance personally), and so - for the first time since its formation in 1967 - the Language Board had lost its broad consensus of Cornish speakers and with it, something of its authority.

Misgivings soon emerged from other sources. Oliver Padel, then Place-names Research Fellow at the Institute of Cornish Studies, agreed that the '. . . new system is a great improvement upon the old. . .' but felt that the new reliance of orthography upon phonology had gone too far: '. . .in my opinion, lt removes itself undesirably far from the spellings of the Middle Cornish texts. . .'.[77] Price was similarly equivocal. He admitted that 'The "revival" has recently been put on a significantly more scholarly and reliable foundation by the work of Ken George . . .' but continued to believe '. . . that "revived" Cornish is not authentic Cornish'.[78] Murdoch, in his 1993 survey of literature in the Cornish language, felt that 'It is beyond the scope of this work to discuss the various alternatives for revived Cornish, although the absence of an agreed standard probably does little to help the furthering of the literature'.[79]

Thomas, then the Institute's Director, was more forthright in his criticism. Although recognising the academic value of George's work upon the history of Cornish phonology, he felt that its findings were inappropriate to the process of language Revival. Thomas took particular exception to the 'phonemic' re-spelling of his home-town (Camborne) as 'Kammbronn', the intrusive 'K' and unusual double consonants having furnished an ambience that was in his opinion distinctly un-Cornish. He concluded that although the Institute '. . .is entirely sympathetic to the Revived or Modern Cornish movement our feeling is that the Language Board has taken an unjustifiably wrong turn . . .'[80] in adopting George's 'phonemic' system.

To some extent the opposition to the changes reflected a generational gap, with the pre-1970s generation tending to oppose the 'phonemic' innovations and the bulk of the newer generation accepting the Language Board line. Many younger people saw 'phonemic' Cornish as re-equipping the language to meet the challenges of the twenty first century, while the older generation saw it as an abandonment of the work of this century. Thus the Gorseth Council, dominated by the older generation, while accepting both amended and 'Unified' Cornish for their annual competitions, decided in 1988 that 'Unified' Cornish would remain as the basis of their ceremonies.[81]

Wella Brown had emerged as a principal supporter of George's 'phonemic' revision, and in response to objections insisted that the new Cornish was merely '. . . the Revived Cornish of Mordon and Caradar with a reformed pronunciation and spelling. Let there be no mistake about this'.[82] Far from abandoning the work of Nance and Smith, George and the Language Board were only improving upon it. However, Brown did consider it important to renew the criticism of Late Cornish pronunciation, rehearsing the already familiar arguments against the speech of West Penwith and dismissing the belief that '. . . perhaps if one were to speak with homely Cornish accents it would suffice'.[83] This renewed aspect of the debate was significant, for already, as we have seen, from the early 1980s several Cornish speakers had been voicing their support for the future development of 'Unified' along what they considered 'Traditional' lines, taking their cue from the direction of *Kernewek Bew* and arguing for further Late Cornish innovations in Revived Cornish.[84] But the renewed objections to Late Cornish were aimed rather at the work of Richard Gendall, another senior member of the language Revival, one who had shared the misgivings regarding 'Unified' but who - in marked contrast to George - had looked to the final historical phase of spoken and written Cornish for his model for the future. Gendall had been encouraged to resume active interest in the language in 1982 - '. . . en vlethan 1982 Rod (Lyon) a screffaz do ve en idn gelwel ve tho comeras radn en dasvounas an tavaz teithiack'[85] (in 1982 Rod wrote to me calling on me to take part in the rebirth of the traditional language).

Gendall and his supporters settled upon the description 'Modern Cornish' for the version of the language that he was to advocate. He considered that the surviving body of literature from the period after the mid/late sixteenth-century (known to scholars as Late Cornish) was extensive enough to construct a comprehensive grammar and orthography without recourse to 'invention'. Thus his *A Student's Grammar of Modern Cornish*, published in 1991, was '. . .a practical, prosaic exposition of every aspect of Modern Cornish, based entirely on textual examples given in their original orthography'.[86] To this 'authentic' orthography was added a historically-matching and linguistically-accessible phonology which, Gendall argued, avoided both the mismatch of 'Unified' and the 'invention' of 'phonemic'. For, in direct contradiction of Wakelin, North, George and Brown, he insisted that the speech of West Penwith was, after all, a clear guide to how Cornish had been pronounced in its Late stage, pointing to the '. . . sounds from St Just, Pendeen, Towednack, St Ives, Newlyn. Native speakers? Yes, Mr G. has heard native speakers'.[87] This was no mere romantic fancy, for in his estimation '. . . the pronunciation system of the older generation of traditional speakers in West Penwith on nearly every point agrees so well with what Lhuyd described . . .'[88] after his special visit to West Cornwall circa 1700 to study and codify the Cornish language. The sounds of twentieth-century English in the far west were still those that Edward Lhuyd, the eighteenth-century Celticist, had recorded from Cornish speakers in the same district more than two hundred years before. Therefore, '. . . it is only Modern Cornish that in addition to its grammar, vocabulary and orthography has a system of pronunciation based on the actual observation of a linguist present while the language was still a living vernacular'.[89]

For those who could accept Gendall's observations on West Penwith (running contrary as they did to conventional wisdom), his argument was a powerful one. To this was added the attraction that, in contrast to 'Unified' (so unashamedly medieval) and 'phonemic' (even more explicitly based on the phonology of 1500), 'Modern' Cornish reached back across relatively few decades to the time when the language was still spoken. Gendall recalled that even into the 1930s fishermen at Newlyn still counted in Cornish - '. . . a vivid and sure link between our time and the days when the language was well enough used to be considered a true vernacular. . .'.[90] There was emotional strength in this argument, providing a sense of historical closeness and continuity for contemporary learners, reassuring them that it was indeed 'their' language and a legitimate part of their personal inheritance. Such 'ownership' and affinity was not only a question of pronunciation and accent, for to the lay observer the appearance of 'Modern' Cornish was (in particular contrast to 'phonemic') reminiscent of the place-names of Cornwall, particularly West Cornwall.

There was also intellectual strength (or at least ideological attraction) in the argument of continuity for those who recognised that hitherto the language Revival had been at root a deliberate appeal to a pre-industrial Celtic-Catholic Cornwall and was to that extent a negation of modernity. Although the post-War Revivalists had proved ready to tackle contemporary Cornish problems, the question of language had sat increasingly uneasily in the maturing political movement of 'anti-metropolitanism'. When reform had come in the shape of the 'phonemic' revision, one effect (paradoxically) was to wed Cornish firmly to the language of 1500, confirming and reinforcing the focus of the early Revivalists. Indeed, George saw this as a strength, '. . . an ideological rationale for basing the spoken language on 1500 is that it just precedes the Protestant Reformation, the *coup mortel* for the traditional language'.[91]

The 'Modern' Cornish model, however, acknowledged the survival of the language into and as a part of Methodist industrial Cornwall (albeit at the margins of the far west), attempting to establish and emphasise the language as a natural element of Cornish modernity. To the early Revivalists, seeking as they were to escape the all-pervading paralysis of pre-War Cornwall, such an idea would have been absurd. But for those in the late 1980s and 90s who recognised and wished to escape the ideological assumptions and aspirations of the Revivalists, 'Modern' Cornish provided an attractive mechanism. For the politically-committed, there was also the attraction that 'Modern' Cornish was perhaps the language, not of medieval religious scholars or indeed twentieth-century romantics and academics, but of ordinary working folk - as Gendall put it, '. . .the native language of my Cornish ancestors, the farmers, fishermen, miners and traders of Penwith and Kerrier, during the last centuries of its life'.[92] And in addition to this potential popular appeal was the curiosity and, later, support that Gendall aroused in the academic world. At the University of Newcastle in New South Wales, for example, 'Modern' Cornish was adopted for teaching purposes, while the Cornish Board of the Celtic Council of Australia (the body which administers Celtic cultural education in Australia) after a detailed study of the options decided also to adopt 'Modern' for its purposes.[93]

Although there was much of import to discuss in the emerging debate between 'Unified', 'phonemic' (later renamed 'Common'), and 'Modern', the discussion was often conducted at a superficial and ill-informed level (on the lines of 'computer Cornish versus the sacred legacy of Nance') and with many of its observers genuinely perplexed. Ray Edwards (later to emerge as an important champion of 'Common'), for example, admitted '. . . there are perhaps grounds for some revision of Unified spelling. . .' but feared '. . .to jump into the unknown water of Mr Gendall's "Cornoak"(sic)'.[94] Tommy Jordan confessed that '. . . all I would require of Cornish Grammar is that it should place the language clearly in the Celtic group. . .' but added that '. . . national credibility, also, stands partly upon Unified, and to say that it is totally invalid is foolish and dangerous talk'.[95] John Pengilly, however, felt that 'Unified' was '. . . invented in the 1920s by middle class hobbyists, it broke all links with genuine Cornish. . .'.[96] That this debate was not confined to the relatively small band of Cornish language activists but had caught the imagination of the general public in Cornwall, was evidenced in the lengthy (and often passionate) correspondence in the popular magazine *Cornish Scene*.[97]

The often bitter and personalised debates that accompanied the 1987-91 period seemed to leave little common ground between the various protagonists, each claiming the purity of their own position and claiming to be the true heirs of the Revival. At first 'phonemic' supporters in particular ignored the existence of other schools of thought,[98] the Cornish Language Board using its historic status to promote 'Common' Cornish as the approved version. But realities forced a reappraisal. The fall in the numbers taking Cornish Language Board exams (to less than half the peak of the early 1980s - see Table 12.1 above) or attending the annual Cornish language weekends were evidence that the switch to 'Common' Cornish had not been painless.[99] Meanwhile, at the end of 1989 Ken George admitted that the use of *DJ* and *TJ* in the new spelling system - which had led to the generally familiar and commonly occuring chy (house) being spelt tji, and had caused most outcry from traditionalists - would be dropped.[100] This made it easier for some 'Unified' Cornish users to accept the new spelling.

Perhaps fearing the long term consequences of washing their dirty linen in public, some of the various language protagonists called a truce in 1991 to produce a document, *The Cornish Language*, which explained briefly the positions and activities of the different groups. Optimistically, the booklet's authors wrote that '. . . this document proves that these groups can put aside their differences as and when necessary'.[101] They explained that '. . . the main differences are in the spelling and pronunciation. . .'[102] but they did not address the real and deep-seated philosophical and ideological contests that lay behind these differences. Pragmatic and peaceful co-existence may yet prove the best way ahead for the language movement, but its activists and participants are unlikely to shed either their historical-ideological baggage or their individual predispositions. Thus the desire to escape the public acrimony of the late 1980s and early 1990s has led not to a better-informed and more scholarly debate based upon mutual recognition but rather to a public silence in which potentially 'damaging' contests in the press have been avoided. Although this truce has ensured that the public has not been reminded of the more negative aspects of the debate, it has not allowed the open and balanced examination of the respective positions.

The future of the Cornish language Revival appears to rest on recognising that the unanimity of the 1950s and 60s will not easily be recovered. In its own way the Cornish language movement reflects that more global uncertainty that has come to dominate intellectual life in all spheres during the 1980s. Future progress rests on a willingness to accept this uncertainty and take note of the often conflicting historical-ideological roots of the language and the Revival. By recognising the existence of both medieval and modern variants of the Cornish language and building channels of communication between them, the Revival movement may be constructing a renewed basis for growth at the same time as widening its appeal to different sections of the community. In this sense diversity can be viewed as a potential strength rather than a weakness.

However, Murdoch felt that '. . . it is not hard to be pessimistic. . .', arguing that the development of literature in the Cornish language would rely not only upon the emergence of a new generation of writers but also would require '. . . an agreed literary standard . . .'[103] and (in an echo of Saunders) '. . . the adoption of themes which are part of a broad cultural perspective. . .'.[104] Indeed, increasingly in the 1990s Cornish language Revivalists of all persuasions have had to remind themselves of Gregor's timely warning to the Celtic world- '. . . let them reflect that languages are not killed: they commit suicide'.[105]

REFERENCES

1. See, for example, Michel Denis, Jean Pihan and Jeffrey Stanyer, 'The Peripheries Today', and Steven Dodd, 'Language and Culture in the Far South West', in Michael Havinden, J.Queniart, J.Stanyer, (eds.), *Centre and Periphery: Brittany and Cornwall & Devon Compared*, University of Exeter Press, Exeter, 1991, pp38-39 and 228-29.
2. See Rosalie Eastlake, 'Cornwall; the development of a Celtic Periphery', unpublished MA thesis, McGill University, 1981 p154.
3. Oliver Padel, *A Popular Dictionary of Cornish Place Names*, Alison Hodge, Penzance, 1988.
4. Charles Thomas, *The Importance of Being Cornish in Cornwall*, Institute of Cornish Studies, Redruth, 1973, p10.
5. For the demise of the colloquial language see P.A.S. Pool, *The Death of Cornish; 1600-1800*, Penzance, Cornish Language Board, 1975 and R. Morton Nance, 'When was Cornish last Spoken Traditionally', *Journal of Royal Institution of Cornwall*, NS7, 1973, pp76-82.
6. Henry Jenner, *A Handbook of the Cornish Language*, David Nutt, London, 1904.
7. For a succinct explanation of this process see Wella Brown, *A Grammar of Modern Cornish*, Cornish Language Board, Saltash, 1984, ppv-vi.
8. Robert Morton Nance, *Cornish For All*, Federation of Old Cornwall Societies, 1929, p11.
9. See Philip Payton, *The Making of Modern Cornwall: Historical Experience and the Persistence of 'Difference'*, Dyllansow Truran, Redruth, 1992, pp128-135.
10. Arthur Quiller-Couch, cited in Tim Saunders, 'Cornish - Symbol and Substance', in Cathal O'Luain (ed.), *For a Celtic Future*, Celtic League, Dublin, 1983, p256.
11. See Jack Clemo, *Confessions of a Rebel*, Chatto and Windus, London, 1949, pp.88-90 for an example of this difficulty.
12. *Kernow*,1, 1934.
13. John J Parry, 'The Revival of Cornlish: An Dasserghyans Kernewek', *Proceedings of the Modern Languages Academy of America* LXI, 1946.
14. A.S.D Smith, *How to learn Cornish*, Arundel, 1947, p20.
15. See Payton, 1992, chapters 8 and 10; and Ronald Perry, Ken Dean, Bryan Brown, *Counterurbanisation: International Case Studies of Socio-economic Change in Rural Areas*, Geo Books, Norwich, 1986, chapters 5-11.
16. R.M.M. Gendall, 'Cornish as an Optional Subject in Schools', *New Cornwall*, 16.1, June 1968.
17. James Whetter, 'Reasons for Learning the Cornish Language', *Cornish Nation* 2.2, 1970.
18. P.J.Payton, 'Language Revival', *New Cornwall*, 17.3, 1972.
19. Tim Saunders, 'Why I write in Cornish', *Planet*, 30, 1976, p29.
20. Bernard Deacon, Andrew George and Ronald Perry, *Cornwall at the Crossroads? Living communities or leisure zone*?, Cornish Social and Economic Research Group, Redruth, 1988.
21. Payton, 1992, chapters 9 and 10.
22. Peter Berresford Ellis, 'The Celtic People: the Linguistic Criterion', *Kernow*, 4, 1989; see also P.Berresford Ellis, *The Cornish Language and its Literature*, Routledge and Kegan Paul, London, 1974, Chapter 8.
23. D.B.Gregor, *Celtic: A Comparative Study*, Orleander Press, Cambridge, 1980, p74.
24. As late as 1979 the Cornish Language Board was still somewhat nervously explaining that its aim was the spread of '... our own national language as a viable medium of intercourse without any political implications', *An Gannas*, 3.4, April 1979.
25. Myrna Combellack, 'Twelve Years' Progress in Unified Cornish, 1967-1979", *Cornish Studies*, 6, 1978.
26. Combellack, 1978, p45.
27. R.M.M.Gendall, *Kernewek Bew*, Cornish Language Board, St Ives, 1972; see also R.M.M.Gendall and Tim Saunders, *Cornish is Fun*, Y Lolfa, Talybont, 1978.
28. *An Gannas*, 3.4, April 1979.
29. See *An Gannas*, 3.11, November 1979.
30. *An Gannas*, 37, January 1980.
31. *An Gannas*, 109, January 1986.
32. Smith, 1947, p8.

33. Wella Brown, 'Stuth an Yeth Kernewek yn jeth hedhyu', paper presented to Celtic Congress, Lannion, July 1981.
34. Chris Jeffery, in *An Gannas*, 39, March 1980.
35. Dorothy May, in *An Gannas*, June 1984.
36. *An Gannas*, 47, November 1980.
37. Kenneth J.George, 'Phonological History of Cornish', unpublished these de troisieme cycle, Universite de Bretagne Occidentale, 1984, p495.
38. Tim Saunders, 1976, p30.
39. Tim Saunders, 1983, pp253-258.
40. See Tim Saunders, *Dalleth Cernyweg*, An Weryn, Redruth, 1979.
41. *An Gannas* 61 [January, 1982].
42. See Chris Jeffery, 'Omsettyans erbyn Kernewek Unyes', *An Gannas*, April 1984.
43. Charles Thomas, 'An Dasserghyans Kernewek. The Cornish Revival', *Old Cornwall*, 6.5, 1963.
44. Cited by Thomas, 1963.
45. Glanville Price, *The Languages of Britain*, Edward Arnold, London, 1984, p134.
46. Price, 1984, p134.
47. Price, 1984, p143.
48. Price, 1984, p142.
49. Martyn F. Wakelin, *Language and History in Cornwall*, Leicester University Press, Leicester, 1975, p86.
50. David North, *Studies in Anglo-Cornish Phonology*, Institute of Cornish Studies, Redruth, 1983, p70.
51. *Old Cornwall*, 8.2, 1968.
52. Thomas, 1973, p10.
53. Thomas, 1973, p10.
54. Charles Thomas, 'The Next Fifty Years', *Old Cornwall*, 7.8, 1971.
55. Payton, 1992, chapters 6, 9 and 10.
56. P.A.S. Pool, 'A Plea for Unified Cornish', *Old Cornwall*, 10. 9, 1989.
57. Thomas, 1963.
58. Thomas, 1963.
59. Brown, 1984, pv-vi.
60. George, 1984, p495.
61. Ken George, *The Pronunciation and Spelling of Revived Cornish*, Cornish Language Board, Torpoint, 1986, p4.
62. George, 1984, piv.
63. George, 1984, piv.
64. George, 1986, p21.
65. George, 1986, p22.
66. George, 1984, p104.
67. George, 1984, p502.
68. George, 1986, p4.
69. George, 1986, p37.
70. The term 'Kernewek Kemmyn' (Common Cornish) was later coined for the revised spelling system, following a suggestion by John King in 1986 (see *An Gannas*, 120, December 1986. This term, an odd choice given the distinctly academic roots of the change, was generally adopted by supporters of the spelling revision by 1989.
71. *An Gannas*, 127, July 1987.
72. Pool, 1989.
73. Pool, 1989.
74. Pool, 1989.
75. *An Gannas*, 148, April 1989.
76. Agan Tavas press release, January 1990.
77. Padel, 1988, p183.
78. Glanville Price, 'Cornish Language and Literature', in Glanville Price (ed.), *The Celtic Connection*, Colin Smyth, Gerrards Cross, 1992, p313.

79. Brian Murdoch, *Cornish Literature*, Brewer, Cambridge,1993, p144.
80. *Associates' Newsletter*, Institute of Cornish Studies, Spring 1990.
81. *An Gannas*, 139, July 1989.
82. Wella Brown, 'The Reform of Revived Cornish', *Old Cornwall*, 10.9, 1989.
83. Brown, 1989.
84. See Rod Lyon, *Traditional Cornish*, Lyon, Nancegollan, 1989, and Rod Lyon and John Pengilly, *Notes on Spoken Cornish*, Dyllansow Truran, Redruth, 1987.
85. *Teere ha Tavaz* 1, June 1988.
86. R.M.M. Gendall, *A Student's Grammar of Modern Cornish*, Cornish Language Council, Menheniot, 1991, p1.
87. *Cornish Scene*, 2.3, October/November 1986.
88. R.M.M. Gendall, *An Curnoack Hethow: Cornish Today*, Teere ha Tavaz, Menheniot, 1992, p1; for a useful account of Lhuyd's activities see Derek R.Williams, *Prying into Every Hole and Corner: Edward Lhuyd in Cornwall in 1700*, Dyllansow Truran, Redruth,1993.
89. Gendall, 1992, p1.
90. R.M.M. Gendall, *A Student's Dictionary of Modern Cornish, Part 1: English-Cornish*, Cornish Language Council, Menheniot, 1991, pvii.
91. George, 1984, p501.
92. Gendall, *Student's Dictionary*, 1991, pl.
93. Letter to Dr Philip Payton from Dr Charles Penglaze, University of Newcastle, New South Wales, Australia, dated 13 September 1993.
94. *An Baner Kernewek*, 46, November 1988.
95. *An Baner Kernewek*, 46, November 1988.
96. *Cornish Scene* 2.4, December 1986/January/February 1987.
97. For example, see *Cornish Scene* 1.4, 1.5, 2.1, 2.3, 2.4, 2.5; for the parallel debate conducted in Cornish see *An Gannas* 120-127, December 1986 - July 1987.
98. See *An Gannas* editorial, December 1989.
99. Compare *Kowethas an Yeth Newsletter*, May 1991, and reports of the language weekend in *An Gannas* in the early 1980s.
100. See the amusing poem by Ken George announcing this in *An Gannas*, 157, January 1990.
101. Wella Brown, Denise Chubb, Ray Chubb, Neil Kennedy, Jane Ninnis, *The Cornish Language*, Cornish Language Board, Agan Tavas, Dalleth, Cossell an Tavaz Cornoack, An Gresenn Kernewek, Kowethas an Yeth Kernewek, 1991, p2.
102. Brown *et al*, 1991, p2.
103. Murdoch, 1993, p150.
104. Murdoch, 1993, p150.
105. Gregor, 1980, pp366-367.

CHAPTER 13

LITERATURE IN CORNWALL

John Hurst

As the Second World War moved into its final phase, an era in the cultural life of Cornwall also came to an end.

'Q.' (Sir Arthur Quiller-Couch) died on the 12th May 1944. Essentially, however, the creative Q. had died long before. Although the years between the Wars and into the Second World War were full of critical activity which shaped the study of English Literature throughout the country - and of the tireless public works for which he was so loved and admired - he wrote virtually no imaginative work after the publication of *Foe Farrell* in 1918. Perhaps the death of his son early in 1919 dried up the creative spark. Perhaps the death in the mud of Flanders of the Liberal ideal to which he was wedded removed some essential inspiration. Whatever the nature of the loss of inspiration (one is reminded of the long silence of Sibelius after the appearance of the 7th Symphony and Tapiola) intermittently throughout the years between the Wars, and on into the Second War, he laboured at *Castle D'Or*, never to finish it.

No dominant figure had emerged in the 1930s and 40s to take the literature of Cornwall forward. As Q. moved slowly towards death, however, there were figures waiting in the wings, and Cornwall in the period after the Second World War would see a flowering of literature remarkable for an area with a population of well under half a million. It is the character of that flowering - both what it is, and what it is not - that forms the subject of this Chapter. What follows does not purport to be a comprehensive survey of writing from and related to Cornwall; that is material for a book that remains to be written. It is the study of a remarkable - and in a way singular - phenomenon.

LIFE AFTER Q.

The shape of things to come was already forming. Late in November 1939 Q. received a manuscript on which his comments were sought. Q. was well known for his generosity to young talent and the author of the novel sent, Jack Clemo, was full of hope that Q. would not only recognise his abilities but also use his influence to further the publication of *Private Snow*.[1] Q. did indeed recognise that Clemo had talent, but it is clear from Clemo's account in *Confessions of a Rebel*[2] that it was a talent he found uncongenial, portraying as it did habits of dirt, open lust and filthy talk! Not a congenial portrait of the Delectable Duchy. Clemo points out, with mild irony, Q.'s simultaneous endorsement of the mild amiability of Lee's *Cornish Tales*. Discouraged, but not deterred, Clemo laboured on alone, deeepening his faith, but also widening his intellectual horizons through extensive reading until the early post-War years saw the appearance of the fine early poems, and the novel *Wilding Graft* (1948).

Clemo's portrait of the harsh realities below the surface of life in the china clay country may have offended Q. The darkest days of the War, however, produced a work which has become the classic account of Cornish working-class life - A.L.Rowse's *A Cornish Childhood* (1942). It is, indeed, a work without illusions, and with undertones of bitterness. Rowse's subsequent career - he had been one of those young Cornishmen whose careers had been furthered by Q.'s direct intervention - had been such, however, that he was able to view the childhood experiences with a degree of objectivity, distance lending proportion. There is also a genuine element of affection in the book for people, as well as for the traditional patterns of Cornish life, already changing rapidly in those early years of the century. In this sense it was an early classic of the nostalgia industry followed rapidly, and still within the War Years, by the more idyllic, more kindly *Shool House in the Wind* by Anne Treneer (1944). Anne Treneer's background in Gorran school-house was altogether more sympathetic and supportive than Rowse's in Tregonissey, so it is scarcely surprising that the book is warmer and more relaxed.

The portrait of a past Cornwall whose character, colour and integrity were endangered, if not already lost, was also emerging as the theme of two very different writers whose origins did not lie within Cornwall, but who had developed a love for and commitment to it.

Perhaps the most famous opening line of any twentieth- century British novel is 'Last night I dreamt I went to Manderley again'. *Rebecca* brought Daphne Du Maurier international fame, and its filming under Alfred Hitchcock's direction and with Laurence Olivier and Joan Fontaine in the leading roles not only ensured that the writer would be able to live in and transform Manderley's prototype, Menabilly, but also projected the image of a romantic Cornwall onto the cinema screens across the world. It was not, of course, her first novel with a Cornish setting. Her first work, *The Loving Spirit*, had been placed in Bodinnick where she had settled. Its picture of the River Fowey was so vivid that it drew Frederick Browning there; they met and were married. Soon after settling there she met Q., whose novels she already knew and loved, and for whose literary judgement she developed great respect, even though he was mildly shocked by her second novel *I'll Never be Young Again* (1932). Daphne du Maurier can, in fact, be seen as writing in the Q. tradition. His seal of approval was made clear in his permission to her to use the title of one of his own short stories for her novel *Frenchman's Creek* (1941) and it was extended posthumously when Q's daughter Foy asked Daphne to complete the unfinished *Castle D'Or*. There are darker undertones in Daphne Du Maurier's work than in Q.'s, and a more open recognition of sexuality, both aspects which must have drawn Hitchcock to the filming of *The Birds*; but she is essentially a traditional, highly skilful writer, and first among equals of those like E.P.Thompson and Winston Graham who have portrayed a Cornwall whose colourfully drawn past has had a potent audience appeal. It is recorded that *Penmarric* (1971) provided Susan Howatch with an income for life.

Like Daphne du Maurier, John Betjeman is not of Cornish origin. Indeed, like her, he is of wealthy middle-class London background. His verse autobiography *Summoned by Bells* (1960) presents many childhood memories, many of them of alienation and humiliation; the most positive are those of a pre-First War Cornwall: '. . . safe Cornish holidays before the storm'. Betjeman's pose as amiable antiquarian conceals a writer tormented by thoughts of mortality, of uncertainty about human purpose and destiny, of tormenting sexuality. His devotion to Cornwall is in part the need for escape from ever encroaching pressures of the twentieth century's erosion of community; but, in the last analysis it is deeper than this. Betjeman senses that there may be a spiritual quality in the Cornish tradition that provides an antidote to the corrosive secularism of the urban culture that is the norm in the modern Western World.

Betjeman's first poems about Cornwall were being written in the early days of the Second World War ('Trebetherick'; 'St Cadoc'). Independent of all these developments a young man in Launceston had taken his first cautious steps into the world of writing. Charles Causley had by the outbreak of War published three plays. The War took him from Launceston for the first time. His Naval experiences provide the substance of much of his immediate post-War writing - his first volume of poems *Farewell Aggie Weston* (1951) and *Hands to Dance and Skylark* (short stories, 1951). It is as if the enlargement of experience given by his time in the Royal Navy, together with the background of voracious reading of anything and everything available to him, combined to trigger the imagination that was to become the authentic (because it was unselfconscious and unassertive) voice of Cornwall. There are few laments in Causley's work for what has been; rather there is an acceptance of what is, for the essentials of humanity with a Cornish face. Knowing and admiring the work of Clemo - acknowledged in 'Homage to Jack Clemo' - and of Betjeman - the more superficial aspects of his antiquarianism affectionately parodied in 'Betjeman 1984' - his imaginative world arises from a dialogue between the realities of Cornish life and those who have heard the 'dark sounds'[3] of life in whatever context.

A CORNISH LITERARY TRADITION?

The early years after the Second World War saw, therefore, a pattern established in Cornish cultural literature that remains substantially unchanged 45 years later. There is no readily identifiable 'Cornish literary tradition'. This is not to imply there is not a great deal of work of high quality with a strongly Cornish face or character. Indeed, the quantity and quality is remarkable for so restricted a population base - as earlier remarked. However, certain characteristics do emerge, which require further examination. Q. does not, in himself, for all his dominating position over many years, constitute a literary tradition, not even when the continuation of his manner of fictional romance through Daphne du Maurier and others is taken into account. An important aspect of Q. is, of course, that though his base remained firmly Cornish, his professional experience lay almost entirely in the older universities and among the academic and political establishment. Again, though he was fascinated by all matters Cornish - he records his excitement at the discovery of the long tradition by which the site of Castle D'Or had been identified with King Mark - he seems to have been far too aware of the great sweep of the European tradition which shaped his views of the character of Cambridge English Tripos to be interested in matters Celtic merely because they were Celtic. Rowse comments, for instance, that despite Q.'s scholarly friendship with Henry Jenner he showed little interest in the Cornish language. 'His devotion to Cornwall was in fact the foundation of an equal devotion to his country',[4] as Brittain says in his admirable life of Q.

Much the same may be said of A.L.Rowse, who in many ways has inherited Q.'s mantle as an internationally recognised voice of Cornwall. Rowse is more concerned with studies directly related to Cornwall; but these, again, are nearly always within the context of his views on Britain's roles in the world, and his studies of the great eras of British (or, more often, English) significance and influence, historically and culturally. It is fitting that Rowse should have turned, in these later years, to write an affectionate and perceptive study of Q..[5] For though, by the accidents of his history, as he often tells us, his career developed as an historian and not, as he might have wished, within the field of literature and as a creative writer, his historical writing demonstrates that he shares with Q. a striking narrative gift. His writing of history, scrupulous in its research methods as it clearly is, lies within the tradition of narrative history exemplified at its best by Gibbon and Macaulay, and in our day by G.M.Trevelyan and C.V.Wedgwood. He shares, too, much of Q.'s approach to his conflicting status as 'Cornishman' and 'Englishman'. Patriotism '. . . to be good must be constructive and not exclusive. It must take justified pride in the great achievements of one's country, not in everything good or bad, just because it is one's own'.[6] But speaking of his relationship with the English as 'A Cornishman, who is sufficiently of them to appreciate them and yet is different enough to see them with a certain objectivity',[7] he nevertheless acknowledges in the closing pages of his *The Little Land of Cornwall* the attractions of the notion of Cornish political autonomy.

If then a dominant strain in Cornish literature is what might be termed the Cornish internationalist, the figure whose roots are deeply embedded within Cornwall but whose sphere of activity far transcends Cornwall, another strain will be seen to be the writer who is rooted not only within Cornwall but also deeply within his or her own community. Of these, within the period in question, Jack Clemo and Charles Causley are pre-eminent, although it will be seen later that recent years have brought to prominence other figures who display a similar pattern of rootedness.

Jack Clemo is of particular interest, not merely because of the intrinsic value of his work, but because he stems from a tradition central to the development of Cornish life, but often uninterested in or even inimical to the Arts - that of evangelical Nonconformity. Indeed, in his origins Clemo presents a striking and puzzling phenomenon; for his early poems are constructed from an astringently anti-aesthetic stance. The view that prefers the stripped pine of a wayside bethel to the splendours of a Cathedral, the encroaching savagery of a clay tip and its contorted structures to the conventional charms of field and hedgerow, produces a craggy beauty of its own in such poems as 'Christ in the Claypit' and 'The Excavator'. It might be expected that a mind developing in a context narrow and confining in the extreme might become inturned, limited in its horizons to a crippling degree. That this did not happen reflects the degree to which Clemo's powerfully emotional perspectives were modified by a sharp and searching intelligence that would find nourishment over areas of experience far beyond those normally available within the day-to-day world of evangelical Nonconformity.

True a staple of the young Clemo's intellectual and spiritual development was the work of the great Baptist preacher, Spurgeon, whose disciplined eloquence provided a strong framework. Soon, however, he was ranging not merely beyond the literature of Nonconformity but widely wherever his powerfully independent spirit might find a kindred individualist - to figures as diverse as Thomas Hardy, D.H.Lawrence and T.F.Powys, and then on to such major continental theologians as Kierkegaard and Barth. Although Clemo speaks with a directness that has rarely been equalled about the life of the clay country (and as we have seen, aroused Q.'s disapproval in doing so), and although he accepted membership of the Gorseth, he has made it clear that he is not interested in much of the Cornish tradition which he regards as dangerously pagan. (Interestingly that other fine Methodist poet John Harris, in the nineteenth century, expressed disapproval of Tennyson and Hawker's interest in Arthurian themes, thinking that they would be better concerned with more immediate and pressing spiritual issues). His mind searches for spiritual rigour wherever it may be found irrespective of local or national boundaries. So diverse influences from the Christian tradition press in on Clemo in his physical isolation on Goonamarris Slip as Bernadette and St Therese of Lisieux become part of a dialogue with William Blake, the Brownings, and Billy Bray. Clemo brings to his art, therefore, the fervour of Methodism in its particular Cornish mode, modified and stiffened by the intellectual rigour of both traditional and modern Calvinism, and the visionary insights of mystics and saints. It is a potent mix, affirming the world of the senses in the context of Christian discipline for which it is difficult to find a parallel.

If Clemo exemplifies a voice of Methodism which adds to John Harris' fervour elements that had not previously found expression, Charles Causley speaks with another, totally distinctive voice. Aware of the work of Clemo and Betjeman, with affection and admiration, his approach is nevertheless entirely his own. For one thing is already emerging from this argument. It is that the creative writers operating in a Cornish context in no way form a 'school' - or even share clear areas of common concern or interest. While more recent writers, such as Don Thomas, Peter Redgrove and Sylvia Kantaris, may be more mutually aware and involved than Causley, Clemo and Rowse, they in no sense constitute a 'school'. There is no major area of focus in the literature related to twentieth-century Cornwall that parallels the Newlyn School or the St Ives painters and sculptors. Causley, Clemo and Rowse are, in fact, products of that very 'separation' into small town units to which Ronald Perry draws attention in Chapter 2, and which militates against the forming of 'schools'. Nor should this necessarily be seen as a matter for regret. It may be that at this stage of its development as a society, with all the dramatic socio-economic change that has been experienced since the War, Cornwall is a potent breeding ground for individual and distinctive visions, rather than of writers creating from a shared vision.

Causley's vision is as distinctive, in its own fashion, as Clemo's. His verse manner has tone of voice that is immediately recognisable, a rhythym and cadence that are all his own. Cornwall, and the past of Cornwall, are the slate on which he writes. As he says:

'all Cornwall is knocking at my door'

('The Seasons in North Cornwall')

Early in his career he gave an interview to Michael Williams for the *Cornish Magazine* in which he said that 'Nobody but a plastic rhinoceros could fail to be conscious of the past in Cornwall. This very dark brooding spirit of the past. Here you learn to live with ghosts'.[8] Many of these ghosts are figures from Cornwall's past - John Polruddon, Charlotte Dymond. Some, indeed, are the daily presences of Launceston itself, like Nicholas Herle who is invoked in 'Dockacre', the voices that spoke 'By St Thomas Water', or the wonderfull voice across the centuries of the Sibard from whom his house in Launceston (Cyprus Well) is named in 'Sibard's Well'. More important, however, than the presences, is of what they speak - as Sibard puts it: 'life's cold truth'.

For if, on the one hand, Causley, the teacher, is the creator of images as bounding with life as 'Timothy Winters' or 'Mary, Mary Magdalene' there is always, near, the awareness of the fragility of that vigour, the thread by which we hang. It is at its most uncomfortably acute, indeed, in some of the poems about children; 'What has happened to Lulu?', 'Death of a Pupil', 'School at Four O'Clock', all spring from that direct loving observation of Launceston, its people and its ways, which are as much his material now as early in his career.

It would be quite wrong, however, to think that because underlying Causley's work is that sense of 'the truth as hard as stone' ('Nelson Gardens') that he is in any sense a sombre or depressing poet. An essential aspect of his tone of voice is a wonderful, understated wit which is often present in the most sensitive contexts. So, such different poems as 'Ballad of the Bread Man' (which must rank among the finest religious poems in English in the twentieth century) and 'Ten Types of Hospital Visitor' treat of 'that which is most serious' with a balance and lightness of touch that proceeds from remarkable emotional pose. For Causley, though he is in no sense a dogmatic poet, is in every sense a religious one. Not that he evokes any transcendence. The God, as in his Bread Man, is 'The God in himself'; and a sense of the mystery of personality and destiny. Again, his positioning in a tradition, of Cornish Anglicanism, which is part of the mainstream, but distinctive, unconcerned with structures, non-centralist, is a source of strength; a slate on which to write.

We come, then, to the third strand in the literature of Cornwall - those, not of Cornwall, who have made it their theme, of whom John Betjeman must be pre-eminent. It is significant that Betjeman is more explicitly concerned with 'the matter of Cornwall' and with what is happening to Cornwall than either Clemo or Causley - for whom Cornwall is the air they breathe, the assumed subject, rather than the concern. Betjeman, with sharp honesty, acknowledges that he is 'part of the problem': 'The visitors have come to Cornwall. I'm a visitor. We litter the cliff with our houses. We litter the cliffs with our shacks. When I was a boy, all this place was open fields. And Cornwall is older than the Cornish'.[9]

There are, in fact, two important strands in Betjeman's writing about Cornwall. The first proceeds directly from his role as a member of the privileged, and to a degree, leisured middle-class for whom Cornwall was increasingly becoming the play-ground and the release. One of his first poems on Cornwall to be published is the well-known 'Trebetherick'. Essentially this is a poem about the pleasures of holidays, from which, in a Wordsworthian sort of way, there is 'life and food for future years' ('Tintern Abbey'); the poem ends with words of thanks for these experiences;

Blessed be St Enodoc, blessed be the wave,
Blessed be the springy turf, we pray, pray to thee
Ask for our children all the happy days you gave
To Ralph, Vasey, Alistair, Biddy, John and me,

Even in a poem as essentially idyllic as this, however, there is a sudden undertone in which he speaks of another face of Cornwall:

. . . the shade of evil
Could stretch out at us from Shilla Mill

The oldest part of Cornwall was the wood as black as night.[10]

One aspect of Betjeman's attraction for the Cornwall of his young days is that it is sufficiently foreign to be stimulating, without being threatening. He speaks, for instance, of 'hills upon whose clinging sides the farms/ Hold Bible Christians'[11] - as if they were strange, but not hostile, natives. The society of Trebetherick, again, consists of the tight circle of his family and the fellow visitors, and the local population, supportive, but separate. On one level, his lament for a part Cornwall is for the invasion of a playground hitherto the preserve of himself and his privileged group; and its consequent vulgarisation:

> Where yonder villa hogs the sea
> Was open cliff to you and me
> The many-coloured cara's fill
> The salty marsh of Shilla Mill.

Cornwall is

> . . . raddled and put upon and tired
> And looking somewhat over-hired.[12]

There are, of course, underlying questions here which Betjeman does not tease out. Neither he nor subsequent writers have undertaken a serious cost-benefit analysis of the impact of technology, and the questions are in fact deep and complex. To focus on Celticity in Cornwall can often be to limit the nature of the enquiry. Recent writing, both fictional and academic, is beginning to tease out the wider issues - Myrna Combellacks' *The Playing Place*[13] and Alan Kent's *Clay*[14] alongside major studies like Philip Payton's *The Making of Modern Cornwall*[15] among others; but the full range of issues remain to be addressed. This book, of course, is an attempt to further the debate and shed new light, tackling those issues of change which alarmed Betjeman.

If on the one hand, Betjeman, like others side-steps the issues, there is another face of Betjeman in his dealing with Cornwall, which is strikingly different. If his fascination with the presence of the Bible Christians has an element of the superficial about it Cornwall was, nevertheless, the agent of his formative spiritual experience. Side by side with cheerful descriptions of holiday Cornwall, somewhat marred by domestic tensions between father and son, and the amusing descriptions of a society circling round golf, and bridge and dances, is the passage recounting his visit to St Ervan church and rectory. The chance encounter with the rector brought him face to face for the first time with the Celtic face of Christianity, admittedly as mediated by the Anglican establishment, but still with its mysticism, its openness to and kinship with nature, its lively awareness of the supernatural intact; the face of Christianity present, in different ways, in R.S.Hawker and Bernard Walke.

Betjeman does not pretend that this experience led him to a certainty that he did not feel. Here, as elsewhere, he balances belief and doubt. The experience is of a different, and more illuminating character to his previous contacts with religion. It is not a Damascus road vouchsafing of certainty.

> . . . Not a sign
>
> Everything looked as it always looked
> But somewhere, somewhere underneath the dunes,
> Somewhere among the cairns or in the caves
> The Celtic saints would come to me, the ledge
> Of time we walk on, like a thin cliff-path
> High in the mist, would show the precipice
>
> (*Summoned by Bells*)

Betjeman's perceptions of Cornwall are not merely to be found within his verse. There is the splendid series of short prose pieces to be found in *First and Last Loves*[17] for instance - on Blisland, St Endellion, Port Isaac, Padstow, and Looe. Here too is his classic essay on *Nonconformist Chapels*, beautifully illustrated by John Piper, which helped many to look in a more informed way at buildings which had often been dismissed as of no interest - Cornish chapels among them. The essays provide numerous insights into Cornish life and Betjeman's awareness of it. His view is, perhaps, best summarised in the closing passages of the essay on *St Endellion*.

> The visitors are there for a season. Mans life on earth will last for seventy years perhaps. But this sea will go on swirling against these green and purple rocks for centuries. Compared with the age of these rocks, the sea's life is nothing. And even the age of the rocks is nothing compared with the eternal life of man. And up there on the hill in St Endellion church, eternal man comes week by week in the Eucharist.[17]

For Betjeman Cornwall is the place where man and nature confront each other most nearly and vividly to define his destiny.

A NEW GENERATION OF WRITERS

As we move on from these figures who came into prominence in the period immediately after the Second World War, but whose formative experiences lie before or during it, we find a literary scene of which the basic pattern is strikingly similar.

The leading figure of that group of writers who take their origins in Cornwall is undoubtably D.M.Thomas. Thomas, born into a skilled working-class family in the shadow of Carn Brea showed early talent and progressed to Oxford, to the Combined Services Russian course during his National Service, and to a Lectureship at Hereford College of Education. After its closure the success of *The White Hotel* (1981) enabled him both to devote his full-time to writing, and to return to Cornwall to live. Thomas himself speaks of the 'two emotional landscapes' of his world - Cornwall and Russia: 'The atmospheric contrasts of the first - wild sea-cliffs and moors, lush river valleys - perhaps have a counterpart in the second; Stalin and Pushkin'.[18]

His family background and experience, indeed, make Thomas almost the archetypal Cornishman. There is the strong Methodist background; before his birth his parents and elder sister had lived in California; Lois, the sister, married an Australian and emigrated; Thomas and his parents joined them for an unhappy couple of years; the departure for education and work; the homing when conditions permitted. And Thomas has done much - and continues to do much - to further understanding of Cornwall, and particularly her literary heritage. There is the valuable anthology of Cornish verse *The Granite Kingdom*.[19] The best work of John Harris has been made widely available through the selection that Thomas edited *Songs from the Earth*[20] and our appreciation sharpened by its sensitive and perceptive introduction. He continues to add to our understanding through readings and lectures within Cornwall.

To the general public, Thomas is best known as a novelist. He conceives of himself, however, as a poet whose tendency to write narrative poems has led him to the type of poetic fiction which is now his hall-mark. His earliest poems, in fact, were a group of highly original Science Fiction narratives and reached a wide audience through their appearance in *Penguin Modern Poets* ll(1968). The Science Fiction mode, however, soon appeared not the most effectivte strategy through which to express and explore the tight-rope on which love and death walk together. They walk together, intimately, lovingly in the poems that stem directly from his Cornish experience and background. At the most basic, most easily accessible level (and not all Thomas's poems yield their meanings readily) there are affectionate elegies for the members of his family, father, mother, uncles, aunts. These poems carry, however, an additional bonus in their wonderful evocation of the details of Cornish life and speech.

> How they loved understatement!
> 'Goin a' drop rain, arr us?' - the sky
> an enraged bladder. 'He've had a drop to drink',
> 'I dear like a bit ride'.[21]

It expressed their landscape; deep labyrinths under the shifted bracken ('Reticent').

Then there is the direct, loving portrayal of his aunt;

> Dear aunt, If Christ had come, as well he might, to you
> You'd have scrubbed his feet with good soapy water

Left from Monday's wash, pocketed a few
Fresh loaves and fishes for your poor sister[22]

('Cecie')

There is, nevertheless, another face to his dialogue with Cornwall. His fascination with the Cornish landscape, is rarely merely a fascination with landscape. Instinctively Thomas discovered a natural affinity with such other Celtic writers as Yeats, Joyce and Dylan Thomas - and in his very different way Jack Clemo - who see sex as numinous, and see landscape as both numinous and sexual. So Thomas's Cornish landscapes have all the sharp particularity of his Cornish people with this added element.

On the humped moor's spine, consumptive miners
turned aside from their plod home to crouch and pass
through the men-an-tol, the ring of granite
I am the men-an-tol, the wind's vagina;
I am the circle of stones grouped around grass.[23]

('Penwith')

Here we are close to the landscape and theme of his first novel, and the only one with a Cornish setting, *Birthstone*.[24]

The plot of *Birthstone* is as much poetic fantasy as conventional novel, and there must be some doubt if its several strands cohere entirely convincingly. Nonetheless, it is written with great verve - Thomas has spoken of his enjoyment in writing it and of his continued affection for the book in *Memories and Hallucinations*, his highly original psychological autobiography. The life of Penwith is wonderfully evoked, many details corresponding closely with many of the poems; but the naturalistic surface overlies a permeating sexuality that governs the direction of the novel. The men-an-tol is at the heart of it; for the ritual crawl transforms the lives of the central characters. Lola, the old woman, is rejuvenated, Hector, on the other hand ages as Lola becomes younger from her experience of the birthstone. There are many other themes. Jo, the Irish narrator is a multiple personality much influenced in her conception by the celebrated *Three Faces of Eve*. Lola and Hector are expatriate Cornish from Grass Valley, California, and a vehicle for the celebration of Cornishness and Thomas' ongoing interest in expatriate Cornish communities. It finds expression elsewhere in such poems as 'A Cornish Graveyard at Keweenaw' (North Michigan). Thomas himself says, '. . . like a panicky cook I threw every ingredient I could think into the pot'.[25] The book has found more friends as Thomas's particular blend of poetry, fiction, and sexual fantasy have become better understood.

Cornwall remains an ongoing theme for Thomas's poetry, although in his fiction he has moved, under the influence of the great twentieth-century

Russian writers, and of his readings in Freud, to a wider canvas for his fiction. He is nevertheless a commanding presence in the Cornish literary scene. As with Clemo and Causley his work has been enriched by its broader perspectives as, similarly another 'provincial' poet, Seamus Heaney, has moved from a focus on the local to a perception of locality broadened by a grasp of a broader sweep of history and tradition.

Throughout the period during which Thomas was developing his art, Cornwall was proving host to a wide range of writers. This does not, however, necessarily mean that Cornwall is in any sense their theme. The direction, for instance of Colin Wilson's work is wholly other, though he has occasionally given a 'South West' orientation to his concerns with the dark corners of the human mind as in his pamphlet *Murder in the West Country*. Similarly, although she has written a few poems on Cornish themes, Cornwall is in no way central to the witty, elegantly crafted work of Sylvia Kanatalis even in contexts, in which, to a superficial view, it might be expected, as in her co-operative sequence with D. M.Thomas.

The case of W.S.Graham is, in some ways, more interesting. Graham, a Scot from Greenock, came to Cornwall in 1943, living first at Mevagissey and subsequently, for years, at Madron. To begin with his work shows little trace of his Cornish setting. The most interesting case is, perhaps, his major narrative poem 'The Nightfishing' (1955). The poem sprang from fishing trips undertaken both in Scotland and out of Mevagissey. Yet the place names used are firmly and consistently Scots. It is as if the Scots inheritance, which remained a major theme of his work to the end is, gradually being modified by and interfused with, the Cornish environment.

One factor in this development was his membership of the convivial group of painters associated with St Ives, his friendships with Peter Lanyon, Roger Hilton, and Bryan Wynter being particularly close. The Newlyn School, as might be expected, had its by-products in literature - notably Norman's son, Crosbie Garstin, himself an illustrator, and Fryn Tennyson Jesse, who started as a painter. St Ives too shows a similar pattern. W.S.Graham's work is more distinguished than any writing that came out of Newlyn, and together with the literary work of Sven Berlin, constitutes a strong cultural statement. The well-known departure from Cornwall of Sven Berlin, and the death of Peter Lanyon and Bryan Wynter broke the impetus of a group which was becoming a powerful point of cultural take-off.

Some of Graham's most appealing poems are, indeed, those which relate to his Penwith friendships, 'Roger Hilton's Watch' , 'Wynter and the Grammarsow', and above all the splendid elegy for Peter Lanyon 'The Thermal Stair',[26] a poem so highly integrated that quotation of line or phrase is impossible. Suffice to say it is imbued with a sense of the environment which fostered their imagination, of their mutual understanding of each other's art, and their kinship and affection. In his maturity, Greenock and Cornwall have fused to a powerful vision.

Peter Redgrove, who came to Cornwall to teach at Falmouth School of

Art in 1965, is a dominant figure among those writers who adopted Cornwall as their base. This is not a context in which to deal in any adequate way with his rich and complex work, but some attention to the appropriateness of Cornwall as an environment for his particular imagination is called for. Redgrove's work is marked by a remarkable imaginative energy. Image collides with image to engender further images as in a controlled nuclear reaction. Like Blake, to whom he is often compared, he cuts beyond the analytic dissections of Newtonian science and the emotionaL and psychological strait-jacket of much Christian and post-Christian thought and practice, to unearth a hidden unity and sources of psychic and imaginative energy. The Cornish setting is not essential to this process, but it is highly supportive of it. Redgrove is aware that Celtic Christianity, much of which has been lost but traces of which remain, had

> . . . a sense of the freshness of mankind, the acceptability of the basic energies that drive him. A Celtic Christian would have said that Man has not fallen; that men and women are equals; that God is in everyone of us; that saints were real people.[27]

Redgrove shares with D.M.Thomas the sense that sexual experience is a channel of the numinous:

> When men and women embrace
> They are a cone of power
> An unbuilt beehive[28]
>
> ('Dr Faust's Sea Spiral Spirit')

The same force underlines the splendid poem 'Dune-Firer' in which a sense of Celtic spirituality and sexuality blend. Redgrove, however, was trained as a scientist and taps sources of energy in intricate, natural and geological processes. He shares, in fact, with that other dominant figure of twentieth-century Celtic literature, Hugh MacDiarmid, the ability to encompass science imaginatively. MacDiarmid's geological meditation 'On a Raised Beach' and Redgrove's 'Minerals of Cornwall, Stones of Cornwall' have much in common, though Redgrove has an imaginative energy, a sense of colour and drama, that is not present in Macdiarmid's craggy splendours.

> Having seen God walking over the burning marl, having seen
> A someone thrusting his finger into the mountainside
> To make it boil - here is the issue of this divine intrusion
> . . . my voice
> Is a squeak buried among the rending of mountains,
> I am a mist passing through the crevices of these great seniors . . . .[29]

Like D.M.Thomas, Redgrove's work has developed increasingly towards a sort of poetic fiction, often in association with his partner, the poet and novelist Penelope Shuttle in a development quite different from the *nouveau roman*. The aridities of the latter seem already to have run their course while the full potentialities of Thomas's, Shuttle's and Redgrove's road probably remain to be discovered.

There is, of course, a substantial number of writers, who have made Cornwall their home and their theme, or who have visited, stayed awhile and then left, for whom Cornwall has provided both setting and stimulus. In the tradition of Q. and Daphne du Maurier there might be counted Winston Graham and E.V.Thompson, residents who have mined Cornwall's past for their well-crafted, highly popular fictions. As with the wide exposure given to Daphne du Maurier by film, so television has boosted Winston Graham from success to best-seller status. Yet one of his best novels is not part of the feted Poldark series, but the meticulously researched *Grove of Eagles* (1963) - which explores, like A.L.Rowse's influential *Tudor Cornwall* (1941) the Elizabethan period when Cornwall's geographical position and degree of social organisation highlighted her strategic importance.

Of those who came, stayed awhile, and then left, imaginatively enriched, particular mention might be made of Rumer Godden and Bryher - the latter the pseudonym of Annie Winifred Ellerman. On their return from India, Rumer Godden's parents lived for many years in St Breward and Rumer spent several long periods with them before deciding to return to London as her permanent base. Her novel *China Court* (1961) is the product of this experience. It traces the fortunes of a family of clay pit owners on the edge cf Bodmin Moor, and gives a vivid picture of that environment. It has a carefully elaborated structure which may puzzle readers until its purpose becomes clear at the end of the novel. The structure may, however, be seen as more elaborate than the substance of the book requires.

Bryher's novel *The Fourteenth of October*[30] (1954) is very different. Bryher met the American imagist poet H.D. during a visit to Cornwall and found, through her, the emotional freedom which her conventional late Victorian upbringing had denied her. A visit as schoolgirl had taken her to the Scillies with which she fell in love and led her to her name. The growing friendship with H.D. completed her release from the bonds of conventionality. As her skills and confidence grew she published a series of remarkable historical novels of which two, *Ruan* and *The Fourteenth of October* had a setting wholly or partly in Cornwall. This novel concerns the state of Britain at the time of the Norman Conquest. Wulf, the central character is carried by the disruptions of the time, first from his Yorkshire home by the Viking incursions, and thence by many adventures to Cornwall. The call to the King's standard at the Norman invasions disrupts again the pattern of pre-conquest Cornish life into which he has settled, and the route of the English forces carried him to servitude in Normandy. Escaping he returns to a changed order in Cornwall, in which its previous autonomy is increasingly threatened. Not only

Cornwall has changed. Wulf's childhood love, Laurel, has turned to his friend Rafe. Wulf sees his destiny in taking up the mantle of leadership he had laid down when he left home, and returns to Yorkshire. *The Fourteenth of October* is both an elegy for a lost Celtic civilization and a lost innocence. Carefully researched, Bryher, nevertheless, wears her learning lightly and the strength of the novel lies in its deft rapid etching of the landscape of Cornwall and the sensitivity of its portrayal of feeling and personal change. Again Cornwall provides the seed-bed which enables Bryher's distinctive talents to take shape. It deserves to be better known.

It could be said, however, of all these works of writers who are not indigenous to Cornwall that, though they are faithful to the detail of Cornish life, by and large they fail to catch its texture. D.M.Thomas, when he turns his attention in that direction, catches the texture of Cornish life unerringly. His stance, however, is too singular, too rooted in the pursuit of his own obsessions, to provide a recognisable voice for Cornwall. For that we must look, among living writers, to Causley and, in a sense, to A.L.Rowse.

CONTEMPORARY CORNISH WRITING

There are, however, new voices beginning to be heard and it is to those we must turn if we are to assess the state of Cornish writing now. Two striking novels of recent date are Myrna Combellack's *The Playing Place - a Cornish Round* (1989) and Alan Kent's *Clay* (1991). Both share a sense of a Cornwall that is lost. Both acknowledge a complicity by the Cornish themselves in its loss.

Myrna Combellack's novel portrays the break-up of a community under the universally applicable forces of the twentieth century, particularly the increased mobility that comes from growing prosperity and swifter, easier communications. Those who come from outside to settle, often in retirement, those who come to visit provide an economic temptation to the indigenous population that is both resented and irresistible. The community is sold out to the twentieth century. All the evils of Pandora's Box are let out. The speech is corrupted, sexuality is warped, the sense of community is destroyed as disaster feeds on disaster. The one positive that remains is the unchanging heritage of Art. Christice, the flawed heroine of the novel, is haunted in the book's closing passages by that crowning monument of the Western European polyphonic tradition, Byrd's 40-Part Motet, *Spem in Alium*, as Hans Castor is haunted in the closing passages of Mann's *The Magic Mountain* by Schubert's great song *Der Lidenbaum*. Is the hidden symbolism here that Cornwall's destiny lies in defining a relationship with the mainstream of British and European culture that recognises Cornwall's distinctiveness without asserting its apartness?

Alan Kent's powerful novel differs from *The Playing Place* in having a more elaborate structure that enables a dialogue between Cornwall's past and its present. Kent uses the fictional device of the journal of a seventeenth-century clerk to the Parish of St Dennis to counterpoint the reality of the clay country before the discovery of china clay. Already, however, the clerk and his vicar sense a doom hanging over the land as technology begins to develop - the doom which works its way out in the cataclysmic climax of the novel as the land, ravaged by technology and greed, wreaks its own terrible vengeance. In this sense the novel constitutes not so much a lament for a lost Cornish civilisation, but an evocation of the potential catastrophe of civilisation itself in the face of unbridled technology. The catastrophe bears a Cornish face and a Cornish meaning, but its implications are wider.

Where then does the literature of Cornwall stand today? A.L.Rowse and Charles Causley have presented us with differing views of Cornish culture and the Arts. In his biography of Q. Rowse remarks that 'The Cornish have not been much of a literary folk - their genius has been all for mining, science and technology - and Cornwall has been mostly written about by others'.[31] The situation is complicated here by the fact that, as Rowse points out, many of those who have been resident in Cornwall and accepted as Cornish (including Q. himself) are only half-Cornish, such as Causley, half-Devonian, or Hawker, wholly Devonian. Observations such as this land us in the difficult and dangerous territory of racial origins and characteristics. Accepting the arguments at their face value, however, an interesting conclusion might be drawn; that imaginative vigour, like biological vigour, springs from hybridisation; that a society that turns in on itself is sterile; one that is open to new influences is the one that produces cultural 'lift-off'. One might push the argument a stage further to claim that the particular engineering abilities of the Cornish of which Rowse speaks came to fruition at that point in time when that particular Cornish strain came into contact with (and subsequently fuelled) the explosion of science and technology that was marked in Britain by the foundation of The Royal Society.

But Causley argues differently: 'We are a creative race. What about the Medieval craftsmen who built our churches... What about the men who did God Almighty in St Austell Church? The only representation of God, I believe, in a Cornish church'.[32] As we have seen already, there is a particular Cornish creativity that finds its literary form in the work of John Harris, Jack Clemo, and D.M.Thomas. All of these are of working-class, Methodist background and serve to disprove the often asserted creative sterility of Nonconformity. All are, as far as can be discerned, entirely of Cornish stock. Again, however, their art takes off at the point at which it cross-fertilises with some aspect of the broader Western tradition. John Harris's best work is moulded in the tradition of Milton and Wordsworth. Clemo, as we have seen, develops in the perspectives of Hardy, and Barth, T.F. Powys, St Teresa and the Brownings. D.M.Thomas acknowledges his debt to Yeats, and Hardy, Pasternak, Anna Akhmatova and Freud. All artists, all creative endeavour, stands on the shoulder of giants.

The conditions which lead to a creative flowering at one point in time and place are inscrutable and unpredictable. That a society fails for long periods to produce distinguished works of art suddenly to 'burst out in to sudden flame' is not a matter of surprise, but a matter of rejoicing when it happens. One thinks of the long creative silence of Hungary, of Finland - suddenly to break the silence in the work of Bartok and Kodaly on the one hand, or Sibelius and Sallinen on the other. That, from the time of the *Ordinalia* to the coming of John Harris there was a literary silence over Cornwall, punctuated only occasionally by the likes of Richard Carew, does not mean that the Cornish are devoid of literary gifts; only that the particular combination of circumstances was not present.

That said, it is important to note, alongside those literary characteristics which Cornwall has, those which it does not, so far, show. Comparison with Scotland is instructive. Twentieth-century Cornwall has not yet produced a figure with so far reaching a mind or so deefined a cultural stance as Hugh MacDiarmid. Nor has she as yet produced a writer with so synoptic an understanding of the 'Little Land' (to use Rowse's phrase) as George MacKay Brown has achieved in Orkney. Alan Kent's approach to fiction shows some affinity with that MacKay Brown and it will be interesting to see if, as he develops, he comes to present that synoptic imaginative grasp. Within the Arts Cornwall has so far presented, at two brief points of time concentrations of activity in which artists mutually stimulated each other - at Newlyn and at St Ives. Both, however, with the exception of Alfred Wallis and Peter Lanyon at St Ives were essentially the result of artists from outside Cornwall coming together. Nothing like this has happened in the sphere of literature. Although the writers all co-operate in readings and lectures, and are joined in mutual awareness and friendship, essentially they do not form School, but operate as powerful individual practitioners each with a peculiar and distinotive vision which may relate more or less explicitly, as the case may be, to Celtic perceptions. MacDiarmid and Mackay Brown, however, have their own giants on whose shoulders they can stand, from the Norse writings of the sagas and the body of Gaelic verse, down through the Scottish Chaucerians and the distinctive chorus of Scott and Burns and Hogg to the twentieth century. It may be that the writers of Cornwall are creating their own tradition, that they are the giants on whose shoulders others will stand.

We are fortunate that all of them share Causley's vision: 'The poet ideally opens up channels, he breaks down the sense of isolation. Art and religion should be breaking down the barriers that separate men'.[33] It is from the marriage of that carefully preserved sense of identity, of which Payton speaks in his major study, with the powerful voices of the Western tradition that Cornwall is finding its distinctive voice.

REFERENCES

1. This novel, along with several others drafted by Clemo in the 1930s, has never been published. Much of the material from this period found its way into *The Shadowed Bed*, first written during this period but not published (after revision) until 1986 (Lion Publishing, Tring). The best current approach to Jack Clemo's poetry is *Selected Poems*, Bloodaxe Books, Newcastle, 1988, and the subsequent *Approach to Murano*, Bloodaxe Books, Newcastle, 1993. The novel

Wilding Graft is available in 'The Cornish Library' series (Anthony Mott, London).

2. Jack Clemo, *Confessions of a Rebel*, Chatto and Windus, London, 1949, especially pp169-171.
3. The phrase, often used by Causley in speaking of poetry, is Lorca's 'sonidos negros'.
4. F.Brittain, *Arthur Quiller-Couch: A Biographical Study of Q.*, Cambridge University Press, Cambridge, 1947, p156.
5. A.L.Rowse, *Quiller-Couch: A Portrait of Q.*, Methuen, London, 1988.
6. A.L.Rowse, *The English Spirit*, Macmillan, London, 1944, p51.
7. Rowse, 1944, p35.
8. Michael Williams, 'Charles Causley' in *Cornish Magazine*, Vol.6, No.1, May 1963. The best current approach to the poetry of Charles Causley is *Collected Poems*, Macmillan, London, 1992.
9. John Betjeman, *Betjeman's Cornwall*, John Murray, London, 1984, p20.
10. Betjeman, 1984, pp45-46.
11. John Betjeman, *Summoned by Bells*, John Murray, London, 1960, p33.
12. Betjeman, 1984, p35.
13. Myrna Combellack, *The Playing Place: A Cornish Round*, Dyllansow Truran, Redruth, 1989.
14. Alan Kent, *Clay*, Amigo Books, Launceston, 1991.
15. Philip Payton, *The Making of Modern Cornwall: Historical Experience and the Persistence of 'Difference'*, Dyllansow Truran, 1992.
16. John Betjeman, *First and Last Loves*, John Murray, 1969.
17. Betjeman, 1969, p212.
18. D.M.Thomas, *Selected Poems*, Penguin, London, 1983, pvii.
19. D.M.Thomas (ed.), *The Granite Kingdom: Poems of Cornwall*, Bradford Barton, Truro, 1970.
20. D.M.Thomas (ed.), *Songs From the Earth: Selected Poems of John Harris*, Lodenek Press, Padstow, 1977.
21. D.M.Thomas, *The Puberty Tree*, Bloodaxe Books, London, 1993, p63.
22. Thomas, 1993, p61.
23. Thomas, 1993, p50.
24. D.M.Thomas, *The Birthstone*, Gollancz, London, 1980.
25. D.M.Thomas, *Memories and Hallucinations*, Gollancz, 1988, p20.
26. W.S.Graham, *Collected Poems*, Faber, London, 1979.
27. Hugh Herbert, 'Faust and Foremost - an interview with Peter Redgrove', *Guardian*, 30 November 1973.
28. Peter Redgrove, *Songs of My Skin*, Routledge and Kegan Paul, London, 1975, p46.
29. Redgrove, 1975, pp108-109.
30. Bryher, *The Fourteenth of October*, Collins, London, 1954.
31. Rowse, 1988, p224.
32. *Cornish Magazine*, May 1963.
33. *Cornish Magazine*, May 1963.

CONCLUSION

Philip Payton

At the Conference on Cornwall at Perranporth in May 1992 Colin Davison, editor of the *Western Morning News* newspaper, drew attention to what he saw as an increasingly significant paradox - on the one hand the growing tendency for both private and public agencies to be organised on a 'Westcountry' (normally Devon-and-Cornwall) basis, and - on the other - the emergence of an enhanced sense of Cornish ethnic and territorial identity. Other speakers noted this paradox, supporters of the Devon-and-Cornwall model welcoming the former development on grounds of economic and administrative efficiency (Cornwall was 'too small') but also recognising that the Cornish identity would be an enduring 'problem' for regional planners. The onus was on the Cornish themselves, it was suggested, to seek an accommodation between the demand for 'regional efficiency' and the desire to preserve Cornwall's distinctiveness.

A further paradox, which was expressed strongly from the floor at Perranporth, was that the Cornish 'problem' which was so evident to regional planners beyond the Tamar was in fact often perceived within Cornwall as a 'strength'. After all, no other county in the United Kingdom (not even a Yorkshire, let alone a Bucks or Berks) could boast an identity that was so distinctly regional or national, and no other county could claim a status in some respects similar to those of Wales, Scotland or Northern Ireland. This distinctiveness, it was argued, was potentially an enormous 'strength' in marketing Cornwall at home and abroad, especially in the European Community (now Union) where continental Europeans were sympathetic to the notion of historic regions but were perplexed by attempts in Britain to create artificial, functional regional entities. 'Cornwall' (an historic region) would strike a chord where 'the South West' (a bureaucrat's construct) might not.

More paradoxical still was that success had thus far eluded the quest for 'regional efficiency'. For all its up-beat optimism, the Devon and Cornwall Development Company (itself soon to expire) had not measurably improved the relative socio-economic situation of Devon let alone Cornwall, while decades of sustained and energetic Regional Development policies had led only to a lop-sided economic profile in which Cornwall's peripheral condition had not only been perpetuated but in fact had become more complex. As this book itself has shown, despite (or because of?) the distinctive and (in their separate ways) very 'Cornish' contributions of tourism and the extractive industries, Cornwall had remained a low-wage economy, with the practical application of the Devon-and-Cornwall model leading to the re-location east of the Tamar of executive and managerial positions, of other resources, and of decision-making powers. Even when, in the early 1970s, there was a real expansion of employment vacancies in Cornwall (associated with the 'branch factory' phenomenon) there was not a fall in the rate of unemployment, the post-War years having witnessed the unexpected (even in 1952) arrival of a mass wave of employment-aged in-migrants. Despite the planners' hopes, this in-migration did not lead to a permanent reversal of Cornwall's socio-economic condition. As well as contributing 'imported unemployment', the process of in-migration had caused significant strain on the Cornish housing market, often to the disadvantage of the indigenous Cornish.

And yet, in the crowning paradox of all, it was the impact of the policies and processes outlined above (and discussed in depth in earlier Chapters) that accounted for that enhancement of Cornish ethnic identity which - as Davison noted - was at odds with the Devon-and-Cornwall model. It was not just that these policies and processes had failed to 'deliver' (in itself a potential cause of discontent) but that they had had deleterious effects which were bound to provoke reaction. Far from being submerged under the weight of change, the Cornish identity was being mobilised and strengthened in new ways. From the rise of political anti-metropolitanism to the emergence of 'opposition' economic policies, and given cultural expression in a range of activities from rugby football to the new 'Cornish novel', 'Cornishness' emerged as an increasingly important determinant of attitudes and behaviour. It was, when all is said and done, a re-defining Cornishness that was born in disadvantage and grew-up in response to sometimes traumatic socio-economic change.

This book, it is hoped, has gone some way towards explaining (if not resolving) the paradoxes noted above and identified in earlier Chapters. It is not the task of this book *per se* to suggest 'the way ahead' for Cornwall but, as Ronald Perry observes in Chapter 3, it is customary to offer visions for a Cornish future. It is commonplace to assert that Cornwall is at 'the cross-roads', and certainly Cornwall has to make some important choices about its future. However, in many areas those choices will be made for Cornwall by outside agencies, in issues as crucial as the Euro-constituency, local government reform, and sub-regional planning. But, as Ronald Perry also notes (in Chapter 2), the Cornish are eternal children of hope, and there is no shortage of visions for Cornwall. Mebyon Kernow, for example, envisages Cornwall taking its place in a unifying Europe: 'Our vision of Europe is one that recognises the strength of international co-operation but respects the diversity of local traditions'.[1]

Interestingly, as this book was being written a debate emerged which appeared to offer three distinct visions for the future of Cornwall.[2] The debate was prompted by serious and persuasive suggestions that Cornwall (or at least very large parts of it) should be designated a National Park. The Cornwall Branch of the CPRE held a conference to discuss the idea, and in arguments that were familiar elsewhere in Britain but were given a particular Cornish hue, it was asserted that unbridled development was leading to environmental degradation and the disappearance of a distinctive Cornish landscape. The answer, it was asserted, was National Park status, a view that was embraced by what seemed to be an 'unholy alliance' of newcomers determined to preserve their 'Cornish dream' and some Cornish nationalists bent on creating their Celtic-rural idyll.

Predictably, such a vision was anathema to the developers themselves, with John Caff of the Devon and Cornwall Development Company arguing that National Park status would merely perpetuate problems of unemployment, low pay, low investment. The answer was to create a dynamic sub-regional economy, with a better infrastructure (more roads) which would attract business into Devon-and-Cornwall from outside and bring the sub-region up to at least the same economic standard as the South East. In other words, the standard orthodoxy (with all its conventional wisdoms, and all its misplaced optimism) was again being articulated, despite the uncomfortable evidence which suggested that the application of such policies over several decades had failed to make any significant improvement in Cornwall's relative socio-economic condition.

A third position also emerged, however, not unlike that suggested by Ronald Perry in Chapter 3, in which both the 'National Park' and 'development' visions were rejected. Preserving Cornwall 'in aspic' was no solution, but neither was a set of policies which had already proved ineffective and indeed deleterious. Instead, returning to an emphasis upon Cornish 'strengths', it was argued that policy objectives should be both more modest and more realistic but also innovatory, aiming for internally-generated and self-sustaining economic activiites. Here locational advantages (not least the maritime dimension) should be identified, with ethnic and territorial identity seen as a positive factor in the planning process. To be successful, however, such a strategy required the strengthening of Cornwall's intellectual infrastructure, the acquisition of institutions and decision-making capabilities, the marshalling of resources in Cornwall (rather than Plymouth or elsewhere), and the unequivocal articulation of a Cornish regional status in both Britain and Europe.

In reality, of course, the continuing debate is inevitably more complex and multi-dimensional than the simplified categorisation above suggests, with the choices to be made perhaps less stark. However, as Colin Griffin, Chief Planning Officer of Cornwall County Council, remarked at the CPRE conference: 'The way forward can only happen if Cornwall is viewed as an entity, and all authorities and agencies that could implement changes can agree a common objective'.[3]

REFERENCES

1. *Western Morning News*, 31 December 1992.
2. *Western Morning News*, 26 February 1992.
3. *Western Morning News*, 14 March 1992.